Creating historical drama

Creating

historical drama

A guide for the community
and the interested individual

By George McCalmon and Christian Moe

Foreword by Louis C. Jones

Southern Illinois University Press / Carbondale • Edwardsville

To Our Wives

Foreword

THIS VOLUME is concerned with the conception, gestation, bearing and raising of historical dramas. It is especially useful for those involved in such dramas as will draw upon a whole community for various kinds of support. As one who, in his time, has sat through scene after scene of ill-written, ill-cast, ill-produced pseudo-historical rubbish, I welcome with a hearty huzza this clear guide line to all concerned.

If there is the stuff of drama in a community's story, then there is good reason to make of it a pageant, or a biography-drama, or even an epic-drama. To recreate the world of those who preceded us, their conflicts and decisions, is to throw our own lives into perspective. But to write and produce such a drama successfully is to avoid a thousand hidden rocks and shoals known only to the very experienced.

Professors McCalmon and Moe have charted the channel and analyzed each danger with the utmost hard-headedness. There is no dreamy optimism befogging this book; it is full of practical experience, wrung from the successes and failures of scores of such dramas presented all over America. The emphasis of the authors on solvency, on careful budgeting and on community relations balances the necessity for respectable historical research, for dramatic writing and interesting presentation.

The segments of the American story are worth telling and retelling but, if they are to be produced effectively on the stage, they must move and entertain and enlighten. And they must banish dullness, for drama is the antithesis of boredom, and history made dull is a betrayal of the past.

Louis C. Jones

New York State Historical Association
Cooperstown, New York

Preface

The need to provide sound bearings for the organizing, writing, and producing of community-oriented drama is the burden of already published books. This one takes as its special province a process that transforms into drama materials belonging, broadly viewed, to American history. Our aim is to improve this process and to elevate the calibre of such drama. While the book addresses primarily the nonspecialist, it hopes to rally the talents and experience of professional historians, educators, and theatre artists in behalf of creating historical drama.

Throughout the text the reader will encounter a frequent use of the historical present tense. This is designed not to deceive but to enliven, and to suggest that there are gains in viewing reenactments of community experience as part of history's continuum. Dramas no longer performed are, therefore, discussed as if they are now being witnessed. But a reader, if he is so moved, need only turn to the appendix for the production data on the title in question.

We acknowledge with appreciation the cooperation of a large number of writers, directors, local historians, librarians, and sponsors of producing groups across the country who responded to our queries. We are especially grateful to Darwin Payne for furnishing the illustrations in the text. For advice and helpful reference materials we are also indebted to Roger Sherman, Samuel Selden, Catherine Fennelly, Fred Rath, William C. Trotman, Mark R. Sumner, and Eleanor Porter, and to the Jamestown Corporation, the Institute of Outdoor Drama, the Sturbridge Village, and the New York State Historical Association. In addition to those on the acknowledgment page, we extend thanks to H. Darkes Albright, Archibald McLeod, and Carolyn Moe, for evaluating and editing portions of the text; to Elizabeth Kenyon, for editing the complete text; to Martha Fellows, for preparing the final manuscript; and to Vernon Sternberg, Director of the Southern Illinois University Press, for encouragement and suggestions, goes the authors' particular gratitude.

George McCalmon
Christian Moe

January, 1965

Postscript

IN APRIL, 1965, before he could see this book in final published form, George McCalmon died. He was a man of honor, industry, and great warmth, a gentleman and rare. His achievement, his Arlecchino spirit are not forgotten.

CM

Acknowledgments

Acknowledgment is gratefully made to the following for permission to quote copyrighted and other material:

To the New York Folklore Society, Cooperstown, New York, for the excerpt from "Aggressive Humor on the East Branch" by Herbert Halpert.

To Harper & Row for the use of the Play Appraisal Form adapted from *The Playwright's Art* by Roger M. Busfield, Jr. Copyright, 1958, by Harper & Brothers.

To Appleton-Century-Crofts for the use of material adapted from *An Introduction to Playwriting* by Samuel Selden. Copyright, 1946, by F. S. Crofts & Co., Inc.

To Cornell University Press for permission to include "Raisin' the Devil" by Robert Gard from *The Lake Guns of Seneca and Cayuga* edited by A. M. Drummond and Robert E. Gard. Copyright, 1942, by Cornell University. For permission to produce this play, address all inquiries to Cornell University Press, Ithaca, New York.

To Dodd, Mead & Company for permission to reprint "Forging the Fifteenth Amendment" from *Laugh with Leacock* by Stephen Leacock. Copyright, 1930, by Dodd, Mead & Company, Inc.

To Charles Scribner's Sons for excerpts from *Abe Lincoln in Illinois* by Robert Sherwood, pp. 189, 190–92, 203, and 220. Copyright, 1937, 1939, Robert Emmet Sherwood.

To Anderson House, Hinsdale, New York, for the passage from *Valley Forge* by Maxwell Anderson. Copyright, 1934, by Maxwell Anderson. Copyright renewed, 1962, by Gilda Anderson, Alan Anderson, Terence Anderson, Quentin Anderson, and Hesper A. Levenstein. All rights reserved.

To Fred Carmichael for permission to include *One for the Lord's Day.* All rights reserved. For permission to produce this play, address all inquiries to the author, Fred Carmichael, Dorset Playhouse, Dorset, Vermont.

To Mrs. Booth Tarkington and Doubleday & Company, Inc. for the quotation from "The Pageant of the Table Round," copyright, 1913, by Booth Tarkington. From the book *Penrod* by Booth Tarkington. Reprinted by permission of Doubleday & Company, Inc. and Mrs. Booth Tarkington.

To the University of Texas Press for permission to use excerpts from

A Cloud of Witnesses: The Drama of the Alamo by Ramsey Yelvington. Copyright, 1959, by the University of Texas Press.

To Barrie Stavis, Ethel Theodora Rockwell, Charlotte McLeod, Marjorie Barstow Greenbie, and Emmet Lavery for allowing us to quote from their works go our especial thanks.

Contents

List of figures

List of tables

Creating historical drama

I. The scope of historical drama

RESIDENTS of an Israeli agricultural collective bulldoze a temporary amphitheatre out of a mountain and celebrate their quarter-century anniversary by producing a drama about the Maccabean War. With a flourish of colorful silk and samurai sword, a Japanese city performs a dramatization in the compound of an ancient castle whose history it depicts. In honor of the coronation of Elizabeth II, an English town recreates its inheritance from the beginnings to the days of Queen Victoria. Citizens of a village in the Bavarian Alps don Biblical costume once every ten years to portray in a Passion Play the last seven earthly days of Christ. These efforts exemplify history-based dramas fostered by communities throughout the world.

Such dramas are engendered by communities in the United States as well as in nations abroad. Several counties, for example, in a northwestern state join forces to do a drama using historical material for a centennial celebration; a town in the same state pursues a similar course. A midwestern university observes its founding with a dramatic work about its past. Students at a southeastern elementary school turn thespians to reenact a short play concerned with their locale's Civil War history. A play centering on a contemporary scientist composed by a fledgling playwright is produced by an eastern college; and the new work of an experienced regional dramatist—not written for the commercial theatre of Broadway—reveals to patrons of a west coast civic theatre group an old legend of the area. A New England church transforms its chancel into a stage to revive an event in biblical history. Members of a western chapter of a national fraternal society apply greasepaint to recount their organization's backgrounds. And a southwestern power company theatrically glorifies its past in a civic amphitheatre. In each of these instances, materials of a historical, biographical, legendary, and biblical nature are put to dramatic use. To identify them all, we shall use the broad term "historical drama."

We also notice that in all the above cases of such drama some kind of fostering group is involved: a town or a city, a church, a nation or world-wide religious sect, a local organization or its national affiliate, a state university or an elementary school, a civic group or special-interest club. Each of these entities has certain values, objectives, interests, and activities that unify its members and lend it a particular character. Let us therefore consider here any one such body as a community, whether geographic, institutional, or organizational. Although many such groups and places represent a part of the larger whole—that is, the larger community—each is a community unto itself bound by individualized aims and activities. For clarity's sake throughout, we shall use "community" in an all-inclusive sense. To us the term implies any town, city, state, or region, as well as civic, regional, national or international group or institution that has particular interests and characteristics. And while a wide variety of such communities generates historical dramas on a world-wide basis, we shall be focusing on experiences in the United States. Yet our material also will be applicable to communities in other lands. Additionally, our chief concern throughout centers on the creating of historical drama in the community from writing to production.

What is historical drama?

Although several general examples have been offered, we need now more closely to ask ourselves "What is historical drama?" Dramatic writing, as we customarily use the term, can be cut out of the whole cloth of our imagination and invention. *Historical* dramatic writing, however, begins with a fabric either of facts or of legendary happenings currently accepted as the same. This fabric is then embroidered upon by the imagination and invention. The warp and woof of historical drama are factual events in the life of an actual person or group of persons, a town, a nation, a social institution, a religious movement, or even humanity at large. But the dramatization must use material which can stir an emotional response in an audience—thus making such material dramatic as George Pierce Baker once pointed out—and which can be adapted for the special requirements of the theatre.[1] Because drama by its very nature must be dramatic and adaptable for the stage, the writer usually has to select, arrange, and modify the data of personalities and events. He does this in order not only to clarify a personal viewpoint—to embody, in effect, an idea or theme—but also to arouse in his audience a feeling that it is reliving the past in terms of the present. Hervey Allen, the author of *Anthony Adverse*, implies that the historical novelist and the dramatist have similar responsibilities and problems in this regard. The former's function, says Allen, "is to produce a complete illusion in the reader's mind." He continues:

> In effect, the historical novel is simply a door through which the novelist leads his readers into other times than their own. But it is not a door to a storehouse of records and specimens of the past. The novelist's

door is the portal of a theater. Once the reader passes it, what he sees going on is not the actual past, but a drama arranged by the author *about* the past. The reader may then succumb to the spell of the dramatic illusion, but that is not to say that he has been deluded into thinking what he sees is the real past, any more than a man who buys a ticket to a play showing the assassination of Julius Caesar has a right to complain that he has not seen the actual event.[2]

Although Allen's appraisal cannot be directly applied to every type of drama based on history, it issues a warning that the playwright should bear in mind. When dramatizing history, he must generally take, out of theatrical necessity, varying degrees of license with the facts. Nevertheless, those facts always remain as the basic material of the dramatic action.

Admittedly every dramatist fashions his characters and dramatic action out of the "facts" of his own existence—that is, out of his observations and reflections on the life and society around him. The writer of historical drama, however, is consciously concerned with giving dramatic life to specific, factual events and personages out of the past. Clifford Odets draws from his personal experience of the Depression to write *Awake and Sing.* In that play he projects the story of a fictional Jewish family in the Bronx caught in a web of clashing personal desires and obligations. On the other hand, Federal Theatre Project writers, focusing on the same period, delineate the economic consequences and problems arising out of the Agricultural Adjustment Act of 1933. The result is *Triple-A Plowed Under,*[3] a socio-historical drama, the action of which is based on actual events. The drama obviously serves to "document" and interpret those events.

Any dramatist may place imagined events and characters in settings that are removed in space and time from his own experience; in so doing he seeks a yeasty milieu for the fermentation of his dramatic—and fictional—story. Maxwell Anderson in *The Wingless Victory,* for example, combines fictional characters and the Medea legend and sets them in early nineteenth-century puritanic New England to heighten a modern comment on racial prejudice. This is not the approach of the historical dramatist, as we use the term. Arthur Miller, on the other hand, more closely coincides with our meaning of "historical drama" in *The Crucible* when he relies on actual court records and the names of real persons connected with the Salem Witch Trials of 1692 to disclose the effects of Puritan superstition and mass hysteria. Yet Miller, like Anderson, is being critical of his own day, for *The Crucible* points unmistakable parallels to the McCarthy investigations of the 1950's.

What subject matter the writer chooses to deal with, and the extent to which it is derived from factual events and actual humans of the past, furnish a touchstone for recognizing historical drama. But another factor in describing the term—implicit in *Triple-A Plowed Under* and *The Crucible*—is the *motive* or *intent* represented by the historical drama itself. Frequently the *personal* intent of the dramatist is not discernible either to himself or to his audience, and this is as true of the historical dramatist as of any other. Such an academic teaser as "What's the author's purpose in writing the play?" is often difficult if not impossible to answer. He may not know himself! But in the case of historical drama, one aspect of the writer's intent remains fully evident: his desire to revivify past or present persons and events in order to project a dramatic experience. This will be an integral part of his overall intent, whether he wishes to commemorate an incident in the founding of the local high school; to depict the highlights in the existence of a humanitarian cause, a community of religious zealots, or a woman physician; or to find answers to contemporary problems by revealing parallels in the past.

Forms of historical drama

Most contemporary writing, fictional or nonfictional, takes a certain structure or form chosen by the writer to give his materials unity, clarity, and meaning. Broadly conceived, drama includes such diverse though related forms as the full-length play, the one-act play, the skit or sketch, the dramatic monologue, the radio drama, the television drama, and the screen-play. To a large degree, these forms are determined by the dramatic medium employed. Media like radio, television, the motion picture, for example, have distinctive forms of drama because each medium has its own intrinsic and special requirements. When it exists, the presence of a "live" audience introduces to the theatre experience certain built-in structural characteristics. And, also, the presence of such an audience gives rise to the broad term "live" drama—the focus of our attention in this book. It is useful, therefore, to see what dramatic forms potentially are suitable for the treatment of history.

Three major types of "live" drama can utilize historical materials in the way we have indicated earlier. First and most familiar to the playgoer is "biography-drama," which focuses on the lives of actual personages and centers its appeal to the audience in the related actions and reactions of its characters. Most frequently, one historical character predominates and unifies the action. Examples of "biography-drama" are such full-length plays as Robert E. Sherwood's *Abe Lincoln in Illinois*, Emmet Lavery's *The Magnificent Yankee*

(Oliver Wendell Holmes), William Gibson's *The Miracle Worker* (Anne Sullivan Macy), Dore Schary's *Sunrise at Campobello* (Franklin D. Roosevelt), and *The Crucible*. Also included in this group are dramatized "religious" histories: Jean Anouilh's *Becket* and T. S. Eliot's *Murder in the Cathedral* (also about Thomas à Becket), John Osborne's *Luther*, and Christopher Fry's story of Moses, *The Firstborn*.

A second form of historical drama is "pageant-drama," commonly a series of loosely linked episodes, unified through theme rather than characters. The form usually presents a panoramic life story of a social, political, or religious community. Most often it is produced and performed by the community itself for a specific occasion and may or may not be repeated. The name of the community frequently appears in a title as evinced by *The Kansas Story*, *Castine*, or *The Pageant of Newark*.

The third major type of historical drama is a more recently developed one referred to here as "epic-drama." Its form combines the large scope of the pageant-drama with the character concentration and involvement found in biography-drama. Since it is still in a state of evolution, its characteristics of shape and style are not yet standardized. For the most part epic-dramas deal importantly if not principally with heroes such as Theodore Roosevelt, Thomas Jefferson and Sam Houston, or with national struggles epitomized by a regional community like that of the Cherokee Indian; and it is the loftiness of theme or character that justifies the use of "epic" to describe them.[4] Fostered by communities, epic-dramas like Paul Green's *The Lost Colony*, Robert Emmett McDowell's *Home is the Hunter*, and Kermit Hunter's *Unto These Hills* are presented every summer.

Within these three major forms there exist many gradations and variations. These are in large part determined by the individual communities and playwrights fusing their common desire for expression. In passing, two briefer forms can be mentioned which are actually dramaturgical abridgements of two of the major types: the pageant-drama episode—such as the brief historical playlet frequently given in elementary schools to honor a national holiday, and the one-act biography-drama of which Betty Smith and Chase Webb's *Lawyer Lincoln* or Thornton Wilder's *Mozart* are representative. In the latter group can be included the growing number of approximately hour-long historical plays for children like Charlotte Chorpenning's *The Indian Captive* (Mary Jemison).

Later chapters will allow more extensive explanation of all these forms. Moreover, our focus throughout is on these dramatic forms of "live" theatrical presentation: the pageant-drama, the biography-drama, the epic-drama, and their related forms. Many requirements and demands of these major types of historical drama can also be applied when treating similar subject matter in other media like radio, television, and the motion picture.

The demand for history and its drama

A lively interest in history exists in our time. We, as a people, have an appetite for historical material that is expressed vividly. We flock to historic sites and museums in an eager way. Family groups plan vacation trips or weekend excursions to such places not simply because they will derive "good" from the visit. They look for fun, too; and fun is what often results, mainly because of the enlarged family facilities provided by park authorities at historic sites, and of the visual and auditory methods that museum directors have developed for interpreting our heritage. A reconstructed ship or village means more to the spectator than a faded old print on a wall cluttered with countless other old prints or the mute ruins a mile from an information center. Seeing guides wearing period costumes with authority—or even waxwork figures in tableaux doing so—may bring back the past more vividly than a portrait or stone statue. Hearing the recorded voices, actual or impersonated, of figures out of the past, or the sounds and cries of conflict at the overlook of a famous battleground lets young and old relive our yesterday with new understanding. At the Palace of Versailles, for instance, moving multi-colored lights and disembodied sound—the voices of kings, queens, mistresses, soldiers, and mobs—allow the visitor to hear, and almost see in his imagination, the daily ceremonial of Louis XIV, the angry rabble of Paris hammering on Marie Antoinette's door, or the signing of the peace treaty of World War I in the Hall of Mirrors; and some eighty other historic sites in Europe—and several in the United States—enthrall tourists by similar means.[5]

Visitors to Old Sturbridge Village, an outdoor museum in Massachusetts consisting of a restored century and a half old New England hamlet, are treated every summer to daily performances of a short drama based on an aspect of early New England life; each summer brings a new drama on a different aspect. In the South at Richmond, Virginia, four historic buildings— the Wickham-Valentine House, the Robert E. Lee House, St. Paul's Episcopal Church, and the Confederate Museum—present for a few months each spring short theatrical performances ranging from an organ recital and a choral group singing songs of the Civil War period to a reading of a portion of Stephen Vincent Benet's John Brown's Body and a dramatic sketch in which Jefferson Davis receives the news of Dahlgren's Raid.[6] And, on a more commercial level, in New York City's Freedomland a tiny historic America is molded out of two hundred and five acres where the young and parents young-in-heart can experience history by ducking crossfire at a Civil War battlefield, by fighting the Chicago fire, or by riding an ore bucket to an old Southwest silver mine. A growing number of parks and museums throughout the country bring history to life by realizing its dramatic potentialities.

Museum attendance appears to be on the upswing. At least ten leading eastern historical museums disclose notable attendance increases in recent years.[7] Furthermore, visitation to historic areas administered by the National Park Service has increased more than sixty percent from 1956 to 1960.[8] And historian Allan Nevins avers that over thirty million Americans visit our national historic shrines each year in Virginia alone.[9] Those whose affair it is to test the interests of tourists are pretty much agreed that—next to scenery— historic houses, sites and museums are the greatest attractions to the American family on the move.[10]

Whether on the move or curled up around a good book at home, Americans continue their infatuation with history. When one looks at random at the racks in the neighborhood bookstore or drug store, one sees an array of history titles among the magazines and paperbacks, not the least of which are those biographical histories designed for youngsters. At the local newsstand one might also see a copy of *The American Heritage*, a periodical with abundant, colorful illustrations and vividly written articles that are based on sound scholarship. It is, as periodicals go, expensive. And yet its subscription list soared from 80,000 to 300,000 in its first four years.[11]

Neither are books based on historical material lacking in their capacity to entice readers. The greatest American best sellers have been Margaret Mitchell's *Gone With the Wind* and Kenneth Roberts' *Northwest Passage*.[12] As a matter of fact, at least one historical novel has been listed among the "top ten sellers" almost every year from 1933 to 1959.[13] Over this same period, fictional and nonfictional works dealing with religious history have soared in publication and sale—Lloyd Douglas' *The Robe* stayed on the best seller list for thirty-two months! One need not check annual summaries in *Publishers Weekly* to realize the impressive popularity during the past decade of fiction and nonfiction in the areas of biography, history, and religion. Future trends in this direction are impossible to foretell, but certainly many readers have indicated substantial interest in these three subjects in recent years.

In spite of the handicaps inherent in two industries that tend to waste their creative talent on trivia, television and the motion pictures have respectively produced some popular programs and films of a historical and biblical emphasis. In the television field, a series like "Profiles in Courage," which dramatizes intrepid personages of American history, has been successful during its year or so network lifetime; and, hopefully, it will solidify the fine tradition of such former historical drama series as "The Great Adventure," "Our American Heritage," and "You Are There." Then, too, events and figures out of biblical history frequently are recreated in programs sponsored by religious groups. Biblical sources over the last ten years have been the subject of many motion pictures, the scope and inherent spectacle of which readily lend themselves to giant cinema screens. Historical subjects, too, appear to be enjoying some revival among the movie-makers. Attendance figures attest to the popularity of such films as The Ten Commandments, Ben Hur, Cleopatra, Lawrence of Arabia and How the West was Won, all spectacles with biblical or historical reference which temporarily have taken viewers away from their television sets.[14] However, owing to the currently unpredictable nature of the film industry, it is dangerous to say this reflects a trend toward presenting large-budgeted screen plays with such subject matter. (And since such films often are lacking in merit artistic or historic, many may say "amen.") Whereas television is the greatest offender, neither the cinema nor its rival medium has realized its obligations to a history-minded public.

While both television and the motion picture have disappointed many of their warmest boosters, the recording industry has—within recent years— grown in quality as it has in quantity. And our understanding of history is the richer for it. Auditory historical footnotes in vocal and instrumental music, for instance, often bring us closer to the "feel" of a period than printed documents. Listeners gain an indescribable immediacy from excellent spoken-word recordings, either from edited tapes of authentic occasions or "on-the-spot" reenactments of such historic moments as Lincoln's 1861 inaugural address. Moreover, sales of such records show a modest but gradual increase.[15]

In the commercial theatre the historical play is frequently considered anathema at the box office. Yet plays treating biographical and religious materials are gaining greater acceptance. In addition to those plays previously mentioned, recent Broadway seasons have witnessed the critical and/or popular success of such biographical dramatizations as A Man for All Seasons (Sir Thomas More), Dylan (Dylan Thomas), The Diary of Anne Frank, and The Andersonville Trial (Captain Wirz, Confederate prison commandant). More than once biographical musicals like The Unsinkable Molly Brown, Fiorello! (LaGuardia), and Ben Franklin in Paris have caught the favor of audiences.

In the last two decades the theatre on-and-off Broadway has seen productions of plays spun out of biblical history like Gideon, The Sun and I, The

Flowering Peach, Between Two Thieves, and *The Sign of Jonah* for example. And competing in the commercial market place, Archibald MacLeish's *J. B.* has proved that the relationship between God's man and man's God can be dramatically provocative in our era. The success of *J. B.*, aided perhaps by controversy among theologians, has prompted the director of religious drama at New York's Union Theological Seminary to observe "a readiness among people generally for plays which will reaffirm something of the dignity of man." [16] Something of this yearning for reaffirmation underlies the attendance of individuals, year after year, at the large-scale epic-dramas that have become annual open-air presentations in some regions, first in the Southeast and more recently spread to other sections of the country. The attraction of such perennials as North Carolina's *Unto These Hills*, Virginia's *The Common Glory*, and Kentucky's *The Stephen Foster Story* has been a compelling one.

Our national longing for the past recently has been reflected in the scope of the nation-wide Civil War Centennial. Taking inventory of historic events within their borders, more than forty states—usually coordinating their efforts with local communities—planned a calendar of activities often revealing dignity and imagination. [17] To illuminate the aspects of a controversial war, many communities featured such events as commemorative ceremonies at historic shrines, restoration of old forts, music festivals, costume balls, and reenacted battles both North and South. In all of these events the avowed purpose was to observe the past, to develop local interest and enthusiasm, and to provide enjoyment for audiences that crossed regional lines. To be sure, the total scope and success of the Centennial cannot be judged at the time of this writing, but such activities in themselves are nothing startlingly new. A hearty interest in our history has been growing in our nation for many decades.

Our national enthusiasm for the vivid presentation of history cannot be denied. We are ready and willing to interpret a heritage that enriches us as a people.

Why dramatize history?

Assuming a strong national enthusiasm for the past, and granting the many avenues of expression open to us, why should we turn to drama as a means of fulfilment? Why dramatize history? This is a complex question to be given an over-simplified answer before taking up the substance of later chapters: what the principles and practices are that yield the best historical drama. And although one of these chapters explores some specific causes of why communities dramatize their history, one important consideration demands our awareness at the outset stemming from the nature of the drama itself.

Philosophers, artists, and scientists generally agree that the drama has a social origin. It is an experience shared publicly rather than privately. In the cultures of the aborigines and in less primitive ones, Oriental and Occidental, the enacted drama functions as the symbolic core of the community, representing a way of living both similar to others and yet peculiar to the specific culture as a whole. Drama which reveals the universal in man, comments playwright Arthur Miller, is honored throughout the world. "Today," continues Miller, "as the world appears to be most definitely split politically, art and especially theatre quite clearly demonstrate that his [man's] deeper identity is universal." [18] Our community of today and the theatre which it creates—if attuned to its respective local heritage—can contribute importantly to our emotional and spiritual growth as citizens.

We all have heard the phrase that "a play *exists* only in performance." While we may have tired of listening to this refrain of the stage director during the junior-class play or the community theatre rehearsal, it nonetheless is true. Without an audience, that is, we cannot have a dramatic experience: it is created solely in and by us when we gather to rediscover common hopes and to share a common self-discovery. When we as an audience respond with immediacy and intensity, the power and wonder of the communal experience is felt. This communion of feeling spread among us is what lends singularity and eminence to the theatre. Claiming that the theatre appeals to the sense of neighborliness in man, the late actor-director Louis Jouvet adds that it "both uses and creates reactions of sensitivity and bonds of affection and friendship. These are the essential acts. Transmitted . . . these acts create in turn a spiritual community and identity." [19] Thus it is that the theatre joins our own life with the life of our community in an experience direct, viable, and dynamic.

To communities that pride themselves on alert and progressive leadership, historical dramas—in scope and complexity subject to local aims and resources—offer opportunities unlimited for the recreation of historical material. The audience, the production and performance personnel, and the community itself stand to profit on many counts. For the audience involved in the creative acts of making history live again, the main satisfactions come from forging spiritual links with the past which, in turn, create "a spiritual community and identity." The presentation of such an effort calls on various individual talents and group specializations. Purposeful leadership in the community needs to find ways of adapting a number of human resources to the inception of the dramatic idea and its development into a full-blown production. Only the limits imposed by the scope and demands of the production scheme should bar conscientious workers from contributing to the general endeavor. For the community itself, far-sighted leadership provides the beacon light to express something in our heritage which we cherish and wish to celebrate. With spiritual benefits, there also accrue social, educational, and often economic gains to the community with the vision and the dream to recreate its history meaningfully and vividly.

Finally, let us not forget that a wealth of history imprisoned in the past cries out for dramatization—it cries out from the dust of library shelves, from historical markers entangled by weeds, from national shrines as lifeless as their own cold stone or marble. Let the community search out this history. And, when its resources appropriately measure to the task, let the community bring its history to vibrant life through a communal effort rewarding to participants and spectators alike. This is an obligation that the community may well owe itself.

II. Recognizing the dramatic in history

IN COOPERSTOWN, New York, Louis C. Jones, director of the New York State Historical Association, is a man with a hankering for the unconventional idea. He effectively runs two popular museums, and in one of them—the Farmers' Museum, which displays the tools and artifacts of early Americana—the visitor finds that he is allowed to touch almost everything. Instead of being rebuffed by the usual "hands off" policy, he is actively encouraged to push an antique carpenter's plane or take a supervised turn at the flax wheel. And out back, in a reconstructed early New York village, his children can buy some old-fashioned penny licorice in a country store or ride in a Conestoga wagon behind a team of proud-footed horses.

People wishing to get a broader background of history come from many states every summer to attend the annual Seminars on American Culture in Cooperstown. There informal classes are offered in a wide spectrum of subjects ranging from frontier folkways and pioneer cooking to the conservation of paintings. All of these activities are the result of Louis Jones' characteristically off-the-beaten-track ideas. In 1958, he had another such idea, and he came to see us about it: New York State was about to celebrate its three hundred fiftieth anniversary, and he thought of scheduling a seminar on the writing and producing of historical drama. "We haven't done this kind of thing before," he said, "but it looks like a good time to start. I foresee a rash of pageants and commemorative dramas, and believe some of these people would appreciate your help." It didn't take him long to convince us. As he rose to go, he added, "And don't forget to tell them how to recognize what's dramatic in history! Not everybody knows."

And not everybody did know. One earnest gentleman was keen to write a drama on Albany's Joseph Henry, the physicist who perfected the electromagnet. The major scene of the projected script consisted of Henry's going through a series of intricate steps to improve the tiny mechanism. A sampling of the detailed "action" went something like this:

> Henry looks at the bent bar of soft iron, a foot long and half an inch in diameter. He carefully takes some silk and wraps it a number of clockwise turns around the bar. Then he . . .

We pointed out to the gentleman that such minutiae could hardly furnish the action of a dramatic scene. For one thing, the intricate movements so described could not be seen by an audience. For another, an audience would not find them dramatically interesting merely because they were historically authentic. However, we added, if Henry's internal action—that of pitting his mind against an uncharted area of knowledge—were externalized, spectators might find him dramatic. Furthermore, if Henry's previous actions showed that he urgently wished to solve the riddle of electromagnetism, then his act of discovery (when properly simplified) could be made dramatically meaningful to an audience. Scientific investigation does not necessarily lie outside the realm of drama, as some effective works have proven. The gentleman realized that he had not been thinking of his idea in terms of its illustration on the stage, and he proceeded to revise it from that viewpoint.

"Dramatic" is a word used carelessly. A youngster runs into a room and falls on his face: he has made a "dramatic entrance." An excitable woman stretches the truth for the gain of a good story: she "dramatizes things." A teen-ager foresees catastrophic results from a trivial incident: his parents say he is acting "too dramatic." All of these situations may bear ingredients of the dramatic as the term is discussed in the following pages. But still it is astonishing the number of people who can, in such instances, intuitively sense the dramatic without having the slightest idea of what it really consists, what it basically demands, or how it can be consciously recognized. For those concerned with historical drama, such intelligence is important indeed.

Far too many historical dramas are as lifeless as a roadside marker partially because their writers and sponsors fail to realize and express the most dramatic elements inherent in the historical material available to them. Therefore, although we grant that there exists in humans a rather intuitive perception of the dramatic, our aim here is to sharpen our *conscious* awareness of dramatic material in history's pages and people.

The drama of personalities

In order to glean the dramatic from history, we must first realize that drama is fashioned out of the sadness and laughter in the happenings of everyday experience. All drama is hewn out of the basic materials of life: human personalities, their loves, their longings, their clashes. And so, we must train our powers of observation and our insights and apply them to the life around us. Our eyes and ears must be open to the myriad details that make one person different from another: faces, clothing, movements, vocal patterns, and other idiosyncrasies—outer signs that reveal the inner person.[1] We must see how some people talk with their hands, some with their eyebrows, or some with scarcely a movement of the lips. The character of a person may be expressed in as simple a habitual gesture as twisting a handkerchief or pushing a hat back on the head. We must know the gait of a young woman in a hurry or the rhythmic tempo of a laborer shoveling dirt.

Our ears must be attuned to the noises of Main Street at midday or to a throng of townspeople watching fireworks on the Fourth of July. The vocal patterns of people, we must realize, reflect their age, their occupations, their geographic origins, and their inner emotions. The bank clerk from Atlanta has a casual drawl that in no way resembles the clipped bite of the high school English teacher from New England. And a teen-age daughter gives a different inflection to "All right, I'm going," when gaily leaving on a date than when reluctantly trudging to her room to do homework. If we are to understand and interpret human motives and action—that is, to understand what makes people tick—we must be aware of the externals of human personalities.

At the outset we must know people in order to discern the dramatic in life and in history. But it is often an easier task to observe the external traits and inner motivations of those around us than it is to "know" people who now belong to history. Having to remove the latter from the winding sheets of the past, we then must breathe life into such persons: first, by thinking of them as ordinary human beings and, second, by selecting their extraordinary qualities, great or small. The figures of the past do not entirely reveal themselves through their deeds or through the best-known facts of their lives. A contemporary artist's sketch of a man's glance or gesture on a specific occasion may reveal a great deal more. And a diary's testament to daily habits or private feelings can do likewise. Capable of realizing the man or woman in the actual figure, we are better armed to perceive the dramatic quality of such a person.

Commonly, effective drama usually revolves around one or more central characters that are in themselves "dramatic." Sometimes the leading character is an individual hero (often called the *protagonist*); or sometimes the leading character is a collective hero—composed of many people, like a community or a particular group. But even when a collective hero exists, one or a few persons who represent the whole group are usually emphasized. Generally, it is held that the greatest source of drama is the dramatic character; and if this be granted, what touchstones do we seek which can be used to test the dramatic silver of the historical figure? Let us look at three figures, disparate in time and place, as they briefly are sketched.

NEW ENGLAND-BORN JOHN BROWN abandoned an early intention to study for the ministry and tried his hand at more than four business enterprises only to find himself bankrupt at the age of forty-two. At fifty-two he had lived in four states, married twice, and fathered twenty children. During his lifetime he developed a strong hatred for the institution of slavery. Following five of his sons to Kansas, he became a conspicuous figure by joining anti-slavery factions to fight pro-slavery settlers in pitched battles. Abolitionists in the East gave him support. Two years before the Civil War began, he proceeded to carry out a scheme for facilitating the escape of fugitive slaves and encouraging a slave insurrection. With a party of only eighteen men, he attacked the federal arsenal at Harpers Ferry, Virginia (now West Virginia). His forces captured and briefly held the arsenal until they were overpowered by local militia and federal troops. Ten of his men, including two of his sons, were killed. The uprising he had hoped to provoke did not occur. He was convicted of treason and hanged, and he became a martyr to the anti-slavery cause.[2]

THE APOSTLE PAUL was born the son of a Roman citizen and raised as a Hebrew. As a young man, he felt that the gospel of Christ was an effrontery to established Judaic law, and, as a Pharisee, he took an active part in the persecution of the Christians. However, on the way to Damascus, he later claimed, he saw a vision of Christ. He was thereby converted to the Christian faith and spent the rest of his life as a missionary, spreading the doctrine of Christianity throughout the Roman Empire. Eventually imprisoned by the Romans for causing disturbances, he was sent to Rome as a captive. It is generally believed that here he was executed, in the reign of Nero circa 62 A.D.[3]

IN 1764 MEHITABEL WING was the quiet Quaker wife of an Irish farmer named William Prendergast who lived in Quaker Hill (now Pawling), New York. Holding his land on perpetual lease from the manor lord, her husband resented having to pay a sizable rent while not being able to own his land. Although his Quaker wife shared her sect's abhorrence of violence, he raised an army of a thousand farmers and continually harassed the manor lords up and down the Hudson Valley. Soon British troops went to the defense of the patroons and defeated the farmers, who resisted by force of arms. Mehitabel persuaded her hus-

*band to surrender and was at his side when he was brought to trial.
During the proceedings, the unprepossessing girl in her Quaker dress
countered the damning accusations of the attorney general by ad-
dressing herself to the court and winning the sympathy of both the
spectators and the Chief Justice. But despite her efforts, her husband
was convicted and sentenced to hang. Mehitabel abandoned the conventional role of stay-at-home housewife and rode eighty miles on
horseback directly to the Royal Governor, from whom she gained a
reprieve for her husband and a petition for a royal pardon. Then she
rode the eighty miles back to Poughkeepsie, without taking time for
rest, and saved her husband from the gallows. The royal pardon was
granted six months later, and the Prendergasts returned to their farm.*[4]

Whatever their dissimilarities—and there are many—these three persons
share common qualities. We must observe first of all that they are persons *not
content.* They are restlessly dissatisfied with something in the world around
them.[5] Doubtless, John Brown is not only galled at a life of persistent failure
but also is enraged by the institution of slavery. The Apostle Paul reverses his
discontent with Christianity, which he feels a threat to established Judaic law,
to a discontent with a world that he thinks needs the gospel of Christ. And
Mehitabel Wing refuses to accept the alternatives of her husband's leading the
life of an outlaw or his leaving life as a rebellious traitor. Dramatic heroes
usually have this quality of active discontent. How compelling a hero would
Hamlet be were he sufficiently satisfied in his position as Prince and heir to
the throne of Denmark? Imagine the result if Hamlet refuses with an indifferent dismissal his ghostly father's command to avenge a foul murder and an
ill-begotten throne! There would be, of course, no play, or certainly no exciting
drama like the one we know. Instead, Hamlet strives against his own pro-
crastination and against his uncle's forces ultimately to thrust home his
vengeance.

The three figures considered here are not merely restive and dissatisfied.
Although history and daily experience reveal such people in abundance, they
do not approach the dramatic until they set out actively to do something about
their source of contention. Restlessness, especially when coupled with discontent, connotes action. Paul is hardly tranquil when he decides to throw down
the gauntlet in defense of Christianity. Mehitabel Wing battles as strongly, if
less violently, against British authorities that would hang her husband as John
Brown does against the institution of slavery. All these persons are positive
individuals possessing strong wills, who struggle hard for or against something

in a time they think out of joint. They fight! They contend relentlessly, sometimes excessively, for something in which they believe. In such combat they may even willingly sacrifice themselves and, in some cases, their families. (John Brown lost three sons in his struggle against slavery and left his wife a widow.) They refuse to compromise abjectly, to give up the fight half way. Quaker though she be, Mehitabel Wing proves no exception to this, because she primarily struggles in defense of her husband's life and future welfare and persists until victorious. The dramatic historical figure not only actively opposes a source of discontent, but also reveals an uncommon intensity of purpose.

It is worth noting that the major obstacles encountered by our three figures can be objectified or represented by human opponents seen in action on stage. The court and militia of the state of Virginia, the townsfolk of Harpers Ferry, and the federal troops are all embodiments of the obstacles opposed by John Brown. Similarly, the Judaic judges and Roman soldiers set against Paul, and the British Colonial authorities confronting Mehitabel Wing, are embodiments of the obstacles antagonistic to these two persons. (Most of these forces are representative of large, less tangible obstacles like the institution of slavery or governmental or religious authority. They manifest the abstract in human form.) Greater dramatic potential is present in these portraits because their struggles can be objectified on stage to show us human forces in conflict. An important corollary follows from this factor (suggested also by the earlier example of scientist Joseph Henry).

Figures out of the past who are not doers, but rather thinkers whose struggles largely are internal (i.e., minds pitted against abstract ideas, scientific concepts, or problems of creating an art work) are difficult to transform into stage characters because the obstacles that buffet them are not easily capable of externalization. The inner turmoils of a John Brown or a Paul or a Mehitabel Wing—whether these clearly can be perceived or reasonably deduced—in large part can be illustrated by the external events of their lives.

When winnowing the dramatic grain from the chaff of historical personages, the severity of the barriers apparent in such lives must be considered. Our three figures, in order to put their lives and their immediate world back into balance, encounter weighty forces against which they must contend persistently. The odds usually are against them. The power of the state and federal governments and the regionally established system of Negro slavery confront John Brown. The established Judaic religion and the strength of the Roman Empire oppose Paul's efforts to spread the Christian faith. Also, the Apostle's own firm belief in Judaic law before his conversion creates an earlier hurdle for him to overcome. Mehitabel Wing comes face to face with British colonial law which sentences her husband to death. The fact that these people encounter barriers that appear difficult, indeed sometimes impassable, makes for struggles that cannot be swiftly won. An extended struggle is demanded. This is a vital point when we realize that the fountainhead of most effective drama is the vigorous combat of a hero with opposing forces that can withstand heavy onslaught. Without such a barrier equal to or stronger than the leading character's exertions, a drama lacks sufficient struggle for the substance of its story.

Another aspect of the dramatic figure can be revealed by a close look at our three sketches: each has undergone some change as an individual. John Brown starts out as an unsuccessful nobody and ends up as a violent military leader and martyr to the anti-slavery cause. The Apostle Paul is transformed from a firm Pharisee who persecutes Christians to a leading zealot and missionary of the Christian faith. The quiet little Quaker girl Mehitabel Wing blossoms into a dynamic woman. All three have moved relentlessly from one state of mind to another. Their willingness to fight for something has wrought in them some significant change. A full dimension of their being has stood revealed in the conflict which their struggles have fomented. Man, by nature, grows and develops. But in the case of dramatic personalities, the change is often swift, radical, and seemingly inevitable.

Conflict is initiated by a decision. Consequently, these figures have made some major decision that has affected their destiny and development. That decision may have been to incite a slave insurrection, to abandon one faith to embrace another, or to forego Quaker forbearance and the established role of a farm wife. People whose decisive actions cause them to change and develop are dramatic.

Resembling a climber deciding to scale a dangerously steep mountain in order to reach its summit, a dramatic character has an earnestly desired destination, a goal of some kind. Usually such goals are acceptable, or at least understandable, to an audience. To effect eventually the freedom of Negro slaves, to override a legally administered death sentence in order to save a husband's life, and to spread the Christian gospel are the specific objectives of our three figures here, and, as such, will find general audience acceptance. Even the controversial figure of John Brown really is not an exception. Although his violent methods might be in question, his ultimate aim generally is approved by spectators. (We note, incidentally, that often the goals of a dramatic historical figure are in advance of his own time and accepted only by later generations. While this feature is no prerequisite to choosing such a figure for dramatization, it undoubtedly heightens dramatic interest.)

Deeds and goals are largely responsible for determining the admirable qualities of a person. Yet Paul and Mehitabel Wing and John Brown are dramatically attractive to audiences not primarily because their acts and goals might be commendable but because those goals are the product of some yearning common to all men: self-fulfilment, or freedom, or survival, or love. These figures gain a universal quality because they struggle for something that all persons strive and long for. A John Brown, therefore, gains in stature not so much through his deeds as through his urgent desire to serve as an instrument to free his fellow man from bondage.

Universality, and the quality of the admirable, are vital factors when we consider that an audience comes to the theatre unconsciously wanting someone to root for. It wants to participate vicariously in a drama's action by consciously or unconsciously associating itself with a hero for whom it can feel some measure of sympathy and rapport. Of course, dramatic literature reveals exceptions to this principle. Yet, we will do well to listen to veteran playwright Howard Lindsay's comment that unless a writer can "write as well as Lillian Hellman" (whose fictional heroine in *The Little Foxes* ruthlessly dominates a southern family), he is unwise to attempt a villainous protagonist.[6] The idealism of a John Brown or a Paul, or the quiet determination and womanly acumen of a Mehitabel Wing are traits that an audience likes and esteems.

Frequently, historians do not agree in their opinions of a particular person from the past. There may exist more variant interpretations of an Alexander Hamilton, a Napoleon, a Franklin D. Roosevelt, for instance, than could be found in fiction or dramatic literature. Furthermore, even the *facts* of persons' lives may vary according to different historians. A writer doing research for a television project amusingly points out that facts as given by historians often resemble gossip that becomes garbled in the retelling. As one example, she says that three conflicting sources told her that

> EITHER "Gulian C. Verplanck . . . despite his Federalist and aristocratic background . . . *began uttering heresy as early as 1790.* Perhaps it was the influence of Edward Livingston with whom he studied for two years." . . . Or Gulian C. Verplanck was born in *1784* and entered the office of Edward Livingston in 1801. . . . Or Gulian C. Verplanck was born in *1786* and studied law with Edward

Livingston. . . . Or Gulian C. Verplanck was born in 1786 and studied law with Josiah Ogden Hoffman. . . .

Any way you take it—and despite his Federalist and aristocratic background—Gulian C. Verplanck was uttering heresy at the age of six or the age of four.[7]

The winged bird of "historical truth" is often elusive and not easy to net! [8]

However historians may disagree in their interpretations of the past, a theatre audience often shares strong preconceived ideas of noted historical personages. The legendary image of a man may frequently be more vital than the man himself. When this image presents a portraiture of near-perfection and worshipful esteem, the dramatized subject may tend to resemble a plaster saint. Robert E. Lee is one example. Cherished by those south (and even north) of the Mason-Dixon line as the man who best dignified the Confederate cause, this general in grey with his quiet ante-bellum charm and wise paternal visage has challenged the pens of notable writers like Stephen Vincent Benét and Paul Green, to mention two.[9] George Washington, too, is a vexing figure to dramatize. There are few effective dramas with "The Father of Our Country" as a leading character.[10] Our first President has become an abstract national symbol of patriotic perfection: the gallant soldier-statesman who chopped down the cherry tree and never told a lie. Rarely does Washington emerge in the drama as anything but a lifeless statue. The myth overcomes the man. A figure whose public image possesses no human flaws may be most dramatic and yet, paradoxically, most difficult to dramatize.

By the same standard, a noted figure of history whose image is that of a villain is not easily transformed into a dramatic protagonist, even if fresh historical evidence offers some substantiation. More than one abortive historical drama has attempted to present Benedict Arnold as a sympathetic protagonist. He is delineated as the brilliant and courageous field officer with aristocratic leanings who, not getting the recognition he deserves, turns traitor to the patriot cause in the American Revolution. But this would not set well with an audience that expects its historical villains to be villains and not heroes. Mentioning this phenomenon, English playwright and critic William Archer once advised that

historians may indict a hero or whitewash a villain at their leisure; but to the dramatist a hero must be (more or less) a hero, a villain (more or less) a villain, if accepted tradition so decrees it. Thus popular knowledge can scarcely be said to lighten a dramatist's task, but rather

> to impose a new limitation upon him. . . . The theatre is not the
> place . . . for proving . . . that Nell Gwynn was a lady of
> the strictest morals, or that George Washington was incapable of telling
> the truth.[11]

Happily, however, the legendary image of a personality may render him more dramatically interesting than he was in fact. The popular image of John Brown is that of the long-bearded, Jehovah-like visage of the John Steuart Curry painting. And the preconception of Brown as the martyr to and the prophet of emancipation generally enables an audience to accept this man without holding against him his violent methods and fallible judgments.

Yet let us not accept the above quoted comment of William Archer as sacrosanct. The apt dramatization of certain figures clouded by myth can prove exceptions to the rule. A case in point is evinced by the dramatization of Daniel Boone in a recent regional drama dealing with the first permanent Kentucky settlement.[12] Boone was far less outstanding and influential than his myth has made him. He did not discover or first explore Kentucky; he did not lead the first band of pioneers into the state to establish the first settlement. And, against the best interests of his fellow frontiersmen, he hired himself to the powerful Transylvania Company, controlled by Tidewater speculators, which illegally had purchased from the Indians almost the entire present state of Kentucky. Boone was commissioned by the company to establish a Kentucky settlement, conceived by its proprietors as the start of a semi-feudal domain under which Kentucky settlers would have the same status as European peasants. Boone's short-lived settlement at Boonesborough was a poor rival to the first Kentucky settlement—an independent one—at Harrodsburg which staunchly refused to acknowledge the authority of the Transylvania Company.[13] Neither history nor the drama reveal Boone as a villain. However, the drama depicts Boone (who is not the protagonist) as a crafty, unheroic backwoodsman not resemblant of the Boone myth. The portrait is dramatically interesting and in performance has been accepted by the audience. A carefully-wrought characterization of a myth-surrounded figure—particularly when serving as a secondary character—can utilize historical evidence shattering a legend and still be effective.

When casting about for major dramatic characters in history, then, we search for restless, positive people with strong wills and unfulfilled desires who under pressure struggle hard for something, who come to blows with obstacles not easily overcome, and who succeed or fail with a touch of magnificence.[14]

The touchstones by which are tested the dramatic qualities of historical figures may appear to be oversimplifications of the obvious. But our chief purpose in stating them is to heighten and strengthen a constant, conscious awareness of what such qualities are.

The drama of events

Even if we now can perceive personages who kindle the fire of drama, how do we recognize historical events that can be fanned into dramatic flame? Not every history is dotted with John Browns or Prendergasts or Pauls! And maybe we are more interested in exploring panoramically the life of a town or social group or an institution. Obviously, some of the same brushstrokes seen in the texture of dramatic historical portraits serve as telltale marks of the dramatic period or event. Dramatic occurrences contain dramatic people. And events have the quality of drama when they embody conditions or circumstances that have to be restored to equilibrium. We should be on the lookout for events that encompass people who, like the figures previously considered, actively struggle against formidable forces in times of crisis. For example, taking a glimpse at the early history of a Mormon settlement in Utah, we discover the following details.

> OGDEN, UTAH, was settled by Mormons in 1847, and was laid out as a town three years later by their leader, Brigham Young. Disaster besieged the settlers from the start. There were floods and disease and Indian trouble; and yet, in spite of the hardships, the people established a firm, expanding community. But still more calamities were to befall them—grasshoppers, droughts, hard winters—and, by about 1857, anti-Mormon feelings had become rampant throughout the nation. There were harsh antipathies toward the Mormons' practice of polygamy and their virtual autonomy in the Utah territory under Brigham Young's governorship. Non-Mormons complained that their rights and federal laws were being made subservient to the rights and laws established by the Mormon church. Federal troops were dispatched to escort newly-appointed non-Mormon officials into the territory and to see that federal laws were obeyed. The Mormons, mistakenly believing that the federal force would slaughter their leaders and suppress their religion, mustered men from Ogden and other communities to participate in guerrilla warfare that delayed the advent of the federal troops. A general amnesty finally was reached, and the new governor was established. In the years to come, civic improvements were made, industries took hold, and the hard feelings between Mormons and non-Mormons gradually eased.[15]

The early history of Ogden is imbedded with the burrs of crisis. Mormon farmers had to battle for survival against onrushing flood waters, crop-destroying drought and insects, and the spectre of starvation. Cholera appears as a formidable enemy, as well as angry Indians and federal troops. The Mormons find that their theocratic form of government and practice of polygamy make them objects of attack by non-Mormons. These are dramatic events because they flash before us the image of an indomitable community. The Mormon settlers struggle against tremendous odds to forge a Zion out of isolated wilderness.[16]

Events in themselves are not dramatic simply because they hold crises; drama is spawned out of the effect of crisis upon the people confronted by, it. If the Ogden Mormons, for example, when beset by grasshoppers, cholera, and Indians had merely given up and moved away without acting against, or in spite of, the critical event, then the dramatic potential of such events would be questionable. Their reactions to the perils encountered reveal their remarkable courage and unconquerable spirit. And often such persons are not famous or familiar figures but little known people who display valor and resiliency when the chips are down. Events which show courageous performance in the face of pressure provide the life-stuff of drama. Historian Bruce Catton once remarked, "The story of the people of America trying to do something, doing the best they can under terrible pressure, exhibiting great heroism, idealism, and endurance, is a story in itself." [17] The persons who epitomize that story, or the saga of any other nation, or faith, deserve the sharp eye of attention.

Events with the germ of drama are not limited to the herculean struggles of courageous people. They may be seemingly insignificant events as well as weighty, jocular as well as serious. Even in the history of the communities sketched above, the ray of the comic spirit may gleam. Which of us cannot see the humor in the practice of polygamy: imagine a Mormon farmer confronted with three angry wives at the same time! With careful research into historical events and into the lives of people, the face of comedy shows its broad smile. It is wise to see it and smile back.

"Well, this is all very fine," a young playwright sighs, "it's not hard to find dramatic highlights of the comic and serious in the rich past of Ogden. But I'm interested in my hometown, whose history looks pretty dull in comparison!" All right, let us take a sampling of the history of what might be this writer's community.

CARBONDALE, ILLINOIS, was founded in 1852 by Daniel Harmon Brush, in company with several friends, because the site looked as if it would be a strategic stopping place on the Illinois Central Railroad. Brush proposed that the town be called Carbondale because it lay in a coal region. Lots were sold only if buyers agreed to prohibit the sale of spirituous liquors. By 1854, the railroad track had been laid, and the first locomotive came. In the 1880's, a station and freighthouse were built, a steam lumber mill, stores, churches, and banks were established and grew in numbers. A teacher's college was established there to train teachers for the region. Late in the century, the prospering town was struck by several bad fires, including the destruction of the college building. However, in the following decades, the town was rebuilt and quietly prospered. By 1947, the small teachers' college had become Southern Illinois University.[18]

Except for a period of fires, such a community hardly gives the appearance of having crises by the score! But when we look closer, we may find a number of events that hold dramatic interest. For example, a lively dispute takes place among the founding fathers over whether the sale of spirituous liquors should be allowed. This is a fiery issue that keeps coming up for a vote—a situation not without its comic aspects. On the day the first locomotive arrived, more than two thousand people came to town to see it; an old man from the hills may very well have fired his gun when the trained passed, thinking it a monster out of Revelations. Some serious problems may have arisen because the town did not have its own water system until early in the twentieth century. And during the Civil War, townsmen go off to fight for the North. But perhaps others join the undercover group of southern sympathizers calling themselves "The Knights of the Golden Circle" who meet in a place not far from town to scheme ways of sabotaging the Union cause. Sympathies undoubtedly are divided in a place as far south as Carbondale. And what about the relations between town and gown, and the growth of the university? And is not the personality of the town's founder, Daniel Brush, worth investigating? And what about the effect on the town of some violent labor conflicts that happen in nearby communities during the twenties? Beneath the patina of the apparently commonplace lies the dramatic.[19]

One must fully explore the life and times of the people who lived during a particular period of history. There will be found daily lives flashing with strong disagreements, spawning crises, provoking conflict, and rippling with laughter. People compete for each other's affection, provide a livelihood in the face of want, and grieve over loved ones lost in wars. Politicians vie for office. Two youths try to win the hand of a local beauty by competing to catch a greased pig. Or perhaps a mistimed explosion of fireworks by an overcurious boy on a village holiday causes temporary panic among horses and people. Little everyday struggles like these are a large part of the history of any community. They are full of drama and should not be overlooked. Furthermore, those small incidents inherently dramatic can even be magnified when they are silhouetted against a background of national events—events such as wars, economic disasters, and times of progress. A town may not bear the marks of a battle and yet have experienced the suffering and anxieties that war can create. And the mood of a town may reflect the mood of a nation. Often small events can be made to appear more critical when viewed as part of the cosmos.

When events can be arranged in a clear, meaningful sequence of cause-and-effect relationships, their dramatic potential is even stronger. They can be more easily woven into a stage-worthy story. Fort Sumter is fired upon and, as an immediate result, the Civil War begins. The Cherokee nation in North Carolina is duped into selling its land to the government and, therefore, is forced to migrate to Oklahoma. A college is destroyed in time of war and, therefore, is forced to close its doors until funds are available. Mormons continue to pursue their highly individual practice of polygamy and, therefore, the national opinion is against them. Of course, the many incidents of which life past or present is composed frequently are not clearly connected or even comprehensible. Fortunately, by looking through the telescope of history we are granted a somewhat superior grasp of the logic and pattern of events than had the people who experienced them. Furthermore, the dramatist normally must take the amorphous material of existence and selectively rearrange it into a meaningful whole—if he is to create a dramatic story for an audience.[20] Drama demands the structuring of experience! Theatre spectators expect to see life on the stage ordered into a comprehensible entity. Therefore, when past events reveal a causal design they possess at the start a valuable potential for dramatization.

Two other criteria for judging the dramatic stem from a pattern of cause-and-effect relationships. First, we may notice in such a pattern that some events foreshadow larger events or conflicts to follow. An act of opposition against the Stamp Act in a town in New England reflects the Revolution to come. A non-Mormon official hotly accuses Mormon leaders of not respecting federal laws and others' rights, and this action foreshadows the sending of troops into Utah territory to enforce federal law and establish non-Mormon rule. A second sign to be revealed in causal patterns is the appearance of some theme or premise that underscores the history of a particular period or community. The Mormons continually must struggle against disaster; after each calamity, they emerge a little stronger, a little more prosperous than before. The pattern reflects an indomitable will on their part never to surrender, however great the obstacles. In a sense, this would be the theme of Ogden. The way people act against certain obstacles can imply an underlying principle or idea of an entire period.

Other touchstones of the dramatic

Events or periods that can be contrasted with each other are good dramatic material. A church burns following festive preparations for an anniversary celebration to be held next day. Community jubilation turns into despair. A period of Ogden prosperity follows a time of severe adversity. Drama feeds on the contrast of moods and incidents. It can thrive, too, on the contrast of characters. How often in history do we find the clash of personalities: Thomas Jefferson and Alexander Hamilton, Abraham Lincoln and Edwin Stanton, Harry Truman and Douglas MacArthur. From the interaction of contrasting personalities can come the conflict—and the humor—of drama.

One of the most dramatic kinds of contrast is *irony*. A state of affairs that culminates in a result opposite to that which was intended may be streaked with comedy or tragedy. The Hessians carouse on Christmas Eve in Trenton, laughing at the helplessness of Washington's starving, barefoot army across the Delaware; and that night the "helpless" army sweeps across the river and captures the revelers in their drunken sleep. And there is the incident of the beautiful Tory girl named Jane McCrea who, journeying from Fort Edward, New York, to the British lines to see her fiancé, is murdered and scalped by Indians hired by the British; the atrocity is used successfully as an anti-British propaganda to recruit volunteers for the patriot cause.[21] Happenings in history that were intended or should have turned out one way, and then turned out another, have the quality of irony. This quality often enhances the dramatic in an event.

More touchstones exist for testing the dramatic in history than can be mentioned here. For instance the personage or event that is unique or suggestive of the romantic or the sentimental is an additional ingredient to look for. But the essential guide marks have been set in this chapter. We know that we must look for the appearance in history of crisis—comic or serious—of causal patterns, and of contrast. We know that historical happenings are made dramatic by the calibre and actions of the people involved. We know that dramatic figures have the will and ability to struggle hard against formidable barriers. In order to realize fully the dramatic, we must *know the motives and actions of people*. If we train ourselves to understand our neighbors, if we look to the behavior that reveals their inner lives, then we are more fully equipped to recognize the dramatic in history. E. M. Forster once remarked that the historian

> is quite as much concerned with character as the novelist, but he can only know of its existence when it shows on the surface. If Queen Victoria had not said, "We are not amused," her neighbours at the table would not have known she was not amused, and her ennui could never have been announced to the public. She might have frowned, so that they would have deduced her state from that—looks and gestures are also historical evidence. But if she remained impassive —what would anyone know? The hidden life is, by definition, hidden. The hidden life that appears in external signs is hidden no longer, has entered the realm of action.[22]

Even more than Forster's historian and novelist, the dramatist deals with action and with the characters of men; and he must recreate history rather than record it. To recognize the dramatic in history—not just a necessary attribute or assignment of the playwright but of others involved in creating historical drama as well—is not enough; we have to recognize and know the human individual also. We can know him as an interacting being, part of that social entity, the community.

III. Why communities dramatize history

IT IS a hot June morning in Williamsburg, Virginia, the now restored old colonial capital nestling in a verdant peninsula between the James and York Rivers. Standing in the outdoor amphitheatre where his drama The Common Glory soon will open for another summer, coatless playwright Paul Green addresses with the impassioned intonation of an evangelist the cast and crew of local college students and citizens. "This is a great thing we're doing here," he says. "We're showing people how this young democracy of ours got its start less than two hundred years ago. We're honoring the men that sweated to make it possible. And to do this you all have to bleed from the navel a little—you've got to work hard!" Caught up by the muscular speaker's compelling sincerity, not a listener fails to respond. And Williamsburg again is reminded of some reasons why since 1947 it has helped foster a drama about Virginia's vital role in the nation's founding. But the will to express so graphically a commonly esteemed heritage for the purpose of commemoration is not confined to Williamsburg or its state. Towns across the country from Anchorage, Alaska, to Jacksonville, Florida, from San Antonio, Texas, to Castine, Maine, throw on the floodlights to honor their past. (Performance data on the historical dramas produced by such communities can be found in Appendix A.)

The commemorative purpose

A commemorative aim is one major recurrent goal of the community keen about celebrating, for instance, the anniversary of its founding, its achievement to statehood, or a famous battle fought nearby. The town of Harpers Ferry in West Virginia marks the observance of its Civil War history and John Brown's raid with a biography-drama—Wallace Dace's The Prophet —about the fiery abolitionist. Illustrating a river town's colorful heritage, Peoria in Illinois taps the talents of its citizens to put on Kermit Hunter's Thunder on the River. The pageant-drama traces the history of this city on the Illinois River from the time that Père Marquette landed on the shores of Lake Peoria through the pioneer years to the present day. Seattle, Washington, ushers in its centennial with Glenn Hughes' The Dream and the Deed, a theatrical panorama of its growth from a settlement of twenty-one persons in

1852 to a twentieth-century city with a population of almost five hundred thousand in 1952. Kansas portrays its first hundred years of statehood in Ruth and Val Rosing's *The Kansas Story.*

Some communities honor their heritage by means of dramas presented over a period of several months in a single year or even in many years. In the coal-rich hills of "West-by God-Virginia!" Beckley since 1961 annually produces Kermit Hunter's *Honey in the Rock,* originally written to celebrate the centennial of the state's severance from Virginia to form its independent status. West of the Alleghenies, the Bluegrass community of Kentucky's Harrodsburg since 1963 memorializes its title as the state's first permanent settlement—even predating that of Daniel Boone's at Boonesborough—by presenting Robert Emmett McDowell's *Home is the Hunter.* Set in the grandeur of the Great Smokies at Cherokee, North Carolina, *Unto These Hills* chronicles each summer the story of the Cherokee Indians as a way of memorializing their traditions and tumultuous past. In the same state, Boone preserves and transmits its rich pioneer heritage by yearly presenting *Horn in the West,* the action of which is set in the Southern Appalachian Highlands between 1770 and 1780. In the serrated and ruggedly majestic North Dakota badlands, Medora perpetuates the area's history by dramatizing T. R.'s adventurous days in the region in Thomas Patterson's *Theodore Roosevelt's Life in North Dakota* (originally entitled *Old Four-Eyes*). San Antonio and later San Marcos in the Lone Star State pay tribute to early Texan valor and sacrifice at the Alamo in Ramsey Yelvington's *A Cloud of Witnesses.* And these are not all of such community-oriented dramas.

We can see that a commemorative function exists not only in geographic communities but also in religious ones. A prime instance of the latter is the Mormon Church which offers every summer the dramatized story of its religious bases at Hill Cumorah, near Palmyra, New York. The place of production marks the location where Joseph Smith, founder of Mormonism, is considered by believers to have received the divine golden plates of the Book of Mormon. The pageant-drama *America's Witness for Christ* by H. Wayne Driggs and Harold Hansen salutes the origins of this sectarian community. In California where men are expected to match the mountains, the Franciscan Order venerates the memory of Friar Junipero Serra in *The Trek to Sierra Cross.* We see recreated the efforts of this courageous priest who began to build the missions that became the state's pioneer settlements. In San Francisco, the Paulist Fathers herald the hundredth anniversary of their order (the Missionary Society of St. Paul the Apostle) by outlining the life of another courageous priest who also is their founder, Father Hecker, in Emmet Lavery's *American Portrait*. And, on the occasion of its fourth centenary, the Society of Jesus offers in New York City Richard Breen and Harry Schnibbe's *Who Ride on White Horses*, a biography-drama treating the seventeenth-century Catholic martyr Edmund Campion. On a small scale, the First Friends Church of Richmond, Indiana, rejects traditional Quaker distaste for theatre by telling of its origins in Esther Jones and Naomi Pyle's *A Sense of Destiny* as part of an anniversary celebration.

In addition to our religious or church groups, many organizational or institutional communities perpetuate their history and traditions through the drama. In this category can be included state universities or elementary schools, business and civic groups, Girl and Boy Scouts, police departments and Chambers of Commerce, service clubs and garden clubs, historical societies and other special interest groups of all kinds. As part of New York State's Year of History in 1959, Dolgeville Central School, for example, puts on a modest pageant-drama encompassing the town's origins. It is intended for and acted by students of the school. As the official Seattle centennial drama recalling the city's past, *The Dream and the Deed* by Glenn Hughes is produced by the University of Washington. To pay tribute to that section of the country from which it gets its name, Western Reserve University presents Lynn Riggs's *Toward the Western Sky* for the Greater Cleveland community to experience. In Utah, Brigham Young University stages R. Don Oscarson's *Sand in Their Shoes*, a musical drama about the exploits of a Mormon battalion in the military campaign against Mexico. Educational groups do not stand alone in such endeavors. The Benevolent and Protective Order of Elks and a water and power company extol their development by respectively producing *The Elk Story* in Hollywood and *Twin Titans* in Los Angeles, California. And Scottish Rite Masons inculcate a sense of group pride in initiates by having them witness privately a dramatization of their organization's history. The diversity of participating groups in efforts of this kind is not unusual.

By recreating its common tie with historical experience, a community serves as a forceful medium of expression for its members. By reaffirming common values, interests, customs, and objectives in the illustrating of its past, it makes its citizens aware of their collective uniqueness and thereby can renew and strengthen community unity. To instill, then, this sense of collective pride, the community embraces a commemorative purpose. The dramatic reenactment of its heritage develops as an expression of strong local or group interest and feeling for the history of a community and its people.

Social purposes and advantages

Linked to a community's purpose in paying homage to the past is the complementary objective of reawakening and energizing community spirit and morale. The pattern of many locally sponsored historical dramas, for example, reflects this aim to stimulate a sense of community self-esteem and the will to future endeavor. The College of William and Mary in Virginia presents *Hark Upon the Gale* to honor its past and the 350th year of Virginia's history. On the occasion the President voices the hope that "the students and faculty of today and tomorrow will play as essential a part in the creation of our fundamental national ideals as did the honored men of our past." An enthusiastic spectator of *The Kansas Story* at Topeka writes the editor of a local newspaper that she feels compelled to reread the state's history because her regional pride has been whetted. Twenty-two western North Carolina towns in the isolated area of the Great Smoky Mountains forget local differences and organize to promote their area through an annual production of *Unto These Hills*. Four communities are brought closer together in a joint effort to produce *The Miracle Worker* on the lawn of Helen Keller's birthplace, Tuscumbia, Alabama, enacted by the local community playhouse. The people of Stevensville, Montana, help effect a clearer understanding of a racial problem by taking an analytical look at that part of their past concerning the local Salish Indians in *A Tale of Bitter Root*. Bert Hansen of Montana State University, who supervises the writing and production of this pageant-drama and many others in the Northwest, feels that such an activity cuts across racial and cultural barriers to solve group problems and facilitate social unity.[1]

Social solidarity is also enforced by a community's inspiriting of local pride not only in itself but in its nation. Williamsburg's *The Common Glory* records how the strivings of Thomas Jefferson and other Virginians help lay the foundations of our national government in the years 1774 to 1781. Roger Sherman, once the drama's talented scenic designer and now its able general manager, has spectators local and nonlocal tell him how impressed they are with the community's contribution to the total history of the nation. A proper nourishment of local and national pride can beneficially strengthen community spirit. Ideally, the inciting of such impulses does not exceed the bounds of good taste and proper proportion by becoming "childish flag-waving in the pep-rally tradition," as Harry Davis, veteran director of such dramas, has put it.

Spectators of and performers in a community-sponsored drama can be directly edified as to their own heritage. This helps to quicken local and national self-regard. By this means, also, a community can communicate to newcomers the knowledge of its traditions and values so that as future or new citizens they may successfully function within it. During the early decades of this century pageant-dramas like Thomas Wood Stevens and Percy MacKaye's *The Pageant and Masque of St. Louis* in 1914 and Stevens' *The Pageant of Virginia* in 1922 consider as one of their aims the teaching of democracy and its meaning to the many immigrants flowing to America from the old world. And today the aim to educate and enlighten citizens new as well as old, native as well as foreign, juvenile as well as adult, inherently is a part of dramas disclosing our democratic heritage.

Many communities realize that dramatized history can have meaning for children. "I'm undoubtedly the most unusual donkey in the world—I can smell gold!" says a talking wooden ass named Ezekiel whose special talent lets his prospector-owner make the first discovery of golden nuggets in Idaho. And, thereby, a marionette play on the stage of a tiny portable theatre reveals to elementary school children in Boise, Idaho, an important event in the state's history. The play, *Ezekiel's Nose*, is the first of a number of specially written scripts which the Idaho Historical Society and the local Junior League serves up to youngsters as palatable helpings of Idaho history. Cedar Bluff, Alabama, exercises the same purpose with "live" drama when a high school teacher acquaints her students with an event in the town's Civil War past by authoring and producing a small biography-drama performed by them and for them.

And it is not uncommon for children's theatres attached to universities or civic leagues to open the curtain on locally-written history plays for children. The Junior Service League of Red Bank, New Jersey, for instance, dramatizes local history about Molly Pitcher and the Battle of Monmouth for audiences at county schools by means of *Sergeant Molly* by Mrs. Donald English and Mrs. Emily Wingerter. Children as well as adults can learn about their local legends and history, and even have a greater capacity to imagine the historical scene. Knowledge about their past is thrust into the hands and heads of the youth when they watch the epic-dramas of such communities as Williamsburg, Boone, Manteo, Cherokee, Beckley, Medora, Harrodsburg and of such towns —previously unmentioned—as Kentucky's Murray and Bardstown. Such dramas produce educative effects. By revivifying heroic American figures and events they help spur an interest in history. Dramas like *The Lost Colony*, *The Founders*, *The Common Glory*, and *Unto These Hills* are seen by thousands of school children. Their souvenir programs, which contain articles by reputable historians, are sent to school libraries and are often used as reference material. Historical dramas of all kinds, when conceived and performed with artistry and truth, can educate the young.

Communal groups put history on the stage to teach their traditions and beliefs. Church groups, for example, foster religious-historical dramas to strengthen existing faith and inspire faith where none exists. A spectator at the Mormon Church's Hill Cumorah pageant-drama is met by a well-mannered student from Brigham Young University who takes down the former's address as a potential mailing list prospect and points out the several information booths where church literature and further details about Mormonism can be obtained. And during the performance of the dramatized Book of Mormon a narrator intermittently expounds the basis of this Church's faith with the partial aim of gathering new sheep into the fold. The Central Congregational Church in Rhode Island's Providence asks its assemblage to be stimulated by new attitudes and fresh interpretations of commonly held ideas. Roger Williams is seen in a new light when the chancel becomes a stage for James Schevill's *The Bloody Tenet*, after the performance of which members of the congregation—so the church reports—could "no longer hold a romantic view of Roger Williams without challenge."

Although a growing number of church groups use the stage to illuminate their traditions, such groups hold no monopoly on historical drama with a religious focus. At Pineville, Kentucky, an organization composed of a cross-section of local citizens is responsible for the annual summer-long appearance of the choric religious drama *The Book of Job* arranged from the King James translation. Orlin Corey, who is the drama's director as well as its adapter, says its major purpose is "to make an exalted contribution to American religious life through drama," while also assisting "the economic life of the local mountain region." Not only Job but the Apostle Paul has been the subject of community-sponsored dramas without direct church affiliation. For three summers Roanoke, Virginia, has featured Kermit Hunter's *Thy Kingdom Come*, which deals with Paul's days as a Pharisee to his last hours before Christian martyrdom in Rome. In all of these dramas local citizens generally get a chance to participate.

Related to historical drama's educative aims and accomplishments can be group harmony resulting from the experience of communal participation. Under the proper conditions, the latter furnishes another major means of fortifying community unity and morale. Lusk, Wyoming, has found this out. Between the Black Hills and Cheyenne in a land of rolling plains and cedar-and-pine-covered hills, this western town recreates every summer the story of how the nearby Rawhide Buttes got their name. Eva Lou Paris' *The Legend of Rawhide* spins a tale about a headstrong young midwesterner in a California-bound wagon train who is skinned alive by Indians in reprisal for senselessly killing a Sioux maiden. Local citizens join together to furnish the costumes, provide the covered wagons and teams, and turn actor; and one cannot tell townsman from rancher under the Indian make-up made of iron ore paint from a nearby mine. The editor of the local newspaper says that the pageant-drama has been a unifying factor between town and ranch people by bringing them together in a common effort. "As most rural towns," he further remarks, "we've seen considerable loss of population and discouragement, but the pageant has been a focal point of pride that's been very healthy."

Many communities find that group cooperation is an advantage that evolves out of joint participation in the creating of a historical drama. The authors of a commissioned pageant-drama in Castine, Maine, at first find fellow townsfolk reluctant to contribute any effort in putting on the sesquicentennial drama concerned with their town's history. The lack of time and the press of other obligations are pleaded as an excuse. But when the citizens are told that the responsibility of producing their own town's dramatized biography lies with no one but themselves, they slowly and reluctantly begin to accept parts and production duties. Rehearsals are haphazard. People come and go as they please. Neither unanimity of purpose nor coordination of action is apparent. Gradually, however, a kind of group spirit starts to emerge and people begin to fit into their roles. When scenes now are rehearsed, the local actors begin to behave as they do at a real town meeting; and they also seem to sense how their ancestors behaved and to personate them as only family can. The production of the play is sold out and the box office demand for more than a hundred extra seats cannot be met. And Castine discovers that it is "not an involuntary association of people confined to a municipal area, but . . . a community." [2] Stimulated by the success of the community effort, the town repeats the drama a second year with equal enthusiasm.

Cooperative effort through participation furnishes a community's need to offer opportunity for the self-expression of its members. We have to admit that in our day technology and automation encourage a sedentary life. Positive activity and participation is lacking—and passive amusement is the rule and not the exception. Yet active participation ensues when people can work and share in a cooperative enterprise usually directed to some social end. Many a community achieves this goal through the effective presentation of a drama founded on its history.

Such a community project reveals not only people's capacity for group cooperation but also latent or not fully realized personal resources as well. An Indian carpenter proves a talent for scene construction by building a fort for the *Fort Laramie Treaty Pageant* at the Cheyenne Agency near Pierre, South

Dakota. In Montgomery, Alabama, a dance instructor blossoms as an effective choreographer by dint of her efforts in a Civil War Centennial pageant-drama. And an educator and historical society president turns out to be a competent dramatist on evidence of his four pageant-dramas about the Iroquois Confederacy offered in consecutive years at Naples, New York. The University of Kansas at Lawrence gives an opportunity to new playwright Richard F. Stockton by producing his *The Trial of John Brown*, a biography-drama dealing with that prominent figure in the state's pre-Civil War history. And Reed College in Portland, Oregon, provides regional dramatist Jane Erickson with performances of *A Mighty Fortress*, a biography-drama about a brutal Indian massacre from Oregon history.

Communities have been pleased at the mutual advantage of allowing fledgling playwrights to try their dramaturgical wings and of permitting experienced regional dramatists to test their work through the reactions of local audiences.

The community's opportunity for learning techniques of theatre practice and developing artistic powers is particularly apparent in the case of productions which use the services of a number of local citizens. A high school teacher in Boone shows so much theatrical promise that he plays the leading role in *Horn in the West* and later becomes its director. A local housewife in the same production assists with the drama's wardrobe and after several summers becomes the show's costumer. A young Cherokee boy who once walks onstage with his mother in a crowd scene now is cast as an important character in *Unto These Hills*. This production at Cherokee, by the way, introduces audiences to the first epic-drama written by Kermit Hunter, who has since had over twenty-five such dramas performed in various regions of the country. And he finds time to aid communities in organizing productions of his work. "The creation of one of these dramas," remarks this lean and taciturn playwright, "is a combination of many people, and the script is just the beginning." [3] While basically a writer, Hunter also has been, during a versatile career, a chamber of commerce secretary, newswriter, church organist, lieutenant-colonel of infantry, business manager of a symphony orchestra and a professional baseball team, and a college teacher and administrator. This broad background equips him well for his present position as Dean of the School of Art at Southern Methodist University. A native of West Virginia and the mountain country west of the Alleghenies, he understands his material and is less concerned with waving the flag than with discovering the true character of the American past depicted in his dramas. Other such regional dramatists as Thomas Patterson, Ramsey Yelvington, Jack LaZebnick, Wallace Dace,

Robert Emmett McDowell, Jane Erickson, E. P. Conkle, Frederick G. Walsh, Gladys L'Ashley Hoover, and John Ehle have seen their first efforts in this form performed to community theatre-goers. Additionally, the large number of students from local colleges and universities appearing in these dramas use the results of their training later in teaching or professional theatre careers. Students and local citizens alike receive basic preparation in all phases of theatre from acting and stage managing to scenery construction and business management. And similar results in college and school communities are, of course, self-evident.

Various levels of participation in a community effort to dramatize its past can be cited. In many cases, participating citizens prepare and execute most or all the phases involved from the initial planning through a drama's writing and production to the selling of tickets. In a pageant-drama presented by the College of William and Mary, for instance, every participant from playwright to usher is a past or present member of the college community. And the experience of Maine's Castine provides a parallel example. With varying modifications, such cooperative efforts kindling a vital community spirit hold true with larger communities as well. In Utah twenty-eight citizens of Ogden's Mormon community combine their energies to produce annually since 1951 Roland and Helen Parry's *All Faces West*, a musical pageant-drama about the trek of the Mormon pioneers from Illinois to the Salt Lake Valley. The authors are inhabitants of Ogden. The cast, production crew and staff are drawn from local residents who offer their time and talents free of charge. Two local counties contribute substantial cash gifts. The local newspaper offers free publicity. One summer a change of theatre site is necessitated. Within three months the community committee with volunteer help transforms a barren hill into a stage, provides parking facilities for 2,500 cars, moves 7,000 folding chairs into the theatre area within a local park, and builds the housing for lighting facilities. The success of this three-performances-a-summer drama is indicated by an average attendance of more than 18,000 people.

Other examples of such community efforts come to mind. The citizens of West Virginia's Beckley—school children, civic leaders, farmers, businessmen, housewives—contribute cash gifts ranging from fifty cents to $3,000 to raise more than $7,000 to help cover production costs of *Honey in the Rock*. Contractors give material. Local radio and television stations donate free time for publicity announcements. And the joint effort culminates in a seven year community and state project to celebrate a centennial with a drama that proposes to run for several summers. Its cast of sixty is made up of local citizens and college and university students from the region. Residents of the local and regional community truly share in creating this historical drama.[4] Other annual dramas supported by communities in North Carolina, Virginia, Kentucky, North Dakota and elsewhere rely heavily on local personnel for their planning, production, and performing. Williamsburg's *The Common Glory*, for example, frankly announces that first consideration in the casting of the *dramatis personae* each season is the possible use of Virginia's talent. Cherokee's *Unto These Hills* employs a good portion of the local population, both Indian and white, as cast, crew, and service workers. Boone's *Horn in the West* year by year increasingly recruits its participants from the immediate locale. And Kentucky's Murray does the same with *Stars in My Crown*, an epic-drama about Alben W. Barkley and the establishment of TVA in the region.

Where a cooperative community effort has been lacking, historical drama frequently fails. This is sometimes true in a metropolitan area with its diversity of standards, values, interests, and goals. Such factors as vast geographic and demographic size, heterogeneity of population, and diversification of interests render unity difficult to achieve. In Pittsburgh, for example, *The Golden Crucible*, a bicentennial drama of the city's pioneer and industrial past designed to run for an entire summer, closes in the red several weeks early. One problem is that an important segment of the community, organized labor, is not adequately represented on the executive committee directly responsible for the production. Union troubles ensue and pickets parade before the theatre entrance on opening night. This blight on the production's start foreshadows further difficulties. Local residents appear reluctant to support a drama of their own history and stay away in droves. The production of Paul Green's *Faith of Our Fathers*, centering on a critical period in our first President's life, suffers a similar fate in Washington, D. C. Intended to run ten years, it closes in two and not without losses. The playwright complains he has to spend more time negotiating with politicians to get funds and positive action than on composing the drama; and the results show it.[5] The city does not support the production. Today, the cooperative community effort and spirit necessary to engender successful large-scale and long-range historical dramas appears more easily effected in the small or average size community rather than in the metropolis. When the presentation of such drama does not arise out of the combined will and effort of the community its chances of success are small.

Economic goals and advantages

One purpose and advantage of locally offered historical dramas can be an economic one. Geographic communities, for example, are generally alert to methods of improving themselves economically by encouraging local spending, attracting industry, and cultivating tourism.

Indirect financial advantages accruing from the production of drama dealing with history are greeted gleefully by local boards of trade. As visitors, attracted by the community announcing such a drama, we may go to the locality, patronize its merchants, and incidentally, add to the local revenue by spending money. We may fall under the spell of the scenic attractions of the area, thus profiting its hotels and motels, restaurants and shops, and the shoe-shine boy on the corner. Some North Carolina communities, for example, continue to reap the rewards of tourism early associated with the outdoor epic-drama movement beginning with Manteo's *The Lost Colony*.

Samuel Selden, former chairman of the Theatre Arts Department at the University of California at Los Angeles, is a soft-spoken, self-effacing man who never boasts that he has probably advised and directed more dramas of this kind and knows more about them than any other person in America. But he takes pride in these productions, having played a major role in the genesis of many while heading the Carolina Playmakers at the University of North Carolina; and one particular point of pride is *The Lost Colony* which he supervised in various capacities for its first two decades. Mr. Selden likes to point out that the drama, with an average seasonal attendance of 50,000 (in a typical year in the fifties), helps indirectly to bring its home locale of Dare County from $500,000 to $750,000 a year. He sees how the income has affected the whole pattern of living in the little town of Manteo whenever he recalls the unpaved streets and unpainted houses of the late thirties and compares them with the prosperous appearance of the place today.[6]

The Lost Colony is typical of the financially rewarding results enjoyed by other North Carolina towns.[7] The State's Department of Conservation and Development estimates that every summer traveler spends ten dollars or more each day in the towns he visits. In Boone, a banker reports that the volume of business rises thirty percent when *Horn in the West* opens. Furthermore, the fact that the operating costs of such dramas are often in the neighborhood of $100,000 through a regular summer season indirectly contributes to community prosperity. The major part of what is spent in meeting payrolls, maintaining the physical plant, purchasing the necessary materials for scenery and costumes goes to the rooming houses, restaurants, and merchants in the local area. Despite direct losses usually in the seasonal operation of *Horn in the West* and *The Lost Colony*, their communities—frequently voted state aid by legislators—keep the productions going because indirect profits arising from them are so substantial, spiritually as well as materially.

One drama in North Carolina is unusually prosperous because of its location on the Cherokee Indian reservation in the Great Smokies. At the end of the first year of *Unto These Hills*, the stores along the main street of Cherokee report that their income jumped up $250,000. This drama of Cherokee history has been sufficiently successful to turn back more than a half a million dollars into constructive aid for the Cherokee. Net proceeds from the production permit the erection of a reconstructed Indian village, the purchase of an Indian museum, the establishment of college scholarships for Indian boys and girls, and a year-round school of fine arts and crafts. Indirect gains from the development of the enterprise include the initiation of new employment and industry for local citizens and the promotion of the National Parks and Forests within the region.

It must be frankly stated that the majority of summer-long outdoor epic-dramas rarely meet operating expenses. The financial benefits are those indirectly received by community merchants, restauranteurs, motel owners, and service station operators.

On a more modest basis than Cherokee, communities divert profits from historical drama productions to civic improvements ranging from children's playgrounds to the building of local historical museums. Sixteen miles down the Ohio from Pittsburgh, in Ambridge, lies a cluster of buildings marking the once extant communal theocratic society of Old Economy. Its buildings and properties have been in part preserved and restored through state and individual subsidies resulting from the success of the annually presented *Man's Reach* and also from the culinary triumph of the tasty German-style dinners available to audiences before the performance. The drama features the nineteenth-century religious settlers of Old Economy. Further west, returns from Lusk's *The Legend of Rawhide* give the town a community building and sufficient funds to repeat the drama several days every summer. In Missouri, the town of Hermann—founded by German settlers in 1837—is able to present each spring since 1952 a new pageant-drama based on an aspect of local history. Profits from an annual Maifest are substantial enough to restore handsomely three historic buildings in the town and to offer annually the May festival and a historical drama.

In Pipestone, Minnesota, where for centuries many Indian tribes came to quarry the red stone used in making the calumet and the war pipe, an

Indian pageant-drama centered on Hiawatha is performed for three weekends each summer. Howard Severson, the secretary-treasurer of the local men's club sponsoring it, feels happy that "the presentation has done more to promote the community and the Pipestone National Park than anything that has happened here so far." In an average season approximately 18,000 people watch the drama. "And you can imagine the benefits," adds Mr. Severson, "of having so many people come into this town." Profits go toward the physical improvement and maintenance of the grounds and properties connected with the production, thus also adding to the attractiveness of the area.

Let us realize, however, that the contribution of material gifts to a local area or organization is neither the sole criterion of economic success nor the most prevalent. That some productions (with or without annually allotted city or state subsidy) make sufficient profits to be offered year after year is a heartening sign, however, that such success can be achieved. In addition to the experience of Lusk and Hermann, this pattern is true of several other pageant-dramas as well as larger and longer-performing epic-dramas.

As a general rule, locales featuring pageant-dramas for one specific occasion feel it a solid accomplishment when sponsors end up in the black. Such dramas, of course, frequently spark local prosperity during the two days or two weeks that they run by adding an alluring attraction to a civic celebration. Sometimes, given normal circumstances and reasonable weather (if a drama is produced outdoors), particularly well planned and executed dramas do bring in a modest return. Peoria, for example, is encouraged by a substantial profit from its *Thunder on the River*. Sometimes a community does not expect to make money—many towns do not charge admission to such productions—and provides funds for this kind of situation.

Contrariwise, a community sometimes loses money that it is not prepared to lose! One frequent cause for such a deficit is over-budgeting, but there are many others ranging from inclement weather to the breaking out of an epidemic near production time. On another level, some long-range epic-dramas planned for a summer or several years do not even meet operating expenses let alone capital outlay. The examples of dramas at Pittsburgh and Washington testify to this fact, as do *Voice in the Wind* at Ruskin, and *Florida Aflame* at Safety Harbor, Florida; *Chucky Jack* at Gatlinburg, Tennessee; *Thunderland* at Asheville, North Carolina; *Bound for Kentucky* at Louisville, Kentucky; *Forever This Land* at Petersburg, Illinois; and *The Confederacy* at Virginia Beach, Virginia. On the positive side, however, historical dramas of various scopes and kinds, when carefully planned and astutely managed by their sponsors, are and can be solvent. And the most effective ones arise out of a genuine interest in the community welfare not motivated solely by the anticipation of financial gain. Nevertheless, as any good businessman will tell us, group spirit or morale is hardly strengthened when a community loses money it is not prepared to lose. Solvency and social advantages—howsoever nonmaterial—are closely intertwined.

The need to entertain

Community *esprit de corps* dims quickly when a historical drama is dull. Members of an audience consciously anticipate that their emotions and/or intellect will be stimulated by what they see and hear; in short, they expect to be entertained. What does this imply in terms of dramatized history? It means, first, that artistic standards must be high. It means that a production must create a lively tapestry of music, color, dance, spectacle, and story which stimulates the spectator to relive the past. It means that the playwright must create a dramatic and essentially truthful vision of living history. It is an unhappy fact—engraved in the memory of many—that entertainment is a consideration too often forgotten. (As one consequence of this, the word "pageant" is box office poison in some locales.) A pageant-drama of the history of education in North Carolina runs for hour after hour. The audience leaves and the players play on. At two o'clock in the morning, recounts a departing onlooker, two sleepy children are the only spectators watching the final scene. In a New York town a pageant-drama supposedly based on local history becomes a dull plethora of sheer spectacle highlighted by drum corps girls holding American flags. In a Wisconsin community, an under-rehearsed centennial drama lasts for three minutes, so its author tells us, before the leading actor forgets his lines and confuses the rest of the cast by jumping far ahead in the script; and all the lights go out because someone has shorted a cable. Needless to say, none of these above experiences is very entertaining to the spectator.

Yet history can be entertaining, as many dramatic productions prove. If we go to historic Bardstown, Kentucky, we see audiences at Paul Green's *The Stephen Foster Story* fully enjoying the American composer's infectious music which is interwoven with the story of his early career. And children and parents alike are captivated by the exciting union of music, dance, color, and story in Cherokee's *Unto These Hills*. But these epic-dramas have no premium on entertainment. A playscript composed and produced with taste and skill has pleased audiences watching different kinds of historical dramas produced by schools, churches, universities, community theatres, towns, and cities. Let us remember that entertainment becomes a palpable reality in effective historical drama.

When citizens are asked to contribute their time—and usually their money—to witness a locally sponsored event, they have the right to expect entertainment. And this applies to a drama founded on community history as well as to the high school band concert or the ladies club fashion show. The drama cannot escape this responsibility to entertain simply by virtue of the halo effect of local history. And it cannot do so merely by exhibiting performers to fond relatives and adoring friends or by advertising a free show. Alert communities realize this responsibility; when they assume it by sponsoring a public presentation, they harness the best energies and talents possible. In the case of historical drama, this charge demands that the playwright create effective drama which will be well executed through the means of theatrical production. Yet entertainment is the obligation not merely of the playwright and the director, but of all concerned. It will result from careful planning, skill, taste, discipline, and plenty of hard work.

Entertainment is interrelated with commemoration, education and enlightenment, economic improvement, and cooperative communal participation as major aims motivating communities to dramatize their past. The prominence of such goals depends upon the individual nature, resources, and collective objectives of the community itself. Its success with such goals rests on its own effort and judgment. Yet, above all, the purpose of entertainment— the most persuasive voice on behalf of other aims—must be perceived.

The possible advantages of artistically conceived and presented community drama can only be effected through knowledgeable and dedicated human leadership. If a community is interested in stimulating or maintaining this kind of drama, it must furnish the most capable leadership possible for what it wants to do.

IV. Leading and organizing the community

"GAD," he was fond of saying, "you've got to believe in the native talent of people. What's more, that this talent can be nurtured. Nurtured by certain men and women—leaders, if you like—endowed with a green thumb." The late Alexander Drummond himself had that green thumb, as hundreds of Cornell University students can testify. His pungency of teaching theatre and his unabashed devotion to American drama nurtured the acting and playwriting talents of men and women who left Ithaca remembering him with affection. Many of them developed in their own or newly adopted communities another pet idea of this academic cocklebur: "The foundation of a popular culture or art in this country really rests, you know, with the human interest of a community in its own creative efforts."

Yet any community, Drummond would have agreed, has to have the resources, imagination, skill, industriousness, and cooperative effort necessary to communicate effectively its art—and a historical drama is an example—to an audience. Desire is never enough.

Seeking dynamic leadership

As communities vary in factors leading to their founding, so they differ in the common elements that appear to generate a pride in group planning and achievement. There are not ready-made patterns or formulae to explain why one small community in Tennessee, for instance, seeks persistently to establish and realize creatively certain social goals while the next town down the valley —of similar age, size, and seeming character—drowses off into a spiritual and economic slumber. When it comes to shaping collective desires to achieve certain goals, communities fall into four general categories in which such desires are: generally recognized and acted upon; generally recognized and dissipated in half-hearted attempts to put something into action; vaguely recognized and gradually forgotten if not ignored; and unrecognized and so ignored. If we are to read the sociological smoke signals, most communities are led to act, whether to improve their transportation system or their industrial art education, by the vision and persuasiveness of a dynamic individual. As it is with the larger social aims, so it is with the program of organizations yearning to produce historical drama.

Such organizations are led to activate themselves by leaders who more often than not come from a wide range of backgrounds, tastes, training, and professional ways of life. They may be a local high school English teacher, a college president, or a city librarian linked to the community by vocational and humanitarian ties. They may serve their fellow citizens as minister or priest of a local congregation, or editor of a chain of regional newspapers, or head of a city recreation department. They may hold their town's welfare high in their altruism as its butcher, baker, or calendar-maker. Sometimes they may be amateur historians concerned about their town's upcoming anniversary or county commissioners disturbed with the challenge of improving recently acquired civic properties. Whatever their ethnic or religious indebtedness or however they reached their present social status, these persons share a common attachment: they have their roots in the community, either by nature or adoption; and they have a civic-minded care for its future.

Qualities of leadership

These, then, are the leaders of a special community task force. Ideally, they possess such vital qualities as intelligence, imagination, persistence, and the ability to dream practical visions. They not only dream; they act. With persuasiveness these leaders speak cogently of community goals. They write a prospectus and pass copies of it to judiciously screened persons. In the prospectus they point out the advantages to a community which creates drama from the marrow of its history. Such advantages (as those mentioned in chapter III) derive from a group effort that sights its standards of entertainment high, encourages the development of creative ability, stimulates the imaginative life of a community, stresses strong social values, and that—through skillful artistic expression—makes attractive the traditions and aspirations of the common heritage. Such leaders set before the appropriate group a vision of what is possible to accomplish; their mission is to convert the listeners to the dream. The calibre of the leadership is measured by the attractiveness of the dream and the practical means of realizing it. A "practical visionary" is likely to be the best leader for initiating the production of historical drama.

Methods of initiating support

Given such a leader, his first step in mobilizing the community for action is to appraise its human resources. The actual structure of the sponsoring or producing organization, whether it be newly formed or already existing, comes later. What he seeks initially is neither an executive body nor the individual who has had "two years of summer stock and was almost cast in a Broadway musical." What our "practical visionary" seeks is a nonsectarian informal planning committee, a group of socially responsible, influential, and articulate persons, representative of professions and industries within the geographic community. Since these persons are to serve as a sounding board for his projected idea, considerable thought should be given to the composition of the committee.[1]

In the formative stages of stimulating the planning committee, the leader need not force or settle issues hurriedly. Much better for him to encourage the more far-seeing and respected citizens to discuss the proposal among themselves, and be convinced of its desirability; thus he gains from their considered opinion. This collected opinion, coupled with the prestige of its spokesmen, will be of much help later. What is more, some of the spokesmen may be potential key persons in the actual sponsoring organization. Furthermore, a wise leader invites more persons to the informal planning meetings than are reasonably expected, knowing that even all those who do attend these frankly exploratory meetings cannot be expected to serve further in an active and constructive way.

If other groups or individuals from surrounding communities have presented forms of historical drama, the informal planning committee often finds benefit in the testimony of their experience, provided that they do not set themselves up as experts. State-supported institutions particularly can sometimes delegate trained field workers to counsel on organizational problems within local regions. In a number of states, university extension divisions not only provide theatre or sociology personnel available for consultation but also instructive printed materials at no or little cost. Extension education policy in New York and Wisconsin, for instance, has enabled Cornell's Mary Eva Duthie and the Wisconsin Idea Theatre staff under Robert Gard to carry their enthusiasms and seasoned skills to groups within their respective states. Other educational theatre authorities, moreover, have frequently at personal sacrifice and without institutional support generously given administrative and technical advice to new or established theatre groups within and beyond the confines of their states.[2] The availability of such help continues to be widespread. Exploring available sources of expert advice from outside the community, an informal planning committee is better armed to consider the leader's idea for possible acceptance or rejection.

Having gained what he hopes is the gilt-edged approval of an informal though influential committee of citizens, a leader is now moved to work out with them the matter of who will sponsor the envisioned program. Tact, discrimination, and perception are involved in this decision. It must seem like a joint decision of the best thinking of the committee. Judged by local needs and conditions, what structure of organization is best qualified to administer the rather formidable task of producing historical drama? In general, three types of sponsoring organizations function to produce pageant-dramas, epic-dramas, or biography-dramas no matter if the communities are large or small. These types are: (1) an individual as sponsor; (2) an existing group or organization; (3) a freshly formed group or organization.[3]

Types of community sponsorship

The individual as sponsor

The day of the individual producer is pretty much of the past, even in the commercial theatre. In this context we find persons incorporating on a profit-making base, investing their own (and others') money and capabilities in order to make more money. This kind of privately-financed sponsorship has resulted in productions of such historical dramas as Sidney Howard's Yellow Jack, Arthur Miller's The Crucible, Norman Corwin's The Rivalry, Robert Bolt's Man for All Seasons, and Martin Duberman's In White America. And from the privately-sponsored Little Golden Theatre comes a musical production of Young Abe Lincoln by John Allen, Richard Bernstein, and Arnold Sundgaard (a recent successful exploration of the commercial theatre's use of dramatized history for child audiences).[4] In today's commercial theatre, the individual sponsor is rare. This fact is also true in the noncommercial theatre.

Although they are a dying race, rich men with philanthropic yens still exist in the community environment. A retired businessman may wish to express his philanthropy in terms of history or religion or art. In many cases the contribution of a site or building or art collection to the community is welcome, of course, and results in a desirable and fitting memorial to the donor and his family. But it is probably not useful to the community for an individual—even if he wishes to do so—to assume sole responsibility for producing a drama of historical happenings. This approach is an open invitation to dwindle the group initiative, to deaden the community's nerve for feeling solidarity and identity, and to rob its members of their share of the communal birthright. If, as we have said, history dramatized is a form of group expression, there are substantial reasons for avoiding the individual who, with the best of motives, offers a package deal to the community. Only in this avoidance can "group unity" be more than a catch phrase.

An existing group as sponsor

Another type of historical drama sponsorship, tailored to size from locality to locality, is the organization already established and operating in the community. We need to observe quickly, however, the distinction between tingling interest to serve as theatrical producer and qualification to do so. Not all organizations are structured and equipped to plan and carry out the complicated enterprise that is the business, craft, and art of producing drama. Some otherwise resourceful boards of trade, in their innocence, have discovered this the hard way. Likewise, more than one historical society has yielded impulsively to a sudden urge to "throw together" a sesquicentennial pageant, only to run head-on into barriers of neglected problems. Three days before the opening night we hear anguished cries of "I thought you said you would take care of the lights!" or "Joe invited the governor to address the audience, but he forgot to check on a public address system! How can we afford to rent one now? We're way over our budget!"

A group already accustomed to solving the problems of play production would seem to be a logical choice for assuming the role of sponsor. And indeed this is what is done in some localities by existing little theatre or college dramatic groups. For example, the Kings Mountain Little Theatre of North Carolina forms a loose confederation with five other small civic theatres along the South Carolina–North Carolina border to produce for six consecutive summers *The Sword of Gideon* by Florette Henri. This epic-drama of the important battle of Kings Mountain and its significant victory for the frontiersmen at a critical point in the Revolutionary War is staged in the amphitheatre of the Kings Mountain National Military Park. Through the jointly conceived and operated project, the federated sponsors of *The Sword of Gideon* are able in part to rise above the charges of insularity and inbreeding frequently leveled at existing groups. The civic community as a whole often views such a group— not without some justification—suspiciously, imputing to it cliquishness and narrow-mindedness (or long-hairedness, depending on the prevalent moral climate). But that bias aside, there is the real consideration of whether the existing little theatre or church group is qualified to handle the many human and technical elements called for by the various forms of historical drama. These may include, for instance, large-scale use of actors, singers, and dancers —many of them untrained—in combination with multiple scenic and costume changes, all to be coordinated under stress of time and limitation of space. If done out-of-doors, furthermore, the productions pose special problems not usually present in the indoor theatre.

Some existing organizations, however, are admirably suited to assume the responsibilities of production. As we indicated in Chapter III, school systems have built-in or self-contained units for sponsoring a program of dramatized history. This ranges from the informal classroom situation through the assembly program to the more formal audience-centered performance involving the general public. Such programs are scaled to various educational aims and practices, not all uniformly commendable. The seriousness with which boards of education regard "dramatics" is reflected—to take one indication—in the provision of adequate equipment and facilities for conducting an educational theatre program. We see how a program operates to its credit in the case of Penfield, New York. The fifth grade pupils of one of the elementary schools begin the sesquicentennial celebration of the town with an indoor production of scenes from the life of Daniel Penfield, the founder of the community. This production, in the well-equipped junior high school auditorium, is the opening gun of a four-month observance of Penfield's one hundred and fifty years of history. Later, as part of the celebration, the dramatic club of the senior high school writes and produces *The Caleb Hopkins Story*, based on an amusing bit of history when one James Wadsworth visited the cabin of Caleb Hopkins and volunteered to take the town of Penfield as a gift "for it was worth nothing." Both of these productions, organized under the guidance of teachers and performed in educational facilities by students for their peers, are prologues to two different historical enactments presented by Penfield adults, one of them by the Rotary Club. Here is a community relying on already established groups functioning as sponsors within a widely-implanted cooperative project.

At the other end of New York State, in Chappaqua, Westchester County, the local Dad's Club, a group of men in the community active in various youth projects, underwrites the annual Junior Class production at the high school. For some years two Dad's Club members, a professional writer-composer team of James Leyden and Lee Benjamin, have been conceiving and directing musicalized histories for the teen-agers to perform. These annual musicals do so much to unify the Junior Class members and the nonfaculty adults who work with them that the Chappaqua Board of Education is solidly in support of this collaboration, a healthy blend of town and gown. Excellence in production is in part attained even without alienating the faculty through extended rehearsals and disregard for school scheduling problems. The Leyden-Benjamin duo believes in brief but intense periods of preparation.

Among the well-established sponsoring structures no group surpasses college and university theatres in their opportunity to produce a variety of historical dramas. As a group, educational theatres—this includes elementary and high schools as well as institutions of higher learning—are in a favorable position to subsidize all or part of the costs of production. What is more, in their students they have a kind of "captive" personnel looking for guidance in releasing their creative talents, and in their directors they have the insights and skills to shape the drama to theatrical ends. (They do not, unfortunately, always realize their obligations to foster the cause of the unestablished playwright or the established one seeking production, whether in the campus or larger community.) The production of original plays has been a most important aspect of the college community's self-realization in efforts of this kind, the geographic spread of which can be indicated by a few samples. Berea College in Kentucky, wishing to celebrate its centennial, commissions Paul Green to write *Wilderness Road,* "a parable for modern times," for production in a native stone amphitheatre atop a sequestered hill owned by the college. In the Northwest director Horace Robinson of the University of Oregon Theatre explores regional backgrounds by producing *Mirror in the Sky* by Jessamyn West, based on the life of John James Audubon, with an accompaniment of original music. The University of Georgia Theatre headed by Leighton Ballew, offers a premiere of Jack LaZebnick's biography-drama of a Civil War firebrand. Ballew produces *John Brown,* in the midst of the institution's embroilment with racial integration, simply to "work with a new script that has vitality and interest and a protagonist who demands poetic treatment." [5]

Paralleling the campus theatre organization as a potentially regular sponsor of drama is the local church. The revival of interest in drama currently cutting across denominational lines, in this country and elsewhere, has been reflected by an increase not only in the number of its advocates but also in the forms of religious drama and its creative possibilities. In Chapter III we touched on some reasons for this swell of interest. Undoubtedly it does exist, and more churches are gradually coming to see how the drama can abet the serious aspects of their life and work. Operational procedures, for successful producing, however, are not always understood or practiced. Means need to be developed at the local level if the church community stands to use theatre to advantage. Fortunately, enlightened guidance becomes increasingly more available on the international and national scene, and along with it a gradual relaxing of sectarian rigidity.[6] One recent example of the mutual benefits derived from both local and national church bodies is a production of *The Bloody Tenet* in the Central Congregational Church of Providence, Rhode Island. This verse play is a work jointly commissioned by the Providence congregation and the Department of Worship and the Arts of the National

Council of Churches of Christ. More of this kind of collaboration is inevitable.

Producing units, other than church and school affiliated, are plentiful across the nation. A few examples reveal that limitation of workers is no index of the ability of established groups to succeed as play producers. In West Virginia, the Harpers Ferry Area Foundation develops originally to carry out civic projects, specifically in cooperation with the National Park Service. Then, to awaken local concern with the historical significance of the vicinity, the Foundation incorporates into the Harpers Ferry Civil War Centennial Association. The second organization, claiming twenty-seven family memberships, simply adopts the same bylaws and officers as the Foundation. The Association becomes responsible for presenting, on four days in October, 1959, the Centennial Observance of the John Brown Raid. Central to the occasion is the production of Wallace Dace's *The Prophet*, a biography-drama on the life and death of John Brown. During the four-day celebration the community plays host to approximately 65,000 visitors by conservative estimates.[7] When we realize that the population of Harpers Ferry is less than seven hundred, the magnitude of the project strikes home. It is a tribute to the willingness of a proportionately large number of individuals in a small community to take cooperative possession of their past. In so doing they enlarge the symbolic core of their communal life.

In the town of Pipestone, Minnesota, the Exchange Club, which annually produces *The Song of Hiawatha*, is composed of a group of thirty-five men whose slogan "unity for service" is linked with the National Exchange organization. The site of the production, a natural five-acre land-and-lake-stage, is adjacent to the Pipestone National Monument, established some years ago to "preserve for future generations the quarries and the surrounding sacred areas used by many Indian tribes." The producers of this well-attended pageant find that it helps to promote civic pride in the educational attractions of the Pipestone area.

The producing structures of the Harpers Ferry and the Pipestone organizations are formed under the sympathetic eyes of the National Park Service, a federal agency also smiling favorably on the production of *The Sword of Gideon* in the Kings Mountain National Military Park. Other epic-drama sponsorships, such as those of *The Lost Colony* on Roanoke Island contiguous to the national shrine, Fort Raleigh, and *Theodore Roosevelt's Life in North Dakota* in the Theodore Roosevelt National Memorial Park, have similar cooperative arrangements with the National Park Service. On the state level there are occasional instances of outright subvention of productions; but it is more usually a matter of the state's granting permission for use of acreage and/or buildings. An interesting example of the latter has occurred at Old Economy, a tiny village tucked between the Ohio River and Ambridge, a western Pennsylvania city seared by blast furnaces and industrial strife. The Pennsylvania Historical and Museum Commission administers Old Economy. For years the people of the area have been generally apathetic to the village's uniqueness. The final home of the now defunct collectivistic Society of Harmonists, Old Economy one day proves irresistible to a handful of history-minded individuals, among them two local school teachers, a newspaper editor, a lawyer, and the curator of the archives of this nineteenth-century utopia. Under the laws of Pennsylvania this group incorporates as the Harmonic Associates, whose primary goal is to activate a greater general interest in the state museum and to encourage the restoration of the site. "*Man's Reach*," says John Barner, one of the founders of the Associates and its business manager-producer, "has been our vehicle to reach that goal."

In Illinois the eyes of the good-humored lady twinkle a reply to the question. "Peoria? Its name *is* the joke of a nation, I admit. We're a river town, yes, famous for bourbon whisky and caterpillar tractors. But many of us take pride in its past. And, what's more, hope for its future." Standing impressively behind Mrs. J. E. Blackmon's words is the organization called The Arts and Sciences Federation of Peoria Area, composed of twenty varied groups working together to enrich the life of their community. To display the unified cultural sources in the third city of Illinois, the Federation sponsors "Fair in the Park," a late afternoon festival in the municipal grounds. Offered are book bazaars, indigenous arts and crafts exhibits, puppet shows, horticultural and science demonstrations, and plenty of music to make more digestible the family picnic. Then at 8:30 P.M., as a climax to the festivities, comes *Thunder on the River*, a commissioned pageant-drama written by Kermit Hunter, calling for actors, singers, dancers, and production crews totaling seven hundred and fifty Peorians. When Mrs. Blackmon, as general chairman of "Fair in the Park," sizes up the headache of her job, her eyes take on an earnest look. "Such an ambitious undertaking," she says, "takes faith and constant cooperation. I'm seeing a great deal of both, which accounts for the zest in our project." A total attendance of 19,000 paid admissions in six nights to *Thunder on the River*, with a net profit of approximately $7,000, testifies to Mrs. Blackmon's claim. Peoria's multi-pronged organization exemplifies how delegation of responsibility plus theatrical know-how can spell success in a community.

The decision as to the type of organization most effective for sponsoring historical drama is, in brief, a crucial one. Its eventual structure depends on local social and economic conditions and the alchemy of human beings. Sensitive and sensible leadership will be appreciative of the potential strengths and weaknesses residing in the community, and make its judgment accordingly. Regardless of what form the organization takes, however, it requires sufficient formality and permanence to serve these three principal functions: to make executive decisions and administer them, to assume responsibility for all financial and contractual agreements, and to ensure continuity of action from year to year—if this seems desirable or even remotely possible.

A new group as sponsor

In many cases the formation of a new rather than the use of an existing organization has advantages not to be lightly dismissed by the community. The purposes of the old group—no matter how commendable and valuable— may be extraneous to those essential for successful theatre management. Even if in harmony with the project, the personnel of the old group may not be qualified to serve the goals set up or to budget necessary time and energy to the rigorous commitments demanded. Furthermore, unhappily but conceivably, the members of the established organization may bear petty animosities or blow up rivalries that are inimical to the welfare of the project. On the obverse side of the coin, the purposes of a nascent group may be structured to newly conceived communal ends and may capitalize on the vigor arising from fresh challenges. A new organization may appeal to promising but untried talent at large, thus uncovering needed fresh leadership; it may likewise encourage an open attitude, ready to take into partnership the best thought and most constructive deeds of all segments of the community.

If the informal planning committee favors—for reasons subject finally to local conditions—the setting up of a new organization, there may be legal advantages. Experience shows that a historical society or association or a civic anniversary commission, wisely formed, gains not only organizational status but also legal protection for itself and the individual members by becoming a nonprofit corporation. The legal involvements of incorporation vary from state to state and sometimes seem overcomplicated. The costs of incorporation, however, are relatively inexpensive and the benefits many. Whatever the contents of the new constitution and bylaws, the articles of incorporation need to express clearly the purposes of the organization. A random sampling of organizations indicates how they upon incorporation adapt their major aims to hastily-contrived or well-conceived ends. One group is devoting its energies to fulfilling a project that attracts hundreds of visitors annually. This is the Abe Lincoln Players' production of *Abe Lincoln in Illinois* in the alfresco setting in the New Salem State Park. A not-for-profit corporation, the Players officially declare that they wish, simply, "to perpetuate a part of the Lincoln history in this Land of Lincoln."

In the small town of Boone, North Carolina, the need for sustained community effort over a period of years to realize notable ends is exemplified. Nestled in a picturesque Watauga County setting of the Blue Ridge Mountains, Boone is far from being densely populated. For several years a small group of Booners—spearheaded by Mrs. Constance Stallings, a local jeweller, and Professor D. J. Whitener of the teachers college located in town—dreamed of a mode of "collecting, preserving, and transmitting the historical heritage of the people of the Southern Appalachian area," and so they wrote this into their charter when they incorporated not-for-profit as the Southern Appalachian Historical Association. After months of detailed planning, the Association was able to realize its sponsorship of an epic-drama when *Horn in the West* opened in 1952. Since then, in the Daniel Boone Theatre, this story of hardy Appalachian pioneers has been presented every summer. While the Association's original plans of adding a museum and a Daniel Boone Village to the area's resources have not yet materialized, the average citizen in Watauga County sees social and economic gains roundabout him that can be attributed, indirectly at least, to the theatrical child of the Association.

Williamsburg, in Tidewater Virginia, has a relatively small population, too. But it has something else: a restoration of the town, courtesy of Rockefeller millions, to its colonial handsomeness and appeal. This serves as a potent lure for thousands of visitors yearly. When the Jamestown Corporation decided in 1947 to produce *The Common Glory* it asked for a charter as a private "educational, historical and benevolent" corporation whose primary purpose was to present dramas or pageants dealing with the early history of Virginia and the United States. This clearly valuable educational objective has been carried through by the annual summer-long presentation of *The Common Glory*, and concurrently for the seasons of 1957 and 1958—an acknowledgment of the 350th anniversary of the first permanent English settlement in the New World—by the presentation of another Green drama, *The Founders*. Because *The Common Glory* over the years has been performed so much and viewed by so many, the Jamestown Corporation became aware that the saturation point for audiences may well have been reached. With considerable foresight the producers in 1964 replaced *The Common Glory* with *The Founders*, tentatively planning to alternate the two dramas at intervals of several years. Although not specified in its statement of primary intent, the corporation has adopted as policy additional educational projects: the training of Virginia students and teachers in theatre crafts and practices, the encouragement of playwriting as an art form, the establishment of scholarships in drama at Virginia institutions, and the eventual assignment of its two amphitheatres to the civic and college communities.[8]

Structural organizations in sponsorship

When a community of whatever size, shape, and claim to uniqueness feels the urge to produce historical drama, there are countless organizational patterns for it to follow. No common pattern will solve the myriad problems posed by any single community. The four diagrams which follow (*Figs. 1–4*) are merely suggested as workable layouts in the structure of responsibilities of which any sponsoring group must become aware. A practical and satisfactory structure can be evolved for any producing organization if in the following diagrams it will distinguish A] the *executive* function as opposed to B] the *business*, c] the *creative* and D] the *interpretative* functions. To those already established play producing organizations these suggestions will appear gratuitous; other groups may, on the contrary, find them helpful. They are aimed primarily at the group for whom production responsibilities are new. Although all four diagrams sketch the general relationships of functions from beginning to end of the play producing process, the immediate focus is on the executive function. In the chapter that follows we shall concentrate on the other three functions: business, creative, and interpretative.

The four diagrams are labeled TYPE I, II, III, and IV. In each the parent or sponsoring organization, operating under its own constitution and bylaws, is a generic term for a historical association or society, a chamber of commerce, a fraternal lodge, a church or board of education, a college or community theatre and the like. Acting for the sponsoring organization is an elected or appointed board or committee in which resides the executive function. In each case there is designated a chief executive officer or General Chairman, and a head or Chairman of Staging, Buildings and Maintenance, Finance and Public Relations committees. The Public Relations committee absorbs promotion and publicity functions; in large-budgeted operations it is often necessary to have these functions handled by separate committees.

The director of the production, for reasons that will become apparent, is always an *ex officio* member of the executive board. Other representation, such as that of the Play Selection and Casting Committee, Legal Counsel, and officers of the sponsoring organization, is sometimes desirable. Some producing groups may wish to co-opt additional personnel; each committee chairman should enlist as many workers as he deems necessary to achieve results.

The four diagrams indicate that the organization pattern for production moves from the relatively simple one of TYPE I to the relatively more complex ones of TYPE III and TYPE IV; from the general and overlapping responsibility

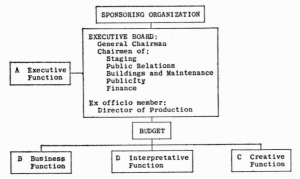

1. ORGANIZATIONAL STRUCTURE: TYPE I. *Serviceable structure where budget is limited and volunteer personnel for producing script is relatively inexperienced; where production is designed for limited number of performances; and where theatre site is familiar to producers.*

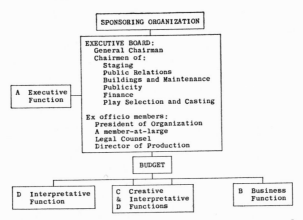

2. ORGANIZATIONAL STRUCTURE: TYPE II. *Serviceable structure where budget is expanded and volunteer personnel is guided by professional director-author or playwright, director, business manager and production designer; where production is medium to heavy in interpretative requirements; and where overall plan calls for performances to be repeated.*

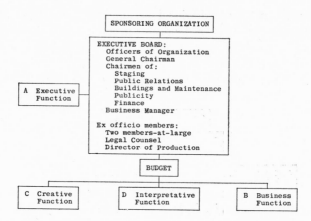

3. ORGANIZATIONAL STRUCTURE: TYPE III. *Serviceable structure where budget is large and script, artistic and technical personnel, and production scheme are items of heavy expenditure; where executive functions reside primarily in volunteer community leaders; and where overall plan calls for repeated performances over weeks or even seasons.*

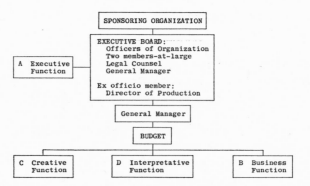

4. ORGANIZATIONAL STRUCTURE: TYPE IV. *Serviceable structure where budget is large and heavy administrative duties warrant employing full-time General Manager on year-round basis; where script, artistic and technical personnel, production scheme, and plant maintenance are items of heavy expenditures; where General Manager supervises budgetary matters and coordinates all artistic, business, promotional, and personnel decisions; where overall plan calls for repeated performances season by season.*

of the committee structure to the specific charges of the specialist; from the modified technical problems of the light, inexpensive production to the intricate and complex ones of the heavy, expensive production.

TYPE I offers a workable scheme where the budget is low and the volunteer personnel for creating, interpreting, and carrying on the business of production is relatively inexperienced; where the production is designed for a few performances; and where the theatre site or stage is familiar to the producers.

Production duties in all the organizational patterns can often be combined: the people in charge of costumes can also be responsible for make-up, for instance, and one committee may be able to function as both box office and house managers.

TYPE II is useful when the sponsoring organization has the resources of an expanded budget and semi-experienced personnel, with perhaps a paid author-director, business manager, and production designer guiding a predominantly volunteer staff. Given a proper supply of initiative and enterprise among the executive board, this organizational pattern is recommended for medium to large-scale productions to entertain audiences for a number of performances.

TYPE III points out a serviceable plan of responsibilities and relationships for groups sponsoring large budgeted dramas, especially those requiring many persons for the business, creative, and interpretative functions of the presentation. This pattern tends toward the policy of hiring at least the artistic directorate (those responsible for the various artistic aspects of production) if not everyone other than the persons involved in the executive function.

TYPE IV suggests an organizational structure that is similar in aim and scope to that of TYPE III. The major difference comes with the employment of a full-time year-round General Manager who assumes responsibilities delegated in other plans to various committees. In general he supervises budgetary matters and coordinates all artistic, business, promotional, and personnel decisions affecting the repetition of a production season after season.

Responsibilities of the executive board

The names by which an executive board is known vary widely (General Steering Committee, Executive Committee, Board of Governors, Board of Trustees, etc.). For ease in discussing the four types of organizational structure the generic term executive board serves, and each diagram is so labeled. This group is charged with powers to settle all matters of general policy, including that of the appointment of the artistic directorate, the selection of the script, and the scale upon which it is to be organized and presented. It decides the time and place of performance, and fixes the price of admission, if any. This body is directly responsible to the sponsoring organization for the allocation of finance and the general control of funds, including that of a prescriptive budget—this latter framed in consultation with a production's artistic directorate. Meeting frequently to consider items of urgency, the board's business is conducted expeditiously when its membership is small rather than large and unwieldy. Nonetheless, it should also provide means to elect other members as the need arises.

The general chairman

This is a key position to fill. If he is elected to the post by majority vote of the sponsoring organization, and accepts it with enthusiasm, the chances for cooperative responses from his colleagues are good. Among his major qualifications are the ability to carry the confidence and respect of the community as a whole and the experience in getting people to realize their potentialities. He must be able to allot enough time to the executive functions of the production to secure the unity of organization and directness of execution that the project requires. His business is to coordinate the work of all other members of the body. In doing so he needs to retain veto power over decisions of committee chairmen in order to avoid stalemates when different individuals may be at variance. While he gains strength in being able to "pour oil on troubled committeemen," he increases his stature—through exercising his prerogatives as chief executive officer—by placing the good of the community above that of any single individual, himself included.

The chairman of building and maintenance

He is responsible for the construction or renovation of existing conditions of the physical plant. Of course, if the production is to be staged indoors on an adequately equipped stage with an adequately designed auditorium, his work is reduced considerably. But if the decision is to have an out-of-doors presentation, his work becomes more complex. Its obligations embrace securing a proper site; preparing a suitable auditorium and stage; attending to an adequate supply of electricity and water; building or providing in some way offices, concession stands, restrooms, pathways, and parking lots; and installing dressing-rooms and work areas backstage, as well as lighting and sound amplification systems. If the chairman himself is not a building contractor or an architect, he should feel free to recruit both, along with cornering the advice of various kinds of engineers, including a sanitary and electrical one.

The chairman of promotion

This person's responsibilities ordinarily are two-fold: what is called *promotion* and what is called *publicity*. Briefly, promotion deals with long-range public relations concerned with "selling the idea"; publicity deals with short-range objectives in "selling the show." When the aims and complexity of the organization warrant it, there is gain in dividing the goals if not the methods within the operation—and separate chairmen justify their office. The Chairman of Promotion at the outset seeks answers to several fundamental questions. What public relations are necessary and suitable for a particular production? How much can be budgeted to make the job efficient? Answers are conditioned by variable factors in the community context.

Involved with cultivating goodwill through an understanding of sponsoring organizations' goals and ideals, the promotion man seeks to create a sufficiently favorable image in the community mind so that people will feel the need to support the organization's aims. He organizes a speakers bureau, public discussion and forum programs and much word-of-mouth promotion. He works closely with the director in a campaign to fire up volunteers to participate as workers and performers. He cares for visiting dignitaries and provides refreshments and entertainment for the entire production staff. When performers and others come from outside the community, he sets up a clearinghouse for their temporary living quarters. A personable, widely and favorably-known individual brings attributes to this post. A leading realtor, an incumbent city councilman, or local travel agent frequently makes an excellent choice.

The Chairman of Promotion also must inspirit business competency as well as goodwill from the executive board. Richard Hoover, the imaginative and tough-minded general manager of the complex business operation of the Pittsburgh Playhouse, asks pointedly what line of thought makes board members "believe that the exchange of dollars for entertainment and culture is any less a business than the exchange of money for any other merchandise or service?" [9]

It is necessary, then, for the holder of this post to organize a systematic campaign to promote group action manifest by hard work, constructive personal involvement and dedication, and financial support when needed. The executive board hopes that this collaboration will result in a production satisfying the needs of many individuals—those who plan, write, perform and, as an audience, experience the drama. If an audience fails to attend the theatrical event, the entire enterprise can be written off as a gigantic waste. To avoid this result, public relations must function effectively. And the same is true of publicity.

The chairman of publicity

His is the duty of seeing to it that the public knows about and attends the historical drama. In order to attract attention and stimulate interest, he deals generally with newspaper stories and advertising, printing and placing leaflets, posters, and outdoor signs, and with radio and television coverage—all gauged to the scale upon which the sponsoring organization wishes to present the drama. On behalf of large-budgeted, long-term productions of epic-dramas or pageant-dramas, he may be wise—after careful screening—to turn the execution of the job over to a professional impresario. The responsibilities are heavy, but many an enterprising and imaginative amateur publicity chairman, man or woman, has acquitted himself well in this post. A local newspaper editor is a "natural" for it. Other possibilities are the owner of a printing establishment or an employee of an advertising agency.

The chairman of staging

His responsibilities fall into two categories: the procurement of materials and equipment for the physical production; and the enlistment of personnel to design, execute, install, and maintain in working order the audio-visual effects required by the script. Often he receives donations of such goods as lumber, paint, and fabrics through personal appeals to local merchants; in emergencies, he may have to expedite the delivery of critical materials. The artistic directorate and he work closely in the preparation and running of the production. Frequently, a local hardware store owner or an industrial purchasing agent makes a sound appointment here.

The chairman of finance

He is responsible for the receipt and disbursement of funds connected with the operation of the production. This includes the management of the box office and the stewardship of tickets, should they be used. In consultation with the other members of the executive board and the director, he frames a prescriptive budget, has it approved so that the business, creative, and interpretative functions can proceed. He is prepared to render financial statements at each annual or regular meeting of the executive board. A banker or insurance company officer is a strong possibility for this responsible post.

The director

His artistic responsibilities and relationships will be described in the next chapter. In addition to being in full charge of the production itself, he is also concerned with all of the executive functions. He must know what is planned and accomplished by all committees. He lends his versatility, ingenuity, and experience in this form of theatrical presentation to the manifold situations facing the board. If such a trained and skilled theatre director is not available for supervising the production, the executive board needs to think twice before proceeding with it. At any rate, the worst possible solution to the matter is to appoint to the directorial chores two or more well meaning but inexperienced local artists with "a flair for the dramatic." One well meaning director is bad enough. But two can create only confusion. From this result dismay and frustration, to the general deterioration of the entire project.

The budget as a function of the executive board

Not all members of the executive board are expected equally to understand the intricacies of accounts payable or the fine print in the insurance policy. But all members can benefit the body and themselves by taking a realistic attitude towards business transactions. Any kind of theatre operation —no matter what its objectives and structure—must be based on practices of sound management and a balanced budget. These are civic virtues properly esteemed. Being business-like and management-wise about its production, the executive board early considers the necessity of making a budget, an educated guess of the expected income and cost of production. (This is where, incidentally, the presence of bankers and businessmen on the board pays off.) If the production is to live up to its potentials, it will need material things and human services, and these obviously cost money. And in these expensive days it will be more rather than less. Financial support for the enterprise is necessary. The two decisive questions facing the Chairman of Finance and his cohorts are: How much money is needed? Where is it coming from?

Both of these budgetary questions will be centrally treated in Chapter v. There they will be examined in the light of larger issues, social, artistic, and technical. These issues relate to factors of the physical location of the production, the authorship of the drama, the theatrical embodiment of it, and the promotion of it. These factors are mentioned here only because the last three of them touch upon a commercialism that repeatedly creeps into the historical drama production picture.

The commercial company's relation to the community

Scarcely has the local Chamber of Commerce or county centennial commission announced its plans for an upcoming commemorative event than there arrives a representative of a company specializing in the putting on of pageants or "spectaculars." He proposes a real service. His company will offer the local organization expert advice on the selection and rehearsal of actors, on a publicity campaign, and on the ways of taking the best bite out of the advertising dollar. Further, his company will provide, on contract and at considerable profit to itself, the dramatized script or "book," the scenery, lighting, costumes, sound, an electric organ and organist, together with a director who is "an ex-Broadway actor." This substantial package deal is tempting, admittedly, to the General Chairman of the executive board, whose experience around town does not include remembering how the last centennial committee handled things.

To their credit these commercial companies do provide considerable promotional adeptness and technical skills. Their "pageant masters"—to borrow the British term—generally are earnest, hard-working individuals of ability who know what it takes to whip four to five hundred assorted bodies—grabbagged in a "casting auction"—into presentable condition within a two-week period. Notwithstanding the research data turned over to them by local historians, the companies also provide scripts frequently well sprinkled with stereotyped historical events and characters, fundamentally unrelated to the community's past. Most of the scenes are so written that they can be presented just as well in Punxsutawney, Pennsylvania as in Blue Earth, Minnesota or in Frostproof, Florida. Of the episodes usually provided an early one is referred to as "The Twilight of the Red Man," with Troop 23 boys in breechcloths lighting fires in front of wigwams (although such structures were probably never used by the Indians indigenous to the locale). Another reliable opening scene is "The Coming of the White Man," always in Conestoga wagons (regardless of whether the first settlers in a given territory ever traveled by this mode of transportation). And just to prove that history can be fun, the script often features "Early School Daze" and "Gay Nineties" and the inevitable can-can girls, leading a distinguished North Carolina historian to comment wryly, "The company furnishes the costumes and the community the cans." [10] This is burlesque claiming to be history, a masquerade of a community's past.

With few or no roots in the community, there is little wonder that the pageant-company representatives—be they writers, technicians, or directors—regard the historical drama at hand as just another job. Each community resembles every other community. To develop insights into a town, to discover what makes it tick, we believe that writers and production directors must take soundings of it, get to know its citizens as they work and play. But beyond the applying of a pernicious formula to all communities—and thereby missing the essential aim and uniqueness of each—the commercial producer fails on another count. He robs the members of the community of the experience of creating together a product that they themselves plan, and produce in a combined act of self-expression.

Successful sponsorship a long-range involvement

"The human interest of a community in its own creative efforts," to return to Alexander Drummond's phrase, is not readily awakened or easily realized. *Castine, The Legend of Rawhide, A Mighty Fortress, Thunder on the River, Home is the Hunter*—these and other productions—were once only gleams in their dreamers' eyes. But they were nurtured and developed with the hard work of many persons over many months. Effective planning for the maturation of such community projects as we have cited in this chapter does not happen over the weekend. It calls for a long-range involvement requiring the best possible leadership and business acumen that the community can muster and sustain. This leadership functions in some type of executive structure. Only when the executive board stabilizes the organizational foundation can the production personnel begin to function. It is on this foundation that we continue to build the production of the drama in its business, creative, and interpretative phases.

v. Energizing the community's resources

A GROUP sponsoring the production of historical drama must, in prescribing a budget, grapple with many mutually related issues of policy. Decisions on these issues stem mainly from a thorough study and recognition of the community's resources, actual and potential. And budgetary matters, as a fact of modern life, bridge across these decisions.

Before trying to answer "Where do we raise the money?" the sponsors need to ask, and answer, "How much will the project cost?" If the production of a historical drama is worth the collective involvement of many individuals, it is worth doing well. Its sponsors should see that the financial resources are deployed to support artistic ends and not dissipated on nonessentials. Whereas an outlay of considerable amounts of money does not guarantee a production of distinction, a business-like concern for fiscal matters is compatible with artistic achievement.

The business motives of the sponsor

In the preparation of a feasible budget, some cautions need to be italicized. Examples of small communities such as Harpers Ferry, Pipestone, and Boone, evince that the size of a community need not be a handicap. Strict analogies, nonetheless, are dangerous. We have been approached by well-intentioned persons representing small towns who are aglow at the thought of creating historical drama in their communities. Having heard of the monetary success of such long-running dramas as *Unto These Hills* and *The Common Glory* in thinly populated areas, these persons are eager to do the same thing back home. When we tell them that these particular productions have annual budgets well into six figures, they respond with something akin to "Oh, but my home town couldn't manage anything like that—we'd go bankrupt!" Perhaps they would, especially if they are bent on emulating these two enterprises. Their mistake is in assuming that *Unto These Hills* and *The Common Glory* operate in geographic locations and under conditions that are typical. Each in its own way has uncommon circumstances and special features responsible for its financial drawing power. So we admonish our well-intentioned friends to go home and cut their dramatic coat according to their community cloth.

With respect to anticipated production dividends, the experience of

The Institute of Outdoor Drama is worth passing on. The Institute receives a steady flow of inquiries from persons seeking advice on getting projects started. Its past director, William C. Trotman, has shared our skepticism for the motives of persons hoping to initiate productions for reasons that are primarily economic. "Our critics accuse these productions of being tourist traps," comments Trotman, an energetic and alert Winston-Salemite, "or the answer to depressed communities by aiding area redevelopment." Acknowledging that some outdoor historical dramas have served as an impetus to community economy, Trotman blends bond issues with idealism by adding, "I have never been ashamed of a theatre just because it can pay for itself; I have never been particularly proud of a theatre that can do no more than pay for itself." [1] Although Trotman resigned from his post in 1964, his credo is continued in the person of the Institute's present director Mark R. Sumner, a Tarheel with a background as writer, stage director, and theatre business manager.

A community, regardless of size, that imagines implanting dollars with its history will produce the cornucopia of financial well-being, is asking for trouble. Fully apprised and honestly objective citizens work for an appropriately-scaled and judiciously-managed project fitted to the capabilities of their community.

The preparation of the budget

Ideally only those material goods and human services and efforts that express and enhance the qualities of the dramatic presentation need budgeting. It is sound business and healthy group psychology for the Chairman of Finance (or, if he exists, the Business Manager) to prescribe to his executive board a simple budget estimating the total receipts from all sources and all the ways in which the receipts are to be expended. These expenditures are those declared necessary by the best informed, qualified persons for the preparation and performance of the drama.[2]

Specimen budgets

In the specimen budgets that follow, ticket sales and other sources of revenue are included under INCOME. The spending of money for personnel and production goods comes under the heading of EXPENSES. Taking into account increasing costs, future developments, emergencies, and human fallibility, it is wise for the sponsors to prescribe a small profit. A "guesstimate" gauges by the rule of thumb that the total expenses should be 70 percent to not more than 75 percent of the possible income. No matter how heavily budgeted the enterprise, this formula can be applied proportionately to projects variously scaled.

The box office income in four of the five hypothetical budgets is estimated at 75 percent of the maximum seating capacity of the auditorium. The fifth one, identified as Budget B, operates on the policy of no admission charge. None of these budgets is meant to be imitated per se. Yet each is organized to illustrate practical considerations in estimating the income as well as the expenses involved in producing a particular form of historical drama. Assumed are certain group aims, phases of growth, human resources, and physical conditions as they might exist, in entirety or in part, in a given community.

Following each specimen budget is a commentary pointing out evidence of soundness in the conjectured planning. The worth of each commentary is increased where it points out as well unwarranted managerial risks and errors of judgment.

Budget A – small-scale pageant-drama

ASSUMPTIONS: Pageant-drama, a first production by newly-formed religious youth group in city of 100,000 in Northwest. Two performances given during Lenten season in church hall, room with no permanent theatrical equipment accommodating 250 persons. Written and directed by experienced drama teacher in local college on volunteer basis, assisted by church musical director. Playwright adapts, to some extent, materials for available talent. Rehearsals concentrated in three-week period. Performed by 35 students of high school and college age, all members of group, formed in part to experiment with religious drama. Some are members of local choral groups, a few belong to college or high school drama organizations. Nucleus of them function on costumes, properties, scenery, and lighting crews. Make-up done by volunteers with outside experience. Church furnishes chairs for audience, and areas to construct and store technical materials. Church assumes utilities (light, heat, water) on its general operating expenses, and promotes production through newspaper releases and regular church bulletins. Church office handles advance ticket orders. Production costs met by sale of tickets.

EXPENSES

Scenery and Properties	$ 40
Lighting (rented)	60
Costumes (constructed and borrowed)	130
Make-up	20
Tickets and Programs	30
	$ 280

INCOME

(Ticket sale, maximum capacity:
2 performances with 250 @ 75¢ = $375)
Ticket sale, estimated at 75 percent of capacity $ 280

COMMENTARY: As initial production of group, this unpretentious project has reasonably good chance of breaking even or clearing small profit. With no rent or expenses for light, heat, or other accommodations, no salaries to meet, no advertising expenses, budget can be limited to necessary items of production. Using staging mode of simplified horse-shoe pattern, there is minimal amount of scenery needed, with more emphasis placed on costumes and flexible lighting effects. Costumes made from materials provided at costs by local church member, adapted from robes, etc., borrowed from church and local schools. Around $1600 worth of lighting equipment rented from college theatre, installed and operated by experienced college student, member of new religious youth organization. Audience potential limited but decidedly active: composed mainly of church members interested in this first attempt to stage church-related drama; of faculties representing high school and college, attracted by presence of all-student cast and by reputation of playwright-director; and of friends of cast. If this project is given a carefully rehearsed performance based on a well conceived script, chances are that it will prove to be a rewarding experience for all concerned. If promotion is adeptly handled and the weather cooperates, near-capacity houses should result. With enthusiasm shown by members of audience and possible surplus of $40–$50, the group might be encouraged to plan for future productions and to organize program on permanent basis.

Budget B — *medium-scaled pageant-drama given annually*

ASSUMPTIONS: Pageant-drama produced by historical society in town of 2500 in agricultural center of Northeast. Two performances given each year in rent-free attractive natural amphitheatre accommodating 1000 persons, located in municipally-owned tract with good parking and picnicking facilities. Budget presumes four previous productions written by same author, a local person using similar format and some repeated materials from year to year, but introducing two or three new scenes annually, all tied in with local history and ethnic traditions of settlers of community. Nominal fees paid to playwright, local director, musical director, and experienced narrator imported to lend vocal authority. About 200 adults and children participate as performers and technicians on volunteer basis. Rehearsals spread over four weeks. Performances begin in late afternoon and end at twilight, thus eliminating expensive costs for stage lighting. Expenditures for scenery and properties account for new elements added, the bulk of physical materials being re-used and adapted as occasion demands. Most costumes borrowed from interested neighbors, all new costumes made by members of historical society. No fixed admission charges; production expenses met by donations from audience; deficits, if any, absorbed by individuals in sponsoring group; profits, if any, devoted to improving local historical sites or public facilities.

EXPENSES

Personnel

Playwright	$ 150	
Director	200	
Musical Director	100	
Narrator	100	
		$ 550

Production

Scenery and Properties	$ 150	
Sound Equipment (rented)	100	
Costumes (for new construction)	300	
Printing of programs	50	
Musical supplies	50	
		650
Total Expenses		$1,200

INCOME

Estimated donations at door (based on previous year's collection)	$ 900	
Sales of articles made by sponsoring group members	150	
Total Income		$1,050
Estimated Deficit		$ 150

COMMENTARY: On two main counts, this is risky business operation. Since there is no admission charged, income is dependent on donations, which are dependent on caprices of weather. Unsettled weather or interrupted performances (as of previous year) could result in unpaid bills hanging over sponsors' heads. On other hand, folks from town and outlying districts find appeal in pleasant surroundings for picnic followed by entertainment. Needed are: (a) regularized system of predicting income, and so enable sponsors to budget for systematic improvements for physical production; (b) initiation of training program for developing new writers, directors, and performers to replace the playwright and director, both of whom have been connected with production since its beginning. Steps need to be taken quickly before presentation becomes stale to audience and unprofitable for entire community.

Budget C – *biography-drama within season's bill*

ASSUMPTIONS: Biography-drama of historical figure produced by civic theatre group of ten years' standing in city of 150,000 in Southwest. Four performances given in building and with equipment owned by group which presents four different productions each season. Experienced director, technical director-designer, and business manager paid nominal fees for services concentrated in evenings and weekends. All other participants on voluntary basis. Capacity seating of auditorium 400 persons; auditorium comfortable and attractive, although its air conditioning system is inadequate. Backstage area with adequate space and equipment for construction of scenery and properties. Wardrobe has fair supply of early twentieth-century costumes, one reason for choice of script. Permanent lighting equipment accumulated over ten years, some of it homemade, but adequate. Drama written by established playwright calls for cast of 18, period of action 1900–1935, with two simplified settings. Production expenses estimated do not include expenditures such as light and heat, insurance, new equipment, etc., so that any profits for this production are absorbed in general operating expenses. (Estimated income ignores possibility of season ticket money which, pro-rated for each of four productions of season, would alter the actual income figures.)

EXPENSES
    Personnel

Director	$ 400	
Technical Director-Designer	250	
Business Manager	250	
Custodian	125	
	——	
		$ 1,025

Production

Scenery and Properties	$ 200
Lighting	20
Costumes (rented and borrowed)	180
Make-up (special wig)	50
Scripts	25
Royalties	125
Advertising	200
Box Office	100
Programs	75
Tickets	50
Reserve Fund (general operations)	250
Miscellaneous	100

		1,375
Total Expenses		$ 2,400

INCOME

(Ticket sale, maximum capacity: 4 performances with 400 @ $2.00 = $3,200)

Ticket sale (estimated at 75 percent of capacity)	$ 2,400	
Advertising in programs	150	
Total Income		$ 2,550
Estimated Gain		$ 150

COMMENTARY: With ten years' experience, theatre organization has worked out well-proportioned and efficient budgetary items, especially with season ticket plan bringing in substantial sums in advance and guaranteeing nucleus audience for productions. Business manager's main problem is to sell separate performances to general public. Choice of this particular historical drama made because dramatic material thought to have relevancy to local history and because playwright born in Southwest. Additional gamble taken on possibility of script attracting actors not normally interested in performing for group. Production economy through using wardrobe stocked with recent acquisitions from well-known local family and director and technical director-designer's agreement to adapt scenic demands to be constructed and shifted by available volunteer help. Relatively high advertising line on budget result of business manager's hunch that in spring of year competition for attention would be strong from other civic organization events, drive-in-movies, television. Unpredictable wave of hot weather could endanger box office income. If executive board could borrow sufficient money to pay for job, theatre in this circumstance should install good air conditioning system to attract customers regardless of heat waves. With theatre organization evidencing sound business management, bank loan is good investment for both parties.

Budget D – epic-drama within bicentennial celebration

RESOURCES: Epic-drama produced by specially formed county drama commission as part of county's bicentennial celebration. County of 50,000 population in Southeast region. Six performances given out-of-doors after dark on high school athletic field with adjacent facilities donated by local school board. Permanent stands and temporary bleachers furnished by bicentennial committee seat total of 2,500 spectators. Experienced artistic directorate comprised of paid director, technical director, costumer, and stage manager is augmented by assistant director, two assistant stage managers, and a sound engineer, also paid. Drama performed by 165 local volunteers, many of whom double as stage hands, properties crew, seamstresses, etc. Rehearsals concentrated in four week period. Advertising and house management aspects handled by volunteer committee, tied in with general bicentennial program. Management costs, seating and care of audience, advertising and promotion underwritten by county funds. Production income aimed to cover operating expenses. Some physical materials of production (stage platforms, scenery, costumes, sound system) provided at cost by local businessmen. Production income derived from admission fee of $1.00 for adults, with children admitted free.

EXPENSES
Personnel

Playwright	$ 500
Director	400
Technical Director	300
Asst. Director	150
Stage Manager	150
Asst. Stage Managers (2)	100
Costumer	100
Sound Engineer	150
Custodian of school	20
	$ 1,870

Production

Stage platform	$ 300
Scenery	200
Costumes (construction, borrowing, rental)	500
Sound Equipment	100
Lights in field (during rehearsal)	60
Lighting equipment (rented)	2,000
Express charges on lighting equipment	250
Mileage for transporting out-of-town personnel	100
Miscellaneous expense	200
	3,710
Total Expenses	**$ 5,580**

INCOME

(Ticket sale, maximum capacity: 7,500 @ $1.00 = $7,500)

Ticket sale (estimated at 75 percent of capacity)	$ 5,625	
Concessions for food and beverages (share)	250	
Total Income		$ 5,875
Estimated Gain		$ 295

COMMENTARY: County commission sponsoring production makes intelligent use of local resources in arranging for use of high school facilities (athletic field, stands, dressing rooms, rest rooms), which are adequate for project. Considering amount of money received and time put in on production, including their travel time, the trained theatre personnel in charge are contributing services for next to nothing. (The director, for example, averages about $2.00 an hour, considering his preparation, travel time, rehearsals, and performances.) An effective production of a good script would make this a high-calibre yet inexpensive investment for the county. Major item of production expense charged against lighting equipment (instruments, cables, control board) which must be of special capabilities not available locally. High school students in domestic science classes help to make costumes, others borrowed from local citizens, with military uniforms rented. Budgetary expense of $100 for transporting artistic directorate, technicians, and large number of performers from outside town decidedly underrated by budget-makers, particularly because performers would be needed for more rehearsals than anticipated and a considerable number of private car owners would require reimbursement. Except for this oversight, fiscal view is promising. Because of the special nature of the occasion, there is a good chance that the 5,625 paid admissions estimate would be met and an estimated operating gain recorded.

Budget E – preparation and first season of epic-drama

RESOURCES: Epic-drama produced by regional historical association in town of 7,000 in picturesque section of south central state. Sixty performances scheduled for new amphitheatre constructed on site of pioneer settlement with funds appropriated by State government. Maximum seating capacity 800 spectators. Experienced playwright commissioned to write drama, experienced musician to write original score. Experienced theatre personnel form leadership for production staff of 70, all on weekly payroll. Artistic directorate comprised of director, stage designer, costume designer, lighting designer, musical director, choreographer, and stage manager. Managerial and production assistance comprised of 2 assistant stage managers, and 10 stage crew members. Actors, singers, and dancers total 50 performers. Some qualified locals included on staff, but all of artistic directorate and majority of performers imported. General manager employed full-time to handle first year administration and operation.

EXPENSES FOR PREPARATORY AND PERFORMANCE PERIODS, FIRST YEAR
Personnel
Artistic directorate (7)

Director	$ 2,400	
Stage Designer	1,600	
Costume Designer	1,200	
Lighting Designer	1,200	
Musical Director	1,200	
Choreographers	1,200	
Stage Manager	1,200	
		$ 10,000
Production assistants (12)		5,000
Performers (50)		25,000
		$ 40,000

EXPENSES FOR PREPARATORY AND PERFORMANCE PERIODS, FIRST YEAR (cont.)

Production Equipment and Installation

Scenery and properties	5,000	
Costumes	4,000	
Make-up	150	
		9,150

Production Operation and Service

Lighting and Sound	300	
Scenery and Properties	300	
Costumes	400	
		1,000

General and Administration

General Manager; and Business Office,
Box Office, Theatre Maintenance Personnel;

Public Relations Manager	21,000	
Utilities and Heat	500	
Telephone and Telegraph	850	
Advertising and Promotion	12,000	
Travel	1,000	
Office Supplies	2,400	
Postage and Freight	800	
Office Repairs	100	
Insurance	700	
Interest on Notes	200	
Rent	600	
Maintenance	2,000	
Miscellaneous	1,500	
		43,650

Royalties

Playwright (minimum)	3,000 *	
Composer	500	
		3,500

Total Expenses of Production, Management and Promotion		$ 97,300
Estimated Cost of Building Theatre	$ 90,000 **	
Estimated Cost of Installing Permanent Equipment and Seats	23,200 **	
	$113,200	
Total Cost of Production Preparation and First Year Operation	$210,500	

EXPENSES FOR PREPARATORY AND PERFORMANCE PERIODS, FIRST YEAR (*cont.*)
  Income for first year of operation
  (Ticket sale, maximum capacity, for 60 performances @ average price of $2.25 = $108,000)
  Ticket sale (estimated at 75 percent of capacity) $81,000
  Souvenir program advertising and sales (net)   14,000
  Concessions for food, beverage, cushions, etc.   5,000

                  Total Income for First Season $100,000

                  Estimated Gain $ 2,700

(* If drama is repeated, in subsequent years a playwright might agree to a percentage of the gross or a percentage of the $3,000. This would be fair to the producers in a lean summer when income and expenses are not favorable.)
(** The subtotal of $97,300 shown above for management and promotion does not include the expense of building and equipping a permanent theatre. The initial construction cost of the building might run from $50,000 to $175,000 or beyond, depending on the topography of the original site, nature of the design, the materials used, and the kind of labor available. The installation of "permanent" lighting equipment and control board, electrically amplified sound system, electric organ, and auditorium seats could amount to between $20,000 and $30,000. The figure of $113,200 shown above for the cost of the theatre plant represents estimated amounts appropriated from state funds. This original capital outlay is not expected to be amortized and is so specified in the state contract.)

COMMENTARY: To make this operation economically feasible, local sponsors would need to raise initial guarantee fund of $70,000 to $80,000 to allow the General Manager to establish the business and promotional aspects of the project and to meet production costs and current operating expenses before revenues come in. Exposure to weather and rigorous use during season would require good construction and equipment in all production aspects; special weatherproofing precautions raise costs. Costumes would require constant laundering and repair. Ticket sale income predicated on average night attendance of 600 paid attendees, a mark demanding skillful promotion to reach. Also predicated on perfect cooperation from weather, a highly unlikely situation. One rain-out means average loss of $1,350, two rain-outs a loss of $2,700, or the equivalent of estimated profit. In a big-business operation a balanced budget for first year is unlikely and the sponsors should be prepared to make adjustments in succeeding years. In most optimistic terms, they could then hope to balance out an average budget during this period provided they could maintain: (a) a high level quality of performance with its resultant favorable word-of-mouth promotion; and (b) a large quantity of widespread and persuasive publicity. Meanwhile, enough supporters of the idea must continue to believe that the overall indirect benefits of the project provide the community with sufficient rewards.

Qualifying factors in budget-making

To frame a prescriptive budget the executive board tries to answer hundreds of questions that are seemingly concurrently raised. Although no formula can be imposed on the budget-makers, they do come closer to eventual financial reality by taking a stand on four salient factors: authorship, physical location of the presentation, methods of producing it, and cultivation of its favor in the minds of the community. Frequently interrelated policies concerned with such factors determine the stand taken.

Looking first at the question of the production's physical location, the problem of space is resolved by considering existing resources. These may range from a historical site to an existing theatre structure. If there is a historic site strategically located in the community and adapted to the purpose of production, we often find evocative gains in this association with the past. Specific sites may be indoors, directly or indirectly connected with historic events or characters. (Examples of potential indoor and outdoor settings are discussed in Chapter VI.) If the site has already been restored through the interest and care of a private organization or public agency, the financial obligations in adapting it for production purposes will be minimized. This is the case in Budget E, where the pioneer settlement is assumed to be reconstructed in somewhat its original condition. It is possible, in such cases, that only the actual production items—lighting and sound equipment, for instance—will have to be included under expenses.

If no adaptable historic site is available, the search continues for suitable facilities. They may turn out to be the rent-free city park, as in the circumstance assumed in Budget B, or the donated high school athletic field, as in Budget D. In the situation assumed in Budget A, the church furnishes without charge a hall to accommodate the production, the facilities to construct scenery, props, and costumes, and the chairs to seat the audience. Even when facilities are not donated to the sponsors, rental and utilities charges in public or semi-public buildings and areas are likely to be minimal.

Important but often overlooked in the selection of an outdoor location are the factors of sight lines and acoustics. To compensate for poorly arranged seats, money must sometimes be expended to assure each spectator a clear view of the acting areas. Where amplification of speech and musical effects is thought necessary, the finest equipment available demands a high priority; even though it means sacrificing other items, a high fidelity sound system, adapted to the physical location, should be obtained. Unless a production is scheduled for an extended run, the rental rather than the purchase of such equipment is a reasonable decision.

Tooting river boats and rumbling freight cars (such as punctuate the outdoor production of *The Golden Crucible* in Pittsburgh) and shrieking jet planes (such as break the illusion barrier of *The Confederacy* along Virginia Beach's waterfront) are visual as well as aural distractions in the alfresco setting. These are problems ordinarily beyond budgetary control. But insect control is another matter. In heavily shrubbed areas insects have been known to set up sounds vexing to audiences trying to listen to dialogue; and in certain seasons the mosquito menace mobilizes insecticide squads to lessen the noisy competition between the self-protective slaps of fully-dressed spectators and those of half-naked Indians. Costs mount as the insects acquire immunity to the insecticide.

Aural and visual equivalents of the preceding distractions abound in the indoor situation also, their correction usually amounting to substantial outlays of funds. Visitors to college and high school auditoriums across the land readily recall the poorly conceived sight lines from flat auditorium floors and strangely positioned balconies; they recall the inability to understand the spoken word because of banging steam pipes or noisy air conditioning systems. When the rental costs of the hall are a budgetary consideration they need to be agreed upon in advance. So do additional changes for adequate public utilities and the use of permanent stage equipment. Adequate space for technicians to function and performers to costume themselves and await entrances is similarly important. The availability of space for rehearsals and technical preparations, which may call for additional rental fees, is another key factor in deciding on the physical location of the presentation.

A second significant factor the executive board faces in determining the budget is the staging of the script. To give theatrical life to the playwright's imagined world, performers must be selected and rehearsed, physical accoutrements designed and built, and music and dance—if they are central to the production scheme—composed and fused with dramatic action and technical effects. To accomplish this function there is always at least a modicum of expense with the materials of production—as indicated in the five specimen budgets—even though all of the human services may be voluntary. To coordinate the hundreds of disparate production elements into a special unity is the proper sphere of the artistic directorate. Looking at the specimen budgets we see that for the artistic directorate—which omits author and musical composer and includes stage director, designers, musical director, and choreographer—the funds typically allocated to this personnel form a wide variety of percentage of the total expenses: Budget B—$300 of $1,200 or 25 percent; Budget C—$650 of $2,400 or 27 percent; Budget D—$950 of $5,580 or 17 percent; and Budget E—$10,000 of $97,300 or 10 percent. Subject to the requirements of the script and its treatment by the artistic directorate, this leads to a general observation: where salaries are allocated for the directorate, they appear in inverse ratio to the total production costs. This is a consistently common pattern, for an increase in the scope of the production and its corresponding overall budgetary claims usually requires wider distribution of funds for more physical materials and more participating personnel, as a comparison of Budget B with Budget E demonstrates.

In formulating the prescriptive budget the executive board must find tentative answers to key questions. What is the minimum number of personnel essential to a commendable standard of performance? How many "extra" performers and helpers can be excluded without impairing a high level of production? Supposing it is decided that a sizable number of volunteer "extras" for a county-wide celebration, assumed in Budget D, need transportation from outlying districts for final rehearsals and performances? Are they to furnish the transportation themselves or is this a legitimate expense to be charged against the production? On another tangent, is the entire production personnel covered by a blanket accident insurance policy? These, and many more questions yield no facile answer. But finding solutions to all of them further tests the executive board's courage, intelligence, and ability to reach a common goal.

More often than not items of equipment and other physical goods consume a big piece of the budgetary pie. Is it wise to rent some and purchase others of these items? How many can be borrowed for a specific production; and if any can, should they? What, furthermore, is to be the policy on donations by local merchants, and what kind of public recognition will be given them? Some penny-wise-and-pound-foolish producers regret too late their decision to "economize" on such items as cheap (and outmoded) sound systems or borrowed (and ill-fitting) colonial militia uniforms, to the detriment of the drama's success in entertaining audiences. The framers of the budget need seasoned advice from those experienced in contemporary theatre practice in order to strike a happy balance between financial expediency and artistic judgment.

Some communities, large and small, do not always have among their ranks persons endowed with the special training and experience so essential to the planning and performing of community-centered dramatic productions. Until these qualifications are on tap locally—a situation to be desired and encouraged—it is necessary for the sponsors to decide whether for their purposes they allot funds to attract experienced theatre talent from outside the immediate community. To give satisfactory expression to their project, the sponsors may wish, after detailed consideration, to go beyond their boundaries to employ some or all of the artistic directorate, the performers, and the technicians. The decision to budget funds for such purposes may prove a sound investment; it is sometimes possible to count among the dividends an improved calibre of production, which in turn swells community pride and increases cooperation. The question of salaried personnel, weighed with other production factors, is fundamental in erecting the financial structure of the entire project.

In addition to general planning for the promotional aspect of production discussed in Chapter IV, publicity presents the third important factor of budgeting. To accomplish the goals of publicity and promotion, there are many kinds of communication available to the sponsors. Listed here are only those most commonly used; the special resources of the community will activate others. They are divided between media of communication "free" and "paid."

Under "free" publicity and promotion

Personal word-of-mouth response, preferably favorable

local newspaper stories, interviews, pictures, and editorials, also preferably favorable

telephone campaigns

radio and television public service programs

printed announcements and bulletins of special interest groups, such as schools, P.T.A.'s, churches, service clubs

guest speakers and oral announcements at meetings of the groups mentioned above

displays in stores, banks, libraries

school or church chimes playing selections pertinent to the current production

photographers' picture-taking sessions

Under "paid" publicity and promotion

newspaper and periodical display ads

printed brochures and postcards for mailing

printed or silk-screen posters, leaflets
radio and television commercials
highway billboards
car stickers for automobile bumpers
official stationery

Some sponsoring groups, relying entirely on free publicity and promotion, omit any related item of expense from their budget. This is the case suggested by Budget A. Large-scale continuous operations, on the contrary, frequently allocate as much as one-eighth of the total production budget to promotion and publicity, as assumed by Budget E. In this instance, $12,000 is appropriated to the year-round campaign to "spread the word" about the production on a national, regional, and local level, distributing it over such items as display advertising, direct mailings, billboards, and radio and television coverage.

In the circumstances under which Budget C theoretically functions, let us assume that the executive board of the civic theatre group decides to meet the competition from other local theatrical productions, drive-in movies, and television spectaculars by budgeting the advertising on its historical drama higher than usual. In addition to its standard campaign of direct mailings and display ads, averaging $75 per production, it makes a special appeal to teachers, students, and history buffs by allocating an additional $125 for radio commercials, newspaper ads, and a motorcade through the city with actors in costume. In the Budget A situation, however, we may assume that a "captive" audience is fairly well assured without an advertising expense through the media of church bulletins, oral announcements, student newspaper stories, and word-of-mouth broadcast by the thirty-five performers. Adult members of the congregation, interested in seeing for the first time a dramatic production staged within the church property, help to swell the attendance.

Free promotion and publicity is always doubly welcome as long as it is appropriate, exciting, and in good taste. But how much to spend on paid advertising is an open question, for there are no certain measures for determining what precisely is effective and just when it ceases to be so.

Procuring the financial means

Having some idea of the budgetary dimensions of the projected historical drama, the sponsors now face the frequently thorny problem of raising the necessary money. No matter how the producing group is structured, it requires the financial credit or facilities that this credit will buy. Financial assets channeled into either capital investments, or production operations, or both, are required. The project seeks underwriting of sorts: this means a guarantee fund that stands to pay all expenses incurred in the process of producing the drama. Methods of securing this underwriting are diverse.

An indirect method practiced by new organizations with slim capital is that of volunteering to offer dramatic entertainment especially fashioned for events within the community. Learned bodies such as chemical engineering societies or mental health associations often look for after-dinner programs; and large industrial corporations or utilities companies are sometimes pleased to have the local civic theatre group dramatize some developmental aspect of their manufactured product. In such circumstances the underwriting of the performance clearly belongs on the hosts' account. The performers gain some experience, a little extra money for their treasury, and—perhaps more importantly—good will for any money-raising hopes they may have in the future when they announce plans for a drama's production. Donations of gifts and materials and human services by the public utilities and corporations with local connections are welcomed by the recipients; and as "theatrical angels" the donors are correspondingly enabled to give their public image a splendid halo effect.

There is a commendable practice, unique in the United States, of having educational institutions subsidizing all or part of the performance of a wide range of drama. In such an educational setting the production of historical drama enters as an inevitable function of the regular theatre program. This accounts for the presentation of it and the encouragement of its writing, especially on college campuses, as indicated by such productions as *The Cry of the Jay* (treating the domestic upheaval of a southern family during the Civil War) at Mississippi Southern College and *More Love, Brother* (concerned with clashes of principles within the Shaker Society) at Western Reserve University; both scripts are written by women students, Mary Ellis and Miriam Anne Cramer, respectively.

Paralleling this development of the campus theatre, dramatized history also finds a place in the offerings of the less securely subsidized civic theatre. Attesting to this are the productions of such biography-dramas as Howard Fast's *The Crossing* (whose central figure is George Washington) at the Dallas Theater Center, and Aldyth Morris' *The Damien Letter* (about Father Damien, Roman Catholic missionary to lepers at Molokai) at the Honolulu Community Theatre. And, as several dramas noted earlier have shown, educational institutions frequently count among theatrical blessings dramatized his-

tories celebrating their past. They finance suitable productions of these not
only to memorialize certain occasions, but also to stake a well-placed hope that
entertained audiences will be disposed to contribute to the future financial
health of the institution.

"Yes, but how do we raise the money," we hear the patient historical
association treasurer ask, "we don't have wealthy trustees or a well-heeled
school board standing behind us!" This is a fair question; any answer must be
a qualified one, pending a thorough study of all the factors influencing the
specific situation. Historical societies, chambers of commerce, service clubs
have experiences that can be cited. These and other nonsubsidized groups are
frequently forced to devise means to back their community-related drama. The
procurement of funds for this purpose often causes them to shake down their
organizational treasury or dip into their respective pockets. But at least such
groups do have some financial equipment with which to work, and by virtue of
their existence as a group they presumably have standing in the community,
with borrowing power and ingenuity to plumb their own resources and those
of like-minded friends. They are likely to cultivate the support of teachers,
social workers, clergymen and other professional persons sympathetic to their
special goals and who, even though they have no private capital to contribute,
can pave the way towards released space and helpful facilities. They are often
in a position to know what official doors can be opened upon government
assistance in various forms. They can, in short, survey all of the constructive
techniques for procuring money and take positive action with the ones that
seem most adaptable to their aims.

In addition to trying to raise funds, producing groups with modest
objectives and shoestring budgets may turn to public-spirited citizens for donations of production materials, equipment, and volunteer help. Materials often
obtained at no or little cost are invaluable to the inventive technical director;
from hardware merchants, he may receive supplies of hardware, rope, and
paint; from lumber dealers, rejected or unused sections of lumber and beaver-
board; from department stores and warehouses, large wooden or corrugated
paper boxes; from textile mills and tailor shops, mill-ends or discarded fabrics;
from demolition companies, wooden doors, metal railings and lighting fixtures,
fireplaces, and the like. Other sources of procuring production goods for
properties, costumes, and scenery are local museums, second-hand furniture
stores, and the attics of private citizens. Useful production equipment donated
or sold at token sums includes hand and power tools, ladders, and sewing ma-
chines. Trucks and trailers are often loaned, as well as volunteer help, especially when the exact nature of the work is defined in advance. The production

operation assumed by both Budget A and Budget B implies that some adeptness on the part of the production staff and some good will on the part of the community combine to give each project some financial stability.

Methods of raising funds

According to John H. MacFadyen, former Executive Director of the New York State Council on the Arts, in the history of patronage of the arts, potential means for their support have emerged successively in the following categories:

the benevolent individual
the philanthropic foundation
educational institutions
business and commercial corporations
labor organizations
municipal, county, and some divisions of state and federal governments.[3]

The sponsors of historical drama must analyze these sources of support to discover which of them are legitimate resources of their own community.

The secrets of fund-raising are no monopoly of the management consultant specialist along Madison Avenue. In the common domain are various fund-raising methods developed in association with the flooding enthusiasm for visual, musical, and performing arts. The methods are not mutually exclusive, and two or more may be combined with benefit. One obvious method resorted to is the outright solicitation of donations. These may come from well-disposed individuals, large corporations, small businesses, and local or regional foundations. But foundations and other philanthropic organizations are not likely to open up their checkbooks unless local initiative demonstrates tangible evidence of its own ability to arouse collective giving. No gift is too small to accept, of course; a single gift, on the contrary, may be too large, if it has a debilitating effect on the community driving force.

An often duplicated plan calls for an incorporated association composed of local merchants, banks, service clubs, private citizens, and the like. This association conducts a subscription campaign to underwrite the entire production costs against loss: this serves as a guarantee fund, not to be called on except in the event of loss. As a barometer of community confidence in the project, the subscription plan is excellent.

Another method of proven worth, particularly where the production connects with a commemorative aim, is the preparation and sale of a printed booklet with pictures and text of significance to the local history. Without receiving any government funds, small communities finance their projects— such as the one organized by the Harpers Ferry Centennial Association, Inc.— by selling advertising in a carefully-edited, attractive Centennial Book, which in turn produces revenue through its sale. The sale of tickets for the historical drama itself swells the income, so that well-managed group efforts often report a solvent operation with an overall profit.

The floating of bond issues proves effective in a community needing large amounts to initiate a large-scale project. With this method the sponsors sell bonds of various denominations, repaying the principal on the bonds as profits will allow and meeting interest notes at specified intervals. The method allows The Pioneer Days, Inc. organization of Ogden, Utah, to underwrite the production expenses of *All Faces West*, receiving additional aid through appropriations voted by city and county officials. In Jacksonville, Florida, a nonprofit educational and historical corporation, the Ribault Quadricentennial Association, sponsors a production of *Next Day in the Morning* through pledges from Jacksonville businessmen.

Another commonly practiced method of fund raising seeks municipal, county, or state appropriation sufficient to support all or part of the expense of production. At Bern, North Carolina, the 250th Anniversary Committee established by the city fathers places before the public an epic-drama, *The Third Frontier*; its committee members receive funds from the municipal government to cover the anticipated deficit of production. *The Kansas Story*, produced by the Kansas State Centennial Commission, is supported in time as well as money by business, educational, and civic organizations in Topeka and Wichita, the two cities where the elaborate musicalized history of the Sunflower State is performed. City and state agencies combine to furnish a guarantee fund to the Centennial Commission for its sizable expenses in producing the giant pageant-drama.

In this connection an important trend becomes discernible with the formation of local arts councils in the United States and Canada, which join together as national arts councils with annual meetings, regular publications, and interchange of ideas.[4] This results in pressure being exerted not merely on state but on city and county agencies to appropriate public dollars for the enhancement of the cultural life in their communities.[5] For historical drama producers, technical assistance and professional counsel from government and arts councils may also be regarded as potentially valuable resources. To regard their availability as the panacea for all the organizational ills of the current project, however, is ingenuous; finding the critical ways and means of producing a satisfying drama must remain finally the difficult lot of the sponsoring group itself.

Budgetary factors in theatre construction

A most critical problem confronting the sponsors is obviously the choice of site for producing their drama. If a suitable theatre structure is donated, money is released for other purposes. If a theatre structure has to be rented, this is a budgetary item ordinarily encompassed. But if to fulfill the aims and requirements of the project a theatre structure (auditorium and stage) has to be constructed or rebuilt the financial responsibilities take on major proportions. Building costs and union labor scales being what they are, even the most compact and unadorned architectural arrangement ties up relatively heavy capital expenditures. Seat for seat, cubic foot for cubic foot, the cost of building an indoor theatre normally will exceed the cost of constructing a roofless amphitheatre without weight-supporting walls. The extent of difference is so dependent on such variables as design, function, materials, size, etc., that it is foolhardy to try making estimates.

Because of the complexities involved in modern building construction, sponsors—for budgetary if for no other reason—need to surround themselves with the best available technical advice in studying the building schemata. Every part of a projected theatre construction, indoor or outdoor, "must withstand careful examination," according to theatre consultants Burris-Meyer and Cole, "and merit inclusion in the building on the basis of effectiveness." [6] So care must be taken, we are told; but care means delay, and delay leads to increased costs. If a limited budget will not provide all the elements as first envisioned by the sponsor, what is to be done? When this question is directed to Arthur Cogswell, the architectural consultant for the Institute of Outdoor Drama, he sounds as if the question is familiar: "Compromise is the soul of architecture. You can't get everything you want on the budget you have in the time available." Then, warming to his subject, he explains: "Here we have four people—an architect, a producer, a playwright, and a designer. And no one of them can get everything he wants. . . . Each must learn the others' desires. Each can adapt to the others." [7] As the architect further reveals, this compromising determines the ultimate usefulness of the structure.

If the project requires the erection of a new building, land needs to be acquired as a site for it. This site is sometimes donated outright by an individual or an educational or charitable organization. Gifts and popular subscription of capital funds may, however, have to pay for land as well as building. Supposing the site is leased from a land-owning public agency, a county park commission, for instance, at a minimal rental; there are yet heavy expenses possible not only in the construction proper but in the grading of the land, constructing roads and perhaps parking lots. If the cooperating businessmen of the town furnish building materials and supplies at cost and if at least part of the construction work is blessed with volunteer labor, a considerable portion of the capital fund can be diverted for items more closely related to enriching the actual presentation.

John B. Lippard, a practicing architect living in Charlotte, North Carolina, has designed the amphitheatres for large outdoor historical dramas, including *Honey in the Rock* and *Horn in the West*. A gentle-spoken Tarheel, Lippard cautions working with a shoestring budget, a situation he has encountered in community projects. "When we work with private groups," Lippard observes, "sometimes they can scrape up more money. But the theatres that have been built by governmental agencies are rat races. Everything has to be approved by the state legislature, [Department of] Conservation and Development, and the park boards." [8]

There are admitted drawbacks to dealing with governmental agencies and seeking financial aid (sometimes as the price for being a pawn in a political chess game). Nonetheless, experience indicates that in various sections of the country the resources of public trusts and offices can be explored and the cooperation of officials—once the red tape is cut—exceedingly helpful.

In West Virginia, state legislators finally are convinced of the merit of subsidizing the construction of an amphitheatre in Grandview State Park; when, after seven long years, a historical association finds the necessary $75,000 to meet the production costs of *Honey in the Rock*. Virginia's Department of Conservation and Development contributes to the construction of an amphitheatre, on land donated by the College of William and Mary, a state institution in Williamsburg, providing the producers of *The Common Glory* match the state's spending dollar for dollar. In return for the state's contribution towards construction, the Jamestown Corporation deeds its theatre plant immediately to the College of William and Mary and retains use of it on a rent-free lease arrangement. In Kentucky, the Department of Parks agrees to finance at Harrodsburg an amphitheatre with chairs, and organ, lighting equipment, and sound system installed. With the theatre site located at the Pioneer Memorial State Park, the sponsors incorporated as the Fort Harrod Drama Productions raise the amount necessary for production operations; they present, subsequently, *Home is the Hunter*. These and other examples point to the active collaboration between public and private funds in support of community theatre projects.[9]

On a smaller scale, in Hermann, Missouri, the town officials make the municipal park amphitheatre available to the producers of an annual Maifest pageant-drama rent free when they elect to do it outdoors; some years they prefer staging it in the local high school auditorium, with space and equipment donated. In Pinellas County, Florida, the Park Board cooperates with the University of Tampa Drama Department, assisted by two nearby chambers of commerce, to produce *Count Philippe's Wild Orange Tree* by Sydney and Marjorie Barstow Greenbie. This production, an example of coordination of town, gown, and public agency, is presented in a county-owned park, the original site of Count Odet Philippe's estate which nurtured the first citrus grove on the west coast of Florida.

Whatever the means chosen by the sponsors for fund-raising and for producing materials and human services, the various steps in the campaign must be carefully announced and clearly defined. And the announced goals should be pursued with patience and pleasant determination, seasoned always with an ethical sense recognizing the need for honoring in the name of the producing group all promotional claims and financial obligations.

The creative-interpretative functions of the sponsor

Having considered budgetary and other financial aspects of the projected dramatic production, we now examine other important resources uniquely the lot of the community: the author, those who direct and perform, and the personnel forming the managerial and general production staff. Sponsors, of course, in practice do not really settle the matter of budget first, independent of these other factors. A number of critical budgetary decisions obviously hinge on what demands the script itself makes and the interpretation imposed on it by the producers. From every view it is essential to choose the drama or the playwright and at least the director as early as possible. Other key members of the artistic directorate need to be added swiftly. For it is their personal involvement in the initial planning and the benefit of their practical knowledge that enhances the chance for a satisfying production.

In the previous chapter we charted four diagrams (*See Figs. 1–4*) representing organizational patterns for sponsoring groups. Types i through iv are those that, under given conditions, may vary markedly from community to community. In progressing consecutively from *Figure 1* through *Figure 4*, we move from a relatively simple to a complex production task, from a depend-

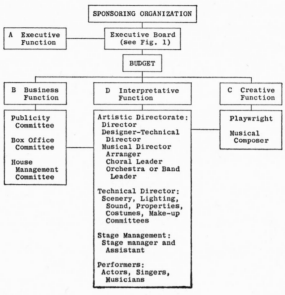

5. PRODUCTION STRUCTURE: TYPE IA. *(Extension of Organizational Structure:* TYPE I.*)*

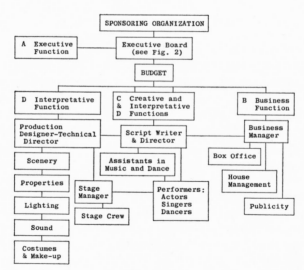

6. PRODUCTION STRUCTURE: TYPE IIA. *(Extension of Organizational Structure:* TYPE II.*)*

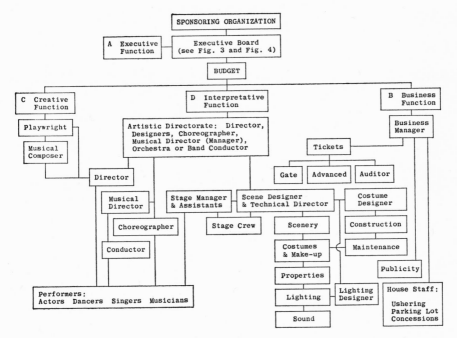

7. PRODUCTION STRUCTURE: TYPE IIIA. (*Extension of Organizational Structures:* TYPE III *and* TYPE IV.)

ence on a relatively untrained to an experienced theatre personnel, and from a commitment of a relatively limited to an expanded business operation. Let us attach to these Types an added structure suggesting the creative and interpretative functions necessary to the process of play production. Production Structure TYPE IA is an extension of Organizational Structure TYPE I, TYPE IIA an extension of TYPE II, and TYPE IIIA serves the production purposes of both TYPE III and TYPE IV. In the case of the last two Types, it is proposed that the organizations they represent have generally similar aims, their executive and business functions differing by the presence of a general manager in TYPE IV.

Regardless of what type of production structure seems most promising, the playwright and the musical composer contribute the *creative* functions of writing the drama and any original music integral to it. Those who give meaning to and embody in theatrical terms the drama created are the interpreters of it. Chief among the persons who contribute the interpretative function is the director, in whom resides the responsibility for making all final artistic decisions of the production. Joining him in the artistic directorate are the other major interpretative agents: the designers of scenery, costumes, and lighting; the choreographer; the musical director, sometimes serving as choral leader and arranger; and the orchestra or band conductor. In most instances, not all of these specialists are required; and often their functions, when required, are absorbed by fewer individuals. Further interpretative duties are placed on the technical director and his production assistants and the stage manager and his assistants. Actors, singers, dancers, and musicians add interpretative meaning to the script. An individual frequently assumes in a production structure more than one function: a director designs the lighting effects, or an actor conceives and executes the masks for dancers to wear. In some uncomplicated production set-ups it is possible for a relatively few staff members, aside from the performers, effectively to interpret the script.

Type IA structure

In the completed structure, we assume that a playwright finishes a script; if he senses the need of an original musical score to support it, he enlists the aid of a composer. In this pattern, the artistic directorate is composed of a director, a designer who doubles as technical director, and a musical director, who may arrange existing music if the playwright and director request it, and who may train and lead the singers, and conduct the orchestra or band. These assignments may, of course, be turned over to others. Under the technical director's leadership, committees work on scenery, lighting, sound, properties, costumes, and make-up. The stage manager and his assistants administer the decisions of the artistic directorate, bringing the performers into coordination with the general and specific interpretative aims of the production. In this proposed structure the actors, singers, and musicians constitute the performers.

TYPE IA structure recommends itself, but is not limited to, the production of a small-scale pageant-drama that features enactment, singing, an original musical score, but no dancing. It is an adaptable structure for the production of a biography-drama, where published rather than original music is used, and the musical director makes his own arrangement for a small-orchestra accompanying group singing as part of the dramatic action.

Type IIA structure

Here we see the dual functions of creating the script and directing it fused in one person. In this case the artistic directorate resides in two chief interpretative leaders: the director, who interprets his own creation; and the production designer-technical director, who exerts control over all production details. Under the director's supervision, responsible assistants carry out his ideas by training the singers and dancers separately, enabling the director to relate their performing specialties to a coordinated whole. The stage manager continues the interpretative function by serving as administrative aide to the director, judging always whether in final rehearsals and performances the meaning of the script as interpreted by the directorate is being maintained. Where the script does not call for it and a capable musical director is not available, no live musicians forming a band or orchestra are included. If musical effects are employed to enhance the script, they can be taped on high fidelity equipment and balanced during the performance by a sound operator.

This TYPE IIA structure is perhaps suitable when the author-director and the production designer are exceptionally experienced and skillful theatre persons, for much depends on their ability to keep large numbers of inexperienced performers and backstage workers constructively busy with a feeling of progress. Both persons will find their burdens lightened considerably by the presence of an alert, tactful, and objective stage manager. If these conditions exist, the TYPE IIA pattern is adaptable for the production of small to medium-sized pageants and biography-dramas.

Type IIIA *structure*

To satisfy the creative function of this organizational pattern, let us assume that the playwright furnishes the script and the musical composer the accompanying score. In this type of structure, often suitable to large-scale heavy-budgeted pageant-dramas or epic-dramas, the artistic directorate functions with an increase of specialists: in addition to the director, there is a designer each concentrating on scenery, costumes, and lighting; a choreographer; a musical director, who stands by as choir leader; and an orchestra or band conductor. The scene designer sees that the director's overall interpretation is expressed visually through costumes, make-up, properties, and lighting. And the technical director (he may be doubling as scene designer) coordinates all visual elements with the auditory elements and the performers' active use of them.

The stage manager's staff administers, as usual, the job of coordinating performers and material elements in the actual performance. Beginning with the final rehearsals, the administering of the concerted group effort is a responsibility of the stage manager, whose job calls for him in TYPE IIIA and other Types to be in charge of all back-stage and on-stage aspects of performance; handling the routines of operation and the quick-thinking judgments imposed by unexpected happenings are his constant responsibility.

The costume designer not only supervises the execution and rental of the complete wardrobe, but often maintains the garments through the production run. The lighting designer, similarly, may not only plan the lighting effects but supervise their performance operation. If a "live" orchestra or band is used, the musical director may conduct the musicians as well as train the singers. Mainly for reasons of economy, musical scores are frequently taped and then become the responsibility of the accoustical engineer and the sound controls operator. When the musical score is early committed to tape, this serves as a decided asset for the choreographer in training the dancing personnel.

Qualifications of the playwright and composer

The playwright

The script chosen by the sponsors for production may be in print or in manuscript form, never performed or performed hundreds of times. If it already exists in readable condition, what makes the sponsors decide to produce it? They are likely to be influenced in its favor if its subject matter promises to have general appeal for the community. But this alone will prove a tepid reason if the script does not also have strong dramatic legs to stand on.

If the play is yet to be written, this can be done by a team of two or more authors, but unity is more likely to occur if a single author assumes the responsibility for the entire script. The sponsors should not mistake academic exercise or a flair for turning out garden club skits for playwriting ability. Ideally, the person the sponsors need to look for to create their drama is maturely knowledgeable of human relations and sensitive to his world. Not only does he possess talent as a writer but he has a genuine interest in the materials of history, and specifically those out of which drama evolves. While he may not have previously written a historical drama, he has to his credit evidence of other scripts alive with some special kind of theatre vitality. Additionally, he shows a capacity for working well with others, especially the director, and for revising the script, meeting deadlines, and otherwise adjusting to the pressures of play producing.

The sponsors of historical drama need to search constantly for playwriting talent within the community and to provide nourishment for it when discovered. When such talent is not harbored locally, the sponsors should unhesitatingly look beyond the community limits for the most promising writer who best realizes the aims of their project. In seeking this person, they should canvas the recommendations of authorities of local or regional reputation in the field, examine and insist upon carefully-chosen cross-checked reactions to all scripts submitted, and reserve the right—where a script seems close to fulfilling their needs—to insist upon detailed revisions under close guidance of the director or any other designated specialist in playwriting. (Sponsors should investigate the information services of specialized agencies listed in Appendix C. A companion source of guidance and technical advice, in a wide range of matters, awaits sponsors in the drama departments of college and universities, in local or nearby civic theatres, and in regional and state arts councils.[10]

The composer

Once the form of his dramatic idea crystallizes, the playwright and the director are the best judges of whether a musical score will strengthen the script. If the need is affirmed, a composer with strong dramatic imagination, capable of understanding and creating a score with contrasting changes of mood and vividly colored effects, is likely to succeed. Through appropriate choral and instrumental components of the score, his music reinforces and heightens the dramatic expression rather than competes with it. If no such score is promised, and the playwright and director feel that music is a necessary coordinate of the drama, then available music suitable to dramatic ends should be chosen and arranged by a competent musician aware of the theatrical nature of his assignment.

Qualifications of the artistic directorate

The director

Ranking in importance with the sponsors' choice of the playwright stands their selection of the director. Without sensitive and understanding direction, the finest of theatre projects will fail to realize its potential. If the playwright creates the script, it is primarily the director who translates it into a language meaningful in the theatre. This is a deceptively simple-sounding assignment, but one that demands unusual human and professional attributes. Some decisive qualities, apparently common to successful directors of community-rooted drama are: knowledge of the crafts of the theatre; appreciation of related arts, especially music and the pictorial arts; sense of artistic taste; organized skill in planning in advance; insight into individual psychology; patience and respect for persons involved in a collective endeavor; and dedication for the ideals and purposes of the theatre. Rarely does a Broadway-inured director, unaccustomed to dealing with inexperienced personnel, limited budgets, and a different cultural climate, possess these qualities in satisfactory proportion. By comparison directors with successful experience in local and regional civic or educational theatre programs are likely to rate strong consideration.

Whatever the organizational form of his producing unit, the demands on the director are complicated and demanding. Over the stretch of weeks and long hours, he must wear at least four hats: that of the artist, the diplomat, the coordinator, and—when occasion requires—the evangelist. As the chief interpretative agent of the author, he makes the major artistic decisions on how to reconstruct in stage practice a vision that the creator records on paper. He evaluates the suggestions of his individual collaborators, judging wherein they enrich the overall intellectual, emotional, and abstract patterns he seeks to synthesize. He coordinates the work of the performers and the designers of setting, costumes and make-up, and lighting, and approves the results of the technical executants. When his co-workers turn confused or discouraged he bolsters their faith in the joint undertaking.

Once the script becomes a personal and group commitment, the director initiates and exerts control over all aspects of the production. And as he moves into the final phases of rehearsal, the director knows that it is the total impact that counts with an audience. So he pretends to the role of audience, seeing, hearing, and experiencing the performance for the first time. In this way he can evaluate the success of the group effort; by testing audience responses, desired or undesired, the director appraises the quality of his concept and the thoroughness of its execution. From his place in the audience, his judgments of intelligibility, timing, coordination, and concentration are useful for performers, his contribution to maintaining high levels of achievement is also an index of his understanding of group morale and insight into individual psychology.

The choreographer and musical director

In our types of production structures we have included in the artistic directorate the choreographer, the musical director, and, when necessary, the orchestra conductor as interpretative agents. Their functions and aims resemble but subserve those of the stage director's interpretation. In addition to being trained musicians, they need to be able to stimulate the best efforts from their performers often under exacting and competing pressures. Frequently they are required to sacrifice musical emphases for more important dramatic ends. Not all musicians or choreographers are able to reconcile themselves to this necessity. Before final commitments are made to and by these persons, the director should be encouraged to explain the artistic functions of music and dance in his interpretation of the drama to be produced. With views clarified, the persons involved can then decide if they continue to be interested in collaboration. A clear-cut agreement at the outset will induce mutual respect in all responsible artists.

Designers of setting, lighting, costumes

More standard collaborative agents functioning in the directorate are designers of scenery, lighting, costumes, and, in some cases, make-up. Sometimes these assignments are carried out by the same individual, but more frequently in heavy productions where time is stringent modern practice calls for a division among specialists. No matter what his areas of specialization, a designer is, like an actor, an interpreter who stamps his own personal comment on the script, but subordinate to the total impact desired by the director.

Designers state a visual meaning through physical materials chosen for their line, color, fabric, and adaptation to practical stage function. The costume designer plans each costume for its appropriateness in the dramatic context, its theatrical expressiveness, and its "wearability." Make-up is regarded often as an extension of costume design. The scenic designer attempts to create an atmosphere appropriate to the imagined place of action, to make the scenic environment more expressive of the emotional content of the script, and to afford the safest, cheapest, and most flexible construction in which to perform the action. Lighting is so integrated with scenic and costume design that they are usually conceived of in terms of the other. Through controlled use of intensity, direction, and color of illumination, the lighting designer synthesizes the animate actor with the inanimate physical materials of the theatre.

In their own local or regional community the sponsors of drama may discover suitable personnel to staff the necessary artistic directorate of their project. If these resources seem not readily discernible, there are state and national agencies geared to help in the search for men and women trained and experienced in the key interpretative functions.

Qualifications of the performers

The collaborative agents who speak most directly to the audience are the performers. The ideal performer is one who acts, sings, and dances superbly. Since this is an ideal seldom attained even in the commercial theatre, the practice among community theatre directors is to cast the strongest possible combination of candidates on the basis of their vocal and physical attributes, their stage experience, and on what skill or skills are demonstrated in the auditions. Singers are welcomed by the musical director of a drama requiring a chorus and/or soloists; but if they are unable to adapt themselves to roles calling for controlled acting or dancing the stage director is likely to find them of limited use. A dancer with an expressive body, however, can frequently contribute valuable acting in at least subsidiary roles. The most versatile performer, though, is regularly the actor who, although not gifted with an operatic voice or terpsichorean grace, senses the dramatic implications of a scene and "acts his way" through a moderately simple song or dance.

The performer's task, then, regardless of his training or background, is to express the dramatic and musical ideas prescribed by the playwright and composer according to the agreed-upon interpretation set by the directorate. But attainment in acting or dancing or singing adjusts itself not only to the creator's attitude but also to the performer's own comment on that attitude. He makes a personal comment and in so doing aspires to the potential status of an artist. Not everyone can excel in the performing arts. The quicksilver of a performer's talent shines out from the most unexpected corners. Its prediction is indeed rare. But once it is recognized in an individual, directors of dramatic production observe that his growth and achievement respond to certain attributes. These are his powers of *observation*, the awareness of life; *sensibility*, the development of sensory responses; *imagination*, the ability to recombine his experiences into something new; and vital *coordination of voice and body.*

Almost every community can furnish people with natural although untried acting ability that may be used at first in minor and non-speaking roles. Assuming the will to develop their individual resources, these persons may attain necessary vocal and bodily control that can be made dramatically serviceable under sympathetic and careful direction. The case of a drama at Tin Top, a microscopic spot in Texas, is typical. Its director Junius Eddy, then professor of theatre at Baylor University, casts theatrically inexperienced townspeople in thirty roles. "I expected the production itself," says Eddy, "to be unfinished, with considerable forgetting of lines, mixing-up of action and business, and a general air of amiable confusion about it all." What else could be expected from a group of people with no previous stage experience whatsoever! Much to his suprise the presentation turns out to be genuinely affecting. Little of the action or business is changed or forgotten. Many of the actors handle themselves like veterans.[11]

Qualifications of the backstage and business personnel

Backstage personnel

Granted a full complement of performers, the artistic directorate still falls short of the mark if it fails to include other interpretative personnel in its planning. As reference to the production structure types indicates, these are the backstage workers, selected by the technical director or production designer. In many hours of the preparatory period, these technicians construct and paint scenery, borrow or build properties, install lighting or sound equipment, and cut out and sew costumes. In the final rehearsals and performances many of them in their various capacities are indispensable to the smooth running of the production. Without their attentive and reliable cooperation, the most imaginative of artistic flights remains grounded.

Business personnel

Finally there are those persons, elected by the business manager, who round out the business function of the enterprise. Chosen with an awareness that their "on view" relationship with audiences results in important impressions, they include the publicity staff, the ticket sellers and general office force, the ushers, and—often in outdoor situations—the parking lot attendants. All of these persons win friends for the theatre through a pleasant, alert, and business-like attitude towards the spectators. Their general effect cannot be overestimated.

Factors involved in selecting personnel

It is the rare city or town that does not possess some human potentials that are worth seeking and training for production involvement. Although local citizens often do not have specialized training in theatre responsibilities, they may have equivalent experiences or talents that fit them to function effectively as members of the production team. A banker, an accountant, or a lawyer, for example, may readily swivel into the business manager's chair. A restaurant cashier or physician's secretary may supply valuable traits of personableness and accuracy in dealing with box office problems. A costume designer sometimes finds mothers who can construct costumes as skillfully as—and perhaps more willingly than—they make their daughters' formal gowns or mend their sons' blue jeans. The writing of program notes and publicity releases may be just the outlet for the limpid prose of the high school English teacher or the feature editor of a local college newspaper. Senior citizens and 4-H clubbers with a facility for using tools may employ them to build window seats, re-cover period furniture, and fabricate home-made lighting equipment. And the inevitable "Willy Westinghouse" in the community does not need a second call to install and operate a stereophonic sound system.

The advantages of using predominantly local personnel are self-evident. They are close at hand and therefore more readily available, although here the question of vocational and domestic obligations cannot be ignored. Housing does not pose a problem, nor should ordinary social relationships between company members and the local citizens. Moreover, the native involved in the production with or without remuneration frequently generates unsuspected feelings of respect and pride in his heritage. These are emotional ties fingered casually by the average "outsider."

Although theatre-trained persons from within the community offer substantial advantages to the historical drama project, it is advisable sometimes to draw upon the larger community—be it county, region, even the state beyond—for help. Often a community finds limitation in its ability to recruit a sufficient number of local personnel willing and capable of filling the production ranks. Furthermore, a script and its interpretative treatment may place such demands on extended acting assignments, spectacular choreographic movement, intricate choral or instrumental music that a thorough scouring of the town indicates that these demands cannot be met by untrained locals. In this instance, it is wise to import trained, experienced talent to ensure success. Generally, the artistic directorate knows of suitable talent that might adapt itself to the requirements of the script and the local situation. Most directors look with favor upon talent that can be scouted on the college, university, and civic theatre training grounds within the region and across the state. This is a source turned to by such large-scale continuous enterprises as *Honey in the Rock, The Stephen Foster Story,* and *The Lost Colony.*

The advantages and disadvantages to using nonlocal personnel are mainly relative to the nature of the individual community and the specific goals of a particular production. If the nonlocals do not furnish clearly superior qualifications over local personnel, then there is no advantage in calling on them.

Generally, however, the final group product will benefit by imported training and talent manifest in such areas as acting, dancing, singing, and technical departments. One advantage lies in the economy of time. When such personnel is recruited, assuredly their acquired skills and imposed disciplines will guarantee that the director can attain more gratifying results in the beginning rehearsal period. The director, for instance, does not expect rehearsals to be held up because actors, through sheer inexperience, fail to learn lines and basic movement. He expects, further, that the level of achievement attained in the early performances will be sustained through succeeding ones. Undisciplined and unseasoned actors are not often capable of this sustainment.

Considering the possible disadvantages to contracting imported personnel, there is first of all the additional time consuming process and expense of interviewing, screening, and otherwise testing persons in various localities apart from the home base. Secondly, nonlocal personnel must ordinarily receive sufficient compensation to take care of their room and board and other life essentials away from home. College actors and technicians, for instance, require at least a minimum living wage; with more mature and skilled persons of proven ability, the salary ascends upward on a sliding scale. Another problem has to do with adequate housing facilities for and within the economic reach of the outsiders. Sometimes an executive board member or the business manager arranges for unoccupied school dormitories to be rented for the duration of the out-of-towners' stay. Or negotiations with private home owners result in accommodations being put at the disposal of the visiting personnel. Where nonlocals contribute their services to a production, it is customary of course for the local sponsors to provide lodging and board for the period of final rehearsals and performances.

Two possible sources of friction arise sometimes when nonlocals are thrust into the local context. One is the inherently natural resentment of townspeople, eager to participate in the production, against outsiders assuming roles or technical responsibilities which the former feel, rightly or wrongly, belong to them. In addition the fact that the nonlocals receive money increases the resentment. This situation needs to be anticipated by the executive board and both parties (the outsiders and the locals) conditioned to its possible development. An early statement of policy by the sponsoring group, explaining the reasons underlying the importation of outsiders, helps to temper the local sense of injury.

People involved in theatrical production—particularly during the dress rehearsal and performance periods—do a major part of their work in the evening hours. This leads to a second cause of possible friction. Adaptation on the part of both locals and imports is necessary. The outsiders need to compromise with the local mores as they understand them; the community needs to allow the outsiders to function effectively by compromising with a situation that is uncommon to its citizens.

Healthy relationships are encouraged between a group of nonlocal personnel and the community at large when the executive board:　1] provides for sufficient and adequate housing before the arrival of the group, the accommodations being within a three-mile radius of the theatre;   2] arranges for the company as a whole to have access to its own isolated social quarters, preferably with food and drink service and opportunity for group relaxation;   3] emphasizes to the artistic directorate the need for selecting outside personnel socially mature and balanced as well as talented;   4] explains to the outsiders community idiosyncracies to which adjustments might be required; and   5] reminds the entire company before rehearsals begin that as representatives of the production its behavior in large part determines the success of the community's relation with the production.

In our examination of some resources that the community can mobilize for its artistic task force, we have concentrated so far on the potentials of money and human creativity. The ability to procure funds, materials, and services to initiate and operate a drama project (of whatever magnitude) is one measure of community health. Continuing efficient management of the affairs of a project is necessary to accomplish fully the two fundamental tasks of its sponsors: to maintain a high quality of theatrical product, and to provide community service. These aims involve not only the uncovering of talent but also its first-class cultivation. A seriously managed community theatre project regards as important a long-range systematic training of playwrights, directors, actors, designers, and technicians, and the younger the better.

We turn now to two other community resources: the human beings forming the audience, and the place of enactment, the physical theatre.

VI. Evaluating the audience and determining the production site

The audience

Two major types of audience

IT IS a cool summer evening in a midwestern town. On the fairgrounds a ferris wheel whose lights form a bright-moving circle in the sky carries a burden of happy people that have come from town and country. Nearby, the roar of a small roller coaster blends with the delighted laughter of people enjoying themselves. Entire families, from grandparents to babes-in-arms, are there. Presently, the high school band appears and wends its way through the crowd, heading toward the adjoining high school athletic field. Family by family, the people begin to leave the carnival amusements and troop along behind the young Pied Pipers. As the band halts and re-forms on the grounds of the athletic field, the crowd members pass their tickets at the gate and take seats in the grandstand facing a stage erected on the field. And as the band plays its finale and the stadium lights focus on the stage, the shuffling and the chatter fades. Now comes the moment akin to that in every theatre in the world: the moment of anticipation.

Here, perhaps, anticipation is keener than usual. Only rarely do these people see live drama. On occasional trips to the city they may see a production put on by a touring company, or in their own town they may see an annual high school play; but their play-going experience since the old days of Chautauqua has been restricted. Most of them have been seeing drama only in the movies or on television.

Now, at a cost only a bit more than the local movie admission, these families are about to see a special kind of drama, one that tells about their own ancestors, their own town, their own memories. It is a pageant-drama depicting their own history as a highlight of a centennial celebration.

The spectators recognize a good many of their friends and neighbors as actors in the production, and costumes or properties they have contributed or helped to make. Possessing a personal sense of their history, they respond eagerly when new aspects of it are revealed. Carefully they watch for the appearance of remembered figures and notable events. Because the production is capably written and presented, the onlookers' attention is sustained. Their children watch the action with wide-open eyes, fascinated by the color and movement, the music and dancing.

As the playwright observes the crowd, she is pleased that the drama is successful. This success is attributable partially to the fact that she has known for whom she has been writing and has evaluated her audience correctly.

This night marks the fruition of efforts to observe the town's anniversary with a drama reviving the past. In this community the active president of the chamber of commerce conceives the idea and discusses it at informal planning sessions with influential citizens. The idea is thoroughly considered and approved; the chamber of commerce president with representatives of the planning committee spark the formation of a sponsoring organization (similar to TYPE II; see fig. 6) directed by an executive board to consider and carry out the arrangements. In its early meetings the executive board learns that a local girl doing graduate work in theatre at the state university has been recognized as a talented student playwright. Her playwriting instructor strongly recommends her and offers to supervise the writing of the script. On this basis the board engages the girl, providing an equitable stipend for her services.

The student playwright accepts the community's proposal. After her initial research—with which the town historian offers helpful assistance—she discovers that the town history extends over a long span of time that has no particularly rich dramatic period, event or legend. Furthermore, the committee points out to her that the drama is intended primarily for the local populace, the audience being comprised of people coming from an area within, say, a twenty-mile radius of the town. The writer is also told that the community cannot afford to hire outsiders. Consequently, willing and qualified local people will execute the production. The director of drama at the local high school, for example, will act as stage director. Armed with this knowledge and a few additional facts, the playwright reasonably chooses to compose a small-scale pageant-drama capable of being economically presented on a temporary stage erected on the athletic field of the local high school. There are bleacher seats for one thousand people. Since the committee has estimated with valid approximation that three thousand spectators may attend, it judges that three performances will answer the seating demands. Advance consideration of the potential audience pays dividends to both playwright and community.

In another state, a community of similar size is planning a historical drama of its own, and has established a sponsoring organization (similar to TYPE IV; see fig. 7) to this purpose. However, prominent in the minds of this organization's executive board is the idea not only of vividly recreating a rich community past but also of attracting tourists to the area. The local state park that encompasses a reconstructed pioneer village already draws numbers of transient visitors. The community also lies proximate to several arterial highways. Seeking professional advice, the sponsoring group engages an experienced business manager to supervise the details. A historical novelist in the region is commissioned to write a script aided by the advice of an experienced director who will stage the drama. The history of the locale, the writer finds, can be focused on that eventful time when the town's early frontier settlement is firmly established. Additionally, he learns that the potential audience is estimated—on the basis of a careful survey—at a figure between thirty and forty thousand people. Thirty percent of this figure, it is presumed, will represent local spectators and those from a nearby metropolitan center, and seventy percent will be drawn from transient visitors during the summer months. It is also anticipated that a portion of this number will be drawn from a metropolitan center not far away.

The nature of the community's past, the potential audience to be attracted, and the town's facilities for accommodating visitors are large factors in the final determination to produce an epic-drama designed to run through the summer and, if feasible, to be repeated for several years.

Waiting for a performance to begin, the playwright sees the audience arriving at the new park amphitheatre, the construction of which has been financially underwritten by a state agency. Seats are provided for approximately five hundred people. The spectators are mainly tourists who have visited the historic sights of the locality that afternoon and will spend the night at a motel or hotel in town. Their knowledge of the area's history is slight, for the most part, but their interest has been initially aroused by the day's sight-seeing. Furthermore, these people have witnessed drama in the motion pictures and on television, and certainly many living in or near metropolitan areas have seen live theatre provided by touring shows if not also that offered by educational or civic theatres. Generally, these spectators as a whole are more theatrically sophisticated than an average local audience. While difficult to gauge accurately the characteristics of any heterogeneous audience, we may surmise that these theatregoers having bought their tickets expect to experience a capably produced, colorful, lively drama based on the locality's history. Most will expect the same level of production and entertainment value of the historical drama as they would of a touring show from Broadway. After the lights dim and as the performance progresses, the playwright observes the audience's interest in the story and its pleasure in the lively songs and colorful folk dances.

Sitting in the back row, the playwright feels some sense of satisfaction that his drama appeals to an audience of whose general nature he has been given some inkling beforehand. Had the community's planning been blind to any evaluation of the potential audience, his drama might have been less successful.

In both of these hypothetical productions, estimating the audience has been a necessary step in the accomplishment of major objectives, for audiences differ markedly in composition as well as in size.

The audience of the first illustration is made up of people having a common origin in the community. Furthermore, its numbers can be accommodated by spacing performances over a period of a few evenings. Because this group can be regarded as homogeneous as well as indigenous, several factors are obvious from the start. First, the local townspeople consider themselves active participants in the dramatic event; many will have contributed time, labor, and possessions to help put the production on the boards. Secondly, because the production represents a strong community make-up, the local audience may not expect a professional level of production; but they will earnestly and self-critically eschew lackluster performances based on a dismal script. Gone are the days when people were captivated—if ever they were—by overlong, stultifying spectacles pretending to the name of drama. Thirdly, because this kind of indigenous audience is interested in the total span of its history, it usually is content to see the past represented in a panoramic sweep of episodic scenes projecting reasonably accurate portraits of past events and personages. Furthermore, such an audience is easily disturbed by errors in fact or unwarranted distortions of characters. After all, the events are known and the ancestors are revered. Admittedly, the local spectator likes to hold in his mind's eye—or maintain in the eyes of his neighbor—a gilded image of the fruit of his family tree without a close look for any worms lurking inside. Although a dispassionate historian may prove that an outwardly beneficent town father actually had the scruples of a scalawag, the playwright must chart a course guided by his conscience, his firm knowledge of the historical facts, and his dramatic necessity in terms of the script.

Under the proper conditions, there are several major advantages in having an indigenous audience. Such an audience is keenly interested in the history depicted, receptive to community performers, and proudly aware of its own active participation. And, nonetheless, it anticipates witnessing a relatively entertaining dramatic production.

In the second illustration, again the community has had to ascertain, by various measures, the composition and size of its potential audience. Since this community wants to embark upon a long-range project aimed in part at attracting tourists, the sponsoring group undertakes a "feasibility study." The study first considers the number and capacity of restaurant and rooming accommodations available in the town, and then determines the frequency with which the latter are used during the proposed season. Because the results are encouraging, the group takes a sampling of motel and hotel guests in the area. By direct interview or printed questionnaire, transient visitors are asked such questions as: "Where are you from? What are you planning to do this evening? Would you be interested in going to an outdoor historical drama if one were presented? Are you interested in the history of this area?" More than ninety percent of the answers indicate some enthusiasm for the offering of a historical drama. Now conscious of the potential audience susceptibility to being attracted (and taking into account the potential playgoers of a nearby metropolis), the community plans a summer-long epic-drama with the hope that it can be repeated for several years.[1]

To this drama comes an audience that is predominantly heterogeneous, originating from a variety of places and backgrounds. This audience is hardly expected to be as familiar with or as personally interested in a locality's past as an indigenous audience would be; nor will it demand a detailed representation of such history. Furthermore, scarcely regarding itself as a participant in the production, but rather as a spectator only, this audience strongly expects to see an entertaining dramatic story, produced with artistic competence.

While each type of audience has characteristics which distinguish it from the other, both local or nonlocal spectators create certain basic, physical demands that must be considered. People must know where the drama is being performed and how to get there; they must be able to get there with ease and have a place to park their cars; and they must stand an even chance of gaining admission when they arrive. Basic, too, is the inevitability that people become hungry, thirsty, and sleepy. An example of the experience of one community thrusts forth the necessity of coping with these problems. The Brush and Palette Club, a community art group in Hermann, Missouri, wishing to raise sufficient funds to restore a crumbling rotunda, decides to have a May festival inviting visitors to see this historic river town founded by German settlers in 1837. Along with other events, a pageant-drama is planned to celebrate the "Maifest." Widespread advertising tells of fine old homes, exhibits of pioneer life and river lore, German food, folk dancing and singing, and the drama. The town of twenty-five hundred is astounded when a horde of more than thirty thousand visitors descends upon the little community for its two-day festival. A traffic jam begins three miles out of town. Drivers park their cars outside the

city limits and walk in. "By then," relates Mrs. Anne Hesse, the leader of the
sponsoring group, "people were getting hungry, and we couldn't feed so many.
Every eating place . . . was sold out of food. People who wanted to stay over-
night slept in their cars." [2] The fifteen art club members stand helpless, faced
with the task of showing over thirty thousand visitors the sights of the town.
Nor is there any solution to finding for a substantial portion of this crowd
sufficient seats in the high school auditorium where the drama is to be presented. While receipts from this first Maifest more than pay for restoring the
decrepit rotunda, a full year of complaints follows. Bloody but unbowed, the
group repeats the event annually in the years to follow, but after the extremity
of the opening year, the number of spectators attending the festival settles
down to an estimable number. Now there are no complaints from visitors.
Hermann knows its audience and is prepared.

Factors related to attracting and caring for audiences

Outlined below are major audience-related factors involved in attracting
either a local or an out-of-town audience and in attending to their care and
comfort. Most of these factors apply to either an indoor or outdoor presentation, short-term or long-term.

I.   Appeal and Announcements
  A] Publicity
      1. Telling what, when, where, how much, and why one should come
      2. Appearing in newspapers, on radio and television, on strategically
         placed posters, and (if the budget allows) throw-away flyers,
         movie trailers, car bumper stickers, etc.
      3. Accenting other interesting attractions in the area: parks, historic
         sites, galleries, museums, resort areas, objects of scenic interest
  B] Highway Signs and Markers
      1. Advertising signs placed when necessary along main highways and
         roads leading to place of presentation
      2. Directional signs that clearly mark routes to place of presentation
  C] Accommodations
      1. Eating (and, if necessary, sleeping) accommodations nearby pro-
         vided for and publicized
      2. Picnic areas near site of presentation

II. Accessibility
    A] Parking
        1. Large, well-lighted, well-drained, hard-surfaced parking space near the place of presentation
        2. A staff of well-trained parking attendants
        3. Adequate arrangements with local and/or state police for free flow of traffic on main highways and roads prior to and following performances
    B] Well-marked, well-lighted entrance to place of presentation
    C] Box office
        1. Reserved seat tickets preferable
        2. Available at conveniently placed spots in town as well as at a box office at entrance to place of presentation
        3. Telephone at the box office for accepting orders for tickets

III. Comfort and Care of Patrons
    A] Absence of distractions during performance
        Location of site planned to preclude (whenever possible) the intrusion of outside lights or noises of cars, trains, planes, watercraft, etc.
    B] Rain shelters
        If performance is outdoors, provision of cover for patrons in event of inclement weather
    C] Foyer space
        If performance is indoors, provision for interior standing room when audience is not seated
    D] Temperature
        If performance is indoors, adequate heating is desirable during cold months and air conditioning during warm months. At any time, proper ventilation should be assured
    E] Comfort facilities
        1. Rest rooms
        2. Drinking fountains
        3. Concession stand(s)
        4. Pay telephone
        5. First aid station

F] Baby-sitting service (optional but often desirable)
G] Audience placement
   1. Well-trained ushers
   2. Comfortable seats
   3. Aisles providing easy access up and down
   4. Sufficient number of well-marked fire exits
   5. Good sightlines from all seats to the stage
   6. Good acoustical conditions

These factors vary in degree of importance, depending on individual circumstances. Publicity, for instance, must be more widespread if the purpose is to attract an audience from a distance; and it must be more "permanent" if the plan calls for repeating performances over a long span of time. Similarly, the problem of parking space can be simpler if the production is to be for a local audience on a short term basis; in such a case, temporary parking space such as an open field may be used. Of course, other factors exist that cannot be detailed here.[3] (See Appendix C for detailed sources of such information.)

Such audience-related factors in the presentation of a historical drama enormously affect the selecting of a theatre site, whether it be an actual existing facility or a potential location. As pointed out, the above considerations may be modified to suit distinctive local requirements and available facilities; no general specifications exist which will be applicable in all situations. When selecting a location for the dramatic presentation, the potential audience and its needs must be soberly and thoroughly evaluated.

The place of presentation

The indoor theatre

ADVANTAGES AND DISADVANTAGES: Indoor presentation has several practical advantages. When an existing theatre building is put to use, there are available, at the least, a stage, seats, and usually some lighting equipment. According to the technical demands of dramatic production, supplementary lighting and sound equipment generally can be borrowed, rented, or purchased. Even when some other kind of indoor space (such as a gymnasium, for example) is to be transformed into a theatre, an electrical power source and electrical outlets normally are present. Folding chairs can be arranged for seating, and a temporary platform can be installed for staging.

If an indoor staging area is small, settings can be simplified, in the interests of spatial and budgetary limitations and ease of shifting scenes.

Fluidity of action may be maintained by using an existing forestage for minor scenes and the main stage for major scenes, or by establishing areas of stage space as locales for different episodes through the skillful command of directed lighting. As one effective solution to this kind of problem, one pageant-drama employs as a setting one large neutral unit (consisting of three tall, joined scenery pieces of various heights) in the upstage area, in front of which are placed properties to "set" the many changing scenes as they appear. The actors carry and place onstage the necessary properties for their individual scenes and carry them off again after the episodes are completed. This is done with no inordinate delay in the forward motion of the action.

Advantages to the performers, director, and playwright of producing indoors can only be touched on briefly here. Certainly indoors the relatively close proximity of actor to spectator lessens the extent of aural and visual problems. A sense of intimacy and a strong feeling of rapport can be achieved between actor and audience. And opportunity exists for subtlety and detail in characterization and in dramatic action. Moreover, the playwright has full freedom to create, if he so wishes, small intimate scenes and dimensional characters. Not surprisingly, biography-dramas, small-scale pageant-dramas, and most abbreviated forms of historical drama fare well when presented indoors.

The advantages mentioned are probably the most significant ones in indoor performance; admittedly, several factors may be diminished when the indoor area is especially large (such as a huge civic auditorium) but in most cases they are operative. One factor remains constant: there is less need to take a gamble on the weather when performances are held under a roof.

The disadvantages of indoor presentation (some parallels will be found in alfresco production) are a matter of degree, and depend largely on the nature of the drama and the resources and conditions of a particular community. When improper or insufficient facilities of space and equipment bring about such extreme compromises as to endanger the effectiveness of a production, the latter is of no substantial advantage to the community. Another major disadvantage occurs when a certain type of historical drama contemplated requires magnitude of effect. If the stage area is not spacious, thus restricting the use of large casts, there are limits on the scope of action and spectacle. Furthermore, the flexibility with which broad mass movement can flow from one scene to another also suffers some restrictions within the confinement of a typical indoor stage.

In a community there may be more than one building potentially useful as an indoor theatre. Considerations affecting the final selection of a place include the material dramatized and the dramatic form chosen, the size of the

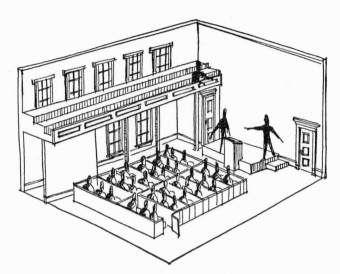

8. MEETING HOUSE AS PLAYHOUSE. *The interior of this building (similar to the reconstructed meeting house at Old Sturbridge Village, Sturbridge, Massachusetts) approximates that of many old churches. The pulpit space serves as the main acting area.*

9. LEGISLATURE CHAMBER AS STAGE. *The audience is seated in the gallery.*

potential audience, and the budget available. The place of presentation suggests itself quite obviously when sponsoring organizations have access to a playhouse or command their own. Production sponsors such as schools, colleges or universities, summer stock companies or civic theatre groups, usually lie in this category. Occasionally, churches and museums possess their own theatres and/or auditoriums which can house historical dramas.

HISTORIC OR CIVIC BUILDINGS AS POTENTIAL PLACES OF PRESENTATION: When sponsoring groups are not their own landlords, they can exercise their imaginations in exploiting their unique resources. Historical drama can be offered in a building (if it is appropriate) where some of the actual events took place decades, even centuries ago. In Sturbridge, Massachusetts, for instance, stands Old Sturbridge Village, a restored hamlet representing New England of a century and a half ago. Visitors are treated to short dramas in a reconstructed meeting house (fig. 8). Even in the halls of stage legislatures, short biography-dramas centering on historical debates can be performed while visitors watch from the gallery (fig. 9). The Vermont Historical Society, for example, observes the centennial of the state's entry into the Civil War by producing Louis P. Peck's *The Appropriation* to an audience of three hundred fifty people seated in the chambers of Montpelier's House of Representatives.

A community may look upon a civic center or a town hall as a potential playhouse. A simplified illustration of this is Tin Top, Texas, which exhibits *Early Days in Tin Top* on a temporary stage consisting of a raised platform at one end of the community center; curtains at the rear and on the sides of the stage are used to conceal a backstage area. A town hall in Maine employs its small stage for *Castine*. A summer resident of the small town, a horticulturist, recruits men with axes and trucks to obtain greenery to decorate the inside of the hall as an "aboriginal forest" that delights for two evenings an audience totaling three hundred people. The larger community of Jacksonville, Florida, sets up a stage in its large, arena-shaped municipal auditorium for a two-week production of *Next Day in the Morning*. One end of the arena is blocked off to provide space for the stage; the spectators sit not only on the permanent seats in the galleries but also on temporary seats arranged on the remaining area of the arena floor. This type of arrangement offers the advantages of a large seating capacity and an expansive area for a broad sweep of action (fig. 10).

THE CHURCH CHANCEL AS PLAYHOUSE: Size is not always a criterion, however, for indoor presentation. Religious groups often hearken back to

their traditional kinship with the theatre by offering drama in a church sanctuary (*fig. 11*) or in a parish hall. The Central Congregational Church in Providence arranges it chancel to suggest Roger Williams' room and the interior of
an early New England church for *The Bloody Tenet*. St. George's Episcopal

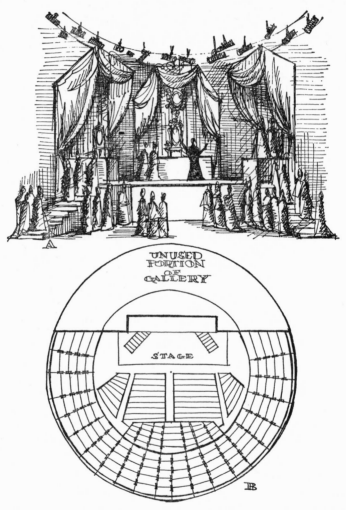

10.   MUNICIPAL AUDITORIUM AS PLAYHOUSE.   A] *A two-level stage is set up at one
end of the arena. As the floor plan* B] *indicates, galleries and temporary seats
arranged on arena floor provide audience seating.*

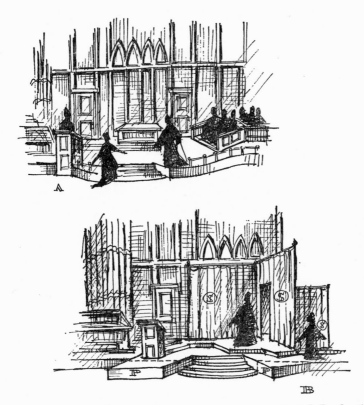

11. CHANCEL ARRANGEMENT FOR A DRAMATIC PRESENTATION. a] *Production uses existing features of chancel.* b] *Modified use of same chancel using platforms, steps, and screens (indicated by* **S***).* **P** *indicates platform segments added to existing edges of chancel floor.*

Church in New York adapts the architectural features of its sanctuary to the needs of a nativity drama, *The Curate's Play* by Nathaniel Bank. The chancel rises above the level of the nave by a number of steps, permitting proper visibility as well as space for the action to take place on the raised level. A choir sits in stalls to one side of this area. A narrator stands behind a pulpit on the nave floor. In the rear of the chancel is placed a high, skeletonized framework serving as a background for the drama, which combines episodes of the nativity with an allegorical contemporary story. The dramatic action calls for actors to move up and down the aisles of the nave for entrances and exits, to arise from the pews, and to use the doors of the chancel. Written for chancel presentation, the drama utilizes a good deal of the sanctuary as its "stage" and gives the onlookers the feeling of participative involvement. In the same city, Christ Church Methodist presents Orlin Corey's adaptation of *The Book of Job*. The "stage" is a high platform in the nave of the church, behind which is hung a black velvet cyclorama that masks the altar. From high on the side walls lights discover the portrayed Biblical characters slowly mounting the platforms (of different levels) which form the stage. From face to foot the actors' make-up and costumes simulate the glittering color and design of Byzantine mosaics, as if the characters had stepped down from one of the church's stained glass windows. Music provided by the organ resounds through the lofty reaches of the building. Both the churches cited find their chancel stage well suited to their respective dramas.

Scenery, if used in a chancel presentation, should be harmonious with the architectural dignity of the sanctuary. The consecrated nature of the latter need not be desecrated. Reflecting a consensus, director James R. Carlson of the University of Georgia advises that "any additions to the sanctuary should be simple, tasteful, and unobstrusive." [4] Platforms of varying dimensions, steps, and small screens can serve to elevate and augment available acting areas. Church furniture, either in its "permanent" or in rearranged positions, offers appropriate uses. The staging of chancel drama is most effective when modern theatre lighting equipment is employed, so that facilities for lighting need carefully to be considered. Because churches vary widely in their design, acoustical and visual, spatial and lighting factors must be measured against individual conditions and a drama's requirements.

THE LARGE ROOM AS PLAYHOUSE: Churches often have spaces other than the chancel where a drama can be presented, such as parish halls or multi-purpose rooms. Large, open rooms of this kind, whether a school gymnasium, a barn, or even an automobile showroom, can be utilized effectively. There are, however, certain basic requirements to be heeded, such as a minimum width of thirty feet, a ceiling height that allows adequate space for overhead lighting apparatus, and an absence of view-obstructing pillars.[5] Such spaces offer opportunity for various kinds of unconventional staging, e.g., central staging (an acting area surrounded by the audience) or a flexible variant of central staging. These basic patterns of central staging (fig. 12) in themselves do not necessitate a limited space either for staging or for accommodating the audience. (Such patterns logically could be used in large arenas or tents, in addition to the kinds of spaces mentioned above.) Our consideration here, however, is focused on the practical matters of housing indoor productions more suited to limited spatial relationships between audience and actors.

In a full-arena plan, the audience surrounds an acting area (fig. 12A). A three-sided arena, or a horseshoe arrangement, permits the audience to be seated on three sides of the "stage" (fig. 12B). A two-sided arena, or alley

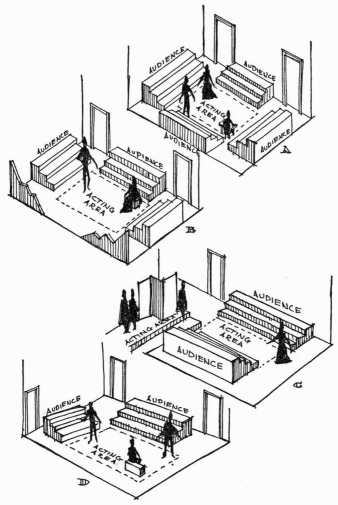

12. CENTRAL STAGING ARRANGEMENTS IN LARGE ROOM. A] *Full-arena plan* B] *Three-sided arena plan* c] *Two-sided arena plan* D] *L-shaped plan.*

arrangement, has spectators seated on either side of a rectangular-shaped acting area that may have a raised stage at one end (fig. 12c). The L-shaped arrangement (fig. 12D) places the stage in one corner of a room, with the audience sitting in rows that meet at right angles facing the stage.

The last three types of central staging allow one or, in some cases, two walls of the room to act as backing for scenery, if desired. It is advisable that the room have several well-located entrances, ideally at least one in each wall, that can be conveniently used as entrances and exits by the players and by stage crew members required to make swift scene changes. Generally, most dramas will require a staging arrangement allowing for from two to four passages for ingress to and egress from the acting area.

If the audience is seated on chairs on a level floor (a condition having its drawbacks), a staggered seating arrangement ordinarily improves the angles of sight for each spectator. Ideally, rows of seats are raised, in a graduated elevation above the acting area, to allow better overall visibility. Seats should be both elevated and staggered, whenever possible. Platform supports providing elevation can be made in modular units, sufficiently graded in height, width, and length so as to be useful as either platforms for seating or for acting levels or setting units. Designed for strength, mobility, and flexibility, these platforms should be capable of being used either separately or fitted with one another in a wide variety of combinations and heights according to the requirements of various productions. Such platforms should not be permanently affixed if genuine flexibility of staging and audience arrangements is to exist. Platform sections should be small enough to be easily handled. In order to be comfortable as seat supports, units ideally should be at least three and one-half feet in depth and in multiples of two feet in length to compensate for the average seat or chair, which is roughly two feet wide.[6] If there is room for three rows of seats on each side of the acting area, platforms can be constructed in at least three heights so that the second row of seats will be elevated above the first, and so on. Such platforms take money and technical "know-how" to build; therefore, a group planning a drama for one brief occasion must carefully consider its budget before making such an investment. If budgetary and other factors do not favor such an undertaking, then carefully positioned seats set on a level floor will suffice. (In the latter situation, it proves wise to keep the number of rows on each side facing the acting area to a minimum for the best possible visibility from spectator to stage.)

The flexible staging situation makes little use of the pictorial or decorative stage scenery usually associated with a conventional proscenium theatre. This fact can prove advantageous to a group with a minimum of budget and trained labor. Because scenery is minimal in importance, stronger emphasis must then be placed on costumes, make-up, properties, and lighting.[7] When the budget makes the purchase of stage lighting equipment prohibitive, the "Willy Westinghouse" of the production team can stretch dollars by adapting for stage use less standard equipment. Window display lights, for example, can be used effectively; and in skillful hands a tin can will furnish the housing for a workable "homemade" lighting instrument.

Central staging requires a high level of performance from actors. Flaws in the acting readily are apparent to the spectators since the performer is in their midst. Furthermore, without the protecting physical distance and the frame of the proscenium theatre, the amateur actor can become uneasy unless carefully prepared beforehand. When an inexperienced cast is employed, this factor needs to be considered. While the basic techniques of acting are still operative, even greater concentration and sincerity of characterization are demanded because of the close physical relationship between actor and audience. With proper direction, the qualified actor can adjust to the open staging situation.

After fully considering the resources of the community and the exigencies of a particular drama, a sponsoring group can determine whether it has a suitable indoor location for presentation. If the decision is negative, then the possibilities of outdoor presentation are considered.

The outdoor theatre

ADVANTAGES AND DISADVANTAGES: The aesthetic value of open-air performance is very strong. By nature we are an outdoor people and feel more relaxed and refreshed when we can take our families to watch events under the open sky. Traditionally, as in Greek, Roman, or Elizabethan times, people witnessed theatre in the open air, and the custom persisted even when the theatre moved indoors. Architects until yesterday, theatre historian James Laver tells us, persisted in treating the whole auditorium as exterior by building little roofs above the boxes and painting the ceilings with clouds and stars.[8] It is not strange that an audience is stimulated by the tonic of the open air to feel a festiveness of spirit. Furthermore, a spectator seated near the very ground where walked the historical figures recreated on stage feels the closeness of the living past.

There are, however, practical as well as aesthetic advantages in outdoor presentations. First of all, an outdoor site often can accommodate audiences of large size more easily than a standard indoor theatre. An open-air amphitheatre is relatively less expensive to build than a satisfactory indoor theatre of comparable size. The usually more spacious stage is well suited to the fluid, spectacular scope of pageant-drama and epic-drama with their frequent changes of scene and large casts. Furthermore, the natural topography may supply much of the stage setting.

Several disadvantages of outdoor presentation can be cited: 1] special aural and visual difficulties may occur because of the extended distance from actor to audience, and lighting and acoustical problems are intensified; 2] stage lighting can involve more expensive equipment than that used in an indoor theatre; 3] there are limits on the sense of intimacy, the detail, subtlety, and depth of characterization; 4] weather conditions affect the assurance of giving every performance as planned; and 5] outdoor exposure can cause swift depreciation of production items and equipment.

Other items could be added to the above list, depending upon the peculiar resources and conditions that exist in the individual community. Unquestionably, outdoor presentation confronts the director, actor, and scenic designer with a different set of limitations and freedoms than pertains to production indoors. The sponsoring organization planning alfresco production follows a wise course when it acquires the advice and, whenever possible, the active participation of persons experienced in producing outdoor drama.

POTENTIAL OUTDOOR SITES FOR DRAMATIC PRESENTATION: There is a diversity of outdoor sites or stages on which to present historical drama. This diversity may include anything from a baseball stadium to the slope of a hillside or a permanently built outdoor amphitheatre.

Sites may be chosen for their historic significance and for the beauty of their natural landscape. On the level lawn of a three-acre garden surrounded by the more-than-a-century old buildings where the Society of Harmonists once dwelled, summer audiences seated on folding chairs watch Old Economy's *Man's Reach*. Scenes are played now on the back porch of the Great House (domicile of the Society's leader "Father" George Rapp), now on the lawn in front of another building, now on a leveled area in the garden, now in a small pavilion beyond the garden. A few tables, chairs, and other properties indicate change of locale. Lights are unobtrusively mounted on upright wooden poles and trees. These, combined with floodlights on the ground fronting the acting areas, focus on the action. Another site which conjures up a sense of the living past is discovered in Alabama's Tuscumbia where *The Miracle Worker* is presented on the lawn of Helen Keller's birthplace. The events of Miss Keller's childhood unfold again where they originated some eighty-two years ago. Beyond a spreading oak, under which she played, lies the

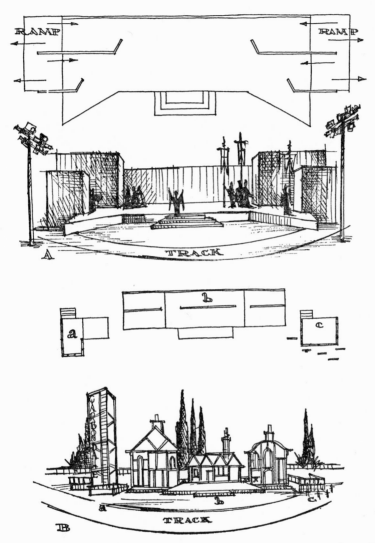

13. STADIUM STAGE. A] *Sketch and floor plan of stage using a neutral scenic background, erected in an outdoor stadium, athletic field, or race track.* B] *Sketch and floor plan using a multiple setting. Scenes are played in front of their designated represented locales, all of which remain in view throughout the course of a performance.*

Main House where the child Helen Keller was born. (Spectators tour the home and grounds before performance time.) To the left is the pump at which the young Helen learned her first word: water. In sight also is the garden house where Anne Sullivan battled the child into dawning comprehension of language. Little or nothing in the way of scenery is added and properties are kept to a minimum. "The place and the play are the thing" remarks the production's director, Ward Wagnon.[9]

Historic landmarks are not the only possible sites for outdoor presentation. A high school athletic field, a fairground, a rodeo arena, or even a racetrack can be transformed into a suitable place for alfresco presentation. (fig. 13A). In commemorating the centennial of Woodrow Wilson's birth, the town of Staunton, Virginia, exhibits for two weeks an epic-drama dealing with this President's life. It is presented on a racetrack within the town limits. In the center of the inner oval and raised about five feet from the ground stands a temporary wooden stage sixty feet long and twenty-four feet wide. It is divided into three sections. Connected by ramps to the left and right of the main stage on a slightly higher level are two platforms serving as separate stages for certain scenes. The major scenic background is a series of tall vertical scenic pieces of neutral color which mask the backstage area and are staggered to allow for entrances of performers and stagehands. The audience sits in a roofed-over grandstand separated from the stage by a wide track. Audience attention is focused on the action by means of lights mounted on the grandstand and on stanchions situated to the left and right of the stage. Stage illumination is also furnished by lighting instruments positioned in the wings. On the field behind the stage, two small trailers with toilet facilities are set up, and tents are put up for dressing rooms, make-up, properties, and costumes.

Variations on this kind of racecourse staging are applicable to presentations in athletic stadiums or outdoor arenas; the principles governing the use of the basic structure are the same for many situations. When settings more suggestive of actual locales are feasible and desirable, scenic façades of buildings, for example, can be erected on a long stage fronting the audience in a multiple setting arrangement (fig. 13B). The individual scenic locales remain in view throughout the course of the drama; the action of each scene is played before its appropriate scenic unit. This approach is used for a pageant-drama produced in Carbondale, Illinois. This kind of stage, however, often is more difficult and more expensive to construct, and more conducive to staging problems, than a stage resembling the Staunton pattern.

Certainly a stadium has the asset of producing adequate seating and other facilities for the audience. Many times a stadium will be equipped with

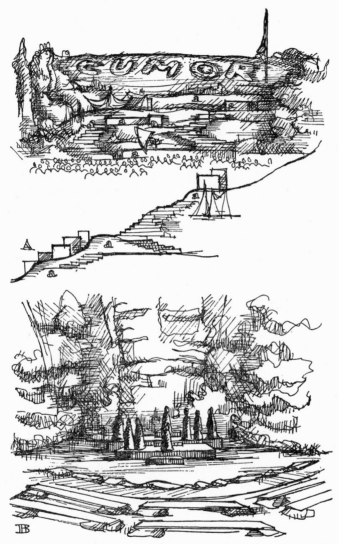

14. NATURE STAGE. A] A mountainside stage similar to the one at Palmyra, New York. The many levels for acting areas (designated by **a**) permit a panoramic sweep of action. Entrances and exits can be made either side of the stage or from tunnels in the mountain. The audience is seated in the foreground.   A] A side view elevation of the stage; acting areas indicated by **a**. B] A civic or state park stage (similar to one at Pineville, Kentucky) backed by a high cliff. Multi-leveled platforms furnish the only scenery.

basic lighting apparatus. With careful and knowledgeable planning, a stadium stage can be simply erected. Obviously, if lighting or acoustical factors pose a host of difficulties, if only a small audience is anticipated, or if the drama is small in scope, a stadium as a site is not the best selection.

Not to be overlooked as possible amphitheatres are natural sites, e.g., open hillsides, sloping meadows, or merely an open place in the woods (figs. 14, 15). Communities can sometimes use such natural stages much as they find them, particularly if a daylight performance is planned; others will have to add at least a modicum of architectural features and lighting equipment. A Mormon community in Palmyra, New York, for example, turns the slope of a hillside into a stage to host a pageant-drama about their religious origins (fig. 14A) annually produced by Brigham Young University. Here on Hill Cumorah is the site where Joseph Smith reputedly discovers the golden tablets giving birth to the foundation of Mormonism. The sloping stage is tiered in four major acting levels. The audience sits on folding chairs on a level area at the base of the hill. Because the audience is a good distance from the stage, microphones are provided to amplify the performers' voices.

A civic, county, or state park can reveal a natural amphitheatre (fig. 14B). Pine Mountain State Park near Pineville, Kentucky, has such a site which serves as an amphitheatre for an annually presented adaptation of *The Book of Job*. The backdrop of an eighty-foot limestone cliff looks down on a level grassy stage which is almost twenty-five feet deep and thirty feet wide. An attractive rock-bordered reflecting pool directly in front of the stage divides the main acting area from the audience. The natural scenery requires little architectural embellishment. A simple complex of multi-leveled platforms furnishes the only theatrical scenery. Two steel light poles stand at the extreme sides of the stage. Dressing rooms, and a control booth for lights and organ, are set up offstage. The audience area is naturally terraced with comfortable seats and boulder-supported log benches, all of which can accommodate more than one thousand onlookers. In Florida's Tampa Bay area near Safety Harbor, *Count Philippe's Wild Orange Tree* is presented in a natural woodland amphitheatre in Philippe Park (fig. 15A). The park lies within the historic estate of Count Odet Philippe, and the drama recounts his colorful life. Surrounded by natural shrubbery, the stage consists of a level, sand-covered playing area framed by the large overhanging branches of two oak trees festooned with Spanish moss. There is a minimal amount of constructed scenery. A small building nearby serves as a dressing room. The spectators sit on wooden benches placed on a natural slope facing the playing area. Because the performance is offered before dusk, the need for lighting equipment is slight. The

15. NATURE STAGE. A] A civic or state park amphitheatre (similar to one in Phillipe Park, near Safety Harbor, Florida) using natural vegetation and an ocean vista as background. Benches facing the stage provide audience seating.   B] A civic or state park amphitheatre (similar to one at Pipestone, Minnesota) with the acting area separated from the audience by a body of water. Except for wigwams, nature furnishes the setting.

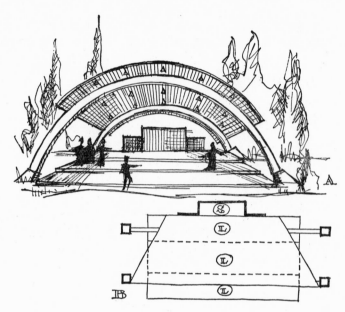

16.   BAND-SHELL PLATFORM STAGE. A] *Notice that four levels can be used as acting areas, that lighting instruments hang on underside of roof.*   B] *Ground plan of stage. Different levels designated by* L, *storage room* S *can house properties and small scenery.*

small-cast biography-drama appears to be ideally suited to the picturesque open-sky theatre.

A lakeside, as well as a mountainside or a park grove, can do duty as a setting for outdoor presentation (*fig. 15*B). Pipestone, Minnesota, for instance, annually displays for three consecutive summer weekends a dramatization of the Hiawatha story on fifteen hundred square feet of ground separated from the audience by a spring-fed lake now filling an ancient pipestone quarry. Across the lake from the Indian tepees that constitute the major properties of the stage action, are placed folding wooden chairs capable of seating five thousand people. Lighting equipment on strategically positioned poles highlights the players. Behind the acting area are a storage building, a refreshment stand, and dressing rooms for almost two hundred actors. Behind the audience are buildings housing lighting and sound controls.

Some communities may have band-shell amphitheatres in their own parks (*fig. 16*). While such structures have been built for musical events rather than dramatic production, they sometimes can with modifications be success-

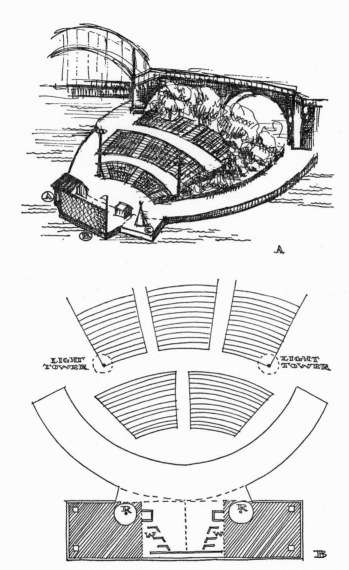

17. FLOATING STAGE. A] A barge-borne stage in an outdoor theatre (based on the *Pittsburgh Bicentennial Gateway Amphitheatre*). Main stage **B** is flanked by two small side stages **A** and **C**. *Walls and roof of* **C** *are not shown in sketch.* B] Ground plan of stage indicates revolving stages **R** and main stage wings **W**. Dotted line designates points at which two barges are connected. Shaded portions indicate roofed areas.

fully used. To the usual rudimentary light and amplification system, additional equipment for theatrical lighting is frequently added. The typical quarter-sphere shape of the band-shell and the level and depth of the platform may cause real difficulties in the shifting of scenery or the movement of dramatic action. However, a band platform in Peoria, Illinois, is successfully adapted to present a pageant-drama of the community's past. The multi-level platform has a total length of more than one hundred feet and a depth of thirty feet. A lighting and sound system are furnished. Tall upstage entrances, an adequate forestage, and three platform levels allow for simplified scenic units and properties to be shifted and the dramatic action to occur without severe cramping or delay. Lighting is employed to establish mood and, when necessary, change of locale. While not all communities will have such adaptable structures, they sometimes can give similar structures out-of-doors a closer look.

Occasionally a vicinity may be in possession of an estate boasting a small garden theatre, with a background of clipped hedges or a conventional arrangement of trees and shrubs. Such sites can be effectively pressed into service if plans include a modestly-scaled drama, a relatively small potential audience, a short run, and a daylight performance. If an evening performance is anticipated, the problems of procuring and installing lighting equipment must give a sponsoring group pause for thought when judging such a site's feasibility for a dramatic production.

An outdoor stage need not even be on land (fig. 17), as Pittsburgh's production of *The Golden Crucible* attests. Located near the city's Golden Triangle at the confluence of two rivers, float two connected barges totaling 156 feet in length and 50 feet in width, providing a main stage and two side stages for the drama of the city's past. Below decks the barges furnish an area for costumes, make-up, and actors' dressing rooms; above decks is space for the three staging areas and for the maneuvering and storing of scenic units and properties. This anchored, self-contained floating stage faces a sloping land-based auditorium. After the production, the barge and auditorium are removed; the site is landscaped to function again as a state park. The staging investment for this particular production is high. Yet the Pittsburgh pattern may be followed along more modest lines.

PLANNING AN AMPHITHEATRE: In most of the examples cited above, a maximum expenditure of ingenuity and energy offsets a relatively modest expenditure of funds. Normally, a community does not find it wise to invest in a fully-equipped, permanently constructed outdoor amphitheatre unless the latter serves a production of extended run or can be used for other purposes.

Planning for such structures should be made in consultation with experienced architects in the field and, whenever possible, with the playwright, scenic designer, and director of the contemplated script. (*see chapter v.*) A community cannot rely entirely on existing models of theatres as guides to constructing its own. Certainly in many current theatres of this type a substantial number of acoustical and lighting problems have not yet been satisfactorily solved. Communities can blaze new trails by building outdoor theatres with exciting new features. Much room for experimentation and improvement exists.

The expense of construction is a factor to be wrestled with at the outset. While generally less expensive to build than an indoor theatre of equivalent seating capacity and total cubic space, an amphitheatre currently can cost from $50,000 to $175,000 without equipment and $200,000 if fully equipped. Expenditures will vary according to the specific conditions of site, size, and the type of technical and physical facilities.

SELECTING AN AMPHITHEATRE SITE: In selecting a site for a permanent outdoor amphitheatre, several general criteria must be applied:

1] *Proximity to area(s) of historical significance, if possible*
2] *Generally favorable weather conditions*
   Careful analysis of recorded temperatures and rainfall is a wise precaution.
3] *Accessibility to and from major traffic routes*
4] *Beauty of surrounding natural landscape*
5] *Topographical suitability*
   a. Natural slope for auditorium cuts contruction costs.
   b. Trees serve as sound reflectors and windbreaks.
   c. Level area at base of slope is needed for stage and backstage facilities.
   d. Level areas for parking lots are needed near entrance to theatre.
6] *Relative freedom from outside intrusions of noise and lights*
   Noise of passing trains, planes, cars, and flashing of lights can distract audience.
7] *Favorable acoustical factors*
   a. Prevailing breezes should blow from stage toward auditorium, to carry actors' voices.
   b. Surrounding fences or walls can help reflect sound.

SIZE OF AN OUTDOOR THEATRE: There are no cut-and-dried rules here. Amphitheatres built for long-run epic-dramas seat from 2,500 to 3,000 people (without requiring amplification for the actors' voices); but many of them do not fill their auditoriums regularly. The current trend is toward reasonable limitations on seating capacity, as illustrated by two outdoor theatres built in 1963 to present historical dramas at Harrodsburg and at Murray, Kentucky. These two theatres seat approximately 850 to 1,000 people, respectively. One reason for the size of the Harrodsburg theatre is expressed by its first general manager, John Cauble, who has effectively steered the initial operations of two epic-dramas: "We would rather play to full houses in July and turn some people away in August, than to play to half-empty houses the first month for the sake of a few extra dollars during the peak second month." (During a typical summer-long run, it is the peak vacation month of August that flushes out capacity audiences.) Additionally, we must realize that visual and aural problems in large open-air theatres can be acute; a smaller theatre may reduce such problems and be more satisfactory. The size of an alfresco theatre should be based on cautious and authoritative estimates, founded on thorough analyses of the potential audience.

Characteristics of open-air theatres

No all-embracing requirements exist regarding the essentials of the physical structure, but a few general observations can be based on outdoor theatres already in existence. Some such theatres are designed to accommodate the presentation of a specific historical drama; others are "nonspecific" in plan. In any case, these theatres typically have a unique relationship to their locale and are integrated with the site. They may include a fan-shaped auditorium and a main stage ranging from fifty to sixty feet wide and twenty to forty feet deep, flanked by two or more smaller side stages. The subsidiary stages are on the same or a higher level than the main stage and normally connect with it by means of ramps or runways. This arrangement allows the action to sweep completely across the spectator's line of vision and enables a wide range of visual effects. Also a diversity of concurrent, as well as independent, action is made possible. With one or two subsidiary stages, settings can be changed while the action continues elsewhere.

As one enters the open-air amphitheatre originally erected for *The Founders* at Williamsburg, one sees a "specific" type of amphitheatre (fig. 18).[10] On the sand-covered stage are thatch-roofed buildings—a church, a store room, private dwellings—all suggestive of the first English settlement at Jamestown; these structures are cut away to disclose their interiors. This setting is

18.   COVE AMPHITHEATRE, *Williamsburg, Virginia. The Founders was performed on this site in 1957 and 1958. Beyond the main stage in the background is Lake Matoaka. (After a sketch by Roger Sherman)*

permanent and remains onstage during the entire course of the action. Beyond the setting lies a vista of Lake Matoaka, effecting a spacious natural backdrop of water and open sky. The stage has neither a roof over it nor a rear wall behind it. A tall stockade wall surrounding the auditorium roughly defines a proscenium opening and conceals the wings of the main stage that curve in a half-circle toward the audience. On the right is a flat, open area marked by a wooden stake bearing totem figures; here, scenes in an Indian encampment and in the wilderness will be played. On the left a grassy slope becomes an acting area for scenes outside the settlement. Rocks, trees, and hedges on the main and side stages form some of the environment of the theatric action. The entire rustic theatre setting blends in with the natural surroundings. Even the seats, which are wooden benches mounted on concrete tiers sloping down to the stage, do not visibly distract from the rustic atmosphere. Planned for daylight performance in the late afternoon, the theatre requires no lighting equipment. While the sun-lit presentation loses some of the magic made possible by stage lighting, it is nonetheless compelling.

Also constructed for a specific play, the Waterside Theatre at Manteo, North Carolina, is composed of a somewhat similar, if more elaborate, arrangement (fig. 19). Planned for evening performance, it displays two tall, capacious

towers representing sixteenth-century blockhouses (typical of the period dramatized) located on each side of the auditorium. These contain lighting equipment which can focus on the production's three stages, the choir stall, and the
narrator's station. Further lighting equipment and a lighting-sound control

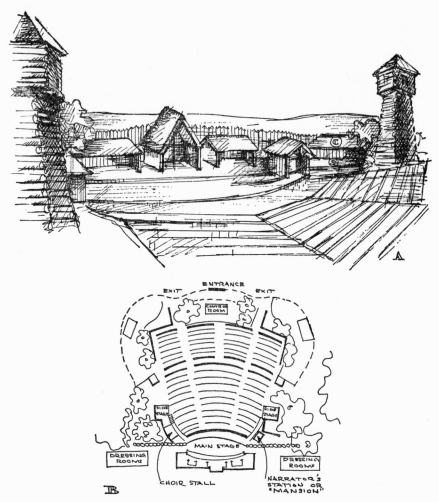

19. A] The Lost Colony at the Waterside Theatre, Manteo, North Carolina. Roanoke Sound lies beyond the stage. Choir stall C and side stage S are at the right in
the sketch. (Based on a photograph in Producing America's Outdoor Dramas)
B] Ground plan of the Waterside Theatre, Manteo, North Carolina.

20. A] LAKE MATOAKA AMPHITHEATRE: Front View, Williamsburg, Virginia. Both
The Common Glory and *The Founders* have been performed here. Lake Matoaka
is seen beyond the main stage **M**. Two lighting towers **T** and two side stages **S** are
discernible in the sketch. B] LAKE MATOAKA AMPHITHEATRE: Rear View. In the
foreground the rear edge of the main stage **M** drops down to the lake; a crosswalk
W below stage level permits performers and technicians to get from one side area
to the other unseen by the audience. Backstage buildings are designated as follows:
dressing rooms **D**, costume room and storage **C**, scene shops **SS**, and property
storage **P**.

booth are installed in a log cabin at the rear of the theatre (fig. 19B). On either side of the audience stand rustic, roofed shelters to protect the audience in case of rain. (Ideally, such shelters provide standing room for a full house and also house rest rooms and refreshment stands.) A stockade wall encircling the auditorium serves as backing for the side stages and extends to either side of the main stage, masking the off-stage space.

The Lake Matoaka Amphitheatre housing alternately The Common Glory and The Founders (fig. 20) is constructed without the specificity of setting of the Cove or Waterside Theatres. Its open, concrete stage can serve equally well for different historical dramas (the fact that The Founders effectively adapts to presentation in this theatre supports such a view). This absence of specificity is an example followed by some of the new theatres being built. One such "nonspecific" theatre is at Murray, Kentucky (fig. 21). It avoids a permanent, specific setting and a specific architectural motif. In this theatre, a panoramic sweep of the area's history is performed on a concrete main stage backed by a white cyclorama. In front of this cyclorama, utilized for lighting effects and projections, is a multi-level architectural unit stretching across the entire upstage area. Without relying on side stages, the action occurs exclusively on the main stage and its upstage unit. Changes of scene are established largely by the introduction of set properties and the use of pantomime and lighting.

While not as picturesque, the neutral, "nonspecific" type of construction in an outdoor amphitheatre can serve in the interests of economy and flexibility (fig. 22). Construction costs may be less when specialized features are omitted from the initial theatre design and when the amount of three-dimensional scenery is reduced by wider use of lighting and projection effects. Furthermore, should the need arise, this type of outdoor theatre can accommodate a different dramatic work, or a variety of entertainment or community events. Concerts, outdoor movies, and religious meetings, represent several events which can be serviced by the multi-use of such a stage.

We recall the case of one community whose epic-drama has run for several seasons. Wishing to offer fresh appeal to attract larger annual audiences, it seeks to present a new drama in an outdoor theatre built specifically for the drama now being done. Unhappily, the sponsoring group finds that its large investment in permanent construction and production items discourages starting afresh to produce a new drama in the theatre. Often the outdoor theatre of neutral architectural design can adjust most flexibly to new conditions and demands.

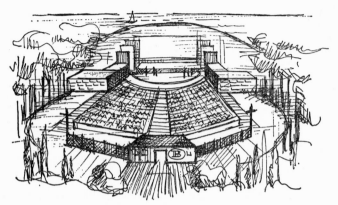

21. Stars in My Crown at the Kenlake Amphitheatre, Murray, Kentucky. Kentucky Lake lies in the background. Box office **B** is seen in the foreground, buildings on either side of the stage house lighting and sound control, dressing and costume rooms, etc. (Based on a sketch in Stars in My Crown 1963 Souvenir Program.)

22. The Stephen Foster Story at the J. Dan Talbott Amphitheatre, Bardstown, Kentucky. Like the Kenlake and Lake Matoaka Theatres, this amphitheatre is of the "nonspecific" type. A lighting booth **L** sits atop a building enclosing administrative offices, box office, refreshment stand, comfort facilities, and rain shelter. (Based on a photograph in The Stephen Foster Story 1963 Souvenir Program.)

PRODUCTION FACILITIES IN THE OPEN-AIR THEATRE: In addition to the overall purpose and style of design of the outdoor amphitheatre, the basic physical and technical facilities must be planned. Lighting of a production, for example, is an important factor in the outdoor theatre, and the problem of finding suitable mounting positions for instruments is not always easily solved. Most existing theatres make use of lighting towers located on either side of the auditorium in such a position that coverage of all stage areas can be attained. The accepted optimum slant for the light to fall on the stage is at an angle of thirty-five to forty-five degrees. Consequently, to approximate this desideratum for stage illumination, decisions concerning the shape, size, and exact placement of the towers (including their distance from the stage) will depend on such factors as the slope of the auditorium, the locations of any subsidiary stages, and the sightlines to all stages. Lighting from towers which normally provide space for eight to ten instruments, is supplemented by lighting from both sides of the stage, from footlight troughs at the front edges of the main and side stages, from the back of the auditorium, and from any additional stations required for a particular production. This pattern, although fairly standard, varies. Cherokee's Mountainside Theatre has a steep slope permitting a stage six feet below the first row of seats (fig. 23). Consequently, it can have some of its major lighting positions located just below this first row. For the control of lighting, theatres must have a control booth affording a view of all stages. The location of the control booth may be the rear of the auditorium, a lighting tower, a space under the first row of seats (as in the Cherokee theatre), or a structure on one side of the main stage. The control booth can house the lighting control board, sound system console, public address equipment for special announcements and narration (and amplification for performers' voices when necessary), and even an electronic organ.

Open-air theatres requires sufficient space backstage for the maneuvering and storage of all properties and scenery as well as for other backstage functions (see fig. 20B). With adequate space for storage, a sheltered area is necessary as a weather-protected scene shop for the construction and repair of scenic units and properties. Even if a production is offered for only one season, the storage of production items enables them to be used again, either for another production or for rental or sale.

Adequate costume rooms are essential. (Few existing amphitheatres allow sufficient space for this purpose, owing either to oversight or to budgetary limitations.) Regardless of the size of its cast, a single production may require more than three hundred costumes to be constructed or rented. Many will have to be repaired or renewed, and most will have to be laundered during a

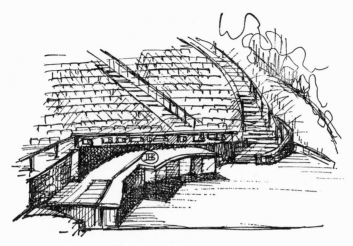

23. MOUNTAINSIDE THEATRE, *Cherokee, North Carolina. The placement of light-ing instruments is seen below the auditorium's first row which is approximately six feet above the stage. In foreground is booth* B *housing lighting and sound control, an organ, and a narrator's station.*

run of any length. Therefore, such space needs to be well equipped with basic costume construction equipment and heavy-duty laundry facilities. Because costumes are often stored in such space as well as in the dressing rooms, such an area should be well-ventilated and weather-tight. In the long run, suitable costume space and equipment represent good economy.

Backstage space is also required for dressing rooms that can provide comfortably for the entire cast. Such space must have adequate rest room facilities, including a sufficient number of showers. In some theatre arrangements, rooms for performers making quick costume and make-up changes will be needed near the stage. If a performer requires costume repair during performance, ideally he should be able to find a costume shop only a few steps from his dressing room.

Performers require space not only for dressing and performing, but also for getting to the stage. Traffic control can become a backstage headache with companies of people having to move swiftly and silently through a number of rapid scene transitions and costume changes. Ideally, all backstage passageways should be wide enough for broad period-style skirts and free of steps which can easily trip the hurrying performer. And sufficiently wide passageways must be provided for cast and crew members to cross freely from one side of the stage to the other unseen by the audience. Also useful is a large space not far from the stage where the entire cast may assemble for instructions or mass entrances. Moreover, a backstage entrance preferably connected with a private parking lot for company members will aid traffic control also.

In summary, many of the above-mentioned details, and others having particular pertinence to an individual community's plans, must be taken into consideration.[11] If satisfactory results are to be obtained there must be foresight in planning the presentation of a historical drama: this means rigorous analysis in evaluating the potential audience, and in selecting the place of presentation. (And such community resources should be known to the playwright if he wishes to write an efficacious drama.)

The four chapters following concern such factors as the writing of a script, the investigation of historical material, and the major characteristics of the forms of historical drama. A grasp of these factors lies not only within the domains of the playwright and director, but also within those of the sponsoring group. The sponsors, if they are to serve as knowledgeable organizers and advisers in the producing of worthy historical drama, must be cognizant of such considerations.

VII. Composing the drama

"WHAT GAVE YOU the idea for your play? How did it come into being?" Throw these questions at an experienced writer and you will probably receive a tentative if not nebulous answer. Where exactly in the creative process an idea or feeling originates sometimes remains forever obscure; the half-formed idea or vague feeling drifting about in the subconscious responds to no timetable but crystallizes when it will and for its own good reasons. There is, nonetheless, more to the creative imagination than mere free-wheeling activity. As soon as the thought or feeling appears as a conscious one, it deserves from its author a responsibility not only for what he does with it but also for knowing why he does it. And it probably will not develop into vital, original, and fresh drama unless it intensely interests the author. If it holds no excitement for him, it will likewise fail to excite anyone else.

Rather than attempt to define an indefinable artistic process, we seek principally to help the person of writing talent who is at the same time an apprentice in the theatre and who is in particular attracted to historical drama. What follows in this chapter is a modicum of theory organized selectively for the apprentice and adapted to methods of solving problems inherent in the playwriting process. (Selected basic terms and concepts dealing with playwriting structure are included in the Appendix.)

These problems of the playwright cannot be unknown to a member of a sponsoring group wanting to function effectively as an organizer or an adviser in the creating of historical drama. This person needs to understand what the playwright's contributions are and what he does. Lacking such an insight, the adviser finds it difficult to judge the merits of a script, commit a group to producing a particular script, and, among other things, deal with or advise a playwright. Regardless of this chapter's focus on matters of composing drama, the layman will profit by sitting beside the apprentice playwright, as it were, and reading over his shoulder.

The emphasis here is on the processes of playwriting and thinking through the dramatic idea rather than on the technique of writing itself. If on the basis of experimenting with the working methods proposed, the apprentice develops an effective method of his own for constructing drama, so much the better.

The playwright searches for materials

A world produces an artist. As a human being, he interacts with that world, regardless of time or place. In works of art this interaction ranges deeply and widely but even though the stimuli—and the medium—of various artists differ, each artist is interested in transmitting his experience to other human beings, each masters techniques belonging to a particular artistic medium, and each studies the materials which express his purpose. These common features among the various arts must be recognized by the playwright.

He also speeds his growth by recognizing important differences between the group experience of theatre and individual and group responses to other artifacts. An Andrew Wyeth completes an oil painting, sells it, and its owner hangs it on his living room wall, appreciating it gradually and privately, according to his whim. But a playwright, a William Gibson, let us say, is dependent not only upon the concerted imagination and skill of other theatre artists to communicate the values of *The Miracle Worker*; it is the audience that bears public testimony to Gibson's attitude towards human courage and devotion, and thus completes the communicative circle. In performance the theatre audience is in effect an ever-present actor contributing to a performance for which he has never been rehearsed. Is it little wonder that no two performances are ever precisely alike?

In the search for the materials out of which to fashion his drama, the apprentice can turn to three major areas of human experience. He can examine his own behavior as an individual, that is, his *psychology*; the accepted standards of morality and ethics, that is, his *society*; and history and myth, that is, his *past*. Here he is encouraged to explore the possibilities stored in the past. But in so doing, he must not ignore the other two major areas, even if he could. Actually he will enrich his findings with sharply observed and deeply understood confrontations with psychology and sociology. Arthur Miller not only relies on 1692 trial documents but also refracts meanings from his personal history to generate *The Crucible*.

In whatever areas the playwright's probings take him, and wherever he locates promising materials, he needs to develop his own approach to the *facts* he encounters. From Holinshed's *Chronicles* Shakespeare borrowed the same facts as did his playwriting fellows; the stories that he apparently read and the Elizabethan world that he lived in were outwardly the same as theirs, yet he transformed the facts with that vast insight into human nature that was singularly his own. In our own native drama different authors confront the same materials inherent, let us say, in the Lincoln facts or the John Brown facts and,

for reasons of background, social conditioning, and personal chemistry, interpret them differently.[1] On the other hand, different materials have been organized frequently to the same end by different playwrights who make similar
thematic statements. Successful playwrights work out their own personal
methods of dealing with themselves, their worlds, and their pasts in searching
for materials.

However individuals may differ in their methods of research, setting
down and testing concepts, structuring the dramatic forms, making revisions,
and the like, they find a common base in the degree to which each author is
endowed with three abilities. These are the powers of *observation, understanding,* and *imagination*. The apprentice needs to mobilize these powers to his
dramatic composition. Observation, as it affects the playwright sharpens his five
senses to such a degree that the nature of his contact with the facts of experience can be recalled at will. Understanding involves his comprehending the
potential relationships in the facts discovered. Imagination is his ability to invent new combinations of related facts gathered from his knowledge and past
experience; at the same time he conceives of characters and happenings with
full emotional understanding. The rate of time it takes for the creative process
to be initiated, developed, and brought to a satisfactory end varies from person
to person, and is gauged by the amount and quality of each playwright's en-
dowment for observing, understanding, and imagining. Since relatively long
periods of time are generally required for ideas to gestate, the process often
moves forward slowly, erratically, and painfully. Apprentice playwrights can
take consolation from the testimony of authors whose goals are gained only
after long and steady grappling with creative problems. Good plays, like good
nondramatic works, are composed by writers who measure what they write
against severe standards of excellence.[2]

Sources of germinal ideas

The *germinal idea* refers to the initial phase of writing which sets creative juices flowing. Not all germinal ideas prove suitable for the purposes of
dramatic action. They must first be exposed, tested, then either developed or
stored away for future use. The apprentice playwright, as he trains himself to
be more observant, finds ideas beckoning from dozens of sources. He begins to
see all around him, in his time-worn relatives, friends, and acquaintances, evi-
dences of humanity to which he has been blind. His sharpened vision con-
vinces him that the materials for thinking creatively are right under his nose.

Almost everywhere he turns, the playwright encounters germinal ideas with dramatic potentials. There are, for example, the two estranged brothers, living on adjacent farms, who have not spoken to each other for years because one sent his children to college while the other refused to make the same necessary economic sacrifice. What line of action could result if the children decide to reconcile the brothers? There also is a quickening effect the playwright receives in listening to a debate on a theory of animal behavior; in discovering the incongruity of juxtaposed names of small towns on a travel map; in watching Girl Scouts around a campfire parody their camp counselors and regulations; in happening upon the classified ad in a large metropolitan daily stating that a young clergyman seeks a new congregation "as far removed from the city as possible." He learns to look regularly in the newspapers and periodicals for the human-revealing stories, the account of trials and disagreements among personalities, and the exploits, adventures, compassions, and vices of persons. He turns to ancient fables for which he seeks modern equivalents; and his blotting-paper memory absorbs anecdotes that he hears. In short, the sources available to the playwright are endless. Those most muscular in dramatic strength are ones to develop.

A germinal idea that initiates with an actual person (as *chapter* II *implied*) is likely to be a manageable one for the apprentice playwright. A dynamic individual promising a strong will and unresolved drive gains, at least in the preliminary phases of writing, a dominant focus. So-constituted a personality lends itself to being conceived of as the *protagonist*, who embodies the central or principal force motivating the main action, or as the *antagonist*, who embodies an equally strong force opposing the principal force. Chapter II's examples of the Apostle Paul, Mehitabel Wing, and John Brown represent the compelling personalities that history provides. Equally valuable personalities may be produced from nonhistorical sources. In either case, dramatic characters do not exist in a vacuum, their qualities being demonstrated only in imaginatively planned interactions spurred by or affecting their character.

The term story has widespread usage; it has a general meaning covering that which can be acted or narrated in words, or conveyed through a series of pictures. It is used here in the narrow sense of written or spoken narration of any length, from the anecdote through the short-story form to the novel. A story is often pounced upon by the playwright as a real boon in trying to get his play underway. At quick view, the story, because it comes packaged as a happening or series of happenings with a formal completeness, seems admirably suited to dramatization. But the playwright needs to approach the story with caution. In the first place, the use of published material without permission sometimes involves plagiarism if not copyright infringement. Secondly, writers frequently become so enamored of the effectiveness of the story, that they fail to regard it only as a germinal idea, believing rather that much of their work has been done for them. This is a delusion, for no narrative, as such, is prefabricated for the stage; it must undergo adaptation of at least some of its parts to be successful in the dramatic idiom. The playwright needs to be further cautioned against pursuing one attractive story after another until he finds himself eventually with a wonderful collection of stories but not a semblance of a play! Probably the apprentice playwright is wise to limit himself to a few stories at a time, testing them for their stageworthiness before turning to a fresh hunt for materials.

Provided that their liabilities and assets are closely observed, stories may, of course, lead to effective drama. The American theatre has been enriched by seasons in which novels were dramatized: Kathryn Forbes' *I Remember Mama* by John van Druten; Herman Melville's *Billy Budd* by Louis O. Coxe and Robert Chapman; Arthur Koestler's *Darkness at Noon* by Sidney Kingsley; Thomas Wolfe's *Look Homeward, Angel* by Ketti Frings; and James Agee's *Death in the Family*, dramatized by Ted Mosel as *All the Way Home*. A profitable pursuit for an apprentice writer would be to compare these dramatizations with the original novels to judge how each dramatist filtered the narrative material through his imagination to give it a different focus for a different life in the theatre.[3]

So much for the possibilities in stories. Writers for the stage also find dramatic strengths inherent in what can be referred to as a *situation*. In a playwriting sense, a situation is an arrangement of circumstances which arrests the attention of the audience and stirs its curiosity and/or emotional involvement as to what will happen next. When an audience begins to worry over the possibility of a conflict and over its outcome, *suspense* is generated. To a considerable degree, suspense is the result of *tension* between characters. Mehitabel Wing (see chapter II), for example, having persuaded her husband to surrender to British troops, finds herself in a potentially dramatic situation when he is tried and sentenced to hang by British colonial law. Feeling responsible for her husband's predicament, she must "do something." Her state of desperation creates suspense: how is she going to act to save his life? Any human being on his way to, or in, or emerging from what is to him a condition of desperation offers the potential of a situation. Suspense feeds upon an active search for adjustment.

To the creative imagination one effective situation suggests another, then a third, and finally a train of ordered *incidents* or events. The latter may be considered from a structural point of view as contrasting and progressive changes in audience concern. Visualizing a germinal idea in terms of situation, then, means to appraise its potentials as dramatic action.

On the other hand a playwright is sometimes attracted to what appears to him as a generally held and accepted view towards human behavior, an *aphorism* or maxim. He may use this aphorism as a germinal idea, hoping to "prove" or in some cases "disprove" its validity in dramatic terms. He wonders if it is humanly possible always to be "true to one's moral conscience," as schoolboys have been admonished for generations, and creates a case in which characters find it difficult to live up to this principle. As a germinal idea an aphorism may have merit if it leads to a writer's conceiving characters who embody various aspects of demonstrating the principle and so structuring their struggle as to affect the audience appropriately. But the envisioned aphorism can be belabored at the expense of dramatic action if the playwright allows his personal conviction to taint the believability of his characters by having them become mere mouthpieces for his ideas. The general effect is that of a didactic statement. History, on the other hand, can often suggest characters and reveal situations that allow the playwright to demonstrate his belief.

Then too, all-pervading feelings growing out of certain geographic places, or mechanically-made sounds, or social conditions may sometimes stir a playwright's imagination. Assume the feeling generated by a large and stately house of the 1880 vintage, shabby beyond repair. Tall grass and weeds overrun the garden, and at the gate a rusty iron fence still guards precariously the house within. At first vaguely aware of a sense of dread or loneliness, the playwright feels an urge to expand his feelings into dramatic concreteness. Or he may respond to other atmospheres: the brightly-lighted diadem of a skyscraper, isolated in an otherwise empty black night; the crackling of snow underfoot in a sunshiny New England forenoon. As he learns to stretch his imagination, he gradually peoples each idea with individuals who make tentative gestures toward a pattern of action. What the practical playwright looks for is the relationship possible between the fact experienced—the germinal idea, that is— and the feeling or view he wishes to express.

For the playwright, as with other artists, the materials of his art are around him all the time. He observes them, as fact, tries to understand them in reference to his personal chemistry, and then imagines them in relationships that for him did not previously exist. By a constant and alert act of mind and will, he improves his seeing, hearing, and understanding of the facts of his everyday life. His system of personal research becomes a matter of habit, as he isolates persons, feelings, attitudes, stories, and situations. He stores in his memory those which strike him as touching, or amusing, or puzzling in the infinitely varied human condition. Those that promise most vivid and complete realization in dramatic form are challenges to his imaginative resources.

Testing germinal ideas

In order to consider the worth of the germinal ideas he has bagged, the hunter-playwright must first visualize such ideas in terms of *dramatic action*. To the concept of dramatic action there are four applications. The simplest form results from the visible *physical* behavior of the actor. As long as it is purposive and expressive, his physical activity—i.e. walking, smiling, fighting, embracing, and so on—gives pantomimic meaning to the script. Physical actions *show* drama rather than *tell* about it.

Dialogue is a second means a playwright has of viewing dramatic action. *Speech* is human activity revealing its speaker searching for, adjusting to, and deciding issues that affect him; its ability to indicate subtleties and nuances of meaning can exceed that of pantomimic movement. Effective dialogue, characterizing speakers and suggesting varied emotional conditions, is full of action.

By selecting appropriate physical activity and speech patterns, the playwright can enlist *psychological* action. Interested in disclosing mental and emotional states in his characters, he knows that speech and external actions can be interpreted as outward signs of characters' subjective desires, beliefs, and motivations—all those changes in thought and attitudes that mark dynamic behavior.

A fourth application considers the total play. A well-conceived play—composed of physical, speech, and subjective actions—is itself a *continuous* action. It involves characters in a pattern of ever-changing relationships progressively moving towards a major climax.

The playwright, then, visualizes a germinal idea that can be expressed in the interrelated forms of dramatic action mentioned. If an author, after putting his idea to vigorous tests, finds that the appeals he responds to would make a better short story or novel, then he is foolish to force it into a dramatic form.

Given the nature of his medium, the playwright must adapt his idea to the physical limits of the stage, to the temporal limits of performance (having an approximate maximum of two and a half hours), and to the comprehension and experience of a group of spectators. Moreover, the medium demands that the playwright's expression be unequivocally clear at the same time that it is swift, emphatic, and compressed. Profound and subtle insights into human nature which the leisurely pace of the novelist allows are sacrificed for different values. A novel, theoretically, can be picked up anytime, anywhere, by the reader who skips here and rereads there for further clarification and additional pleasure and enlightment. But the theatre is a time-space art, presenting its total experience in a calculated sequential order and under a telescoped system of chronology. And, furthermore, while the novel deals with a past that is frequently reported in the present, the stage schedules its action in perpetually present time. "A play is what takes place," Thornton Wilder reminds us, "a novel is what one person tells us took place." [4]

A good germinal idea has potentialities not only for *dramatic action* but for *unity, credibility, completeness,* and *practicality.* One means of gaining unity is through *structure.* To the novel-reader the need for unity is hardly as critical as it is to the member of the theatre audience. In short or long plays, whether they be structurally diffuse (or *extensive*) or *compact* (or *intensive*), a main set of relationships needs to be constantly maintained. Ordinarily, the necessary focus comes through the frequency with which an audience sees (or hears about) characters. Structural unity is likewise condensed, as a general practice, when less rather than more time transpires in the enactment, when there are fewer rather than more changes of locale, and when parallel or subplots are minimized. Generally, the concentrated, closed structure associated with the so-called unities (time, place, and action) is, in principle, recommended. However diffuse and open the intrinsic structure of any drama, its pattern still finds unification possible through structured progressive movement culminating in a climax.

A second important but more elusive means of effecting unification is by *tone.* This is by nature ambiguous for it is the result of feeling rather than of analysis. It derives in part from the personal face the playwright turns towards his material: serious, ironic, playful, depressed, joyful, agonized, optimistic or whatever. His attitude is responsible for the differences between traditionally classified tragedy on the one side and comedy on the other, with all their inbred types falling between. Tone derives in part also from the basic stance his era takes upon art in general. The tone that identifies Joan of Arc as characterized in plays by the German Schiller, the Anglo-Irish Shaw, the American Anderson, and the French Giraudoux is in part tempered by each playwright's personal view of reality; [5] it is also tempered by the respective outlook towards martyrdom, religion, and politics of each author's age and nationality. The identifying tone of a script makes it distinctive from others of the same genre and even of the same playwright. When it succeeds in harmonizing itself with the structural elements—dialogue, characters, idea, plot—the combination makes for an artistic construct of the playwright's original design.[6]

Effective germinal ideas also promise *credibility* in the idiom of the theatre which in large part is based on the actor's moving and speaking in space resulting in strong vivid impressions. Because of these impressions, the theatre audience places great store in the believability of a character's actions and reactions. Life breeds complexity and unpredictability, but stage characters require simplification, consistency, and intensification. Even principal characters can be no more than a concentrate of a few carefully selected aspects of a personality. Salient questions are: Is each character consistent in terms of these aspects? Are his actions the probable and necessary outcome of a given character's desires? Are his words and movements appropriate to the character as we know him? This cause and effect principle, however, operates within the realm of the playwright's imaginary world. Especially in the case of nonhistorical personalities, the judgment of credibility is based not so much on the logic of experience or of rationality as on the premises invented by the author and accepted by the audience.

An effective germinal idea, furthermore, includes *completeness* and *practicality* among its potentials. Completeness infers two things. One is the just and balanced emphasis between the subject matter engendered by the idea and the considerable group effort it takes for humans to compose, produce, and attend it in performance. Faulty playwriting is afoot, for instance, if a full-length script leaves the impression of being an over-extended one-act play; and, on the other hand, a one-act drama should not be so jammed with incidents as to afford no time for developing plausible characters and credible actions. A second aspect of completeness infers an outcome logically developing from the dramatic action preceding it. The conclusion of the drama, in brief, achieves satisfaction by answering an interesting question posed in its beginning scenes. In *Hamlet*, for example, the dramatic question posed early in the action is: will Hamlet avenge his father's death? The outcome of the play answers the question.

Related to the factor of completeness is the germinal idea's promise of feasible realization. A drama arising from the idea faces matters of *practicability*. A production of any drama is worth no effort and expenditure out of proportion to its proposed length and potential values. Factors to be weighed are the time necessary to write and rewrite the script, the appropriateness of the script for the occasion and major purpose of the intended production, and the provision of time and resources necessary—human, technical, and financial

—to establish and prepare an adequate production scheme. A large-cast, large-scale epic-drama in scenario form only, for instance, will hardly be practicable for a small community (with a small budget and a small high school stage at its disposal) facing within six months a three-day centennial. But a small cast biography-drama already in first draft form might be quite practicable under the circumstances.

Examples of germinal ideas

A few concrete examples will serve to test some of the principles established for germinal ideas with potentialities for dramatic treatment. They are representative of ones submitted by playwrights in their apprenticeship. What does each germ promise?

> A YOUNG COLLEGE girl who was driving her father's car against his wishes, is faced with the problem of whether to turn herself in for the accidental hit-and-run death of a seven-year-old boy. Though she was actually unaware of the accident, all circumstances point toward her guilt.

This idea contains a fairly common situation which prefigures dramatic action. A *situation*, in the technical sense, presents the need for a character to choose between two or more alternatives, the consequence of any one of them being of important concern to the character. Situation yields action, and action is plot. Here the girl is forced to choose between the outside chance of going scot-free or of clearing her conscience by reporting herself to the police. If she does the latter, she runs the risk of legal proceedings as well as parental wrath. Yet an internal debate with herself could water down dramatic action and so prove dull. A decision on her part to report to the authorities or confess to her father could release a series of involvements leading to some kind of effective climax. Why did the girl take the car against her father's wishes? An answer to this may uncover a volatile family relationship. Its initial situation and two or three strong-minded, emotionally-involved individuals could produce, with skillful restraint, an interesting one-act play.

> IS THERE VALIDITY in the statement that pride can grow in a man's character as long as and to the extent that it is challenged? That once unchallenged, it will revert to self-illusion?

Absorbing and perhaps profound questions are set down here. The great danger is that they can be answered better in ways other than in drama; in lectures, for example. A writer would solve an important creative problem by imagining characters whose behavior could allow "pride" (not always easily objectified) and its absence to be demonstrated in dramatic action. And he would have to plot the action with lapses of time, so that that subjective life of the characters could increase in credibility. This idea plunges so deeply into the lives of at least three principal characters that an adequate expression in a short play is unthinkable, if it is to be dramatized at all. A novel, in which individual thoughts and feelings could be carefully and singularly presented, is probably called for.

> FAMINE AND PESTILENCE *strike an eighteenth-century Eastern European Jewish community. The chief rabbi brings a suit against God. A tribunal of rabbis is convened to pass judgment on God's responsibility for the tragic events. Great controversy results from the prosecution. The verdict is guilty.*

As with most folklore, this has a built-in completeness about it, but as a tale to be told. Daring to pass judgment on God and then finding Him guilty—this is a challenging and exciting concept. In a dramatization of the idea, the playwright could enlarge the arena for the titanic struggle by suggesting a remoteness of time and place. Knowledge of certain sectarian doctrines and formalities is essential if he is to know what few facts need selection for their theatrical effectiveness. In the trial scene, physical action would be negligible. Highly contrasting personalities and clash of attitudes would have to be imaginatively handled if the trial is not to lose its intensity and sense of direction. There is substance here to warrant a long, continuously uninterrupted one-act drama. With sensitive musical support, this idea might also blend into a worthwhile opera.

> A MAN *of fifty-five is custodian in a city office building. He does his work quietly and efficiently, speaking a cultivated American-English. When the occasion arises and genuine interest is shown by some of the occupants of the building, he holds forth knowingly on history, literature, and philosophy.*

How dramatically useful this human being could be largely depends on the basic drives that motivate him and what goals he has at age fifty-five. If he has no unfulfilled desires, he is not likely to embody a dynamic stage personality. But as the germ is outlined, the custodian could have appeal. Why is this man of apparent refinement and education working in an unskilled menial position? His efficiency at carrying out his tasks indicates that he does not find them distasteful. And he seems to enjoy social contacts. How did he land where he is? What is his past? What are his family relationships? Is he actually leading a double life, the office job being a "front" for something illegal or sinister? The imagined answers could stir up a personality functioning as a primary, or perhaps more effectively, as a secondary character in a short or full-length drama, comic or non-comic.

> A RURAL NEWSPAPER reports that a small house on the edge of town burned to the ground. Its owner, an eighty-year-old man who lives alone, was not at home at the time. Authorities said that there is no insurance on either the house or its contents. A neighbor, who reported the fire, said it is the third time a house on that site burned to the ground.

This idea is attractive on several different levels. If we could assume that the old man with his own hands rebuilt his house each time it burned, he would be entitled to our admiration. He has a splendid independence and courage. He perhaps could believe that, in his language, "spirits" were responsible for destroying his property, yet would accept no help in his personal vendetta against the antagonists. But what climate of probability does the play operate in? Does the old man accept the existence of the "spirits"? Does he see them? On what level of reality are they to be taken by the other characters? By the audience? If the tone of the proposed dramatic action insists on realistic treatment, then the burning down of the house once, twice, or three times could become increasingly impractical. But if the tone allows for fantasy and abstraction, the house-burning effect could be managed with theatrical impact. Elements of music and spectacle could be revealing if properly integrated. An extended dramatization of the material is hardly justified.

> THE INTERIOR of a cottage along a desolate stretch of rocky coast. The cottage is starkly simple, and most of the belongings are unadorned. But there are several things not in keeping with the general tone of the building—a delicate antique chair, lacy curtains, a pair of silver candlesticks, and a large gilt-framed painting of a young girl over the crude stone fireplace.

In a quiet way the qualities of the atmosphere suggested here proposes a dramatic action that could be engrossing. The environment implies two ways of living, two contrasts of physical and mental conditions. The setting could be the home of an elderly pair, a man and wife, a sister and her brother, or two maiden sisters. Either or both persons could have known more affluent days, reflected in the few physical incongruities in the room. It could be the basic setting for an extended action employing time fluidly, in which flashback devices reveal aspects of earlier days sharply different from the life now experienced by the cottage's occupants. Strong but not equally dominant characters would be necessary to compensate for the loss of unity that comes through changes of locale and a widespread time scheme in an extended treatment. Possibly a one-act version could evolve in which an intenser focus would be on the two characters themselves, their interrelations strained or altered or renewed by the introduction of one or more characters from the world beyond the desolate stretch of rocky coast.

> THE DIARY and letters of Narcissa Whitman form the testament of a valiant woman. Delicately brought up, surrounded by comfort and convenience, Narcissa Prentice in 1836 married Marcus Whitman, a medical missionary to Oregon, and spent her honeymoon in a covered wagon. She was the first white woman to cross the continent, at considerable personal and material sacrifice. After maintaining a mission station for eleven years among the Cayuse tribe, the dedicated Whitmans met a cruel death at the hands of those they served. An attack of measles struck down white and Indian children. Dr. Whitman's medicines cured the white children but had no effect on the Indians. The rumor spread that he was poisoning them. Angry Indians massacred the Whitmans.

Narcissa Whitman appears to be a historical figure who produces the dynamics of compelling drama. From the time she marries and starts westward, her life is dominated by goals and deeds that can be painted in broad theatrical brush strokes. She encounters events embodying unexpected conditions that require a continuous struggle for adjustment. There is the wide contrast between the protecting shelter of family and friends in her youth and the almost constant state of uncertainty she had to endure in her maturity. Only after the Whitmans' patient and long-suffering service to the Indians finally resulted in confidence and friendship did the ironic blow strike. The death of Narcissa and her loved ones at the hands of their savage friends is best realized in the fuller reaches of the long play.[7]

A method of developing a script

For illustrative purposes we now shall conjecture how a short play by Robert Gard called *Raisin' the Devil* may have been imagined and developed by its author. The play, appearing at the end of this chapter, has had widespread production in New York and adjacent states. It can be regarded as a successfully managed arrangement of dramatic elements capable of arousing and sustaining audience attention. Its values, appropriately interpreted, engender excitement and laughter, responses apparently desired by the author. Its length, structural pattern, simple unity, and consistency of tone make it suitable for our purpose, namely, to illustrate a process. Through some such process Robert Gard may have arrived at certain artistic decisions in developing *Raisin' the Devil*. No claim is made that he developed it in such a way. Our present aim is simply to conjecture how certain problems facing a playwright might be solved.

Searching for fruitful ideas, a writer browses through folklore and early histories of New England. He is struck by the number of references to early nineteenth-century itinerant preachers or circuit riders, and particularly to one referred to as "Crazy Dow" or "The Eccentric Cosmopolite." One of the most widely traveled men of his time, Lorenzo Dow has earned fame in Ireland and England as well as most of the Eastern sector of the United States from Louisiana to the Canadian forests. The man seeks to save souls by preaching fire and brimstone and to cure bodies by vending "Dow's Family Medicine." Even in the face of stiff competition from an array of contemporary circuit riders, this Dow is singular. The writer responds excitedly to this positive individual possessed with unresolved drives and a prophet's zeal. Dow is of the compelling stuff of drama.

In New Jersey, Georgia, Connecticut, Delaware, New York—everywhere his mission takes him—Dow's exploits stimulate the spinning of tales. Often the tales are the same ones repeated and given probability by the dubbing in of local names and decorations. One of the most frequently recounted tales, appearing in various forms as an anecdote,[8] a sentimental ballad,[9] or a detailed narrative,[10] concerns Dow's raising of the devil. This strikes the writer as an attractive idea, with possibilities worth mulling over. Meanwhile, what other Dow biographical or legendary material stimulates the playwright's imagination? There is the occasion in Saratoga Springs when Dow unwittingly aids Eliza Brown, an ageless burlesque dancer of easy virtue, to trick a wealthy New York importer into being her husband. There is the attempted lynching of Dow by a gang of rowdies at a camp meeting where Lorenzo, fearless and self-possessed, mounts a stump and, preaching a short sermon, wins over the gang leaders who escort him and his wife back to safety.

These stories and others have their fascination. But the playwright must curb the lure to keep gathering fascinating bits of colorful humanity if he is to get to the writing of his drama. He wishes to write a short play strongly focused on Dow, so he rejects the competition that Eliza Brown might bring; he wishes the play to deal with a small number of characters with a minimum of production necessities (such as scene-shifting), so he rejects the episode in which Dow's life is threatened by the rowdies. Moreover, he keeps being drawn to a comic treatment of some kind. So he turns back to the devil-raising story. He recalls several different versions of it and one of the more flavorsome he notes as having been passed on from father to son:

> I heard one time about Dowie [Lorenzo Dow], the great preacher. He went to a man's house and wanted to stay all night. The husband wasn't at home, but the wife said he was welcome to stay because the husband often talked he'd like to see Dowie the preacher. Now she told Dowie, she says, "If you hear an awful noise when my husband comes home, don't get scared, because he generally comes home intoxicated and makes an awful noise."
>
> So finally there was a man come, and he come in very quiet. And Dowie thought that kinda strange, the wife tellin' him he'd hear an awful noise. So he went to sleep. Couple, three hours afterwards, another man come in, and he heared an awful noise—and it was the husband, and the wife tried to quiet him. He [Dow] discovered the first man run to the head of the stairs and jumped into a hogshead of tow.
>
> The lady of the house tried to hush her husband and told him to be quiet because Dowie the preacher was there. He says, "If Dowie the preacher is here," he says, "he's gotta prove to me he's Dowie the preacher by raisin' Satan." So Dowie told him, he says to get the doors all open because when he comes he'll come all aflame. So Dowie he takes a candle and steps to the barrel o' tow and sets it afire——and this feller jumps out and runs—he's all aflame. And this man he fell on his knees and was converted.[11]

This tale is simply and economically told. Strong in dramatic possibilities, it has unity and completeness, the climax is graphically realized, and the pointed conclusion has an almost Biblical cadence: "And this man he fell on his knees and was converted." All four characters are interesting, even the wispy visitor whose predicament allows him to hide in a hogshead of tow. Certain action is explicit; a lot more is implied. Its perspective, however, is that of the story-teller, not the playwright. To structure the elements into a play, the playwright must make some artistic decisions if he is to retain the important relationships and the dramatic focus on the stage. For one thing he does not have a plot for his action. Before he can arrive at this phase of his composition, he can with profit indulge in a process that will stretch his imaginactive powers, a process we call *saturation*. Its value, as always, will shift with the individual user, his material, and his purpose.

Saturation

This process will not assure the playwright of world-shaking results. It simply enables him to soak up facts as a means of gaining authority over his material. Only as the playwright sits in the center of his material can he write with conviction. He will need to know a great deal more about his characters than he ever will use in the play, no matter what its length. It encourages him to avoid vagueness and stereotype in character or incident, mainly the product of routine rather than imaginative habits of thinking. Saturation allows for the invention of new combinations of facts. It aids in keeping the writer's tone consistently firm in the handling of his material, a positive aid in attaining unity. It helps in keeping important relationships in focus, actually a matter of constructing and proportioning the plot.

To begin the saturation process, the writer needs, minimally, one character or an imagined setting. (A Lorenzo Dow conjuring up the devil is a rich legacy, of course.) If he has one of these, the other is not far removed. Neither can exist separately: visualization of character in action forces the creation of an environment; visualization of an environment encourages the invention of character. With the latter the playwright is in a position to set about building up the society that encloses the character, imagining various possibilities in the way of relatives, associates, friends, and enemies.

Saturation with *character* means investing the imagined characters with biographies. These can be organized in many ways. More space and emphasis is normally given the important characters. The following outline proposes character development through such obviously overlapping considerations as these:

A.   External Characteristics:
1] *Physical*: size, weight, shape, etc. (the ways in which he differs from as well as resembles other humans).
habitual mode of walking, standing, etc.; use of head, hands, eyes, etc.
general tonus, state of health.

2] Vocal: patterns of speech, quality of voice, all indices of geographic and family habits, etc.

3] Dress: care and importance attached by individual; as an index of vocation, trade, financial circumstances, historical period, etc.

B. Internal Characteristics:

1] Hereditary: parentage, racial, etc.

2] Beliefs and interests: attitudes towards society, religion, science, etc.; towards material goods and spiritual values.

3] Intellectual: training, education, pleasures, etc.

4] Character traits, in general.

5] Emotional biases toward home, family, friends, business acquaintances, politics, etc.

C. Social Characteristics:

1] Direct and indirect interrelationships with family, friends, associates, neighbors, members of community, etc.

2] Environmental: home, neighborhood, school, church, employment, social strata, etc.

Saturation with *environment* considers:

1] Physical milieu in which the action takes place: a description of what it embraces, what it leads to, what it looks upon—the essential nature of it as conducive to a particular kind of action.

2] The modes of life of the persons concerned in the action—how this is reflected in the setting.

3] The aspect and life of the community (however abstract or concrete this may be) in which the action is laid.

This saturation is an evolving process. One thing the apprentice discovers in it is that his preliminary ideas give way to new emphases. By testing a character in different combinations with other factors, the character's qualities shift. His originally-conceived central character sometimes turns out to be more valuable in a secondary level of importance; or he tests his action in another environment and realizes that this more fully affords the values he wishes to express. He keeps combining and recombining until certain characters "stick" and become integral with the action. Along the way he also discovers that much of his artistic problem is in knowing what to leave out as in knowing what to put in.

Let us apply such a process to *Raisin' the Devil*. Lorenzo Dow is comprehensively and sympathetically treated by his biographer, Charles Coleman Sellers, in *Lorenzo Dow, The Bearer of the Word*. Early in his book Sellers takes his stand on the part legendary, part historical data he collected: "there is little need for separating the chaff from the wheat: all are believable of the hero of this history." [12] In saturating himself with this personality from the past, a playwright has considerable materials to sift out for their usefulness.

The following picture of Dow summarizes some of his pertinent external characteristics:

> Lorenzo was tall and fragile in appearance, stoop-shouldered, with thin legs and arms, with light brown hair hanging over his shoulders, a long beard, a thin nose and bright blue eyes in a pallid face. His dress was unkempt and soiled; like other holy men, he was too absorbed by the divine to consider cleanliness and care for appearances. . . . He came, generally, wrapped in a long black cloak. Sickly and melancholy as he was, he was active and quick and had the similitude of health. . . . His voice was harsh from continual use, and he spoke in gasps and with difficulty, having suffered almost his whole life from asthma— his shoulders . . . "moving convulsively up and down, as he worked his vocal organs as laboriously as a man would work at a dry pump." [13]

Born in Coventry, Connecticut, in 1777, Lorenzo was the fifth of six children born to Humphrey and Tabitha Dow. The family was reared in the Calvinist doctrine. Father and Mother were not enthusiasts in their religious practice, which made them susceptible to the invasion of inflammatory Methodists. Lorenzo was particularly susceptible: he became a convert. When little more than eighteen years of age, he was off on his first mission of spreading the gospel of Methodism.

Other aspects of Dow's personality become clearer with this estimate of a few of his internal characteristics:

> Lorenzo had little dignity and a world of impudence. He would play fearless pranks on camp meeting rowdies; he would verge on buffoonery in the pulpit. But most often he was sober and terribly earnest; godly men, even if they opposed his erratic course, seldom doubted his mission. He had but little schooling, and yet, in his travels, has acquired a vast fund of information of the type which appeals readily to popular credulity. [14]

More details of the life of this wandering oracle are abundantly contained in the biography and other sources. Only one other observation is necessary, however. Dow's brilliance was a superficial one, maintains his biographer, the remarkable store of wit and ingenuity in his composition being what allowed him to hold his own in public life. In the tale that we hypothetically dramatize, this particular characteristic of his begins to size up as a dominant factor in the action.

What of the other characters? In the recounted tale, there are the "wife," the "husband," and the "man." Will they serve the plot unchanged? Perhaps. The playwright delays a final decision on this for awhile, preferring to filter, rearrange, and then test his materials. He does agree, however, that three characters—as yet unnamed—are needed to assist the ingenious Dow in the climactic deed of producing on cue the "Satanic Majesty." And at least three are needed to furnish the exposition and prepare for the climax. A traveling companion to Dow, such as a faithful wife, will only get in the way and tend to dissipate the focus on Dow and his opposition. As to the total of four characters, this number seems desirable if they can fulfill all the dramatic functions the playwright requires. With so few characters, each of the three can be fleshed out proportionately.

In constructing his plot, the playwright asks what ingredients of the tale will serve dramatic purposes. As told, it has an interrupted time scheme, with a lapse of two or three hours after Dow goes to bed. The playwright wisely plans to work for a continuous uninterrupted action and a progressive thrust to the climax. In the account, the climax occurs when a candle is burning, so it can be assumed that the hour is after dark, Dow having gone to bed. The tale also suggests that the house has at least three rooms and probably more, since reference is made to "the head of the stairs." To give plausibility to the tale after the "husband's" return, it must be assumed that Dow is in one room, the "man" leaves another to jump into the hogshead, and the "wife" and "husband" are having an argument in a third. On the stage the fulfilling of such physical requirements will be space-consuming and costly; but the playwright sees a gain in unity by confining his action to a single room. He does sigh regretfully, though, at having to give up the splendid effect of the "man" descending the stairs "all aflame."

How else does the playwright envision the environment? His action is of the period of the Great Revival, the religious awakening which affects persons in both rural and urban areas; but his action, he imagines, is better suited to the isolation of the countryside where neighbors are scarce. He wishes the milieu of the play to reflect the simple necessities and few adornments of a many-purpose room, crudely built and furnished. It is used for purposes of eating, cooking, socializing, and storing tools and other useful articles, such as tow. One door opens out on to the exterior; at least one more leads to another part of the house if the action ascribed to the tale is followed.

In the tale, Dow's connection with the environment is almost by accident, as if he were passing by and stops, merely seeking a bed for the night. The devil-raising incident is consequently a device of the moment. In plotting the action the playwright seeks for Dow an urgency that brings him to this particular house: perhaps he is hunting a person who has thus far eluded him, and, moreover, he does not have time to waste. So the motive power in the dramatic action is Dow's desire to make his local record perfect by converting the last "infidel" and to do it with extreme urgency. This is a strategic decision of the playwright's for it now makes possible an identifying of the other three personalities.

There is no point to the entire conversion idea unless the "husband" offers opposition as the last "infidel." Yet if the "wife" and the "man" are persons already avowed followers of Dow, he will probably recognize them both. Now the playwright begins to test the possibilities of having only the "man" a convert, given to feelings of guilt through association with the "wife." She must have some stigma or other, which makes it all the more crucial to the "man" that Dow does not catch him in the house. In the tale, the implication is that the "man" is the "wife's" lover. Should the playwright pursue this relationship? As he mulls over the plotting effects of such an arrangement, he realizes that it sets up a husband-wife-lover triangle whose development has these disadvantages: it would require too much time to resolve; shift focus from a Dow-husband to a husband-wife relationship, thus diminishing the importance of Dow; shift focus from a husband-as-infidel-to-be-converted to a lover (and wife) as rogue-to-be-reformed, thus altering Dow's primary goal in appearing at the house; and, in addition, suggest an adulterous state possibly limiting the play's appeal for some types of audience (a consideration when contemplating the nature of potential audiences). The writer rejects this alternative.

Of course, Dow's achievement will be all the greater if his "infidel" is engaged in a practice or occupation illegal or beyond the pale of respectability, and is well known in the community because of it. Assuming that the "husband" will make the best "infidel," perhaps he could be a petty thief, notorious and daring. This may work well. What if, rather than a "wife," he has a daughter who could be involved with the "man"? And what if, as a father, he could be concerned about making a profitable deal with a suitor for this daughter?

The "infidel" begins to take on a petty lustre. As for the other two characters, they also start to assume definition. Certainly there are several gains in this new father-daughter relationship: by making the daughter and her suitor young, the writer gains contrasts to the older people; the suitor does not want to be found in the house by either Dow (who will think he is in unsavory company) or the father (who will object to the courting without his consent); the daughter wished to be courted by the young man and therefore protects him against both her father and Dow. The main antagonism to Dow and his goal resides, of course, in the father's attitude toward Dow and his profession.

As his mind simmers over artistic choices influencing characters and what they do, the playwright becomes aware of technical considerations that are the special province of the stage. He thinks of the Devil-raising action. The tale calls for a burning candle to ignite not only the tow (loose fiber of hemp or flax) but also the man hidden in the barrel! Aside from the violation of standard theatre safety regulations with burning candles, the effect of having a person leap out of the barrel and run off stage as if "aflame" imposes too many technical difficulties and acting hazards. A substitute device is required. Perhaps a walking stick, used instrumentally by the actor for other purposes, can be brandished in the air and beaten upon the barrel. And, moreover, ramming the stick into the barrel might trigger a desired response from its occupant. Visually, a substance covering the actor's face and clothing to make him look "unearthly" will enhance the special theatricality of the climax. Molasses or oil? These are too messy, and besides the actor has to remain in the barrel for something like eighteen minutes. The substance must be easily applied by the actor himself and have physical qualities that will not spoil his disposition or his costume. Perhaps flour or a flour-like substance is worth trying. It might have the added advantage of producing a white powdery cloud, giving credibility to the apparition, particularly if the stage lights are dimmed gradually as the action progresses.

The foregoing discussion merely suggests ways of developing germinal ideas and testing their potentialities in character relationships and structuring plots. A recommended next step in gaining perspective is for the author to set down a synopsis. In précis form of some two hundred to three hundred words, the synopsis forces him to eliminate the relatively nonessential and to concentrate on the principal characters and their central involvement. An expansion of this outline to narration, where details suggested by earlier research and saturation are incorporated, can frequently help to crystallize further the playwright's ideas. (An example of using a synopsis to aid in developing a play will be found in Chapter ix.)

Once the writer has gone through the phases of making a saturation, a synopsis, and—as his material and experience dictate—a narration, he can probably move into another phase in the process of composing a play: the making of a preliminary scenario. Here he will be forced to make many more decisions which will determine his script's promise. These decisions will involve details of varying degrees of importance; most of them will be related to the already discussed factors of dramatic action, unity, credibility, completeness, and practicality.

The preliminary scenario

The preparation of a scenario is recommended to the apprentice playwright before attempting the first draft. There are helpful functions that a well-prepared scenario may provide him: 1] in the construction process, a scenario may expose unsuspected problems inherent in the proposed action and hasten their solution; 2] in terms of characterization, the scenario may stir him to bring his imagined personalities to fuller life; 3] upon reflection, the strengths and weaknesses of the designed action—now able to be viewed in its totality and proportioned parts—may become more readily apparent, thus making revision more intelligently possible.

The contents of a scenario vary in practice with different authors, and the apprentice needs to discover by test what, if any, of this method, is adjustable to his own mind and temperament.

We suggest either employing index cards (5″ x 8″ is a good size) or setting up a format on standard business-size stationery. In the former practice, each index card accounts for a separate structural unit and lists the characters and the dramatic functions of that unit, together with a brief description of the action; the cards can be spread out on a table and examined and rearranged at will. The latter method records the same information in a ticktacktoe pattern laid out so that its columns account consecutively for the elements and functions of each structural unit. The preliminary scenario of *Raisin' the Devil* demonstrates its use. Here the structural unit is regarded as a "French scene," when the playwright conceives of the entrance and exit of each character as a change of dramatic potential, marking a corresponding change in dramatic function. Each scene is numbered consecutively, its approximate playing time noted,[15] the characters involved listed, their important actions described, and the significant dramatic functions identified.

At the end of this scenario there is a brief commentary on some of the solutions Robert Gard achieved in the complete play reprinted here. It is instructive to compare the printed play with the germinal idea and its development in the saturation process.

Preliminary Scenario for Raisin' the Devil

Characters:

> DAUGHTER – *a young woman, attractive, in her early 20's*
> YOUNG MAN – *local youth of the same age*
> REN DOW – *a traveling preacher in his late 40's, tall, stoop-shouldered, long beard; wears long black cloak and carries a walking stick; speaks with great intensity*
> FATHER – *a notorious horse-thief, about 55, rough and aggressive*

Time: *in the mid-1820's, late afternoon*
Place: *near Schoharie, New York; a cabin room, sparsely furnished; a couple of chairs, a table and bench; in a corner a large barrel with bunghole in the side; two doors, one leading outside, the other to another room; a cider jug on table*

> Code: D = Daughter; YM = Young Man; RD = Ren Dow; F = Father;
> (YM) = *Young Man hidden in barrel*

French Scene	Est. Length	Characters	Digest of Action	Main Dramatic Function
1	10 min.	D YM	YM, uneasy, tries to leave D. She employs devices to keep him from leaving. He is obviously afraid of F's rough reputation. And since he's recently been converted by RD, YM reminds D of RD's warning that the Devil will get a person who doesn't mind the company he's seen with. D slightly miffed, urges YM to leave. Having won his point, YM decides to linger for a kiss. She suggests that he had better kiss his horse goodbye, since her F covets it. As YM finally is ready to leave, a loud call comes from outside. D peeks out: RD himself is there. YM doesn't want to	Exposition. Preparation for appearance of Devil. Characterization of D, YM, RD, and F. Comic tone established.

French Scene	Est. Length	Characters	Digest of Action	Main Dramatic Function
1 (cont.)	10 min.	D (YM)	be caught here by RD, attempts to hide in bedroom, but D discloses that F's asleep there. So YM is trapped. D suddenly thinks of big flour barrel, almost empty, that can hold YM. He jumps in, she puts lid on it just as loud knock comes on door.	Minor crises to stay or not, ending finally in decision as where to hide.
2	4 min.	D RD (YM)	D opens door to admit RD. He enters suspiciously, looking place over carefully. D invites him to sit down after telling him F isn't home. She offers him cider which he partakes of generously. He keeps probing her about when F is expected. She tells him that her F warned that he'd kill any preacher who set foot in the house. RD is unmoved by this, telling her he'd like to make 100 percent clean record of converting everyone in Schoharie before departing. In the midst of rhetorical outburst from RD on Devil, YM issues large groan from barrel. RD associates noise with barrel, but D insists it came from F in other room. Reprimanded by RD for lying, she says she did it only to save RD's life. But RD is not impressed, and goes into bedroom to find F.	Characterization of RD through his attitude towards room and absence of F. Further characterization of D. Attack on main struggle. Preparation for attitude of F towards RD as preacher. Crisis and subsidiary struggle when YM's groans increases tension.
3	5 sec.	D (YM)	D puts hands over ears, anticipating uproar, but there is only silence.	Characterization in RD's further determination to find "infidel." Suspense built up through D's action.

French Scene	Est. Length	Characters	Digest of Action	Main Dramatic Function
4	4 sec.	D RD (YM)	RD re-enters. Angrily he reports that no one is in other room. D in disbelief runs into other room to see for herself.	Resolution of crisis for D.
5	6 sec.	RD (YM)	RD, alone, walks over to barrel, looks at it curiously.	Preparation for later use of barrel and its occupant. Liaison scene to allow RD to be alone.
6	20 sec.	D RD (YM)	D re-enters, admits that her F must have slipped out of house; she advises RD to leave for his own good. RD echoes his determination to wait for F's return. Evening approaches. They are interrupted by sound of horse being halted outside. RD rises to face outside door.	Preparation for fading daylight. Further characterization of RD and also F.
7	10 min.	D RD F (YM)	F enters obviously a bit drunk, fails to notice RD. RD tries to introduce himself but F interrupts him, thinking he is a stranger come to court D. F tells RD to leave before he loses temper. Finally it penetrates who RD is. F immediately calls for gun. D is frightened. RD tells F he's going to convert him right away because he's got to get on to Schenectady. F threatens RD "for the last time." RD produces warrant he has made out for F's arrest on charges of horse-stealing. RD issues choice to F: either he repents or RD will take him to jail where horse-stealing charges will probably have serious consequences. F inspects warrant and	Struggle over F's conversion mounts. Suspense develops as F threatens to kill RD; D offers resistance; RD oblivious to any danger. Introduction of new element in plot: warrant.

French Scene	Est. Length	Characters	Digest of Action	Main Dramatic Function
7 (cont.)	10 min.	D RD F (YM)	then elects to go to jail and death, if necessary. RD is confused over this turn of events; he asks what it would take for F to change his mind. F says it would take a miracle, citing the case of another preacher who told everyone he could raise the Devil. F maintains it isn't possible, but if he could see it done he might be convinced. RD announces with great confidence that he will raise the Devil. F begins to get nervous, loses his aggressiveness, as RD proclaims he'll do the raising right in the room. This elicits groan from barrel, whereupon RD tells the Devil never to darken the door again, and suddenly rams his cane into the bung of barrel. YM lets out a wail of terror and pain, leaps out of barrel covered with flour, and tears for the door, RD whipping him all the while as he pursues him out of house.	*F's response to warrant creates unexpected situation for RD.* *Demonstration of RD's skill at quick-thinking. He invents trick, the decision to act constituting the Major Crisis.* *Major Climax.*
8	10 sec.	F D	As shouting and moaning subsides outside, D laughs knowingly as F stands paralyzed with terror.	*Major Climax, tempered with Comic Tone maintained.*
9	1 min.	F D RD	RD returns and F falls on his knees, confessing his sins. RD extracts promise that F will give up stealing horses and also force D to go to church meetings. She agrees to this gladly, hoping there to see the recently chased "Devil." After a final admonition, RD departs to perform wedding ceremony.	*Resolution of Climax: RD, his trick successful and his goal achieved, is ready to continue his mission.*

French Scene	Est. Length	Characters	Digest of Action	Main Dramatic Function
10	1½ min.	F D	F, recovering from his experience, partakes of some cider and wonders whether getting religion means giving back things which were taken before his conversion. F greatly relieved to know that he won't have to give back YM's horse. D hopes to make it possible for horse to be taken into family by getting RD to perform a double wedding. She exits while F reacts to this news by taking a swig of cider.	*Outcome of struggle. Minor Crisis when F introduces question of conversion "policy."* *Comic punctuation to Resolution.*

Approximate running time: 27–28 minutes

Commentary on some problems and solutions in the structural process

Scene 1 Although relatively long in proportion to the entire script (about one third of it), this scene is kept lively by introduction of new information revealed through physical action and psychological action. Uneasy feeling of YM justifies quick changes of mind whether to leave or stay. Line of action of both young people clear and direct. Note the placement of action in Schoharie County, famous during this period for its large number of horse-thieves. Observe how playwright integrates this topic with drives of F and its usefulness in concluding the entire action of play. Comic note is established to suggest unifying tone of action.

Scene 2 Although not seen by the audience, the presence of the YM in the barrel creates tensions connected with plot and comedy. The longer RD stays, the more the tensions are increased. Physical action is somewhat limited, in contrast to Scene 1, until after RD rises excitedly and orates. Once YM groans, the tensions build sharply.

Scene 3 Observe the attention-getting values of this very brief interlude: its effectiveness is developed through the dramatic action of contrasting physical movement and unexpected silence.

Scene 4 and 5 These scenes and the next add a structural variety to the plot: they provide contrasting qualities in the rapidity with which the dramatic potential changes. Scene 5 allows the audience to see that RD has not been duped about the sounds coming form the barrel.

Scene 6 In viewing this scene, one may observe that the play's structural variety includes also the quantity of characters used. Taking in sequential order, the ten scenes have this division of characters: 2, 3, 2, 3, 2, 3, 4 (for the major crisis scene), 2, 3, and 2. This factor, combined with others, adds to the progressive movement of the action as a whole.

Scene 7 This scene, as with the others, is itself structured as a miniature play with preparation, development, and resolution of a crisis in which one or more of the characters are involved. Note how the playwright plans that rd's objective (namely, to convert f) is not too easily accomplished. This pronounced reversal, at the moment of rd's apparent success, increases the struggle and resultant tension. The entirely plausible attitude of the f is an excellent device for arousing and elevating new attention patterns. Additionally, the playwright has prepared for the "inspiration" of the Devil-raising. Granted the sharpness and inventiveness of rd, this registers as being entirely credible. The suddenness, vigor, and accompanying noises of the climactic action itself are the logical outgrowth of the previous characterization, plotting, and established tone of the action.

Scene 8 The sharply contrasting attitudes of f and d as we see them reacting to the exit of the Devil contribute strongly to the comic excitement of rd's successful deed.

Scene 9 Observe how swiftly and economically rd's successful invention is resolved. The sight of the repentant f on his knees is an expressive moment.

Scene 10 After the pyrotechnics of the climax, this scene gains by the insertion of a new and pensive quality. It is within the f's character to indicate that his repentance is only skin-deep. This provides a minor crisis in the final scene. The d's decision and resultant action suddenly but appropriately brings the line of action to a satisfying end. The comic tone persist throughout and enhances the unity of the action.

First draft, appraisal, and revision

Putting to use the help that his research and planning can offer him, the apprentice playwright should then rapidly deliver himself of the first draft of the play. Even though he is dissatisfied with certain scenes or characters in it, he should force himself to put down something; the important thing is to start and finish the fullest and most interesting action that he can visualize.

Once finished, the first draft should be put away, ignored as much as possible, while the writer turns to other projects. Only after a fitting interval, when the subjective intensity of writing has diminished, should he return to the draft and view it with as much detachment as possible. With all his powers of objectivity, he needs to evaluate its strengths and weaknesses, as he sees them. If he pretends that the script has been written by someone else, the inexperienced writer may more honestly test his success in handling certain structural and conceptual considerations. One method of encouraging clearer perspective is to apply a series of questions, such as the following appraisal form suggests. (Factors of content, author's purpose, play's length, and the like will influence the value of the individual question; where it is advantageous, the writer should invent more pertinent questions to answer.)

Play appraisal form [16]

A]   Structural considerations
1. *Preparation:* Does it capture attention and arouse interest? Is the necessary information skillfully provided? Are the initial character relationships clear? Is an environment suggested appropriate for the action?
2. *Attack:* Is there a decisive complication leading to the basic struggle? Is it properly timed? Are the opposing forces aligned?
3. *Developing Action:* Is it built into a pattern of continuously interesting complications? Does it have vital minor crises? Are the motives of conflict strong enough to sustain the basic struggle?
4. *Major Crisis:* Is it fully realized in terms of the conflicting forces? Are the consequences of the critical decision clearly shown?
5. *Major Climax:* Is it the peak of emotional intensity resulting from the conflicting forces in the major crisis? Does it merit all the preparation?
6. *Falling Action:* Does it move quickly from the major climax? If there is a minor climax, does it grow out of the major climax? (In some full-length and many one-act plays, this structural consideration may be negligible.
7. *Outcome:* Does it imply a point of view? Does it make a satisfactory commentary on the preceding action? Is it the logical outcome of the basic struggle?

B]   Conceptual considerations

1. *Theme:* Is the total action unified and directed by a central idea? As it is expressed in the play does it seem valid for and acceptable to the intended audience?

2. *Conflict:* Are the human issues in it clearly expressed? Are they important and/or interesting as human issues?

3. *Drive:* Is the desire of the protagonist definite and forceful, likely to win sympathy and/or hold attention? Are the oposing forces strong and interesting enough to be worth the involvement of the protagonist? Do the desires of the opposing forces generate the maximum intensity consistent with the basic conflict of the play?

Because a writer can never be certain how much his prejudices are coloring his judgment, he should seek for his script a reaction from two or three carefully-chosen persons (preferably with directing experience) whose critical views he respects. On the basis of their independent appraisals, the apprentice can then decide which values he wishes to retain and which to eliminate. It is often wise at this stage to make another scenario. Whatever format the scenario takes, the apprentice playwright's aim now is to take a fresh look at the dramatic purpose of each structural unit and of each character introduced. With an overall view of the entire play before him, he can analyze where, for example, scenes duplicate their function, where characters receive too much or too little stress, and where climactic moments fail through improper placement or ineffectual preparation. By analyzing the structural elements in perspective, he will be better able to see what major shifts in emphasis are advisable in his second draft.

This time he should write the draft as quickly as he can, allowing inspiration to account for unplanned ideas, some of which may be superior to those originally plotted. Again an effort should be made to keep the whole play in mind, its parts related as much as possible. Once this revision is completed, the playwright repeats after a reasonable period of detachment from it, his own appraisal of the script. Once more he should seek the counsel of his respected advisers; using their judgment as a touchstone, he can then decide what conscious steps he must take in revising the script. Having completed a second revision, he probably would get most help if he could have, under the guidance of a seasoned theatre director, an oral reading of the entire script, preferably with experienced actors moving about to suggest basic physical relationships. Following this modified performance a healthy discussion of it by actors and a few invited guests could be profitable. From this experience the playwright stands to gain considerable insight into his progress and to strengthen the next draft of the play.

Once he reaches the point where his script is to be staged, the apprentice playwright discovers that rewriting is still imperative. In truth, the playwright's development must remain incomplete until he has gone through at least the experience of rehearsals and performances. From the director of his play, from the actors who perform in it, from the audiences who attend it, the playwright learns that no matter how well he constructs his play, how richly he endows his characters, or how adroitly he turns his dialogue, there is always room for improvement. He knows that there is still wisdom in the threadbare proverb, "plays are not written, they are rewritten."

Raisin' the devil [17]

by Robert Gard

Time: 1825, *late afternoon in summer.*
Place: KING MILLER's *cabin, near Schoharie, New York.*

THE CHARACTERS OF THE PLAY

JENNY MILLER, *the daughter of the horse-thief, King Miller.*
BILL SPARKS, *a young blood of the country-side.*
REN DOW, *a tall, somewhat grizzled, travelling evangelist; he has a slight limp and carries a cane.*
KING MILLER, *a notorious horse-thief; sly and whiskered.*

*   *   *

THE SCENE *is the main room of* KING MILLER's *cabin near Schoharie, New York. The room is sparsely furnished: a couple of rough benches; a center table upon which stands a small jug of cider; a large barrel with bung-hole in its side, in a corner of the room; a couch along a part of the left wall. Doors are right and left, the left door leading outside, the right door to another room of the cabin.*

(BILL SPARKS *is trying to pull away from the clinging hands of* JENNY MILLER, *a pretty girl of twenty.*)

BILL (*in a frightened voice*). Let me go! I'm scared!

JENNY (*after a struggle, pulling him onto the couch*). Sit down, Bill. Here, have some more cider. (*She starts to get the cider-jug from the table.*)

BILL. I can't! I . . . I shouldn't even be here!

JENNY. I'd like to know why not?

BILL (*hesitating*). Well, you're a . . . I mean, your father's a . . . a . . .

JENNY (*without much interest*). Yes, I know. Pa's a hoss thief. (*She pulls* BILL *down beside her.*)

BILL. Yeah, that's it, and I don't think . . .

JENNY (*stroking Bill's shoulder*). What Pa does hasn't got anything to do with you'n me. Come on, Bill, let's you'n me get friendly.

BILL (*as an owl hoots outside*). What's that?

JENNY. Only an old hoot-owl! What you so nervous about, Bill?

BILL. You sure it's all right with your pa if I come here to see you?

JENNY. Well, Pa did say he wouldn't have any young fellers foolin' around here; but shucks, Bill, Pa never meant nothin'.

BILL (*rising and edging away*). Yeah, he never meant nothin', I suppose, when he took that shot at Henry Vrooman. Henry ain't dared to go out alone at night since.

JENNY. Well, if Pa did shoot at you, it'd only be to scare you, Bill.

BILL (*not at all anxious to be scared in that way*). Uh-huh, I see. Well, maybe I'd better go.

JENNY (*rising and catching him*). No, no! Don't go! Why, we're only just startin' to get acquainted. Drink some more cider! You know, Bill, it's mighty nice to have a young feller come 'way out here in the woods to see me. You know, me and Pa don't get out much, daytimes.

BILL. You're sure your pa ain't anywheres around now?

JENNY. I told you he was out in the woods.

BILL (*wiping his face*). I'm kind of nervous. 'Course, I wasn't brought up in the woods to be scared of night-hawks, but . . .

JENNY. You're not afraid of *me* are you, Bill?

BILL. Noooo, not of you.

JENNY. Then let's forget all about bein' afraid. Drink your cider.

BILL (*takes a nervous pull from the jug. After a moment, uncomfortably*). You know Ren Dow, th' preacher?

JENNY. Th' travellin' evangelist? Sure, I saw him once. Him they call th' Peter th' Hermit of America, or some such.

BILL. That's right.

JENNY. And I heard a funny story about him once, too. Seems Ren was drivin' his sled through the snow, and he met a feller comin' t'other way. There wasn't room for 'em both to pass, so Ren he got up in his sled and shook his fist and said, "You git out of my way, or I'll sarve you as I did a feller back aways!" Well, Ren looked so fierce that the other feller wallered right out into the deep snow and back to th' trail again. Then he come up behind Ren, and he said, "Say, Ren, how'd you sarve that other feller?" And Ren, he said, "Well he wouldn't turn out for me, so . . . I turned out for him!" There, ain't that a good story, Bill?

BILL (*nervously*). Uh-huh.

JENNY. And Ren Dow must make a fortune out of that snakeoil of his, even if he won't take a cent for preachin'!

BILL. Yeah. Well, last Sunday Ren come here to Schoharie and started preachin' on that little knoll east of the Court House, and . . .

JENNY (*as* BILL *hesitates*). And what?

BILL. And . . . I . . . I . . . let him convert me!

JENNY. Aw, honest?

BILL. I sure did! Nobody coulda held out against him. It was either come or be damned! There wasn't no hangin' back, 'cause Ren, he said there wasn't but one kind of hell, and that was the hot kind! After that, the whole caboodle just walked to 'im, and give themselves up.

JENNY. They did?

BILL (*just a shade accusingly*). An' you'n your pa's about the only ones ain't been converted here in Schoharie.

JENNY. I wouldn't mind bein' converted, Bill, but th' old man's tougher'n harness leather that ain't had no oil!

BILL. And that's what I mean! You see, it don't look so good, me comin' to see a gal that ain't even been converted.

JENNY. Nobody knows you been comin' to see me, do they?

BILL. Well, you see . . . I went and confessed it to Ren Dow; and he said I'd better mend my ways!

JENNY. Well, some's good and some's bad. Me'n Pa's just naturally bad. Have a little more cider?

BILL. I don't reckon I'd better.

JENNY. Look here, Bill Sparks, you think I'm pretty, don't you?

BILL. Sure, Jenny, I think you're pretty, but . . .

JENNY. An' you ain't mad 'cause Pa's a hoss thief?

BILL. 'Course that don't matter much to *me*, only, supposin' someone was to catch me here? I . . . I ain't afraid of *livin'* folks, but Ren Dow said th' Devil'd get a feller if he didn't take care about the company he was seen with. Said th' Devil was right lively hereabouts, too.

JENNY. Oh, so I ain't good enough for you, ain't I?

BILL. I never said that! Gosh, Jenny, I'm so mixed up. My morals is all twisted outta shape.

JENNY. I guess I don't understand you at all!

BILL. Well, I'm a convert. I reckon I'm a Christian!

JENNY. Oh, so you're a Christian! Well, I don't want you to do anything against your will, so maybe you'd *better* go.

BILL (*rising eagerly*). You see what I mean, Jenny?

JENNY. Well, I wouldn't want to force nobody to stay with me.

BILL (*on his way*). Then I'll just be going. (*He grabs his hat, then hesitates.*)

JENNY. Why don't you go, then?

BILL (*not in such a hurry after all, now that he has won his point*). I was just thinkin' maybe I'd drop in tomorrow to say hello, if you was sure your pa'd be away. (*Hastily.*) 'Course, I couldn't stay.

JENNY. You needn't come at all if it's goin' to hurt your conscience.

BILL. It ain't that I don't want to see you, Jenny; but sometimes when I get to thinkin' about th' Devil, like ol' Ren Dow told about, I get plumb outta my head. Ren said the Devil had a big pitchfork, and a tail of fire, and that he come with snakes and wild beasts, all abreathin' fire!

JENNY. Then I don't blame you for gettin' scared, Bill. All right, you can come ridin' by, and if Pa ain't home I'll give you a signal, like always. And say, Bill . . . (*She lowers her voice.*) . . . if I was you, I'd look close after that fine hoss of yours. Pa's sure took an almighty shine to her.

BILL. To my hoss, Queen?

JENNY. Yeah. I tried to talk Pa out of it, but he said as how he didn't like you anyway, he guessed he'd just try to get your hoss.

BILL. He come right out and said he didn't like me? Whew!

JENNY (*laughing*). You know Pa.

BILL. Say, someday the folks around here are going to get mad, and then they'll do your pa like they done that Mister Van Alstern that murdered Sheriff Huddleston and stole his hoss. . . . They'll hang him! Then maybe he won't be so smart! My hoss! Lawdy! Well, I'd better go see if he's where I tied him. Goodbye, Jenny.

JENNY. Goodbye, Bill.

BILL. You . . . give me a goodbye kiss 'fore I go?

JENNY. You was converted, wasn't you?

BILL. Yeah, but . . . (Looking around to see that nobody is near.) . . . it ain't
a sin to kiss a gal if she wants to be kissed!

JENNY (flirting). Who said I wanted to be kissed?

BILL. Well, nobody. Only the way you been actin', I . . .

JENNY. You can just go and kiss that hoss of yours goodbye, instead!

BILL (starting toward her). Aw . . . (He is brought to a dead halt by a loud
"Hallooooo" from outside.)

JENNY. Somebody's comin'! (She runs to the door and peeps out.)

BILL (transfixed and shaking with fright). Is it your pa?

JENNY. No. It's . . . it's Ren Dow! Ren Dow himself! I can tell by the way he
limps and whips the grass with that long cane of his!

BILL (uttering a loud cry of despair and wishing for the firm rock of salvation).
Ren Dow?

JENNY. And big as life! Where's your hoss, Bill?

BILL. Hid in th' woods! (He looks around desperately for a hiding place.)
Where'll I go? I dasn't let 'im find me! (He runs toward the bedroom
door.) I'll just go in here!

JENNY. No, no! (She gets in front of him.)

BILL. No? Why not? I got to, I tell you. Ren Dow'll put the Devil onto me if
he finds me here.

JENNY. Not so loud. Pa's asleep in this room!

BILL (who has been struggling to get into the bedroom). Huh? Oh m' God!
(He darts back to the center of the room.)

JENNY (running to look out the outside door). Ren's acomin' close, now!

BILL (whispering hoarsely). Help! Help!

JENNY. And I guess you'll be meetin' that Devil right soon, Bill. My gracious,
do you suppose Ren's comin' to try and convert me'n Pa?

BILL (wailing). Lost!

JENNY (hastily turning from the door). Hold on a minute, Bill. If it ain't beneath your dignity, you could get into that flour barrel, yonder. It's big
enough for you, and as it's gettin' dark, like as not Ren'd never see you
at all!

BILL (darting to the barrel). I'd rather stay in it a week than face Ren Dow!

JENNY (running to help). Get in, then. Here, I'll hold the top off for you.
May be a little flour still in it, but that won't hurt you any!

(BILL is no sooner stowed away than there is a loud knock at
the door. JENNY smooths her dress and hair and goes to open. REN DOW
enters suspiciously. He is a tall, somewhat grizzled, keen, travelling
evangelist; he is past middle age, has a slight limp, and carries a long,

stout cane; his black clothes are worn with much travel; a paper sticks from his coat pocket; he wears a black hat. He looks the place over with obvious displeasure before he turns to JENNY.)

DOW. You Jenny Miller?

JENNY. Sure am. And I know you, too. You're Mister Ren Dow, aren't you?

DOW (*half smiling*). I reckon I be.

JENNY. Well, won't you sit down, Mister Dow?

DOW. Your pa to home?

JENNY. He's away right now. (*She pulls out one of the benches.*) Come sit down.

DOW. Uh. (*He sits stiffly.*) So your pa's away, is he?

JENNY. Yeah. (*After a long, uncomfortable pause.*) You . . . was wantin' him for somethin' special?

DOW. Yep.

JENNY. Somethin' I could do?

DOW. I reckon you could, if you had the conviction! (*He pauses, looking at her fixedly.*) I been conductin' service over in the knoll east of the Schoharie Court House. I ain't seen you'n your pa there. I come to persuade ye.

JENNY. Well, Mister Dow, me'n Pa, we don't go into sassiety much.

DOW. I said nothin' about sassiety! That's somethin' th' Devil worked up. (*Fixing her with his eye.*) Young woman, does your pa fear the Lord?

JENNY (*innocently*). Why, I reckon he does. He never goes out on Sunday without his shotgun!

DOW (*starting back*). Huh? Eh? He don't, eh? (*Taking the whip-hand again.*) Hunts on Sunday, does he?

JENNY (*a bit flustered*). Will you have a glass of cider, Mister Dow? It ain't much hard.

DOW (*smelling the jug*). Harder'n stone. Well, might have one mug of it.

JENNY. We ain't got a mug, Mister Dow. Guess you'll just have to tip the jug.

DOW. All right, all right! (*He takes a long, gurgling pull at the jug.*) Ummmmm. (*He puts the jug back on the table and looks intently at* JENNY.) When's your pa comin' home?

JENNY (*glancing cautiously at the bedroom door*). Well, I dunno. You real sure you want to see 'im?

DOW. I want to have a talk with him.

JENNY. Pa ain't long on religion.

DOW (*dryly*). Huh! As if I didn't know that. What d'ye think I'm here for, girl? I never come on no pleasure call.

JENNY. I was just tellin' you, Pa don't like preachers.

DOW (composed). Like as not.

JENNY. And Pa said if ever a preacher come around here he was goin' to kill 'im!

DOW (interested but not much moved). Oh. (There is a short pause.)

JENNY. Well, ain't you gonna leave?

DOW. I'll just wait a spell for your pa.

JENNY. But I just told you . . .

DOW (exploding). Pshaw! I come here to convert King Miller, and I'm gonna do it! I'm gonna leave Schoharie with a clean record of convertin' every man, woman, child, and livin' beast, and nothin's gonna stop me short of the blazes of hell, which . . . (He fixes JENNY with his eye.) . . . is where you'll end up, young woman, 'less you turn from the trail o' enequity you been followin' an' repent! Girl, do you want to be a Christian?

JENNY (frightened). Ju . . . just what does it mean, Mister Dow?

DOW. It ain't what the Baptists says it is!

JENNY (wide-eyed). No?

DOW. No. An' it ain't what the Presbyterians says it is, neither!

JENNY (hopefully). No?

DOW. No! (Bringing his hand down hard on the table.) It's what the Methodists says it is, and don't let anybody tell you different! (Getting up and raising his eyes on high.) When I was a boy I was a wicked swearer: but in the dead o' night I fought two devils on a sea o' ice; and one was weak and t'other was strong; an' th' weak one vanished in a cloud o' flame; and th' other one . . . (He is interrupted by a loud, terrified groan from BILL in the barrel.) What's that?

JENNY. (standing up). That must be Pa!

DOW. But you said he wasn't here! (He starts toward the corner where the barrel is.) Sounded like it come from over here.

JENNY (getting in front of him). No, no! It was Pa, I tell you!

DOW. But you said he wasn't here!

JENNY. I was only tryin' to save your life. Pa's asleep in there. (She points to the bedroom door.)

DOW. Then I'll wake 'im up! (He starts toward the door.)

JENNY. No! Pa's awful when he wakes up. He might just shoot without thinking.

DOW. Bah! He wouldn't shoot me. (As JENNY hangs onto him.) Young woman, you are tamperin' with the Lord's business.

JENNY. You better go, Mister Dow. Come again tomorrow.

DOW (*looking toward the bedroom door*). Sleepin' in the daytime! (*In disgust.*) Another sin against King Miller!

JENNY. Pa does most of his work at night. I guess he's got to sleep sometime.

      (DOW *breaks away and goes into the bedroom.* JENNY *puts her hands over her ears and stands center, awaiting the uproar.* DOW, *however, returns immediately.*)

DOW (*severely*). Young woman, falsehood is a cardinal sin!

JENNY (*trembling*). You still alive? Pa must not be feelin' well today.

DOW. There is no one in that room.

JENNY. What? (*She runs to look.*)

      (DOW, *left alone, walks to barrel, looks it over curiously, turns as* JENNY *comes back into the room.*)

JENNY. Well, for goodness' sake, Pa ain't there!

DOW (*savagely*). Where is he?

JENNY. You might as well go home, Ren. Pa ain't hardly ever in after sundown.

DOW (*with great firmness, sitting down on a bench*). I have come to see King Miller. I will see him if I have to wait until tomorrow morning. He has sinned. . . . (*He is interrupted by a loud "Whoa girl, whoa Queenie" from outside.* DOW *rises, faces the door.* KING MILLER *enters. He is a whiskered, sly fellow of fifty, slouchily dressed.*)

KING (*lurching in*). Howdy, Jenny!

JENNY (*severely*). Pa, where you been?

KING. Nowheres. What you got to eat, Jenny gal? (*Seeing* DOW.) Who's this here? Some feller acourtin' ye? Haw, haw! Got yerself kind o' an old one, didn't ye, gal?

JENNY (*trying to motion her father to silent*). Pa, I thought you was asleep.

KING. Fooled ye, I did. Crawled out th' winder 'bout two hour ago. (*Approaching* DOW.) Well, feller, I don't allow no courtin' of my gal, so you pack!

DOW. Sir, my name is . . .

JENNY (*quickly*). It's all right, Pa. He just dropped in to tell me how-de-do.

KING (*turning away*). Well, git! And you, Jenny, git me somethin' to eat.

DOW. My name's Lorenzo Dow. You King Miller?

KING. Yeah. Now feller, you'd better git, afore I lose my temper. I kin see you're a stranger, but I reckon a gal's good lookin' as mine'd draw 'em from a long ways off. Now I'm lettin' ye go, and ye'd better . . .

DOW. Miller, I came to see you.

KING. I swored I'd kill th' first feller asked fer her hand!

DOW. I ain't askin' for her hand. I'm askin' for you!

KING. Fer me? Oh, ho! ho! ho! What'd ye want with me?

DOW. I been tryin' to tell you, Miller. I'm Lorenzo Dow, the great preacher.

JENNY. Oh, oh! (*She puts her hands over her ears.*)

KING. Dow? Preacher? (*He recognizes the name.*) Th' travellin' evangelist, b'God! Here in m'house! (*Yelling.*) Jenny, git my gun! (JENNY *clasps her father.*)

JENNY. Hold on, Pa. Don't kill 'im!

KING. Lemme go, Jenny. (*To* DOW.) You snake, snuckin' in here behind my back. I'll fix you!

DOW. King Miller, I'll either convert ye, er kill ye. Will ye come peacefully before the sight of the Lord, or will I have to use more unpleasant means to wash away your sins?

KING. Threatenin' me, are you? Oh, ho! Lemme go, Jenny!

DOW. Listen to the words that'll make you a saved man. (*Clearing his voice.*) King Miller . . .

KING. Quit callin' me King Miller. King's good enough fer my friends and my enemies! It don't sound good when you say 'em tergether thataway.

DOW. Tonight I ride on to Schnectady, and before I go I will convert every man, woman, and child in this town. Miller, you are the last.

KING. I'm givin' ye a last chance, Dow. Get out! Scat! If there's anything I can't stand to have around me, it's one of you preachin' fellers.

DOW. I thought you'd resist, Miller, so I came prepared. (*Takes a paper out of his pocket.*) Before I came here I went to the Court House and had myself sworn in as a deputy sheriff. I had, at the same time, a warrant made out for your arrest on a charge of horse stealing—a charge which, I am surprised to find, ain't ever actually been made out against you before.

KING (*sobered a little*). Me, a thief? Haw, haw! Jenny, please git me my gun. (*But he does not struggle to free himself.*)

DOW. I got plenty of proof. How you been usin' Gebhardt's Caves as a hidin' place . . . what you done up on Schoharie Crick. I may as well tell ye right now that the citizens o' this town was fixin' to come in a body and hang you up to a tree over east of the Court House, but I saved you. I pled with that righteous passel o' men to let me touch you first . . . to see if I couldn't save you, Miller, and to keep my record in Schoharie one hundred percent! I won this great boon for ye, Miller. Now, what is your answer? Will ye repent in th' sight o' th' Lord, or will you go with me to th' jail to face a charge for which you will doubtless be hung? . . . To say nothin' o' roastin' through all eternity on th' coals o' hell!

JENNY. He's got you, Pa!

KING. Lemme see that warrant. (DOW *shows it to him.* MILLER *reads slowly.*) "Fer stealin hosses. To wit: June 1st, from Dave Keppel, one black mare. . . ." *(He stops, puzzling out the next words.)*

DOW *(impatiently).* Signed and attested to!

KING *(continuing).* ". . . signed and attested to by Dave Keppel. From Abraham Keyser, one gelding, an old mare with foal, and two mules . . ." *(Excitedly.)* That there's a lie! They was asses!

DOW. Make your choice.

KING *(plaintively).* Now ain't you kind o' takin' advantage o' me, Parson?

DOW. It's for your own good, Miller. What'll it be?

KING. Well, I . . . I reckon you'll just have to take me along, Parson.

DOW *(starting back).* What?

JENNY. Take it easy, Pa!

KING. I hain't givin' up my belief fer nobody.

DOW. But man, it'll mean th' noose!

KING. Maybe so. But ain't this here America? Ain't a man got a right to think as he sees fit? I reckon you can hang me up, Parson, fer I hain't givin' up my freedom of believin' fer nobody er nothin'. Why, that's what our grandpappies fought fer in the Revolution, waren't it? Tim Murphy, and Boyd, and . . .

JENNY. Told ye he was tough, Parson!

DOW *(very impatiently).* Miller, I got no time to waste. Dark a'most now. What'll it be?

KING. Let's go to the jail, Parson. *(Plaintively.)* Never thought my old friends'd turn agin me like this!

DOW. But man, think! *(He is earnest and confused now that his scheme has broken down.)* You got no right to be an infidel! What'd it take to make you change your mind?

KING *(serenely).* One o' them miracles.

DOW. A miracle?

KING. And that ain't possible. So let's go.

DOW. Hold on. Ain't you never heard o' John Sommers?

KING. He 'nother preacher?

DOW. He was took blind. Stayed blind for twenty year. Then one morning he prayed to th' Lord fer his sight, and it come back to 'im.

KING. Lived over'n Sharon, didn't he? Done some preachin'?

DOW. He did.

KING. Biggest liar I ever knowed! Now, I lived about fifty-five year, Parson, an' all that time I hain't seen a single miracle I knowed of. An' that's where all you fellers' arguin' falls down. Feller I once knowed, preacher too, said he could raise th' Devil any time he wanted; but far's I could see he couldn't raise nothin' but th' roof, and he sure took that off whenever he opened his mouth.

DOW. Raise the Devil, eh?

KING. 'Tain't never been done, and 'twon't never be done—'cause, Mister Ren Dow, there ain't no Devil! If there had a been, he'd a got me long ago. Come on, let's go.

DOW. If I raise the Devil for ye, Miller, would ye freely confess your sins in th' sight o' th' Lord?

KING (smugly). Sure thing.

DOW. Miller, I will raise the Devil for you. Right here in this room.

KING. Huh?

DOW (in a deep, impressive voice). I will raise him!

KING. You're bluffin' me, Parson. (But he looks around nervously.)

DOW. Miller, ain't you feared to meet th' Devil face to face?

KING (laughing feebly). I ain't feared to meet any devil you kin raise.

JENNY (hiding her eyes). Pa, he's goin' to do it!

KING. He's bluffin'. All preachers is bluffers!

DOW (in a hollow, awe-inspiring voice). I . . . will . . . raise . . . him! (Sound of a very loud and terrified groan from the barrel.)

KING. Seems like I heard somethin' . . .

DOW. I will raise the Devil that is lurking in your house, and I will drive him away. And if he ever returns . . . (Another groan from the barrel. DOW turns toward it.)

KING (more and more feebly, and edging toward the door). Oh, ho, ho, ho, ho.

DOW. Stand still, Miller. (MILLER halts as though shot. DOW in a deep voice.) Devil, I command you to arise, and to heed the warning of a man of faith. Do not come nigh this house again, until it is cleansed of sin. I will raise you, Devil, into a ball of flame, and I will flog you as you flee! (DOW slips his cane into the bung of the barrel and gives a sharp thrust and twist.)

   (BILL SPARKS lets out a wail of terror and pain; bursts off the lid of the cask; and covered with flour, rises like a wraith; clears the rim of the barrel with a bound; and rushes toward the door, shouting and moaning at each step. DOW pursues him with surprising quickness, *whipping him plentifully to the door and outside it.* KING *stands with mouth wide open, too frightened to move.* JENNY *holds back laughter with difficulty.* BILL *vanishes; his cries may be heard floating back through the darkness.*)

DOW (*re-entering*). Miller, you have seen the Devil.

KING (*falling on his knees*). By God, you done it, Parson!

DOW (*arranging his coat*). Do ye freely confess your sins in th' sight o' th' Lord?

KING. I does, Parson.

DOW. And ye'll give up stealin' hosses?

KING. Yes, Parson.

DOW. And swearin'?

KING. Yer dam right, Parson.

DOW (*to* JENNY). And you, young lady, you'd better mend your ways; or the Devil'll get you, first thing you know. You go to the meetings.

JENNY. Devil'll get me if I do, Parson. But I'll sure go if Pa'll let me.

DOW. King Miller, will ye let this gal go to th' meetin's?

KING. I'll flog 'er good if she don't, Parson.

DOW (*sighing*). Then my duty's done. I must go now to the Schoharie Court House and perform a marryin'. Then to Schenectady. Then to Albany. I hear that they are cities of the ungodly! I see hard work ahead. Goodbye!

MILLERS. Goodbye, Ren!

(DOW *exits, waving goodbye with his cane.*)

KING (*slowly getting up*). What a preacher! (*He goes cautiously to the barrel; thrusts it with his toe; looks into it, sniffing the air.*) Whew! (*He mops his brow.*) Any o' that hard cider left, Jenny? Ren Dow never said nothin' 'bout hard cider, did he?

JENNY (*giving him the jug*). No, Pa.

KING (*shaken*). It ain't every day a feller sees th' Devil in person!

JENNY (*wistfully*). No it ain't, Pa.

KING (*scratching his head*). Jenny, somethin's botherin' me a little bit.

JENNY. What is it, Pa?

KING. Well, I been wonderin' if repentin' means turnin' back somethin' that was . . . borreyed before a feller gits religion.

JENNY. What's on your mind, Pa?

KING. Well, I was out in th' woods behind th' house, 'long earlier this afternoon, and I run onto that Sparks feller's mare. You know, th' one I

took such a fancy to? It an' me just naturally sort of went away together. Jenny, you reckon I'd ought to take it back?

JENNY. I don't guess I'd bother, Pa. (*She throws on a wrap.*)

KING (*joyfully*). You wouldn't? Where you goin', Jenny, gal?

JENNY. Well, Pa, if I can find Bill Sparks before Ren Dow performs that
marryin' he spoke of . . . well, it'll be a *double* marryin', and that
Queen hoss of Bill's 'll be in the family! Bye, Pa. (JENNY *exits.*)

> (KING *gazes after her a moment, shakes his head, sits down on
> the bench, and takes a long swig of cider.*)

CURTAIN

VIII. In quest of background

WE COME UPON a historical novelist—whose quest resembles that of the historical dramatist's—prowling through a museum in search of background for a book about the early Britons and the Norsemen.[1] With notebook in hand, the novelist stalks around a preserved Viking ship, dug from the grave mound where it covered the body of a sixth-century chief. Looking at its long, slim, fierce lines, she weighs how the steering paddle is attached and estimates how much strength a man would have to possess to keep the boat on course in a heavy wind.

In another museum lie bronze weapons, shields, great curved war horns; the author gains permission to hold some of the artifacts. Picking up a Norseman's sword, she notes its decoration and length and asks herself what the original holder's hand must have been like to grasp and wield it; what was his muscular control? She builds up the man from his sword hand. When she puts a great bronze torque around her neck, she becomes immediately aware of the effect it would have on one to wear a metal collar of such enormous weight digging into one's collar bone; it was bound to create a feeling of immense solidity and respectability, comparable with the effect which a starched shirt collar and tie seems to have on a business executive. The huge bronze bosses worn on the chest or waist by the ladies of the same epoch appear proud, splendid, and uncomfortable—and well calculated to stop any running wild in the woods. A glance at a curiously shaped shield patterned with red enamel raises questions. Who fashioned the shield? How did his mind work? What were his artistic concepts? Had they anything to do with his religious ideas? Looking at these brilliant red shields, the author asks, what moved in the hearts of ancient Britons?

By looking at and touching the artifacts of a past epoch, the novelist begins to catch an image of the men of the time. And, similarly, the writer of historical drama gains like rewards from examining these and other types of historical data.

Sources of historical data

In quest of background the playwright must look to source materials for the substance of his dramatic story. Such materials can be commonly distinguished as *primary* or *secondary*. Primary materials represent the original record of a fact, and include diaries, letters, contemporary newspapers, maps, and other original documents of all kinds. Such original data when selected, arranged, and usually interpreted by one or more persons become secondary material. In this category lie biographies, histories, and sometimes even historical fiction. Customarily, materials of this nature appear in written or printed form; but they also encompass iconographic items—or such auditory records as transcribed speeches and oral testimony. To the scholar primary materials are of key importance; they can also hold value for the playwright doing historical research. Yet the writer will find secondary materials—in which much initial research and interpretation have been done for him— equally helpful and conserving of research time and effort. In surveying a comprehensive array of secondary source materials, the playwright will find that interpretations often differ widely and he must follow his own preference. On the basis of such a survey a judicious selection can be made; and frequently the playwright is lured to the view of one or two historians. Since the writer is less a historian than an artist dramatizing history, he justifiably relies to some extent on the work of the professional scholar. In many cases, however, he will need explore both primary and secondary sources to acquire the background necessary for reconstructing events and personages of the past.

Primary and secondary sources mark no inflexible line between the factual and the interpretative. By nature secondary sources most often reflect interpretative opinions. On the other hand, primary sources frequently stand as both factual and interpretative. A contemporary newspaper or periodical account of an event, for instance, is prone to report the facts from the viewpoint of editorial policy. A Southern-born reporter who sent to *Harper's Weekly* an account of fiery John Brown's trial and hanging in 1859 viewed the details of the event through the perspective of an anti-abolitionist mind.[2] Similarly, a personal diary sometimes discloses more of an idealization of what its writer *thinks* he is than a report hewing closely to objectivity. Nor should a writer forget that before the days of radio and the tape recorder, a speech was rarely recorded with full accuracy or detail. Patrick Henry's "Liberty or Death" oration of 1775 was not reported in its entirety until published in an 1817 biography; and then it was based on the accounts of witnesses.[3] That interpretative material is not solely companion to secondary sources need not be further stressed. When capable of distinguishing between them, the researcher-playwright can find profit in both factual and interpretative materials.

Written materials, both of a primary and secondary nature, loom large as chief repositories of historical data. Playwright Theodore Ward digests

Manuel Gottlieb's work on the history of the land question in Georgia during the Reconstruction for the gist of Our Lan', a drama portraying the struggle of a Negro community to hold onto the land given them after the Civil War.[4] Profitable research sources, biographies provide rich veins of informational ore about a person and his existence. To glean material for his epic-drama The Marble Horseman, Ramsey Yelvington sifts through many sources concerning his protagonist finally to focus on Esmond Wright's biography Washington and the Revolution and Samuel Eliot Morison's monograph essay "The Young Washington" (as well as Henry Steele Commager and Richard B. Morris' collection of contemporary accounts in The Spirit of 'Seventy-Six).[5] Emmet Lavery credits Francis Biddle's Mr. Justice Holmes as the principal source for his portrait of the titular character in his The Magnificent Yankee.[6] Robert E. Sherwood's indebtedness to Carl Sandburg's Abraham Lincoln: The Prairie Years when he was composing Abe Lincoln in Illinois suggests that historians who are also poets (Stephen Vincent Benét shares this estate with Sandburg) offer rare blends of imaginative insight and deep familiarity with and remembrance of the past.[7]

Legal documents, and community and court records constitute sources tapped by writers of historical drama. For the biography-drama More Love, Brother treating a midwestern Shaker settlement in 1864, author Miriam Anne Cramer relies on the diaries, journals and other documents of the Shaker society to form the incidents of her story. In like manner, the First Friends Church of Richmond, Indiana, possesses congregational records which Esther Jones and Naomi Pyle find revealing when dramatizing its history in A Sense of Destiny. The official court record arising from the trial of Confederate prison commandant Henry Wirz furnishes the historical models for Saul Levitt's creation of character and situation in The Andersonville Trial. As standard practice, writers of dramas centering on figures associated with noted trials—Lizzie Borden, Leopold and Loeb, Sacco and Vanzetti, Joan of Arc, Scopes, John Brown, Anne Boleyn, Galileo, to mention a few—all draw from the well of the court records involved.

To the discerning eye personal diaries and letters hold revelatory insights into the human personality. Kermit Hunter discovers a sense of humor in Washington's literate but impersonal "Journal" in which the young Virginian recounts an embassy in 1753 to the Seneca Indians during which he gave the Queen of the Senecas a fine coat and a bottle of rum, "the latter of which she prized more highly." This inspires the playwright to write a humorous scene of such a meeting to open The Golden Crucible.[8] And the poignant diary of a sensitive thirteen-year-old Jewish girl hiding from the Nazis is the basis of Frances Goodrich and Albert Hackett's *The Diary of Anne Frank.*

Finding the letters of the men about whom he was writing the closest realization of a habit "to go to life for material," Sidney Kingsley grants the published letters of Jefferson, Hamilton, and Washington as central sources for his penning of *The Patriots.*[9] William Gibson admits his indebtedness to thirty-eight of Anne Sullivan's letters which he considers "among the most extraordinary ever written" as a major fund of inspiration and information for *The Miracle Worker.*[10] Another writer delights in letters sent to a boyhood friend by the youthful Thomas Jefferson in which he vows to sail a flatboat (named after an unappreciative beloved) to distant lands "to be cured of love," and mournfully relates how the pretty speeches he had prepared for the ears of a desirable Williamsburg belle were, when vented, "a few broken sentences, uttered in great disorder, and interrupted by pauses of uncommon length." [11] Actual phrases edited from the letters partially provide the plot and dialogue of a scene in *Hark Upon the Gale* depicting Jefferson as a despondently romantic young student.

Written testimony marks another mine of material open to the playwright. Impressed by Thomas Jefferson's 1774 document "A Summary View of the Rights of British America," Paul Green finds substantiation for his creation of the fiery patriot in *The Common Glory* as a political leader who strongly advocated a break with Great Britain well before the shooting at Lexington.[12] Considering the Bible as written testimony, Maxwell Anderson is inspirited by those passages in Luke describing the visit of the twelve-year-old Jesus to the temple of the Sanhedrin in Jerusalem to center *Journey to Jerusalem* on a dramatic account of the boy's emerging comprehension of his life-mission.[13]

Written texts of public utterances and play texts stand as primary materials in which we search out clues to the speech and actions of past figures and events. Robert E. Sherwood, for example, distills Lincoln's views on the democratic ideal from several of his speeches; and he joins Lincoln's word to his own to compose the stage figure's public speeches particularly his farewell address at Springfield in the last scene of *Abe Lincoln in Illinois.* Play texts of a specific period often hint at the idiosyncracies of the vernacular —the use of certain words and expressions, the imagery, and the dialects—of the people of the time, and consequently often contribute ideas for the drafting of dramatic language. In order to catch the flavor of the speech of a proud lady at the English court in 1693, the author of *Hark Upon the Gale* peruses William Congreve's *The Way of the World,* an English comedy of manners written in 1700, and garners some valuable impressions of idiom and phrase which aid in constructing dialogue for the pageant-drama's opening scene.

Wishing to capture a vivid picture of the Lincoln-Douglas debate at Freeport, Illinois, in 1858, Ethel Theodora Rockwell leans heavily on contemporary reports of the occasion in the *Chicago Daily Press and Tribune* and in other newspapers of the day.[14] Revealing in its editorial comments a decidedly partisan outlook, the *Chicago Daily Press and Tribune* describes Lincoln as the representative of the common man who from his cradle "felt the blighting influences of the dark and shadow which . . . kept the poor in poverty while it advanced the rich in their possessions," and "a man of rare power and of strong, magnetic influence" whose unceasing good humor "accompanies his close logic and smoothes the way to conviction." [15] In this paper at the same time cartoons depict tall and rugged man-of-the-people Abe in a more favorable light than grotesquely tiny and rotund city-slicker Douglas; Abe the Giant-killer slaying Douglas the Little Giant is an image repeatedly expressed in illustrated caricature bearing several rich impressions for the dramatist's use in *The Freeport Pageant of the Blackhawk Country.* Abstract qualities and political ideas are frequently dramatically expressed and theatrically graphic in political cartoons—iconographic sources worth looking into. Despite their partisan tendencies, contemporary newspapers and periodicals offer sharp perspectives into a historical event and the figures that walk therein.

In summary, community records, court records, church records, legal documents, diaries, personal letters, written testimony, newspapers, periodicals, texts of speeches, play texts, histories, biographies, autobiographies, etc., stand as potential sources of written data for the dramatist.

Auditory records also offer prospective dramatic facts for the researching writer. Certainly the advantage is clear in having spoken transcription of a speech delivered on a specific occasion as well as a written transcription of the same speech. We are more likely to grasp attitudes of the speaker toward his material and the reaction of an audience, giving us a clearer picture of speaker and the effect of his speech. Dore Schary listens to recordings of Franklin D. Roosevelt's speeches when absorbing background for *Sunrise at Campobello.* The editorial staff of the Living Newspaper hears speeches dealing with farmers' problems in the thirties as part of their research for *Triple-A Plowed-Under.* Seeking live rather than recorded sources, Richard Morris investigates the yeasty legend of Maggie Tobin Brown, the mining camp girl who became a Denver millionairess; he interviews several of his subject's contemporaries to mold the title character and the "book" for the musical *The Unsinkable Molly Brown.*[16] To fill in the gaps left by missing official records of the trial of labor hero Joe Hill, Barrie Stavis explores as one avenue of research the testimony of living participants. He finds many "quite old, with hazy memories and fancifully embroidered recollections" but interviews "at great length four old-timers with exceedingly sharp and keen minds." [17] Writers thoroughly pursuing a community's historical background must not neglect to talk with its oldest inhabitants who hold memories of its earlier days. Furthermore, such citizens often can supply local legends and traditions. Recordings of events, transcriptions of speeches, oral testimony from living witnesses represent the major types of auditory records that may be drawn upon to advantage.

Frequently those things we can see or touch provide a keen look into the mirror of the past. Museums, historic homes and buildings, private collections or possessions in room, barn, or attic furnish rich repositories of what can be called the scenery and properties of history: furniture, clothing, utensils, maps, and so on. To this list of iconographic data can be added pictures, photographs, television tapes, and films.

Artifacts supply telling sources for research. Looking at Queen Elizabeth's minute hose and tiny, exquisitely embroidered gown on display at Virginia's Jamestown Festival exhibition,[18] we descry a surprising image of the diminutive stature of this powerful ruler; nearby, a glass case of contemporary armor reveals the men of the time to be not much larger. The earlier example comes to mind of the historical novelist who began to perceive the people of an epoch when viewing and handling their artifacts. In another vein, Barrie Stavis closely studies contemporary maps of Harpers Ferry and adjacent states to determine John Brown's strategy in attacking Harpers Ferry; he puts to work his findings in several scenes in *Banners of Steel*. The authors of *Fiorello!* find newsreels invaluable background material on the energetic Mayor LaGuardia of New York and even insist on their inclusion in the production of the musical biography-drama.

Certainly pictures and photographs bear eloquent testimony. What tales of deprivation and despair are told in Matthew Brady's photographs of Andersonville prison and its survivors. What a vision into the pathos of an event is painted into Benjamin West's "Death of Wolfe" or John Trumbull's depiction of the death of Joseph Warren on Breed's Hill. How clearly we glimpse the Yankee determination and impassiveness lining Roger Sherman's visage caught by the Ralph Earl portrait, or the debonair and cavalier quality in the handsome features of Joshua Reynolds' Burgoyne. Iconographic materials, auditory records, and written materials are fruitful soil for the research digger.

Chapter II emphasized the need to explore fully the life and times of the people who lived within the particular period to be dramatized. Only through such exploration can a writer discern the dramatic in order to breathe life into figures and episodes out of the dust of history. And he must remember that the characters of the past thought and acted within the framework of their own period's conception of values, and of their own materials of life. Therefore, it is a playwright's obligation to investigate thoroughly his sources, to seize—as far as possible—a vibrant image of former figures and happenings in order to create a living experience of the past for an audience. A sponsor, moreover, shares this obligation. As an advisor, he should be able to spur community enthusiasm to unlock family diaries or documents, to ramsack old attics for the historical treasures that may be found there, in short, to discover and make available historical data which may contribute to the efforts of playwright and a production of a historical drama. Additionally, a sponsor should know his community's history to the extent that he can judge the success of a script in creating an essentially truthful "living experience of the past."

The advantage of the local historian

A young playwright is commissioned by a college community to dramatize its past, and is asked to meet with the community historian. First "boning up" on the general material in two brief histories, he jots down some ideas for the drama's shape and content and, then, visits the historian. As he stands at the door, he worriedly realizes how little he really knows about the college's history and about selecting and locating (in one short summer) those sources offering necessary background material. The historian is an elderly little man whose eyes smile as he greets his visitor. After some pleasant introductory conversation, the younger man tells his host the sources he has already used; the latter smiles indulgently and suggests a good many more, telling where they are located and whom to see about acquiring them. The older man then relates in astonishing detail some of the significant patterns, personages, and occurrences in the history considered, taking care to distinguish the factual from the unsubstantiated or possibly apocryphal. He learns the writers' incipient ideas for the drama and makes suggestions. He points out some events and persons with which the audience will be familiar and will expect to see with reasonable accuracy. And he cautions the writer on the lack of substantial record available concerning certain periods. Perceiving the help the historian already has lent him, the writer makes an appointment to meet with him again after doing further research. Generously, the historian makes his time and expert mind available.

Throughout the period of composing the first draft, the playwright finds the historian an immeasurably valuable advisor. While the latter does not realize all the problems the writer faces in dramatizing history, he comes to respect the writer's authority of judgment in this area. Reciprocally, the playwright is grateful to have the historian's comments and advice on the accuracy of the script. A cordial working relationship is established, and the two men end up as a good team.

This illustration reveals several salient advantages of a community historian for the writer. The competent local historian knows the history of the community, what is of major importance in that history, and where to find out about it. He can not only aid the playwright but he can also direct the latter to other knowledgeable persons: librarians delighting in tracking the scent of a needed fact,[19] citizens relaxing in the sunny recall of their youth, or tale-spinners animating the indigenous legends or stories not always found in print. Looking back to *Raisin' the Devil* in the preceding chapter, we recall that author Robert Gard drew the substance of his play from a story originally told about Ren Dow by many tale-spinners, and each spinning varied in the telling. In some communities, a competent "historian" may range in occupation from a librarian or high school teacher to the wife of a hardware store owner. Yet whenever factors of time, place, and personalities make it possible, a friendly working liaison between playwright and local historian proves mutually enriching.

Fortunate is the playwright who knows what source materials to look for, where to look for them, and how to realize their values. Yet before the writer can gain sufficient strength to husband his drama, he needs to be familiar with the features and special problems of historical drama's major forms. He must select an appropriate form in which to pour the molten substance of his dramatic idea and his material. The chapters that follow explain the major forms. An understanding of their respective strengths is as necessary for members of the executive board as for the playwright, the director, and the interpretative corps.

IX. Features of biography-drama

HUMORIST Stephen Leacock has composed a brief "dramatization" of an event out of history, wherein characteristic shortcomings of ineptly conceived biography-drama are delightfully and exaggeratedly emphasized.

Forging the Fifteenth Amendment

A Drama of the Civil War [1]

THE SCENE *is laid in the Council room of the White House. There are present* ABRAHAM LINCOLN, SEWARD, STANTON, ARTEMUS WARD, *and the other members of the cabinet.*

LINCOLN (*speaking very gravely*). Mr. Secretary, what news have you from the Army of the Potomac?

STANTON. Mr. President, the news is bad. General Halleck has been driven across the Rappahannock, General Pope has been driven across the Roanoke, and General Burnside has been driven across the Pamunkey.

LINCOLN (*with quiet humor*). And has anybody been driven across the Chickahominy?

STANTON. Not yet.

LINCOLN. Then it might be worse. Let me tell you a funny story that I heard ten years ago.

SEWARD (*with ill-disguised impatience*). Mr. President, this is no time for telling stories ten years old.

LINCOLN (*wearily*). Perhaps not. In that case, fetch me the Constitution of the United States.

    (*The Constitution is brought and is spread out on the table, in front of them. They bend over it anxiously.*)

LINCOLN (*with deep emotion*). What do you make of it?

STANTON. It seems to me, from this, that all men are free and equal.

SEWARD (*gravely*). And that the power of Congress extends to the regulation of commerce between the States, with foreign states, and with Indian Tribes.

LINCOLN (*thoughtfully*). The price of liberty is eternal vigilance.

(In the printed text of the play there is a note here to the effect that Lincoln did not on this particular occasion use this particular phrase. Indeed it was said by someone else on some other occasion. But it is such a good thing for anyone to say on any occasion, that it is the highest dramatic art to use it.)

LINCOLN *(standing up from the table to his full height and speaking as one who looks into the future).* Gentlemen, I am prepared to sacrifice any part of this Constitution to save the whole of it, or to sacrifice the whole of it to save any part of it, but what I will not do is to sacrifice all of it to save none of it.

(There is a murmur of applause. But at this very moment, a messenger dashes in.)

THE MESSENGER. Mr. President, telegraphic news from the seat of war. General Grant has been pushed over the Chickahominy.

LINCOLN. Pushed backwards or pushed forwards?

THE MESSENGER. Forwards.

LINCOLN *(gravely).* Gentlemen, the Union is safe.

This scene, of course, points up some of the common pitfalls which the inexperienced writer of biography-drama often falls into without so much as a push—backwards or forwards. We intend it here as more than an entertaining prologue to this section, and shall refer to it later in the chapter. Such pitfalls are avoidable if one becomes familiar with the general features and problems of biography-drama as a dramatic form. This familiarity will assist the writer as well as those placed in the position of having to judge merits of a script.

Structural features

Like other forms of historical drama, biography-drama defies rigid definition, and only general observations can be made. Obviously, its structural characteristics are similar to those of any effective play.

While sometimes offered out-of-doors, this kind of drama is commonly staged indoors. This factor affects the features of the form in several ways. First, the normally limited expanse of the indoor stage discourages emphasis on large spectacular effects involving mass groupings or action. Consequently, such effects generally are lacking in most biography-dramas, which are likely to favor a preponderance of interior scenes with a limited number of characters. Second, the restraint on spectacle and mass action allows a drama's cast to be as few as the playwright desires. Third, the more compact spatial relationships between actors and audience and among actors permit greater concentration on character delineation and interaction. Movement and gesture in acting, for instance, can be visually detailed and subtle.[2] Furthermore, the greater freedom for intimacy and spatial proximity of performer to spectator indoors enriches content and expression in the dialogue. Normally common demands of indoor production influence the structural characteristics of the form.

Time span in the action and character focus

For its sustenance biography-drama ordinarily feeds upon concrete events in the life of one or more persons, or on legendary happenings accepted as fact. Essentially it contains a situation focusing on some aspect of an actual person's life, and concentrating on a limited period of time. Usually dramatic action begins near a point of conflict, progressively unfolds, and leads to a dramatically consistent culmination. Developing through a series of continuously related (and, ideally, continuously interesting) incidents, the plot consists of an ordered series of casually related scenes. To be most effective, these scenes are so closely related that none can be deleted or transposed without affecting the plot as a whole. Each scene develops out of preceding scenes and contributes to those which follow. Incidents are connected to produce a central dramatic effect.

The period of history encompassed in the action generally extends no further than the life span of the central characters. Concentration on an intensive period of time allows to be disclosed a unified dramatic story centering on the same characters throughout. Below is a random sampling of the time span covered by nine biography-dramas.

Time Span	Drama	Subject
A day in 1825	Raisin' the Devil by Robert Gard (One-act drama)	Ren Dow, Evangelist
A day in early 1800's	One for the Lord's Day by Fred Carmichael (One-act drama)	Early 19th century New England treatment of poor
2 days in November, 1847	A Mighty Fortress by Jane Erickson	Oregon's Whitman massacre
3 months in 1859	Banners of Steel by Barrie Stavis	John Brown
Several months, 1692	The Crucible by Arthur Miller	Salem witch trials

1856 to 1859	The Prophet	John Brown
	by Wallace Dace	
1521 to 1535	A Man for All Seasons	Sir Thomas More
	by Robert Bolt	
1831 to 1861	Abe Lincoln in Illinois	Abraham Lincoln
	by Robert E. Sherwood	
1902 to 1933	The Magnificent Yankee	Justice Oliver Wendell
	by Emmet Lavery	Holmes

The time span in the dramas above ranges from one day to thirty years —and other variations exist. The one-act biography-drama, usually centering on one incident and a small number of characters, encompasses the most concentrated time span. Along with historical time, playing time varies in such dramas. In full-length biography-dramas the action is compressed within one and a half to two and a half hours of playing time; the one-act versions generally run from about thirty minutes to an hour.

Major structural types

Two major approaches frequently are followed in structuring the plot of a biography-drama. The writer centers his plot either on one specific episode in his protagonist's life or on a sequence of events in that life, possibly spanning many years. In the latter approach, significant incidents are selected to reveal character rather than setting up a suspensive plot. Here, playwright George Middleton advises that "the total script must not become a sausage string of one-actors" but that it "must be culminative, it must blend and also build in interest towards completion or climax." [3] Notice with either approach that unity is sought. Whether a biography-drama be diffuse or compact, a necessary focus must be maintained throughout.

The first of the above methods is illustrated by *A Mighty Fortress* which concentrates on one incident in the life of Narcissa Whitman and her missionary family in mid-nineteenth-century Oregon and deals with circumstances leading up to their massacre at the hands of the Cayuse Indians. Representative of one-act biography-dramas, *Raisin' the Devil* also focuses on a single incident. (see chapter VII.)

The second method is exemplified by Sherwood's Lincoln play. In this drama spanning Lincoln's thirty years in the Prairie State each scene cumulatively propels the story forward, revealing facets and motivations of its central character. Sherwood describes the drama as concerning "the development of the extraordinary character of Abraham Lincoln," which was "a long, uncertain process, affected by influences some of which came from within his own reasoning mind, some from his surrounding circumstances, some from sources which we cannot comprehend." [4] The action traces Lincoln's metamorphosis from an indecisive and unambitious procrastinator desiring to be left alone to an aroused and decisive champion of human rights. To show this "long, uncertain process" of Lincoln's growth, the playwright requires the less compact and more episodic type of structure. The subject matter and the writer's intent are consonant with the structural type employed.

Dealing with approximately the same chronology, Florence Ryerson and Colin Clements adapt a similar method in *Harriet*, a drama of Harriet Beecher Stowe's life from 1836 to 1863. The character of Mrs. Stowe is revealed by concentrating on her private life from the time of her marriage to the aftermath of the publication of *Uncle Tom's Cabin*. The protagonist develops from a wife and mother fearful of entering the fight for abolition to a dedicated woman resolved to complete at personal sacrifice the writing of an anti-slavery book bound to effect turbulent consequences. Through the eight scenes changing in locale from Ohio to Maine to Massachusetts and spanning twenty-seven years, unification is preserved by the constant focus on the central character and her development.

Selection, development, and use of historical facts

The historian, ideally, strives "to tell the truth" about the past. To such ends, however, the historian himself is involved in two acts essentially creative. One is an intense rethinking of the historical fact in order to understand it; the other, a desire to communicate skillfully to others his interpretation of the historical fact. These acts lead the eminent British historian C. V. Wedgwood to assert that "any way of thinking about, or looking at, historical facts . . . must be an exercise of the imaginative and discriminating faculties; History in any intelligible form *is art*." [5] Granting that the historian, from this view, may be an artist, how does his attitude towards art and truth differ from that of the playwright?

Major differences exist in their respective attitudes. The historian must use only what is before him; he cannot invent material, neither can he reject material without first making certain that the historical fact will not add to his knowledge and understanding. The playwright, on the contrary, can reject material which seems to add nothing to what *he wishes* to project, and selection of what he regards as the essentials is an important phase of his creative process. Rather than being servant to the facts, the playwright can invent or discard as his purpose directs, for it is his privilege and indeed function as a creative artist "to manipulate and to intensify the truth about life as he sees it. The bare truth is not enough in itself." [6]

The problem for the playwright is deciding how much accuracy to historical data should be sacrificed to suit his dramatic purposes. Modern audiences, representing an age that has made a fetish of accuracy, understandably resent overselection and oversimplification in the presentation of history. Yet the playwright, "faced by the task of putting a shape on almost limitless complexity," as Christopher Fry avers,[7] has the responsibility of sifting out of a welter of details a story simple enough to be understood by an audience that knows nothing, or next to nothing, about it. Today's playwright must attempt, therefore, to heighten and intensify truth about life without *seeming* to distort the historical record. The degrees to which he does modify the facts about which he writes vary with his purposes and methods in dramatizing the material selected.

Out of the often baffling amount of material confronting him, the biography-dramatist has to select, arrange, and intensify that which will serve the truth of history and his own dramatic purpose. Certainly two common criteria for selecting what facts to dramatize are: 1] their significance in terms of the subject, and 2] their dramatic qualities or potential. And the facts that ensure both demands are the fruitful ones. That Lincoln married an extremely ambitious woman is both significant and dramatic. If a playwright's intent, for example, is to show the emergence of Lincoln from an aimless backwoodsman to a man worthy of the Presidency, he cannot ignore Mary Todd who undoubtedly exerted influence on her husband and his career. Moreover, the dramatic values inherent in their stormy courtship and married life—described by Carl Sandburg as the mating of "a slow-going wilderness bear and a cultivated, tempestuous wildcat" [8]—are unmistakable. In creating his picture of Lincoln, Sherwood does not fail to place Mary Todd prominently in the foreground.

Substantiated by a competent biographer, here are facts about Mary Todd that the playwright encounters.[9] She was an intelligent, cultured, ambitious woman who, against the opposition of her family, chose to marry a rough-hewn backwoods lawyer. The lady-shy Lincoln was inevitably drawn to the proudly reared Kentucky belle. Although Lincoln proposed to her and was accepted, he broke the engagement shortly before his wedding day and left Springfield for a brief time. When he returned, he was ultimately reconciled with Mary, and they were married. Lincoln's indifference to social niceties, his untidiness, and his occasional lack of dignity often annoyed his well-bred but hot-tempered wife. And yet she often asserted his abilities and told friends, "He is to be President of the United States some day." While Lincoln apparently treated his wife with patience and consideration, he occasionally lost his temper with her.

Sherwood uses these facts as a basis for several scenes in *Abe Lincoln in Illinois*. Several incidents are in effect seized almost wholly from the historical record—such as Lincoln breaking his engagement, to mention one— not merely because they illumine some aspect of the protagonist, but also because for his purpose the writer cannot invent a better one.

The playwright's decision on "what to use," then, will be first dependent on his motive or purpose. Let us now assume that, as is often the case, a writer wishes primarily to make a comment about his time. He will look into history for those epochs and events, figures and facts, that will best permit a parallel to the problems of his own era enabling him to accentuate a contemporary theme. Written in the midst of World War II when national morale was at low ebb, Sidney Kingsley's *The Patriots*, for example, depicts another period of national crisis when the new nation after the American Revolution wavered perilously between becoming a democracy or a plutocracy. Kingsley wishes to clarify the meaning and demands of the democratic ideal by recalling a challenge that this ideal faced more than one hundred and eighty years ago.[10]

Saul Levitt, author of *The Andersonville Trial*, sees an analogy between the Nüremberg trials of 1946 and the 1865 trial of Captain Henry Wirz, commandant of the infamous Andersonville prison where fourteen thousand Union prisoners died within two years. He perceives that no horror of Dachau or Belsen is unmatched at Andersonville. Consequently, he dramatizes the trial of the Civil War's only war criminal in order to project the timeless question of the extent of man's individual moral responsibility when it is in conflict with authority.[11] The Adolf Eichmann trial occurring after the play is produced further points the contemporaneity of the theme.

Voicing his opinion that most superior playwrights of his acquaintance have been "one-idea men," dramatist Elmer Rice suggests that throughout Robert E. Sherwood's work runs one dominant theme: "The reluctance of the self-centered, sensual man to assume the responsibilities that life thrusts upon him, and his ultimate recognition of the moral obligation to do what must be done." [12] Granting this view, we see why the figure of Lincoln before assuming the Presidency so attracted Sherwood. Furthermore, in 1937 when the drama was in the writing, democratic ideals were in danger of being compromised by appeasement with Hitler; and Sherwood also found in Lincoln a fitting image for the conditions of the pre-World War II era. Authors of such biography-dramas select figures and events from history that resemble the problems and premises of their times.

Other playwrights may wish to recapture an event or figure that contains the germ of an epoch. The story of John Brown's attack on Harpers Ferry, his subsequent trial and its aftermath foreshadow the bloody contest to follow in 1861. In *Banners of Steel*, Barrie Stavis brings into sharp relief the fears and prejudices that cut the pathway to war. Also, he finds in John Brown a protagonist in advance of his time who is punished by his own generation.[13] And in the story of Brown's last exploit, the playwright finds events that follow a recognizable cause and effect progression. The abolitionist wishing to strike a blow against slavery attacks Harpers Ferry; the attack is defeated. He is tried, convicted, and hanged; and his death becomes martyrdom. These incidents are selected and arranged by Stavis into a sequence of chronologically progressive scenes whose historical background is already causally related.

Causal relationships in historical material, however, are not always clear. Here is where the playwright enters the area of unsettled or still debatable fact. The "possibly" and "perhaps" of a dramatist's interpretation of a character proves acceptable where evidence is lacking or conflicting. The playwright often finds he must augment the facts doled out by history in order to explain the motivations of his central character. History does not explain, for instance, how the young, vacillating Lincoln developed into a wise political leader of a nation in crisis. Sherwood, therefore, in order to explain such growth admits that he has perhaps "exaggerated the fact that he [Lincoln] was forever pushed forward by his wife and his friends." [14] In order to dramatize Lincoln's emergence as a decisive man of action, he invents a wholly fictional scene in which the brooding self-doubting young lawyer meets on the prairie a pioneer family whose simple faith and need influence him to take on purpose and direction. At that time, historians indicate, Lincoln felt the free North and the slave South could coexist, and was opposed to stirring up any trouble which could incite war. Yet this invented dramatic motivation exaggerating certain traits to explain his character answers dramatic necessity and effectiveness without distorting the historical portrait.

History, in presenting several views of a man, often confuses perspective or places emphases on idiosyncrasies which blur his basic nature or the significance of his deeds. The dramatist, by the very nature of his art, must synthesize his subject's qualities to make the latter understood by an audience. Therefore, anything not essential to his purpose must be deleted. What if a biography of Thomas Jefferson tells that he was far from an excellent public speaker owing to a troublesome stutter? This fact probably will not clarify Jefferson's role in a drama concerned with our nation's struggle for independence. What if a biographer informs us that John Brown was expert at evaluating the quality of wool when a wool merchant? This attribute lacks meaningfulness when sketching the determined raider of Harpers Ferry. Facts or views which confuse a playwright's essential purpose are best omitted.

Dramatic rearrangement and adaptation of facts

> The playwright's chief stock in trade is feelings, not facts. When he writes of a subject out of history, or out of today's news, he cannot be a scholarly recorder or a good reporter; he is, at best, an interpreter, with a certain facility for translating all that he has heard in a manner sufficiently dramatic to attract a crowd.[15]

These words of Sherwood bear consideration. The closest annotated transcript from the pages of history or biography will fail flatly in the theatre—killed by its own literal fidelity. Effective biography-drama does not attempt to "get all the history in," but seeks to capture the *essence* of that history for the purpose of creating a vivid, meaningful, and truthful dramatic experience for an audience.

Because such drama thrust forth a dramatic story, the facts of personalities and incidents are modified, selected, and arranged. Historic time is condensed, actual events transposed, and dialogue created where suitable words are not available from records. *Banners of Steel* offers an illustration. Playwright Stavis encounters these facts when approaching the record of John Brown and his raid on Harpers Ferry.

> IN 1859 BROWN *proceeded to carry out a plan for facilitating the escape of fugitive slaves and stimulating a slave insurrection. During the summer of that year he rented a Maryland farmhouse near Harpers Ferry. There, with a band of twenty men, he remained in hiding.*
>
> *Needing a housekeeper to cook for the men and to divert suspicion, Brown asked his wife Mary to join him in Maryland. She felt compelled to remain in North Elba, New York, but sent her sixteen-year-old daughter Anne and Martha, the wife of her son Oliver.*
>
> *In his extant letters to his family, Brown showed every indication of being an affectionate husband and father.*

Brown, after an abortive attack on Harpers Ferry, was captured with those of his men remaining alive, was convicted of treason by a Virginia court in Charles Town, and was sentenced to death by hanging.

Mary Brown was permitted to visit him and did so on the day before his execution.[16]

Let us follow a possible process of selection and rearrangement of these facts made for dramatic reasons by Stavis. First, because the actual number of men in Brown's company proved too unwieldy for the stage, he omits several of the raiders from the play and, in several cases, fuses their personalities with those of the remaining men. Second, he thinks it necessary to show the protagonist's affection for his wife and children. He may perceive the dramatic values also of pointing up the family sacrifices made by Brown and some of his men—most of whom were young and many of whom were married. He may have realized the value of depicting the scene between Brown and Mary in jail on the eve of the execution. Since the play's first act begins in October, 1859, in the Maryland farmhouse and the last act ends with Brown's execution in December, 1859, Mary Brown—solely on the basis of actual fact—could only appear near the end of the drama. Yet this is late in the action to introduce such an important character as Mary and her relationship with her husband. While Mary can be mentioned and "talked about" earlier in the play —a letter from her could be read, for example—this choice is far from satisfactory.

For dramatic reasons, accordingly, the author of *Banners of Steel* elects to replace facts with feeling. He rearranges the facts and places Mary Brown, rather than Anne Brown, with her daughter-in-law Martha in the farmhouse where the raiders prepare for their attack on Harpers Ferry. Such a rearrangement serves several dramatic functions. Mary Brown's presence at the farmhouse in the drama's first act introduces that character to the audience, further delineates the protagonist through his relationship with her, and underscores Mary's personal courage in the face of the probable personal sacrifice that confronts her. Moreover, the audience is now sufficiently prepared to accept her only other appearance in the play in the next to last scene of the final act when she visits her condemned husband. Dramaturgical logic would question the introduction of such a significant character at the end of a drama without being brought on earlier in the action. And because the main action deals with the preparation for, and the execution and the result of, the attack on Harpers Ferry, it would be difficult for much of the dialogue to focus exposition on an offstage Mary Brown.

That Martha, the wife of Brown's son Oliver, was present with her husband in the Maryland farmhouse is a historical fact requiring no rearrangement. Through Martha and Oliver, the playwright is able to delineate the poignancy of a young husband and wife faced with the dark uncertainty of Brown's scheme. Not surprisingly, the affectionate relationship between Martha and Oliver, and between Mary and John Brown, crystallizes the courage and sacrifice of all the men and their families.

Mary Brown in 1859 was approximately forty-three years old. Stavis suggests in his stage directions that she be considered forty-eight. The playwright may have felt that adding years to Mrs. Brown's true age would place her in a sharper contrast to young Martha Brown. His purpose apparently is to provide greater clarity of character relationships.

None of these rearrangements distorts the essential spirit of history; rather, each intensifies by means of clarity and compression dramatic qualities in the situation. Nor do they create oversimplification of character or incident.[17]

The human equation

Unless dramatized people and events possess recognizable universal and human qualities, they will fail to live for an audience.[18] Consequently, the playwright searches for such qualities—courage, love, integrity, or whatever they be—in his material. And because these human qualities are most apparent in a man's personal relationships, many biography-dramas effectively focus on a person's private life. In Banners of Steel, for example, we witness Brown's husbandly devotion when his wife visits him in his cell on the eve of his execution. Similarly, Emmet Lavery in The Magnificent Yankee delineates the character of Justice Oliver Wendell Holmes by concentrating on his relationship with his wife and close friends during the last three decades of his life. Central characters of many such dramas embody universal human attributes, human flaws, and inner conflicts which fill out their stage portraits.

The revelation of human weakness as well as strength in pivotal characters aids in making dramatized figures credible and interesting. Lincoln, in Abe Lincoln in Illinois, is both indecisive and firm of purpose, capable of both anger against as well as extreme patience with his wife. Stavis's John Brown in Banners of Steel is stubborn, blind to logical reasoning, short-tempered, but is also rationally motivated, calm, and courageous. In The Prophet, writer Wallace Dace sketches Brown as a vengeful, albeit sincere, abolitionist who cold-bloodedly orders the death of five helpless pro-slavery settlers in Kansas, although later is tortured by his guilt over the deed. Harriet Beecher Stowe's prototype in *Harriet* is delineated initially as being so intimidated by pro-slavery forces that she shrinks from contributing her talents to the abolitionist cause; later, she finds her courage and writes an anti-slavery novel without fear of personal sacrifices involved. Howard Fast's George Washington in *The Crossing* is at times indecisive, hot-tempered, flirtatious, and overly fond of wine, while basically remaining a firm leader in time of crisis. Anne Sullivan in *The Miracle Worker* is at once self-doubting and strong-willed, hot-tempered and controlled as she strives to teach the intractable young Helen Keller. All these dramatized characters experience growth as they overcome weakness to achieve strength. Universally human attributes, often conflicting within the same person, lend credibility and depth through contrast to a stage figure.

A biography-dramatist commonly deals with complex human personalities (with complicated human emotions) which, while they must be simplified for the stage, should not be superficially predictable in terms of characteristics all black or white.[19]

The credibility of historical figures can be shaken if they are made to mouth strong prognostications of the future. For a delightful scene in which a French explorer is mortally pierced by an Indian arrow, Stephen Leacock writes the following stage direction: "... he [the explorer] expires on the spot, having just time before he dies to prophesy in blank verse the future greatness of the United States."[20] Humorously, this directs focus on our point. Historical characters on stage must be reasonably confined to their own epoch exposing no more knowledge of their period or view of the future than would be probable in their lifetime. Few alert theatre-goers will fail to chuckle derisively if George Washington should, for example, possess a vision of the threat of Red China, Benjamin Franklin foresee the hydrogen bomb, or Thomas Jefferson glimpse too accurately "the new frontier" of the late John Fitzgerald Kennedy's administration. A playwright can make a timely comment, or emphasize the irony of the situation as viewed from the perspective of the present, by perceiving similarities or meaningful disparities in past and present history. While the historian may be free to pass judgments on the past in the light of later events, the playwright must reasonably restrict himself to the world of his character. Ideally, dramatized historical figures must be so completely caught up in their own world that, by virtue of their credibility, they are able to catch the present into it too.

Fictional characters

Sometimes the use of fictional characters is necessary to round out and bind together the dramatic action. With such characters, not inhibited by the preconceived ideas of historian or audience, the playwright can then enjoy flexibility. Obviously a fictional character can say and do things that a historical figure frequently cannot without unseeming distortion of the record. Sherwood, for instance, admits that he creates the fictitious character of an old Revolutionary soldier in his Lincoln drama solely to show that his protagonist knew men who fought in the Revolution.[21] English playwright John Drinkwater adds to his cast of characters in *Abraham Lincoln* an imaginary character as a member of Lincoln's cabinet "for the purpose of embodying certain forces that were antagonistic to the President." Pointing out that this device is a dramatic necessity, he further explains, "I chose . . . to invent a character for the purpose rather than to invest any single known personage with sinister qualities about which there might be some dispute."[22] Edith Mirick, depicting the life of Mary Todd Lincoln in *Storm*, seizes upon fictional identities representing Mrs. Lincoln's Washington enemies among senators and society women "for safety's sake, giving more freedom of action with less risk."[23]

Actual facts and personages remain the meat and potatoes of the dramatic ragoût. But the proportional adding of fictional characters can act as a soupçon of burgundy elevating beef stew to boeuf bourgogne. The flavor is enhanced while the meat and potatoes still provide the base.

Dialogue

The most vital factor with which characters from history are enjoined by a playwright is the spoken word. And when serving its chief tasks of forwarding the action or delineating character, effective dialogue possesses rhythm, movement, and is set in a dramatic context discovering a character searching for, adjusting to, and deciding critical issues affecting him (see chapter VII). To cite an illustration, in *Banners of Steel* Barrie Stavis introduces an early scene set in a farmhouse near Harpers Ferry, where under close confinement John Brown and his followers meet to plot the strategy for their attack on the nearby town's Federal arsenal. One of the men, a mulatto named Newby, begins a speech in quiet graphicness:

> I couldn't sleep last night . . . I found myself thinking of my father, that good white man from Scotland, who loved a black slave woman,

my mother, who bought her freedom, married her, had children by her, and who took his black and beautiful wife and the Mulatto children she bore him, and set them free. I am free. . . . And I thought of my wife, a slave, and of my seven children. No. They are not my children, nor is my wife, my wife. They are the property of Jesse Jennings of Warington, Virginia, slavemaster. I thought of many things last night, but of those two, my father and my wife, my thoughts were the deepest. And I thought how there is both good and evil in the world and I asked myself: "Who is responsible for good. God? Then who is responsible for evil? Man?" But man is God's child. God cannot be evil, yet undoubtedly His children are. But how can God not be evil if He has the power to prevent it, yet allows evil to flourish? . . . My soul cries out in the need to believe in God's goodness. Yet I am troubled and perhaps there are others who are troubled also.[24]

This speech reflects the emotional state of the group hiding in the farmhouse awaiting the approach of the critical hour: general tension and edginess increases. The speech particularizes a few essentials of Newby's personality (he is a proud, deep-feeling, compassionate, thoughtful man), his background, and the reason for his being a member of Brown's band. Here is a man aching for reunion with his wife and children; a man searching for an answer to a personal problem, but linking it to the larger question of slavery; a man, with faith shaken, trying to reconcile a belief in God's goodness with the existence of evil; a man seeking support from those whose troubles he would share.

Newby's embroilment with a deeply-wrought search for adjustment gains through a series of contrasted ideas and a laddered colloquy to a climax. He contrasts himself, a mulatto, with the others of the group who are full-blooded Negroes and whites; he contrasts himself, whose wife and children are slaves, with his own father, "a good white man from Scotland"; he contrasts freedom and slavery, good and evil, and God and man. The playwright structures the individual sentences and the speech as a whole to gain a sense of progression. He chooses common words that accumulate imagery in context, and he makes use of compound sentences whose simple free-flowing syntax is abruptly halted by monosyllabic interruptions. He relies on echo words ("wife," "evil," "thought" and "thinking," "child" and "children," etc.) and repeats syntactical arrangements ("who loved," "who bought . . . ," "who took . . . ,"; "And I thought . . . ," (but note the new significance to "And I asked.") A sensitive actor will not fail to respond to the tonal effects and emotional rhythms built into the speech. With word and deed illuminating each other, the actor playing Newby traces an underlying pattern of action that is the character's search for the meaning of his experience.

Catching the flavor of the time

Successful dramatic language in biography-drama commonly avoids what has been disdainfully described by George Bernard Shaw as "modern vernacular seasoned with thees and thous and haths and whithers to make it sound peradventurously archaic." [25] And yet it can suggest the idiom of the time. While the phrasing and flow of the stage speeches must be heightened from everyday conversation, and suitable to the character speaking, it can be understandable to a modern audience while also contributing a flavor reminiscent of the past.

A golden mean between modern speech and the idiom of the historical period is the goal most often sought. The duologue of a common soldier and his commander-in-chief, from Maxwell Anderson's Valley Forge, relies mainly on modern speech, yet the rhythm is still suggestive of an earlier time. General Washington listens to a hungry young soldier named Teague who is unable to understand why he cannot return home for the winter without being branded a deserter. Stressing his need to feed not only himself but a starving family at home, the soldier points to the large number of men who already have left.

TEAGUE: ... More'n that, everybody knows that there's two or three thousand men gone home already for the same reason, and if they was here now they'd be chewing the bark off the second-growth birch like so many cottontails. I don't hold it against you and I don't hold it against anybody because I don't know who in thunder to hold it against, but there's nothing to eat here.

A fellow soldier warns Teague to be quiet but he continues.

It ain't that I'm afraid of a good fight. A good fight's ham and eggs to me. Me and my boy here, we make for home every winter when the grub gets scarce, and we come back every spring when the fighting starts. We're coming back next spring, and every spring, till we chase the goddamn red-coats clear out of Chesapeake Bay, and across the Atlantic Ocean and right up a lamp-post in London town! Fighting's fine, but sitting here and starving down to a hide-and-buttons—I don't savvy it.[26]

The speech illustrates the effectiveness with which modern contemporary speech can be put in the mouths of eighteenth-century figures. Yet we note the use of certain words and phrases that recall an earlier time—"in thunder," "London town," "hide-and-buttons." The adroit handling of a few colloquialisms and vivid images—"chewing the bark of the second-growth birch like so many cottontails," "a good fight's ham and eggs to me,"—suggests a sense of the time and, of course, characterizes the speaker.

After listening to the soldier's preceding speech, Washington tells Teague that his feelings are understandable but will not win the war:

WASHINGTON: . . . But this you should know, sir: if you go home, and we all go home this winter, you won't need to bother about coming back in the spring. There'll be no fighting to come back to.—General Howe will march out of Philadelphia and take over these states of ours. If he knew now how many have deserted, how many are sick, how many unfit for duty on account of the lack of food and clothes and munitions, he'd come out in force and wring our necks one by one, and the neck of our sickly little revolution along with us. So far we've kept him pinned in Philadelphia by sheer bluster and bluff and show of arms. We've raided his supplies and cut off his shipping and captured his food-trains and so bedeviled him generally that he thinks there's still an army here. But every able-bodied man, every man that owns a pair of dungarees for his legs and brogans for his feet, has to look like ten men if this nation's coming through the winter alive.—What are we in this war for? Are we tired of it? Do we want to quit? [27]

Part of the historical details of this speech can be found in a letter of March, 1778, that Washington sent from Valley Forge to Brigadier-General John Cadwalader.

By death and desertion we have lost a good many men since we came to this ground, and have encountered every species of hardship, that cold, wet, and hunger, and want of clothes, were capable of producing; notwithstanding, and contrary to my expectations, we have been able to keep the soldiers from mutiny or dispersion; although, in the single article of provisions, they have encountered enough to have occasioned one or the other of these in most other armies. . . .[28]

Granting that Washington did not speak exactly as he wrote, his written utterances here cannot (and should not) be duplicated in stage speech. Playwright Anderson has kept the truth of Washington's feelings and translated them into the terser phrases and common words of our modern idiom. We observe that it is only a few archaic phrases, the length of sentences and phrases, that remove the writing from that of our own day.

The General's stage speech, like that of Teague's, is basically contemporary to our time. But again certain words and phrases suggest the past, such as, "But this you should know, sir," and "bedeviled." Furthermore, the factual and precise phrases and vocabulary, the relative lack of imagery, the long sentences of Washington's speech distinguish his character from that of the common soldier. Teague's speech is simpler in phrase, rhythm, and vocabulary, and comparatively richer in imagery. Listening to both these speeches without knowing who was speaking, we could easily perceive that two different people were involved. This is a good test of dialogue.

Source materials can tell us something about the speech patterns of other eras but we cannot *hear* the conversation of the past and cannot know *exactly* how people talked. The dialogue of a biography-drama should seem to be plausible, without causing the spectator to protest that "people didn't say that then!" It is dangerous to use slang phrases familiar to modern ears, even if authority exists from history to warrant employing them. Although in 1775 a person may have used the phrase "grin and bear it" or may have referred to a particular young man as a "jerk," this hardly insures that an eighteenth-century character saying the same will not sound anachronistic to today's audience.

Critic John Gassner advises that in writing historical drama, the danger of archaism or derivative literariness grows as the action recedes in time from the present.[29] Gassner believes the problem can be solved automatically by the use of genuine poetry, for the dramatic poet can use contemporary language and speech pattern and still heighten the effect. However desirable, the successful use of blank or metered verse to accomplish the flavor of historical remoteness is rare even when attempted by experienced playwrights. It is ill-advised unless a writer has proven poetic talents.

Exposition

In the earlier speeches taken from *Valley Forge* we are told the pitiful condition of Washington's men, the military situation in 1778, and the desperate condition of a soldier's family during the American Revolution. This abundant expository material is well concealed within the context of a dramatic exchange between a discouraged, hungry soldier anxious to return to his family and his stern but sympathetic commanding officer. There is a critical issue at stake: the soldier, typical of many of his comrades-in-arms, wishes to return home; and Washington must struggle to control the men from deserting and keep his army together to win the war. Moreover, the characters for the most part do not self-consciously state details that the other already knows: Washington does not know the condition of the man's family or the latter's personal reaction to the army's privations; the soldier does not realize the importance of holding the army together throughout the winter. Here is an excellent situation for exposition to be imparted, for the audience to be given (or reminded of, in this case) information necessary for their understanding of the action to follow. This is not to say that exposition can *only* be imparted in such a dramatic context. But it is a principle of biography-drama, as well as any drama, that skillful dialogue must conceal its exposition just as the art of playwriting must conceal its art. Audiences do not like to become aware that they are being fed information.

Biography-drama dialogue must not be overstuffed with factual details. After all, historical drama is not meant to replace the history book. (All the better, of course, if the experience whets the interest of the spectators enough to send them to the history book or biography for fuller details.) In short, we do well to take the warning implicit in critic Wolcott Gibbs' tongue-in-cheek description of unsuccessful biography-drama dialogue:

> History on stage requires a system of running references very unlikely in human speech. For the convenience of an audience, for instance, it is probably necessary for Thomas Jefferson to say, "Just think, it was exactly seven years ago today that I wrote the Declaration of Independence," or for Alexander Hamilton to explain (in 1800) that he would undoubtedly be killed in a duel with Aaron Burr (in 1804). Remarks like these are unquestionably helpful to customers who never survived the third grade, but sound moderately queer when delivered in a theatre.[30]

Needless to say, such drama profits by avoiding "a system of running references very unlikely in human speech."

Use of documents, writings, and recorded utterances

In Leacock's humorous Lincoln sketch, we recall the members of his cabinet baldly quoting phrases from the Constitution. And we smile at Lincoln's line, "The price of liberty is eternal vigilance." (The phrase is not Lincoln's remark but one derived from a speech of anti-slavery reformer Wendell Phillips in 1852: "Eternal Vigilance is the price of liberty"—which, in turn, probably comes from a line from Irish politician John Philpot Curran's speech in 1790 on the right of election, "The condition upon which God hath given liberty to man is eternal vigilance. . . .") [31] While Leacock is merely making a comic point here, the reference leads us to a major observation concerning dialogue in biography-drama.

Great is the temptation to seize avidly upon quoted utterances from the speeches or writings of historical figures; and it is one a playwright can seldom avoid. But a prudent writer, when succumbing, makes sure to edit the material so that it is easily understandable, unobtrusively integrated with the other dialogue, and dramatically interesting to an audience. If the stage character of a Patrick Henry, for example, were to give the entire "Liberty or Death" speech, even the most ardent history buff in the audience would not escape acute pangs of boredom. When such a speech is utilized at all, it must be skillfully arranged to emphasize its most climactic, familiar, and/or forceful portions. Only then may it prove to be dramatically successful. The same is true of documents when quoted in the dialogue.

Returning to Leacock we find him obliquely ridiculing the absurdity of twisting a well-known utterance away from its original meaning. The historical Lincoln is attributed as having remarked: "You can fool some of the people all of the time, and all of the people some of the time, but you can not fool all of the people all of the time." Leacock parodies the phrasing of this into: "Gentlemen, I am prepared to sacrifice any part of this Constitution to save the whole of it, or to sacrifice the whole of it to save any part of it, but what I will not do is to sacrifice all of it to save none of it." This parody also cautions against mixing quoted utterances with the dialogue which the playwright creates for his characters. The literary talent of the writer is too often inferior to that of historical character credited with the utterance or statement. While audiences may delight when recognizing Lincoln's familiar words if the stage figure begins a speech with "Four score and seven years ago, our fathers brought forth . . . ," they will lose their interest swiftly if the next lines sound as though written for a third-rate television drama. Quotations from the writings or utterances of history's figures can have a peculiarly false ring when spoken secondhand, particularly when they are familiar to an audience. It is a challenge, therefore, whenever using quotations, to make them appear a natural part of the character's speeches.[32]

Perhaps by way of summary, a checklist regarding the use of quoted material may be offered. Is the material:

1] dramatically interesting and necessary?
2] easily spoken by an actor?
3] easily understandable to an audience?

4] unobstrusively integrated with the writer's invented dialogue for the character?

5] consistent with the character's nature and attitude?

6] properly edited as to length, clarity, and dramatic purpose?

One of the greatest proofs of the effectiveness of a quotation within the dialogue is that it does not stand out baldly as a quotation.

Development of a one-act biography-drama

Fred Carmichael's one-act drama *One for the Lord's Day* appears at the end of this chapter. By virtue of its length, structural pattern, simple unity, and consistency of tone, the script is suitable for our purpose in illustrating a developmental process. Although the author may through some such process have arrived at those artistic decisions illustrated, no claim is made that he developed his drama in such a way. Our aim here, again, is merely to estimate how certain problems facing the writer may be solved.

One for the Lord's Day is written specifically for presentation in a restored New England meeting house in Old Sturbridge Village. The latter is an outdoor museum in Massachusetts presenting the story of rural agricultural New England in the years 1790 to 1840. It consists of a New England village containing a meeting house, a tavern, a country store, residences, farmhouses with all their barns and outbuildings, gristmill and sawmill, shops housing village craftsmen, and so on. The museum wishes to vivify for visitors the intellectual, religious, and humanitarian aspects of New England life shaping the lives of its people. Therefore, the museum directors decide to dramatize some aspect of New England life by means of a half-hour play presented during the summer in the village meeting house. This building has seats for two hundred and fifty people and a raised platform area adaptable for dramatic presentations. It is estimated that three performances per day will accommodate all summer visitors wishing to see the drama. No admission is charged. The program has been in operation every summer since 1961, each year dramatizing a different aspect of New England life.

Carmichael is commissioned to write a script treating the relief of the poor in a town like Old Sturbridge. A specific set of demands are given him. His drama must have a playing time not exceeding thirty minutes. It must treat a given subject out of New England's past, namely, the poor relief problem, and must do so with accuracy. The production budget allows for only a limited number of actors who receive salaries for their work. And since the drama must be presented in the museum meeting house, its action must be such that it can actually take place there and utilize its natural interior features (see fig. 8). (In the interior of the building, rows of wooden pews face a small pulpit platform which has been extended with temporary additional platforms to allow adequate space for the dramatic action. To the left of the platform, as the audience faces it, is a raised gallery.) Owing to the limitations of setting and playing time, no change of locale or time lapses within the action are permitted.

The playwright, let us assume, in undertaking his assignment first studies the buildings and artifacts of the restored village and absorbs all the "atmosphere" he can. Then he continues his research by investigating his subject and its milieu. He finds that no general history of the poor law in New England exists. The museum historian aids him greatly, however, by providing him with source materials consisting of biographies, diaries, but, in the main, of local histories of various New England towns.[33] The playwright finds Harriet Beecher Stowe's *Poganuc People* (Boston, 1818) a valuable source for learning about the customs and speech patterns of the period. Culling pertinent information from these sources, he gains an emerging picture of New England life from 1790 to 1840. He encounters facts about the poor relief problem like these below:

> THE PROBLEM of state and town poor relief dates back to sixteenth century England. Before then, care of the poor has been the province of the Church. Elizabethan laws required "sturdy beggars"—those not crippled, aged or infirm—to be whipped out of town but also made the parishes responsible for the relief of those born within their own limits. It was this system that colonists brought with them to America. Able-bodied paupers and vagrants were given a warning to leave the community. The system of "warning out" all non-native paupers was similar to the "whipping out" of previous centuries. In the early 1800's many New England towns turned to auctioning off their helpless poor —children, widows, cripples and the aged—to the lowest bidder, a person who charged the town the lowest amount for the pauper's upkeep. Often these auctions took place at the local tavern. The poor were set up before the townspeople and sold off one by one, or family by family. Once auctioned off, the poor were at the mercy of their owners for the term of their indenture. . . .[34]

In the period before legislation was enacted, the disposition of the poor, the playwright learns, was determined by the individual community and executed by a public official appointed to the task. Not only would the community policy be determined at a public assembly in the meeting house, but also the voting members of a township would hear public officials render an account of their doings. Realizing the importance of such an assembly, the playwright familiarizes himself with the nature and function of a New England meeting house. He may have drawn upon such information as the following:

> EVERY EARLY New England community felt the urgent need to assemble together at regular intervals of time for the transaction of public business or the discharge of public trusts. Since the church was the core and the town meeting the center of this self-governed society, it appeared logical to house both civil and religious functions within the same building. The latter, because it was used indifferently as a place for both religious and civil transactions, was called a meeting house. To the early New Englander both functions were equally serious and sacred.[35]

Saturation

Taking stock of the material gleaned from his research, the playwright is ready to begin the *saturation* process. The setting has been determined. The action must occur in Old Sturbridge Village between 1790 and 1840 and must use the meeting house as its background. Since the most dramatically interesting period of the poor relief problem—when the helpless poor are auctioned off—was the early 1800's before poorhouses or state laws were enacted, the question of the approximate historical period resolves itself. In short, an environment is visualized.

Another minimal need to begin the saturation process is at least one character. The society that encloses such a character is known. Because Old Sturbridge is a representative, rather than an actual, village of that period, credible characters must be invented.

The environment being known the playwright visualizes the situation around which his subject can best be dramatized. The requisite meeting house setting suggests one situation: a town meeting in which the citizens debate the merits of saving local funds by auctioning off the poor. Not only does this sound dull, but it also poses several dramatic problems. It will involve too many characters for adequate development in a one-act drama and, therefore, too many actors for the slender budget permitted. Such a scene can easily bog down into a debate never arriving at a dramatic story. There is nothing personal or specific at stake. To be sure, the integrity or conscience of the town or the general fate of its poor can stand in the balance. Yet these are general issues difficult to center on in a short drama. A direct focus on the plight of one person may work better.

As the playwright starts out, a character and a situation leap to mind. A pauper in a New England community is threatened to be sold at auction. This holds specific dramatic interest and sharper focus. Will it solve all the problems of a town meeting setting? The answer is probably "no," so the town meeting is set aside for the moment as the playwright concentrates on the character.

What kind of biography shall the person be given? Is she or he to be a major character who can embody the playwright's humanitarian objection toward the practice of auctioning off the poor? If so, the person probably must be sympathetic and attractive. To best meet this requirement, the character probably can not be a shiftless vagrant. An aged or infirm person, or even a child is a possibility. But the pathetic appeal such characters provoke can swiftly "stack the cards" on one side. All too readily the forces opposing become oversimplified, and the black and white of melodrama engulfs the more genuine "gray" of history. This possibility is therefore cancelled.

What about a man sturdy in mind and body? This selection is soon ruled out. It is unlikely that a mentally and physically healthy male not a vagrant will be a pauper in early nineteenth-century New England. Perhaps a healthy, pretty young woman, married or unmarried who has become penniless, will do? How did she become penniless? If married, she may be a young widow left destitute by the death or desertion of a husband. If unmarried, she may be an orphan left in a state of penury after the death of her parents. Realizing that the one-act form leaves little time for many involvements of plot or character relationships, and that good taste sets some restrictions on obvious sentimental appeals (like that of an orphan, for instance), the writer tentatively prefers to think of the character as a young widow reduced to poverty soon after the sudden death of her husband. One character begins to emerge from the environment.

In order to visualize what other characters will be involved, the playwright first fleshes out the situation toward making it a story. A young widow facing the common disposal of a pauper is a likely protagonist. Her self-respect, happiness, and security are at stake. Confronted with this threat, her objective probably is to find protection from being "sold" at auction and, ultimately, to find security from pauperism. The main line dramatic action will be concerned with whether or not she achieves this goal.

The community policy toward the treatment of the poor can act as an opposing force to the accomplishment of such an objective. Who will represent this opposition? The playwright remembers that townships were free to determine how they would meet their responsibility in caring for the poor; few state laws existed on the matter by the early nineteenth century. The townships' policy toward this duty was carried out by a public official charged with the task. And here is discovered a feasible antagonist.

But the situation does not yet promise a complete action. The playwright examines his outlook toward the material. He considers inhumane the practice of auctioning the poor. He knows that between 1830 and 1860 the practice diminished in New England and gave way to the provision of local poorhouses and, later, state institutions. Consequently, individual communities slowly were to become more humanitarian when dealing with this problem. The playwright wishes his drama to show a glimmer of the humanitarian progress and the changing attitude which eventually occurs. How can this view best be evidenced? The young widow can go to the auction block, or she can do away with herself to save her self-respect. These two alternatives are seriously questioned by the playwright. Both will be difficult to incorporate logically and effectively in action taking place within the meeting house. The first of these may lead audiences to expect on stage an auction of the poor which normally occurred in the local tavern. (And the museum has cautioned the playwright that the history dramatized must be truthfully exact.) The second of these alternatives emerges as being too melodramatic. Either alternative will: 1] render difficult as well as weaken the significant foreshadowing of the community's changing attitude toward the poor—since the widow has been "sacrificed," and 2] require a penetration and an amplification of plot difficult within a thirty-minute drama.

Is there a better alternative? The playwright can have his heroine avoid the auction block, while possibly implying that the local attitude toward poor relief will become more humane. Yes, this choice appears to be the most logical, and also avoids the major difficulties presented by the other suggested courses of action. The problem of how the young widow will be "saved" now arises. A consideration of the other characters to be involved may reveal an answer.

Thus far, the playwright begins to see the following story materialize. A young widow left impoverished by the death of her husband is to be auctioned to the bidder charging the town the smallest amount for her maintenance. A town selectman represents the community position. Terrified by the prospect of being "sold," the protagonist searches for some salvation from this fate. She ultimately finds it. There is an indication that in the future the community will change its attitude toward poor relief.

Yet from this rough sketch arises a substantial problem. In order to achieve sufficient dramatic tension and effectiveness, the threat of the auction must be imminent. If the attractive widow resides in the town, however, friends would have taken steps to help her before the action begins. Furthermore, if the town is callous enough to auction off such an admirable young woman, the latter scarcely will demonstrate a positive hope for a change of attitude toward poor relief. Most logically, the community—through its official representative—will have to become aware of an aspect of its practice hitherto unrealized.

Historical sources tell the playwright that to the puritan New Englander pauperism was akin to crime and that abject poverty was considered evidence of improvidence or shiftlessness. It strikes the playwright that if the widow is not from Sturbridge but fleeing there from another community, several possibilities can be considered: 1] she can still be returned to her home community to face auction, 2] the threat of auction can be immediate, or 3] Sturbridge can encounter for the first time a pauper who defies their prejudiced description, thereby shaking their beliefs. The reason for the protagonist seeking asylum in Sturbridge can be that she has an acquaintance there. Without further hesitation the playwright establishes the young woman as a community outsider.

Thus far in the saturation process, the playwright finds the outline of two characters sketchily conceived—a widow and a town official. Other characters will be needed to furnish exposition and implement the plot. As many as three additional characters probably can be developed. A total cast exceeding five will mean that some characters can only be superficially treated. Seeing the shadows of two characters, the playwright now contemplates what other characters can be involved.

It may be helpful to have someone from outside the community with the perspective to look at its attitudes objectively. Conceivably, such a person can represent the author's humanitarian view toward poor relief. Another New Englander hardly will have an objective attitude. A southerner or westerner? Perhaps, but the playwright is not anxious to get involved with the exposition necessary to establish the character and attitudes of a figure from South or West. Given its specific purpose, the short drama will have little time to spend on anything not relating to New England's problem of the poor. What area outside New England has acquaintance with the latter's poor relief practices? Since the section inherits its poor relief practices from the Elizabethan era, England appears a likely choice. An Englishman is a good candidate. He can come in handy, moreover, for provoking necessary exposition about the English background of poor relief. In order to speak knowledgeably, he can be well educated, a teacher or minister or lawyer, who can register astonishment at such treatment of the poor in a land boasting of liberty and freedom. The American credo of freedom certainly will be familiar to an Englishman. Furthermore, this person—in the interest of tightening character relationships —can be connected either as friend or relative to one of the characters whose point of view differs from his own. The selectman, for example. The Englishman being a visitor, the selectman quite naturally can be showing him the meeting house.

The fact that the action must take place in the meeting house seems to call for another character involved with that place in some capacity and one who can be used to set the scene. Will a minister do well here? This occupation offers a character an excellent excuse to be in the meeting house at almost any time. But by virtue of his education and position in the community, a minister will resemble the town official and the English visitor in social class, educational background, and sophistication. Besides the image of three professional people does not suggest much opportunity for contrast. A distinctly different type of person from the Englishman and the selectman is needed. Will a sexton be a preferable selection? His job will take him freely into the meeting house. A church sexton, being on part time duty only, will customarily also hold a plebian job in the community—a tradesman or an artisan of some kind. Here, then, is an opportunity to create a relatively unsophisticated down-to-earth Yankee with practical views, a representative villager contrasting with the more polished selectman and English visitor. The playwright holds on to this character.

Are any other characters needed? If the widow is to be from another village, it would work well for her to have some friend in Sturbridge. Besides she needs a champion of some sort in whom she can confide. A young man attracted to her? There are already three men to one woman in the cast. And in the early nineteenth century proper widows did not go running to young male friends. What about a relative turning up at the last moment to save the protagonist? That smacks of the improbable "deus ex machina" of Victorian melodrama, and it is not even seriously considered. A female friend? This last choice is seized. Another woman can be useful as a confidante for the widow. And a female will supply needed leavening to the three males onstage. This female friend must be given some reason why she cannot readily take care of the protagonist, otherwise the dramatic problem will not promise any extended struggle for adjustment. If she has a husband or a fiancé, she will have to get his consent. A husband will appear extremely unfeeling if he flatly refuses to let his wife help her friend; therefore, the alternative of a fiancé may work better. The friend naturally will be hesitant to endanger her marital chances by requesting a husband-to-be to provide not only for her but for the widow besides. And the playwright sees the advantage of tightening character relationships by affiancing the widow's friend to a stubborn young selectman holding views unsympathetic toward poor relief. This confidante of the widow is going to be an important character. She will be able to perform valuable functions, character-wise and plot-wise.

Synopsis

An idea of the characters to fill the drama begins to evolve. As a result of further saturation with the characters and the drama's environment, the playwright sketches a preliminary synopsis of the action.

AN IMPOVERISHED young widow, fleeing the threatening danger of being "auctioned off" as a pauper in a nearby town, seeks out asylum with a friend in Sturbridge. There she finds her friend engaged to be married to a selectman responsible for the common practice of disposing of the poor. The official firmly believes in the practice. The selectman and the community duty he represents act as opposing forces to the widow's finding protection. Her struggle provides the main line of action. Having some jurisdication over the widow's situation—both through his official position and his relationship as husband-to-be of her friend— the selectman is forced to a decision either to permit or to forbid the young widow asylum. And he is persuaded to reconsider his official responsibility regarding poor relief. His ultimate decision is influenced by one or more of the following factors: the admirable qualities of the widow and the poignant description of her plight, and the sympathy and support from the widow's friend who is also the selectman's betrothed. The widow's situation is resolved when the selectman allows his fiancée to take care of her friend as he reevaluates his attitude toward pauperism and its amelioration.

This line of development suggests a preliminary way the playwright may structure his germinal idea into dramatic form by concentrating on the emphatically focal characters and their involvement. In the preceding précis, however, the playwright has not dealt with the secondary characters and only has sketched the action. Furthermore, several questions still must be grappled with. How can all the essential exposition concerning the background of the poor relief problem be imparted to the audience? (The museum has asked the playwright specifically to clarify the historical subject for spectators.) What factor chiefly determines the decision of the selectman and, consequently, the resolution of the dramatic action? Since the widow's fate is significantly dependent on the support of her friend, the latter will likely assume a most active role in influencing the final decision. Is there a danger of centrality shifting to the widow's friend?

After mulling over these "unknowns," the playwright expands his synopsis into a scenario. Then subsequent to several drafts, his drama is ready for production. His success can be judged on the basis of the final script which follows, a script effectively tested in performance.

One for the Lord's day [36]
by Fred Carmichael

THE CHARACTERS OF THE PLAY

JONATHAN WHITTLE, a *Selectman of the Town of Sturbridge*
HANNAH BIGELOW, a *young woman from another town*
VIRGIL SMALL, a *storekeeper in town*
JAMES PATON, a *visiting Englishman*
AMY PENNIMAN, *affianced of Jonathan*

Setting: *A Meeting House in Sturbridge, Massachusetts.*

*   *   *

The following is a copy of the Master script as it was originally presented for over two hundred performances at Old Sturbridge Village, Massachusetts. It was presented in the Meeting House and the directions are for that setting. The building has two rear entrances each with an aisle leading down to a platform on which is the pulpit. There are exits left and right from the platform. From the rear of the Meeting House, there is a stairway leading to a balcony which runs the length of the building. For productions in other buildings, the director will have to adapt the movements accordingly.

The costumes are of the early eighteen hundreds. With the exception of JAMES, *the men are in simple, everyday clothes.* JAMES *is dressed for travelling.* HANNAH, *of course, is in mourning; however, her bonnet and collar of her dress are relieved by white.*

(*At the start of the play,* HANNAH *enters from the rear doors. She is slightly dishevelled. She comes slowly half-way down the aisle.*)

JONATHAN. (*from off stage.*) Come along, James, come along.

JAMES. (*off stage.*) Just a moment. (HANNAH *rushes down the aisle, looks for a place to hide, and goes out the small door up left; she closes the door, but it remains slightly ajar.*)

JONATHAN. Step along. Don't spend all your time on the outside. (*He enters.*)

JAMES. (*enters after him.*) Have pity. I am quite out of breath. Ah, tis a most imposing edifice, Jonathan. So clean and simply built.

JONATHAN. We have no time for the artifices of Europe.

JAMES. (*as he surveys the interior.*) And much larger than I would have thought.

JONATHAN. It is only proper that the Meeting House should be the largest building in town. Are not prayers the very backbone of our existence?

JAMES. Assuredly—and are all the Churches in New England made of wood?

JONATHAN. It is the most plentiful material at hand. We use what God has provided and are thankful for it.

JAMES. There is so much for me to learn here.

JONATHAN. How fortunate that you could come at all.

JAMES. But for so short a time. In October, I resume my teaching in England again.

JONATHAN. This is a new post?

JAMES. Yes, in one of our better schools. If it weren't so handsomely endowed, they never could have sent me to survey this new world of yours and report on it.

JONATHAN. Not a new world to us, James. It is the only one we have ever known. Tell me, will Sturbridge occupy much of your Journal?

JAMES. I shall write down everything of interest. For instance, in Winter, do you have any way of keeping this building warm?

JONATHAN. Why, it needs only the heated words of a good parson.

JAMES. Ah, so I've heard.

JONATHAN. Look, James, out here is our Churchyard. Many of our mutual relatives are buried out there.

JAMES. Our mutual relatives! The world grows too large, Jonathan. A great ocean now splits the roots of our family tree in two.

JONATHAN. Our ancestors were already divided, cousin, in their ideas of freedom.

JAMES. There are many types of freedom, Jonathan, but I must admit you seem to enjoy great contentment here in Sturbridge.

JONATHAN. You have been here but a few hours, James. All is not contentment.

JAMES. Is it anywhere?

JONATHAN. In my heart, James, in my heart.

JAMES. Those are the words of a lovesick poet.

JONATHAN. You are looking at a man in Love. (*Laughs.*) Come next month, I am taking Mistress Amy Penniman to wife.

JAMES. My heartiest congratulations.

JONATHAN. She's a good woman. Quite alone since her father died. (*Gestures towards audience.*) We shall be married here, have our home a stone's throw that way and, God willing, send our children to school over there. As a teacher, you will want to see the school. Our school master is a fine man and certainly no pauper—his wages are ten dollars per month.

JAMES. Don't speak to me of paupers. The vessel I travelled on had them swarming in the hold like rats.

JONATHAN. Thanks to mother England deporting them!

JAMES. Be fair, cousin, is it not better to send them here where the opportunities are limitless than to let them rot in jail?

JONATHAN. Opportunity is one thing, but to abandon them on a strange shore to fend for themselves is another. Why, over half the inmates of our almshouses are foreigners, English and Irish.

JAMES. But why? Is there not enough work for everyone in such a large country?

JONATHAN. There is opportunity, yes. A man can live off the land, but those who are not *trained* to do so fall by the way. Even the son of Squire Peasley, born and bred *here*, *perished* when he tried to make his way to Kentucky.

JAMES. I'd heard our paupers were not better off here—jail or an almshouse on both sides of the ocean. They find no sanctuary.

JONATHAN. Our almshouses are barely a sanctuary—most of them are filthy and poorly run! Liquor is used to bribe the inmates to work. The only answer possible is "warning out."

JAMES. "Warning out?" This phrase is new to me.

JONATHAN. If a town warns a person to leave within thirty days, or a year depending on the law, the town is not held responsible for his upkeep. I am a Selectman in Sturbridge and, I tell you, the paupers keep me busy.

JAMES. Are there so many?

JONATHAN. No, but I have to see that they are returned to their settlements.

JAMES. You mean where they were born?

JONATHAN. Just so. In 1767, a law was passed which stated that a man who lived in a town more than a year without being warned out was considered an inhabitant of that town. So you see, I have to step lively if we are not to be overrun with paupers.

JAMES. Is there no poorhouse in Sturbridge?

JONATHAN. There is no need. We have a better and cheaper way of taking care of the poor devils.

JAMES. Let me hear it.

JONATHAN. We auction them off. (JAMES *starts to speak, but* JONATHAN *sees something through the window.)* James, there is Squire Peasley. Come, you must meet him. A fine man and our most respected citizen.

JAMES. This auctioning of the poor . . .

JONATHAN. That problem will keep but the Squire will not. Hurry, James.

JAMES. (*wryly.*) My New England cousin does not want for enthusiasm. (*They are out the back door. Door at side opens and* HANNAH *reappears; she comes to the front of the pulpit, then speaks.)*

HANNAH. Oh, please don't let them do this to me. I have lost so much already, leave me at least my dignity. Please, please. (*Crumples in tears. The rear door opens and* VIRGIL SMALL *enters whistling.* HANNAH *ducks behind the pulpit.* VIRGIL *comes down aisle; carries a broom or gets it from closet later in speech.)*

VIRGIL. (*looks out window half-way down aisle.*) I declare, this here day's so nice I wish I was a young colt again so's I could go runnin' through the fields. But I got responsibilities. Got to check this here Meetin' House afore tomorrow. (*Comes onto platform.*) See it's swept out clean as a apple tree in Feburary. (*Looks at floor.*) Don't look too dirty to me noways. (*Up at ceiling.*) Don't see no cobwebs. And as for . . . (*Looks at audience for the first time.*) Land sakes, where'd you all come from? T'ain't the Sabbath, be it? . . . And you're so diff'rent lookin' . . . Ain't from Boston way, be you? Naw, they don't even dress that peculiar down there . . . You, sir, what kind of rig you call that? Your good woman make it for you? Maybe she needs a pair of specs . . . And you, Mistress, be that all hair or be it a bonnet? . . . Leapin' grasshoppers, I

got it! You're part of the dream I had last night. It was years and years
ago. There weren't no stagecoaches, weren't no Village Green; weren't
even my store over there. Oh—I forgot to introduce myself. I'm Virgil
Small, storekeeper. Well, anyways, I dreamed I was sittin' right here
when it weren't no Meetin' House, it was just a clearin' in the woods
full of Indians. Yes, sir, Indians, and they was holdin' a meetin' here in
. . . what was the name they called it? Wombega—that's Indian for
Meetin' Place. Well, sir, they let me sit down and watch . . . So I must
still be dreamin', but I remember distinctly havin' my breakfast . . .
even had a nice hot piece-a-pie, I was feelin' so good. See? *(Shows stain
on shirt.)* But now I'm on the other end of the stick as it t'were . . .
You've come from the future to watch *me* in *my* Meetin' House . . .
Well, you just sit there and watch but don't make any noise—wouldn't
do for other folks to know our secret, would it? Jumpin' anvils, I can't
stand here talkin' like this. I gotta get to work and sweep up a little.
(Gets broom if he hasn't before.) That's the trouble with people, they
get you to talkin' and the first thing you know, you done plum nothin'.
(Turns back to the audience and squints.) Where'd they go? . . . Folks?
. . . you still there? Nope! *(Starts sweeping.)* Ain't seen anythin' as
strange since Mrs. Perkins' bull thought old Squire Peasley was a cow
and come a-chargin' at him . . . *(Laughs.)* Squire jumped higher than
a sunflower in August. *(As he sweeps behind pulpit* HANNAH *comes
forward and they make a complete circle.)* Is that a loose board? *(Walks
back and she reverses field, too.)* Guess not. *(Turns back and bumps
into her. Gives a squeal.)*

HANNAH. Please, sir, I beg your pardon if I frightened you.

VIRGIL. Thought you was a ghost. What was you doin' behind there?

HANNAH. I'm looking for Mistress Amy Penniman.

VIRGIL. She'd hardly be sittin' behind the pulpit waitin' for you.

HANNAH. Please, sir, don't mock me.

VIRGIL. Who be you? You ain't a guest of Mistress Amy's cause I saw her
this mornin' when she come in for some calico. She didn't mention no
visitors.

HANNAH. She's not expecting me. I've come all the way from Greenville.

VIRGIL. *(to* HANNAH.*)* Greenville? I think you and me better go and see about
this. We don't hold with strangers here.

HANNAH. No, please. I left Amy a note at her house and I came here. I didn't
want to see anyone else.

VIRGIL. What you done? Commit some kind of crime?

HANNAH. No, nothing amiss, I assure you.

VIRGIL. Then why are you so upset?

HANNAH. As children we were the closest of friends. She, of everyone, would not desert me now.

VIRGIL. I better see to this. What you done? Stole something?

HANNAH. Leave me alone, please.

VIRGIL. That's it! You stole somethin'. You're a criminal. Come on. (Starts to take her arm.) The guilty got to pay.

HANNAH. A criminal? That's too kind a word for me. I am a pauper.

VIRGIL. (releases her.) A pauper?

HANNAH. I see you shy away from me. Are you afraid to touch me? Do I have the plague?

VIRGIL. Ma'am. I don't follow the road you're leadin' me down.

HANNAH. That's the way I am treated. If only I were sick it wouldn't be a crime. The town would pay for doctors to take care of me. If I were lame, the town would provide me with a cane, but since I am guilty of this terrible affliction of being poor, they are going to put me up at auction.

VIRGIL. Not someone like you. Why, you're a respectable person. I could tell that from the minute you knocked me into the pulpit.

HANNAH. You mistake, sir. Respectable is not a word we use for paupers.

VIRGIL. I don't hold with this auctionin' off of human bein's noways.

HANNAH. Then you are in the minority.

VIRGIL. No, Ma'am. There's a lot hereabouts that agrees with me. We're havin' a Town Meetin' come Friday week and after that maybe we're goin' to provide decent livin' arrangements for the needy.

HANNAH. Bless you for that.

VIRGIL. 'Course your friend, Mistress Amy, I don't rightly know how she feels. Some folks just want the poor taken care of as cheap as possible. Jonathan Whittle, one of our Selectmen, he kind of heads that group and, since he's Amy's intended . . .

HANNAH. Her intended? Is Amy gettin' married?

VIRGIL. Come next month. Oh he's a good man, Jonathan is. Got a nice bit of property and makes a tidy sum from it, but he's as sour as a green lemon on this idea of Sturbridge havin' a poorhouse.

HANNAH. Perhaps if he were poor, his mind would take a turn.

VIRGIL. (as outside door closes.) Someone's comin'. Get behind there. (Pushes her behind pulpit. Starts sweeping and whistling furiously.)

AMY. (enters and looks around. Comes slowly down the aisle.) Virgil . . .

VIRGIL. Oh, Mistress Amy, you most near sent the spirit flyin' right out of me.

AMY. Has anyone been waiting for me?

VIRGIL. All good things come from the pulpit, Mistress.

HANNAH. (*stands up.*) Amy, thank the Lord, I've found you.

AMY. Hannah . . . oh, Hannah, how good to see you again. (*They embrace.*) I found the hasty note you left. But how come you're here?

VIRGIL. This young woman's in a way of needin' a friend.

AMY. Hannah, what's amiss? Why this visit with no warning? And where is Sam?

HANNAH. Amy, I—I could not bring myself to write you all that has happened.

AMY. Yes, when your last letter came, the snow was still shrouding the hills.

HANNAH. It's my Sam . . . he was taken from me . . . (*Starts to collapse.*)

AMY. Hannah! Virgil, get a chair. (*They guide her to chair.*) Come and rest. Virgil, take yourself next door and fetch some coolin' water.

VIRGIL. Yes, Ma'am. I'll be as quick as a catfish at a worm. (VIRGIL *exits.*)

AMY. Please—Tell me about Sam.

HANNAH. (*to* AMY.) Dear Amy, I didn't know who else to turn to. Sam had worked so hard. He was out there on the land from sun-up till it was so dark you could count the stars. We had the house and land and this year its produce would lighten our heavy debts. Then one day he went out even earlier than usual . . . it was just an ordinary day like any other . . . (*Almost giving way to tears.*)

AMY. There, there, dear friend, tears will only water your sorrow and make it grow.

HANNAH. He didn't come in for supper. When I went in search of him, the moon was already high. I found him lying there on the land he loved, the early green shoots of the grain nodding around him. They had life and he had none.

AMY. Oh, Hannah—Why didn't you let me know?

HANNAH. I tried to earn a living by sewing, by helping my neighbors—anything to repay our debts but I gave way to illness . . . the refuge of the weak. And now, there is nothing left. The fields are empty . . . My neighbors were kind as they always are to those bereaved. But how long can one expect charity to continue? Now I am what is called a public charge. A pauper. This coming Saturday, they are to put me up at auction.

AMY. This can't be.

HANNAH. I am to work in a stranger's home, to face Heaven knows what. Neighbors gave me a ride as far as Sturbridge. I told them a friend invited me. I had to turn to someone.

AMY. You did right. I will think of something.

VIRGIL. (*enters with water.*) Here's the water.

AMY. Thank you, Virgil. Here, sip some of this.

HANNAH. No, I'm all right now.

AMY. Are you sure?

HANNAH. Yes.

AMY. I thank you anyway, Virgil.

VIRGIL. T'weren't a very long trip. (AMY *goes back to* HANNAH. VIRGIL *is left looking at the water.*) Can't let good water go to waste. (*Drinks it.*)

AMY. Hannah, you're not to worry. You're here now and I'll see that you'll be well taken care of, Providence willing.

HANNAH. I don't feel so alone any more. Now that we're together again, but as usual I have nothing.

VIRGIL. Beggin' your pardon, Ma'am, but you still got the house your husband built. They can't take that away from you. That's the law. They have to leave a pauper with a Bible, household utensils, tools, and furniture not to exceed one bedstead and necessary bedding for two persons to a bed.

AMY. He's right. And Jonathan says, too, that you can keep your household furniture up to a total of fifty dollars value.

HANNAH. That's only if you are supported by the town, not auctioned off.

AMY. I'll ask Jonathan's help. Being a Selectman, he knows all about these things.

VIRGIL. Think on it, Mistress Amy. Now, I know'd your Jonathan since we used to go gathering chestnuts together. He's got a will that is just a stubborn as the hardest nut we used to find. He does his duty and the devil take the one who tries to alter his ways.

AMY. But he has a kind heart, Virgil, or I could not love him as I do. He knows the poor are human beings the same as the rich.

VIRGIL. He knows the law is the law.

AMY. But I know Jonathan.

VIRGIL. I known him longer.

HANNAH. Please, don't raise your tempers on my account. I'll go back. I was wrong to leave.

AMY. No, Hannah. Let me speak to Jonathan alone first and everything will be right as tinder.

VIRGIL. Well, you'd better push your friend behind that pulpit agin' 'cause I see Jonathan and his friend sayin' goodbye to Squire Peasley this very moment.

AMY. Quickly, wait back here while I speak to him. *(Starts to push her through small door at back.)*

HANNAH. Oh, Amy—are you sure you're doing the right thing?

AMY. Trust me!

VIRGIL. Too late. They're comin' this way by the gravestones. He's showin' them to his friend.

AMY. *(takes* HANNAH *halfway down the aisle.)* Then wait by the front door. If need be, I'll speak to Jonathan in front of his friend.

VIRGIL. I'd better get back to sweepin'. Mistress Amy, suppose the Squire comes in *that* door. He's likely to, y'know.

AMY. That's right. Hannah, go up to the balcony and hide. No one ever ventures there except on the Sabbath.

HANNAH. But, I—

AMY. Do as I tell you. *(*HANNAH *exits and* AMY *goes back to* VIRGIL.)*

VIRGIL. Better start your feet movin'. They've just about finished readin' every stone in the yard.

AMY. Virgil, you've got to stand by me and help.

VIRGIL. If'n I do, how's about you payin' me the bill you owe?

AMY. Virgil Small, are you trying to take advantage of my position?

VIRGIL. 'Course I'll help. I always be kindly disposed to a gentle woman in distress.

AMY. *(with an idea.)* Oh, she is indeed gentle and what a cook. And her sewing . . .

VIRGIL. Mistress Amy, you get those ideas right out of your head. I'm a bachelor born and bred.

HANNAH. *(appears on balcony.)* Amy—

AMY. That's right, Hannah. Now stay there till I tell you to come down.
    *(*JONATHAN *and* JAMES *voices heard off stage by U. R. door.)*

AMY. Get down, quickly! *(*HANNAH *ducks out of sight.)*

JONATHAN. *(as he and* JAMES *enter.)* . . . Judge Peasley's grandson is a fine, healthy boy. *(Sees the others.* VIRGIL *sweeps energetically.)*

AMY. Good afternoon, Jonathan.

JONATHAN. Amy and Virgil. What goes on here? A small town meeting?

VIRGIL. In a way. Afternoon, Jonathan.

JONATHAN. Amy, I am pleased to present James Paton, my cousin from England. James, this is my wife-to-be, Mistress Amy Penniman.

JAMES. Delighted, Miss Penniman.

AMY. *(curtsying.)* Mr. Paton.

JONATHAN. And this is Virgil Small, our storekeeper.

VIRGIL. Reckon you find Sturbridge a good deal different from your home, eh, Mr. Paton?

JAMES. In some ways, but the peoples of each country are very akin. What a great pity trouble is starting to brew between our two countries again. I fear, Jonathan, that our friendship may be put to the test of conflicting loyalties.

AMY. Must it always be this way? Can you men never sit down and discuss your problems peaceably? Why, if the troubles of the world were left to us women, we could settle them in half an hour over a cup of tea and a quilting frame.

VIRGIL. (laughs.) Oh, I'd like to see that—Generals of the army sitting down and sharing a pot of tea. "Pass me the yella wool, General Washington, and let's have your terms of armistice." (Men all laugh.)

AMY. You can laugh all you want, but we women have more respect for our fellow beings than you men.

JAMES. Jonathan, I think you have a fiery colt here.

JONATHAN. She does have a mind of her own. But Amy, you surprise me. I feel we men have great respect for our fellow beings.

AMY. You couldn't or you would not sell them to one another.

JONATHAN. Amy, this is a strange conversation to be having the first time I show Cousin James through Sturbridge. What must he think?

JAMES. On the contrary, you were starting to tell me about this auctioning of your poor yourself. Please, I am uncommonly curious.

VIRGIL. Me, too, Jonathan. You go and explain it. (Leaning on broom.)

JONATHAN. Don't you have to get along to your store, Virgil?

VIRGIL. No, sir, I'm busy sweeping. (To JAMES.) You see, I'm the sexton of the church, too. I got me more jobs I'm holdin' down.

JONATHAN. You've more business than a man on the town.

JAMES. (amused.) And what does that mean, pray?

AMY. It describes an auctioned pauper—one kept busy at chores by his owner.

JAMES. Ah, there's that word auction again. Come, Jonathan explain.

JONATHAN. It's very simple. When one sinks into a state of pauperism, who is to take care of him? Must we support these poor people from the small savings of the town? Upon my soul, charity is a Christian act, but it can go too far.

VIRGIL. So we auction them off.

JAMES. Just as I feared; we've heard of this practice in England.

JONATHAN. Yes, and the person who bids the lowest amount he will charge the town for taking care of the pauper gets him for a year.

VIRGIL. So the town don't have to pay as much as supportin' him outright.

JONATHAN. It's only a sound business deal, James.

AMY. Dealing in human beings.

JONATHAN. Amy, this is a man's discussion.

AMY. I beg your pardon, sir, I forgot that a woman only bears children and must not concern herself with their welfare.

JONATHAN. Amy!

JAMES. (*stopping the slight skirmish.*) And do people here bid much for these paupers?

JONATHAN. Sometimes they go as high as one dollar a week and even, on occasion, a mite higher.

JAMES. They can use the talents of these people they buy?

JONATHAN. Of course. A good, strong man can fetch a right good price.

AMY. And children, Jonathan, don't forget the children.

JAMES. Youngsters, too?

JONATHAN. But we take special care of them; the boys must be taught to read and write and cypher.

AMY. And when they come of age, they are sent out with but two suits of apparel—one for working days and one for the Lord's Day.

JONATHAN. Of course the town attends to all medical expenses.

VIRGIL. Funerals, too. Plenty get sick and die, y'know.

AMY. (*sarcastic.*) Oh, yes, Mr. Paton, the town pays $10 for the burial of a child over 12 and only $5 for one under 12. (*To* JONATHAN.) Is it cheaper for babies, Jonathan, because it takes less wood for a smaller coffin?

JAMES. Why, Jonathan, you are no more enlightened than we are in England! Is this the freedom your ancestors were so anxious to achieve when they came here?

VIRGIL. Those questions have been asked of him already, Mr. Paton. They only get him all steamed up like a kettle of herbs on a hot stove.

JONATHAN. (*hotly.*) I am not steamed up like a hettle of kerbs . . . kettle of herbs. But I have good reason for my convictions.

VIRGIL. 'Pears you can't talk straight.

JONATHAN. You see, James, if you give the poor an easy life, you're just breeding more poverty.

AMY. But surely a decent almshouse—

JONATHAN. Almshouse . . . almshouse, that's all I hear.

JAMES. But would not a poorhouse be the solution? A place where the poor would be able to live by certain standards and could still carry on a useful life?

VIRGIL. *(chuckling.)* Here we go.

JONATHAN. Many towns already have almshouses, but in short order, they become nothing better than an Inn for the wandering poor. If you take good care to warn paupers out of town, then you're not held responsible.

VIRGIL. You're right there. Why, Mr. Paton, t'weren't very long ago that warning out was quite the thing to do. There was more warnings out flying around than leaves on an October Day. *(Slyly.)* Why even Jonathan, who wasn't actually born in Sturbridge was warned out, if I'm not mistaken. Wasn't you Jonathan?

JONATHAN. Well, I—

VIRGIL. Yes, sir, warned out he was—one of our most respected citizens. Kind of gets out of hand, you see.

JAMES. I best not stay too long or I shall be warned out.

VIRGIL. Jonathan probably's goin' to run home and write it out while you're havin' your supper.

JONATHAN. No such thing.

AMY. There would be no problem if we had a decent almshouse.

JONATHAN. Amy, I will hear no more of it. It is not for you to worry about the poor, they already feel sorry enough for themselves. If they lived by the word of the Lord, if they were God fearing and frugal people, they would not be paupers.

HANNAH. *(from the balcony.)* I am God-fearing, Mr. Whittle. I am frugal. Yet I am branded a pauper.

AMY. *(hushed.)* Hannah . . .

JONATHAN. What are you doing there? Where did you come from?

HANNAH. Not this town indeed, sir. Greenville. Shall I wait here while you warn me out? My settlement will gladly accept me back again to auction me off.

AMY. Jonathan, this is my friend, Mrs. Bigelow, the one I told you so much about. Hannah, allow me to present my affianced, Jonathan Whittle.

HANNAH. *(curtsying.)* Sir.

AMY. And James Paton, his cousin from England.

JAMES. I am honored, Ma'am.

HANNAH. Sir.

JONATHAN. I suggest, Amy, since you placed her up there, that you bring her down at once.

AMY. Yes, Jonathan. Hannah, we will be pleased to have you join us.

HANNAH. I fear you speak only for yourself, Amy.

VIRGIL. For me, too, Ma'am.

JAMES. And I.

JONATHAN. *(backed into a corner.)* Please, Mrs. Bigelow. Do let us meet with you on an equal footing.

HANNAH. As you wish. *(Starts downstairs.)*

AMY. Now, Jonathan, control yourself. I did not know she was coming. But her husband died tragically and she was left alone and helpless.

JONATHAN. Amy, do you realize what you have done?

AMY. She had to turn to someone. *(To JAMES.)* You see, sir, Hannah and I grew up together. That is why she came to me in her moment of need. It was most inopportune with your being here and Jonathan being a Selectman so I concealed her till I could explain.

VIRGIL. And I helped. Don't mind saying I did. Nothing like a lovely lady to stir the better fibres in a man.

JONATHAN. There are many things you do, Amy, which I shall never fully understand. Are we not betrothed? Must you stoop to deceit?

AMY. I do not consider this deceit, Jonathan, only tact.

JAMES. From all I could see, Mrs. Bigelow appears to be far from the dark picture Jonathan has painted of a pauper.

(HANNAH enters.)

AMY. *(goes down aisle to meet her.)* Hannah, please come in. Gentlemen, I ask your kindness in greeting Mrs. Bigelow.

JAMES. Mrs. Bigelow, I take it you find yourself in reduced circumstances and your settlement town does not have an almshouse?

HANNAH. That is true, sir. They prefer to auction off the poor just as Mr. Whittle recommends.

JONATHAN. I do not recommend it. I just think it is the surest course to take.

HANNAH. Have you ever seen an auction, Mr. Paton? Are they held in England?

JAMES. No they are not, and I have never had the occasion to attend one.

HANNAH. Oh, it's a sight to see. It is held at the Tavern on the Saturday night, following the town meeting. The leading citizens are all there, often the worse for liquor. They're boisterous and full of laughter. Spirits make the bidding more heated and the town comes out ahead. First they start describing the paupers to be auctioned. "Here is old Simon, healthy, willing to work. What am I bid?" And the poor person must stand there while his life is thrown back and forth like a ball between children at play. And when he is bought, who knows what kind of home he will find himself in? Perhaps he will have a decent place to bed down at night, more likely not. And for a woman—Mr. Paton, it is infinitely worse for a woman.

AMY. Hannah, please—

HANNAH. (*overriding her.*) Not so long ago, Mr. Paton, I was a respected member of a community and now I have fallen to the point where I am going to be sold—me, a human being, a creation in God's likeness, I am going to be sold. Do they think that pride goes when poverty comes? That human dignity can stand for this abuse? If this is the free world we talk about, the free world our forefathers came here to establish, than I would rather live in a land where slavery is practiced openly and not under the guise of charity.

JONATHAN. (*after a pause.*) Amy, she is your friend, I suggest you take her in your care. Come, James, let us go to my home for tea. Amy, you will join us there as quickly as possible. (*They start down the aisle.*)

AMY. No, Jonathan.

JONATHAN. I beg your pardon.

AMY. The tea will grow cold waiting for me, for I shall be with Hannah. Yours is the tongue of a strong-willed husband, not the smooth one of a man in love.

VIRGIL. Careful, Miss Amy.

AMY. You have vowed you love me, Jonathan, but how deep is your affection for me—would it hurt you to see me degraded as Hannah is?

JONATHAN. This is no time for supposition! (*Starts out again.*)

AMY. Suppose! Suppose I say that you shall not have me for a wife, Jonathan. That you shall have to buy me?

JONATHAN. What's that?

AMY. What if I refuse to wed you here next month? What if I continue to live as I am now? Very soon, the meager money which was left me will be gone and then I, too, will be a pauper. Will you come to the auction sale, Jonathan? Will you sit around the Tavern and drink with the others before the sale starts? And what will you bid for me? One dollar a week? Am I worth that? Is any human being worth a whole dollar a week? When will the asking price be too much and when will you let another buy me? What am I worth, Jonathan, in dollars and pence? What am I worth?

JONATHAN. But, Amy, you are not a pauper. You are a woman of property.

AMY. So was Hannah. And her husband was proud of her. Think how you would feel if I were for sale. (*Pause.*) Jonathan, that is the way Sam Bigelow would feel now if he saw us in this House of Worship.

JONATHAN. But, Amy, my feeling for you . . . I . . .

AMY. Why does a man feel it is weakness to say the word Love?

JONATHAN. If you were ever auctioned off before the townspeople, I . . . I . . . (*Pause.*)

AMY. It is different when it is a person you love, isn't it? Remember all human beings are loved by someone.

JONATHAN. I have only tried to do what is best.

AMY. Oh, Jonathan, if we can give paupers a new suit for the Lord's Day, can we not give them dignity all the days of the year. A man with dignity will not be a pauper for long.

JAMES. I think you may have won your point, Mistress Amy. It was admirably put.

AMY. I must apologize for being so outspoken. Indeed, never before in my life have I acted so rashly. I think, if Jonathan will agree, that we should all retire for tea.

JONATHAN. Yes, yes. By all means.

JAMES. I'm glad to find this young country still follows English customs in finding solace in a good cup of tea. (*They have been going out down aisle.*)

JONATHAN. Mrs. Bigelow, I shall expect Amy to bring you, too.

AMY. Yes, Jonathan.

HANNAH. Thank you, sir.

JONATHAN. After we marry, Amy, remind me never to ask your opinion unless I am prepared for a persuasive argument. (AMY *starts to speak.*) And may it always be as just as this one. (*Exits with* JAMES.)

AMY. (*hugs* HANNAH.) Hannah, I think you will have nothing to fear. You shall come and stay with me until the wedding and then you shall always have a place with us as long as you want it. And we'll find a position for you. With your love for children maybe you can teach the summer session of school? There is need of such a person.

HANNAH. I would love that more than anything.

AMY. Of course, you are still young and pretty and there is many a handsome swain in Sturbridge . . .

VIRGIL. I was thinkin' of suggestin' you accompany me to the applepaging bee over to Widow Persey's this evenin'. I was fixin' to go alone like always, but . . . (*Fades out shyly.*)

HANNAH. I shall think on it. (*Meaning yes.*)

AMY. *(as they start, leaving* VIRGIL *on stage.)* Hannah, sometimes I'm convinced that providence takes a hand in all our lives. I think today has seen the first step toward the end of auctioning the poor here in Sturbridge.

HANNAH. I am sure something guided me to you; and if it has helped, then let us not question how it came about. *(Exit.)*

VIRGIL. *(to audience.)* Well, folks, I didn't think all that was goin' to happen when I first saw you sittin' there. Of course, it ain't a very important part of history when you think of this whole big country. One tree ain't a forest, but it sure makes a shady spot. But I can't stand here talkin'. I got to get over to Jonathan's, for that cup of tea and be sure I got me a companion for that there apple bee. *(Starts to leave.)* When you go back where you come from do a favor for me? Take a bit of this place with you—not only the calm and the peace, but some of the fightin' spirit as well. Well, less you're aimin' to stay here till Amy's and Jonathan's weddin' next month, I guess this is good day. *(He exits.)*

Commentary on the play

Sequence 1 and 2: Hannah, Jonathan, James—The brief and wordless action of Hannah's entrance at the beginning of the play stirs the audience's interest and curiosity. A serious tone is established. However her motivation in hiding from Jonathan and James is not entirely clear.

A chief objective of the play's function when presented at Old Sturbridge Village is to reveal to museum visitors some of the social background of poor relief at this time. Consequently, in the dialogue between Jonathan and James, a substantial amount of exposition is disclosed. Because so much of it relates to historical facts, several transitions from one topic to another are not entirely smooth. And the plot is not essentially advanced. However, the exposition is kept within a dramatic context since it delineates the characters of the two men through their attitudes toward certain facts. Also Jonathan's and James' conflicting viewpoints lend the dialogue a sense of forward motion.

Note that the playwright clearly establishes the Meeting House as the setting for the action.

Sequence 2 and 3: Hannah, Virgil—The reappearance of Hannah provides an active contrast to the preceding scene involving Jonathan and James.

By showing her state of suffering, the playwright readies the audience for the plot to get into motion.

The characterization of Virgil furnishes a refreshing aspect contrasting with the preceding scenes without violating the serious tone first established. Notice the comic qualities that this character provides throughout the drama. Furthermore, the playwright offers to the audience a character with whom they can comfortably participate in the action. Focus apparently is directed on Hannah as a protagonist.

Sequence 4: Hannah, Virgil, Amy—Variety is provided by the introduction of a third speaking character (Amy) within the scene. The scene also prepares the audience for the attack.

The plot and characters have developed considerably since the synopsis. But notice what has happened. The centrality has shifted abruptly from the widow to her friend, who has become the protagonist. In Amy resides the strongest principal force or drive to "do something" about the situation. It is she who forces a critical decision even though she has most to lose by it—her marriage is at stake. And she has strong personal and humanitarian determinations to bring to an end the local practice of auctioning the indigent. The young widow is reduced to a secondary character who is acted upon. In order to seek her goal of protection, she must throw herself on the mercy of her friend who determines to do something about the problem. Thus, we see that in the process of evolving his drama, the playwright's focus may have shifted, deliberately or unintentionally, from the widow to her friend.

Sequence 5 and 6: Virgil, Amy, Jonathan, James, Hannah—The dramatic struggle begins—Amy strives to win asylum for Hannah by changing Jonathan's attitude toward the treatment of the poor. The crisis, which is not clearly defined, occurs here. Having made the decision to try to help Hannah rather than not to help her—thereby not risking her marital prospect, Amy consistently strives to attack her intended's viewpoint. The maximum point of suspense created by the struggle, that is, the major crisis, is never fully reached because Jonathan becomes inarticulate when he should be strongest in meeting the attack of Amy and what she stands for.

The widow's problem has been resolved. The larger problem remains unresolved, but a strong note of hope exists that the auctioning of the poor in Sturbridge will soon end.

Note that the playwright sees that Amy's goal to aid Hannah is not easily attained. Also structural variety is supplied by the increase of the number of characters to five.

At the drama's end, Virgil's speech to the audience completes the dramatic frame created earlier and ends the drama with a personal message appropriate to the production's function in Old Sturbridge.

Summary—The drama is commissioned for the purpose of presenting to museum visitors a social condition in a representative New England village of the early 1800's. Certainly *One for the Lord's Day* clearly exposes the attitudes and practices of relief for the poor during the period. While fictional characters must project the action, they emerge as interesting, credible human beings (historically and dramatically). The action environs a generally logical and interesting dramatic story somewhat weakened by a shift of character focus and the failure of a strong major crisis and major climax to materialize.

In all, we find that this brief drama makes good use of the restrictive demands placed upon it. The history encompassed is accurately depicted. The cast is small. The action occurs within thirty-five minutes playing time; and it takes place entirely within the Meeting House without employing any lapses of time. The architectural features of the building are utilized to good effect. In view of his purpose and the predetermined limitations, the playwright has created a creditable biography-drama despite a few flaws in craftsmanship.

X. Features of pageant-drama

BOOTH TARKINGTON fans recalling *Penrod* hardly will forget the title character's first grim encounter with "The Children's Pageant of the Round Table." It is decreed by his mother that the twelve-year-old Penrod must appear in this pageantry to be presented on the local schoolhouse stage. His specific task is to declaim the sentiments of a character named the Child Sir Lancelot.

> *I hight Sir Lancelot du Lake, the Child,*
> *Gentul-hearted, meek, and mild.*
> *What though I'm but a littul child,*
> *Gentul-heartud, meek, and mild,*
> *I do my share though but . . . a tot,*
> *I pray you knight Sir Lancelot!* [1]

The boy is wary of the assignment. His distrust deepens when he finds himself being costumed for the role by an industrious mother and older sister charged with making him look "as medieval and artistic as possible." Looking in a mirror, he sees himself clad in a pair of feminine silk stockings serving as tights, a shrunken pair of his father's long red underwear cut down to suggest pantaloons, the top of a faded pink silk dress doing duty as a shirt, and an antique gold cape as a mantle. It is obvious to the boy that the original purpose of these articles has not been disguised successfully. Suspicion turns into horror at the thought of appearing in this worse-than-naked condition. On the pageant's opening night, Penrod desperately seeks out a moment of privacy in the janitor's closet, where joyfully he finds and puts on over his stage apparel a pair of blue overalls. His costume thus hidden, and the overalls at least temporarily concealed by his mantle, he enters upon the stage with new confidence. Needless to say, when at the required moment he throws off his cloak, his appearance is revealed to the shock and merriment of the audience, and the downfall of the pageant.

Penrod's suspicion of pageantry is still shared by many, and not without cause. In order to dispel traditional distrust of this much-maligned form, it is the writer's charge to create pageant-drama of solid artistic standards. A knowledgeable grasp of the basic characteristics and problems of this form can quicken the attainment of this objective. Considerations regarding character, dialogue, and dramatic action vary in degree rather than in kind from those of biography-drama. The latter form will furnish a foundation for an understanding of the pageant-drama.

What is pageant-drama?

The term "pageant" connotes many things. In the Middle Ages and in the Renaissance, spectacular festivities were staged to welcome royalty to a city, to honor military heroes home from the war, or to celebrate a coronation or royal wedding. Included in such showings were magnificent parades with richly decorated marchers and floats and lavish palace entertainments. Such imposing exhibitions were termed "pageants," a word also given to the movable wagon stages on which were performed the religious and morality plays of medieval England. Today, the term may be applied to community festivals organized for specific occasions which, though marked by the spectacle of processionals and parades, are free of any dramatic significance. And even beauty contests may be referred to by the word.

Obviously, our concern here is not with events such as described above; nor does a dramatic form (with roots of origin in the Renaissance) called the masque lie within our consideration, except when its elements are combined with those of pageant-drama. Sometimes carelessly dubbed "pageant," the masque tells an allegorical story in which characters, whose actions are symbolic of the spirit rather than of fact or event, are personifications of ideas or ideals, for example, Will, Freedom, Hope, Progress, Education, and so on. Akin to the medieval morality play, the masque's purpose is to present universal truths in such a way as to bring their lessons home. (To give a representative example, the character of WILL aided by FREEDOM and HOPE defeats DRIFT in a struggle for dominance over the American mind.) Its symbolic plot commonly integrates dramatic development, music, and pantomimic dancing. Popular in the first three decades of our century owing to the efforts of playwright Percy MacKaye and others, the masque is seldom presented today. It is not historical drama as such, but merely an adjunctive form of pageantry; it treats the abstract while the pageant-drama deals with the concrete.

Our own use of the term "pageant-drama" refers simply to a type of community drama telling the story of a community's life by recreating significant events in its history, with those events commonly being depicted in a panoramic series of episodes, largely related by theme. It is marked by a lack of conformation to any set pattern of definite characteristics and defies reduction to cut-and-dried rules. Most published pageant-dramas are not helpful as models since they have been tailor-made to suit the demands of a particular area with a particular purpose and place of presentation. Furthermore, the experience and writing skill of their authors varies enormously. Often having scant literary or dramatic merit, many of these scripts for the most part serve as examples of what not to do.

Pageant-drama is treated here as a specific, if flexible, type of dramatic structure. Because this structure is affected by production considerations, three such factors are briefly treated.

Spectacle, music, and dance

Considerations of spectacle, music, and dance described here in relation to pageant-drama are, in the main, applicable to epic-drama.

Spectacle

A pageant-drama may be produced indoors or outdoors. In either case broad projection of its inherent elements will remain a contributing factor to its success or failure. An audience must receive the strongest possible impact from its variety, color, and scale of production. Generally, therefore, all elements of production are on a large and vivid scale. Pageant-drama scenes profit by providing opportunity for mass movement and physical action in terms of colorfully dressed groups. For example, in Ethel Theodora Rockwell's *The Freeport Pageant of the Blackhawk Country* (presented outdoors), a stage direction for one scene describes the active crowds in Freeport, Illinois, on the day of a Lincoln-Douglas debate:

> Across the stage surge the great masses of people who are hastening to the grounds where the debate is to take place. Some are walking, some are riding on horseback, while others come in every conceivable sort of conveyance drawn by oxen, mules, or horses in any number from one to half a dozen. Thronging together are well dressed politicians and prosperous businessmen, handsome well dressed women, farmers and their families, mechanics, children, young men and young women making the day a gala one, delegations from Jo Daviess, Winnebago, Carroll, Edgar and Ogle Counties with bands playing and banners and flags flying, and now and then singing snatches of political or patriotic songs.[2]

This kind of scene is representative of the form's spectacular features which often include music as well as mass action.

Music

Music is vital to the successful pageant-drama; it can convey mood, accompany the dancing and singing, ease the smoothness of swift transitions from scene to scene, and help to sustain a continuing mood or to introduce a variety of moods from different scenes. Whether the music is vocal or instrumental, or both, it can develop cohesive motifs binding together the heterogeneous scenes. When special music can be composed, the results are often the best.

A stage director must make a thorough study of the music to be used in a production in order to know how it can best be interpreted with the drama's text and how it can set the pace and flow necessary for the various episodes through its varying moods and tempos. When original music is composed, he works closely with the composer in order to accomplish the most effective results. And, to aid these artists, the playwright need not hesitate to suggest in his script the purposes he wishes the music to serve, including the moods he wishes it to evoke. A writer, as well as artistic directors concerned, must be aware of the contributions music is capable of making to a script.

Dance

A powerful adjunct to the pageant-drama, when meaningfully and artistically integrated with the text, is solo or group dancing. Here, sufficient variety is desirable. If two scenes, for example, present an uncomfortable similarity, greater contrast may be achieved by means of effectively designed dance sequences. One choreographer of outdoor historical dramas, Foster Fitz-Simmons of the University of North Carolina theatre staff, emphasizes the multi-pronged functions of dance:

> It can be sheer decoration, a pretty interlude in rhythmic movement designed merely to please the eye. On the other hand, it can take over the telling of a story at a particular moment in the drama and do it more vividly and intensely than any amount of words or conventional stage action. It can be employed as a framing device or setting for a particular scene, serve as a transition from one scene to another, or establish and hold a mood. These are fairly broad generalizations, and more often than not they are combined in performance.[3]

A large stage seems to call for large, sweeping movements of the dance. Pageant-drama, particularly when produced outdoors, requires of the director a good knowledge of choreographic techniques, but while the author and director can outline what is needed, only the dance specialist can secure the desired results.

Structural features

The common purpose of a pageant-drama is to excite local pride and civic motivation in a community through the reenactment of its history. Thus two functions are immediately intertwined: to inform or remind a community of its past, and to project a commemorative theme arising from that history as an incentive to future civic endeavor.

Characteristically offering a panoramic view of a community's growth, pageant-drama has been called a form in which the community is the hero and the growth of the community is the plot. Given such a plot and hero, the writer helpfully can think of this type of drama in terms of two major structural units: the *focal plot* and the *connective frame*.

Focal plot and connective frame

The focal plot of pageant-drama is composed of the individual scenes or episodes which taken collectively recreate the life story of a community. These scenes depict events which are usually arranged in chronological progression without necessarily being related by strong cause and effect relationships. Often loosely linked, therefore, such scenes rely heavily on a central idea or theme to furnish a unifying thread weaving all together.

Because of the scope of the historical coverage normally demanded, the time span of such dramas can extend for more than one generation. The College of William and Mary drama *Hark Upon the Gale*, for example, stretches its action from the founding of the college in 1693 to the renewal of its prosperity after the Civil War in 1888—a span of one hundred and ninety-five years. However, the time factor is entirely related to the dictates of the sources, subject matter, and specific aims of individual pageant-dramas as the following sampling of nine dramas suggests.

Time Span	Drama	Subject
1748–1791	George Washington of Young America by *Esther Willard Bates*	*Washington*
1775–1880	Control: A Pageant of Engineering Progress by *George Pierce Baker*	*Development of mechanical engineering*
1850–1951	The Dream and the Deed by *Glenn Hughes*	*Seattle, Washington*

1800–1962	The Kansas Story	State of Kansas
	by Ruth and Val Rosing	
1693–1888	Hark Upon the Gale	College of William
	by Christian Moe	and Mary
1604–1946	Castine	Castine, Maine
	by Marjorie and Sydney Greenbie	
15th Century–	Dolgeville	Dolgeville, New York
1959	by Eleanor Franz	
	(Abbreviated form)	
Pre-Christian	America's Witness for Christ: The Hill	The Book of Mormon
Times–1836	Cumorah Pageant	
	by H. Wayne Driggs and Harold	
	Hansen	
510 B.C–1838	Those Who Bear the Torch	Famous thinkers and
	by Students of Horace Mann School	teachers throughout
		history

It is not surprising that within this generally panoramic pattern, time between scenes leaps over many years. Furthermore, when a broad view of a subject is desired, there is obvious difficulty in directing the action on one central character or even a small group of characters projecting the historical story. Frequently unable to possess the unity allowed by character and a concentrated plot, pageant-drama must lean on the use of a connective frame.

The connective frame consists of one or more devices which explain and help to link the scene of the focal plot by bridging the time gaps between scenes, stressing a binding theme common to all the scenes, and generally unifying the focal plot. These devices may range from prologues, epilogues, and narration to dramatic interludes. Dance, choric chant and song, music, allegorical personifications are elements that may be found in the connective frame. The term represents the structural thread by which the scenes of the focal plot are joined.

Table 1 indicates three major structural patterns (more varieties exist) showing possible relationships between a connective frame and focal plot scenes. Generally, the nature and scope of the subject matter will govern the need for and the use of a framing device. No one example of the three above necessarily is preferable to another. However, the tightest possible relationship between focal plot scenes generally will permit the most effective relationship of those scenes to a connective frame.

Intensive and extensive types of pageant-dramas

Perhaps it will be clarifying to think of pageant-dramas as being either intensive or extensive in scope. Looking at the intensive type first, we find that it concentrates on a limited period of time, often within the lifetime of one or more major characters appearing throughout the focal plot. An example of this type is Roland and Helen Parry's *All Faces West*. In a series of eleven major episodes the authors dramatize the story of a young Mormon family who

1. *Three arrangements of connective frame.*

Pattern A	Pattern B	Pattern C
Frame	PART I	Frame
Scene 1	Frame	Scene 1
Frame	Scene 1	Scene 2
Scene 2	Scene 2	Scene 3
Frame	Scene 3	Scene 4
Scene 3	Frame	Frame
Frame	PART II	
Scene 4	Frame	
Frame	Scene 1	
Scene 5	Scene 2	
	Scene 3	
	Frame	

This pattern suggests large time gaps between scenes. The connective frame is needed and used between or within each scene of the focal plot.

This pattern suggests that each respective Part focuses on a reasonably concentrated period of time, and/or a causally related action. The scenes in each Part can follow each other without an intervening framing device except at beginning and end.

This pattern suggests a short drama that has a sufficiently concentrated focal plot so as not to require a connective frame between its scenes.

with other pioneers of its faith makes the great trek from Nauvoo, Illinois, to the Salt Lake Valley. The span of time encompassed is from 1846 to 1848. Joining each scene is a connective frame, comprised of a singing chorus and narrator, which emphasizes the theme and sets the necessary exposition for the subsequent action. The drama's synopsis of scenes below (similar to Pattern A in Table 1) indicates a limited length of historical time between episodes. (*** indicates connective frame.)

***

Scene 1: Evacuation of Nauvoo, Illinois, early February, 1846.

***

Scene 2: Preparing the Way. Camp at Sugar Creek, Ohio, March, 1846.

***

Scene 3: Beginning the Trek. From Sugar Creek, Ohio to the West, March, 1846.

***

Scene 4: Peace with the Red Man. Near the Council Bluffs, June, 1846.

***

Scene 5: The Mormon Battalion. Camp at Mt. Pisga, near Council Bluffs, June, 1846.

***

Scene 6: Camp on the Plains. Eastern Wyoming, Summer, 1847.

***

Scene 7: The Final Miles. Near Ft. Bridger, Wyoming, early July, 1847.

***

Scene 8: Journey's End. Overlooking Salt Lake Valley, July 24, 1847.

***

Scene 9: Homecoming. Salt Lake Valley, October, 1847.

***

Scene 10: Scourge and Respite. Salt Lake Valley, Spring, 1848.

***

Scene 11: Fulfillment.

In its abbreviated form, the pageant-drama frequently is intensive in pattern. Such brief dramas, which on the average last no longer than thirty to sixty minutes in performance, are written primarily for children. They commonly focus on key events in the life of a historical or Biblical figure or on incidents leading up to an important event. Considerations regarding the full-length form are applicable to this briefer form with two major exceptions: (1) greater selectivity of material is necessary, and (2) when directed at children, story and dialogue must be sufficiently understandable to the age group for which it is written.

Dramas spanning more than one generation which do not focus on any one person or group generally are of the extensive type. *Thunder on the River*, for instance, unfolds the story of Peoria, Illinois, from 1673 to the present day. Transitions in time preceding and following each of the twelve focal plot episodes are facilitated by a narrator and a chorus serving as a connective frame. The synopsis of scenes below reveals the large time gaps between the drama's action episodes (similar to Pattern A in Table 1). (*** indicates connective frame.)

Thunder on the River

***

Scene 1: The French: somewhere along the banks of Lake Peoria, summer of 1673.

***

Scene 2: The British: the high ground along the river, summer of 1765.

***

Scene 3: The Americans: the old settlement known as Fort Clark, summer of 1825.

***

Scene 4: The Steamboat: the waterfront in Peoria, summer of 1832.

***

Scene 5: The Railroads: the village of Peoria, summer of 1854.

***

Scene 6: Lincoln and Douglas: the town of Peoria, fall of 1858.

***

Scene 7: The Farm: a farm in Peoria County, fall of 1880.

***

Scene 8: *The New Century*: the city of Peoria, the period from 1890 to 1917.

***

Scene 9: *Heavy Industry*: the city of Peoria, a summer day in the 1900's.

***

Scene 10: *Vaudeville*: the city of Peoria, a winter evening in 1927.

***

Scene 11: *Crime*: the city of Peoria, any time between 1925 and 1950.

***

Scene 12: *Peoria*: past, present, and future.

Three obvious characteristics of *Thunder on the River's* extensive pattern are the encompassing of a lengthy time span, large time gaps between scenes, and a preponderance of exterior scenes (which more easily facilitate the demands of spectacle).

In either extensive or intensive pageant-dramas the number of scenes can vary anywhere from five to ten to twenty. In performance, such scenes are most commonly presented in one of these four ways: (1) spoken by actors, (2) pantomimically performed by actors while several readers speak the dialogue over loudspeakers, (3) acted in dumb show with one or more narrators describing the background and action of each scene, or (4) acted in dumb show with musical accompaniment and with explanatory narrative printed on the spectator's program. The first way is capable of providing the most artistically effective results and, not surprisingly, requires the greatest effort from all concerned.

Intensive and extensive patterns can be equally effective when a writer works for unity through the skillful use of his connective frame and the careful composing of focal plot scenes.

Theme

A well-constructed pageant-drama must be founded on a definite theme —commonly a commemorative one—arising from the development of a community and the interpretation of that development. Merely to dramatize the chronological sequence of events is not sufficient for the writer; he must dig deeply into the past and find there the roots of the present and the seedlings of the future. Customarily the theme of a pageant-drama emphasizes the strengths of a community's past and, by implication, charges the audience to preserve and perpetuate the example of its heritage by worthy communal endeavor.

The central idea of a pageant-drama must be stressed firmly and clearly. In *Century of Progress*, for example, a figure representing the present year expresses the theme as he speaks to a figure called Progress:

> The future is not up to me, nor to any other year, for that matter. It is, as it has been in the past, up to the people. The progress of Carbondale, the future of Carbondale, rests with its people; so, in a larger sense, the progress of the country, the future of the country, rests with its people. Listen to the words of Whitman, ". . . everything comes out of the people, everyday people, the people as you find them, and leave them; people, just people! . . ."[4]

And the theme of *Castine*, heard in the final words of the narrator, transcends local significance to touch on universal purpose.

> Then our town, so small, so peaceful, so far from all the world's strife and striving, woke to find it is a part of one great world. . . . If Castine is to be what it always has been, a serene and neighborly community of free people, we have to make the whole world a serene and neighborly community as well. . . . The world is now too small for anything but brotherhood; and brotherhood, before it can be universal, must be based upon the principle that all men are created free. Our purpose is a world of liberation not only from the tragedy of war, but from the tyranny of hate and greed, and from the barriers of race and class.[5]

Observe the resemblance of these thematic ideas to the great common theme of pageant-dramas which may be expressed thusly: "Our community has had, through the past endeavor of its people, the strength to grow despite hardships; we seek to maintain this proud heritage and through its example to strive for the betterment of our community." As *Castine* reveals, this thematic idea can link the local premise to a national or universal one.

While on a commemorative occasion one customarily praises one's subject, a pageant-drama is not obligated to do so where praise is not deserved. Effective pageant-dramas may also reveal the past shortcomings as well as the strengths of their subject and may be more interesting for having done so. If a community, for example, at one stage in its history is guilty of fomenting violence or injustice or greed significant in the chronicle of its development, then such a period (if capable of successful dramatization) should not be omitted. A community, like a dramatic character, is the more interesting and dramatic the more capable it is of human flaws as well as virtues. One to two and a half hours of uninterrupted self-praise can be wearing on an audience.

In special cases, the impetus for civic betterment can be accomplished by the frank depiction of an unproud past. We know one writer now dramatizing the story of a western Indian tribe historically noted for shiftlessness, lethargy, and ingratitude. He hopes to stir communal energy now lacking by means of candidly depicting its shameful past while, however, not neglecting to point out potentialities for future improvement.

Ideally a pageant-drama preserves throughout a unity of theme which is the outgrowth of the inherent solidarity and congruity of the materials presented. All the scenes of a pageant-drama should be related to the central idea so that they will have a thematic relationship whether or not their own causal connections are strong or slight. Furthermore, the author must grasp for himself the meaning of a community's chronicle apart from its chronological sequence of events. His must be the larger vision that sees the relationship of past, present, and future and evinces it through his drama.

The making of the focal plot

To meet its function of re-creating a community's history for its enlightenment and inspiration, the focal plot of a pageant-drama is immediately faced with an incontestable demand: it must present vividly the salient historical facts or events in that history and make clear their significance. As one of his initial steps, a writer will find it helpful to select and list the essential historical episodes that must be dramatized. Minor incidents or events are temporarily omitted, realizing that the most interesting of these may be worked into the focal plot at a later stage. A writer needs to estimate at the outset what is the irreducible minimum of essential episodes. Then other considerations will be brought to bear. Do the events that have been tentatively chosen support the drama's theme on which the whole structure is to rest? If the theme has arisen from a sound insight into the history, no problem should exist here. How extensive a connective frame will be necessary to bridge apparent gaps in historical time and subject matter? Here the factor of actual performing time arises. The actual length of time available—two and a half hours or less—limits the possible number of episodes and connective frame interludes. Individual episodes of the focal plot generally should not require more than twenty minutes at most, some considerably less; and individual units of the connective frame generally should not demand more than five minutes at most—many will be considerably less, even to the extent of thirty seconds. With a rough basis for a time scheme in his mind, a writer then determines how many episodes cannot be omitted and how many units of the connective frame will be necessary. Realizing the approximate time available for presentation, he will make further additions or excisions in his material as the case may be. Such initial considerations as these will not only save him a good deal of time in conceiving the focal plot, but also will strengthen his conception.

In the preface to his *Historical Pageant of Illinois*, Thomas Wood Stevens, a noted pageanteer and educator, advances a workable approach to selecting and arranging material for a pageant-drama. Stating his purpose to describe "in a short space of time, a few of the most stirring events in the history of Illinois," Stevens offers the following commentary:

> As the number of scenes is certainly limited, only events as may be considered turning points in the story of the state are chosen; and the ability of the material for dramatic presentation also is a factor in the selection. In most cases, the event itself is so presented as to make clear its culmination rather than the diverse causes which brought it about. To do this, events which certainly occurred during several days are frequently showed as taking place in a single scene; and frequently conversations are transplanted from place to place; such liberties have their excuse in the compression which they bring about.[6]

The compression and transposition of events and utterances mentioned by Stevens vary little in principle in this form from their use in biography-drama. And, in the main, considerations regarding the selection, arrangement, and development of historical facts in the latter form can be applied to the pageant-drama also and, therefore, need but small elaboration here. Owing to limitations of time and number of scenes, pageant-drama does require a particular approach to its material chiefly in two ways: namely that 1] turning points be chosen in the history to be depicted, and 2] only the climax and immediate resolution of these events chosen be reenacted. First, let us deal with the second factor.

For the most part, the events re-created in a pageant-drama must be shown at a point beginning just before their culmination and ending swiftly after their immediate resolution is reached. Diverse events and causes, for example, brought about the battle of Lexington in 1775. Yet Sidney Howard's first scene in *Lexington* shows chiefly the climactic skirmish between the Minutemen and the British troops and its immediate aftermath. To cite another illustration, one scene in *George Washington of Young America* recreates the Braddock massacre of 1755, that successful attack of the French and Indians near French-held Fort Duquesne upon the troops under General Braddock's command. The scene depicts the climax of the attack, culminating in the death of Braddock and the retreat of his remaining forces under Washington's leadership. While the actual events preceding and surrounding the Braddock massacre were numerous, only the climax and resolution of the massacre is seized upon for dramatization. This approach is most necessary in the extensive type of pageant-drama in which a broad scope of history is surveyed. It stimulates the writer to look for the crises in events.

Events selected for dramatization should include, in substantial degree, turning points in the past to be re-created, and the more extensive the history to be covered, the greater the need to apply this criterion. Usually representing the significant events of a community's development such turning points— when they possess inherent dramatic qualities—normally are concerned with some significant act or decision of the community resulting in a crisis directly affecting, or having consequences for, its destiny. The synopsis of scenes of a pageant-drama at the end of this chapter illustrates this point. Those events demonstrating a community act or decision holding consequences for the future are the stuff of stageworthy focal plot scenes. Generally, they are historically significant, dramatic, and representative of a commemorative theme.

"Insignificant" events as material for a focal plot

When dramatizing the story of a community, a writer looks for events significant of its evolution and growth with an eye toward showing how and why these events are indeed significant. To accomplish this purpose, it sometimes is necessary to create episodes based on what may not appear to be important events in a community's history. Suppose, for instance, that records tell us that in 1679 there is imposed upon a New Jersey town the authority of an overbearing royal governor whose edicts curtail the liberties of the citizens. To show their protest, the citizens free by force fellow townsmen who have been unjustly imprisoned by the governor's officials. In so doing, they flaunt their opposition to the governor's authority and laws. The act represents a small insurrection at the time. Examining the town's total history, it is apparent that the citizens before and after that incident maintained their rights and freedom against despotic power. This act of the townspeople, then, aids in shaping the course of their descendants' future. Such an episode may not in the opinion of a historian be a significant event in the development of the town, but it clearly demonstrates the mettle of the community and signifies its progress.[7]

Common demands of a focal plot scene

In composing the historical episodes, the writer will be faced with demands of exposition, stageworthiness, and often spectacle. Let us first consider
the two initial requirements. A focal plot scene has to convey certain factual
information. It should be dramatic as well. But sometimes the writer will encounter material not essentially dramatic in itself—the founding of an institution, a decisive meeting of a policy-making body, the visit of a famous personage, and so on. When such material lacks intrinsic dramatic values, it must
be shaped by the writer to possess them.

As part of its dramatic requirements, each focal plot scene should be
patterned as a miniature play containing elements of exposition, attack, struggle, major crisis, major climax, and outcome (or its prediction). (The reconstruction of a pageant-drama scene at the end of this chapter illustrates a
writer's consideration of such elements.) Often not as tightly bound together
in causal pattern as in conventional dramatic construction, pageant-drama
episodes, therefore, must be more self-contained and complete in themselves.
When we realize that the normal full-length pageant-drama may contain a
total of ten scenes or more in its focal plot, we are aware that the writer is
charged with writing a minimum of ten diminutive plays. The pageanteer,
then, must be an effective scenewright as well as playwright.

Spectacle is another demand often placed upon a pageant-drama. Here a
writer will be tempted to create scenes purely for the sake of spectacle, regardless of their expository or dramatic value. But visual and auditory elements,
too, must be directed toward continually propelling the focal plot forward.
For instance, dances—Indian, folk, or otherwise—should not be inserted here
and there as if separate numbers in a musical revue. While many an effective
episode may emphasize spectacle by intensifying visual elements and subordi-
nating the dialogue, it must possess expository and dramatic qualities as well.
Spectacle having no real pertinence is best omitted. But when spectacle
thrusts forward or visually interprets the focal plot and is integrated with it, it
merits inclusion. And the fact that it places most emphasis on pantomime and
less on dialogue in no way lessens its value or artistic purpose.

Each scene in a pageant-drama should hold dramatic and expository
values and, when demanded, values of spectacle as well. The writer then is
always faced with two, and often three, of these demands in approaching the
scenes to be created. While one of these demands may assume the first position of importance in any given scene, the other two demands must be considered also.

Character

Pageant-drama, whose purpose is to clarify the development of community life, subordinates the individual. As pageant-writer William Chauncey Langdon points out: "The individuals . . . come and go with their generation, even the greatest men of history simply making their contribution to the development of their city or state and then passing on, while the city or state . . . endures through the centuries." [8] Owing to this characteristic trait of pageant-drama, little time exists for detailed characterization within the single scenes with the result that characters are less developed in this form than in, for example, biography-drama. There is, therefore, a substantial challenge for the writer: only a few strokes can be used to sketch the stage portraits of historical figures. Therefore, the strokes employed must be well-considered ones.

The necessary simplification of a character through the use of a few pertinent details is illustrated in a scene from George Washington of Young America.[9] The emphasis throughout this work is on the important events in Washington's life, most of which are significantly representative of the nation's early history. An early scene is set in 1775. Washington is a colonel of Virginia militia under the command of General Braddock; the latter leads a military expedition charged with wresting Fort Duquesne from the French. The action opens with a fierce dispute between the colonial and British troops. Braddock harshly intercedes in favor of his own troops, and is pacified by the Virginia colonel. Nevertheless, the proud, narrow-minded Braddock insults the "untrained colonials" (as he calls them) and ignores Washington's warning that the French and Indians probably plan to ambush them before they can attack the fort. The British general stubbornly insists on using European military tactics of fighting in the open and places the militia, trained in Indian fighting, in the rear. The British are cut to pieces in an ambush and routed by the enemy; Braddock receives a mortal wound. Washington saves the survivors of the panicked British forces as well as his own remaining men by means of a skillful retreat.

The action of the scene requires that a few specific qualities of the historical figure be shown. He emerges as a well-spoken colonial officer, respected but unheeded by the British, and a military leader whose bravery and cautious military prowess enable him to organize the retreat of a badly defeated body of troops. These are the brush strokes of character detail needed for the scenes. In reality, of course, Washington is much more than just a tactful, brave man of action and military leader. He is well-read, skilled in surveying, fond of sports and good wine, uncommon in physical strength and proportion, and (according to biographer Henry Cabot Lodge) at this time a hot-tempered fighter loving fighting for its own sake with little regard for odds or personal safety, a quality which caused him to make many mistakes in the early campaigns of the French and Indian War.[10] However, few of these attributes, with the exception of the last, are relevant to the action, and consequently, are omitted. And Washington's hot-blooded fierceness and recklessness in battle are superseded by his cool-headed and prudent military prowess and authority (which, historically, may well have developed after Braddock's defeat). The historical figure probably is a sufficiently complex human being to possess both sets of attributes, but for the scene described only those pertinent to the action centering on the event are used.

The author of the above scene, Esther Willard Bates, probably has considered the following factors in sketching her character of Washington: 1] what history reveals about the personage, 2] what the person must do within the scene, and 3] what aspect of the person's qualities must be reflected by the action of the scene. These factors provide compass points for character creation within a pageant-drama scene. The selection of detail necessary for characterization in this form is more restrictive than that in biography-drama which tends to focus primarily on character rather than on event and, therefore, can produce stage personages of greater dimension.

The temptation for the writer here is to oversimplify his characters with the possible result that they become uninteresting stereotypes not resembling their actual counterparts. If the major characters in a scene are not credible and dramatically interesting—and this depends in large part upon the skill with which the writer has selected and shaped the details of his stage figures—the event or aspect of the community being re-created also will fail in credibility and dramatic intensity.

Such undesirable results also can stem from another factor. The commemorative theme of a pageant-drama slyly encourages a writer to magnify and idealize the stature of historical figures in order to elevate that of the community. Here again a writer is in trouble if he indulges such a temptation. Regardless of the commemorative aspect of the form, he is not artistically permitted to offer inhumanly flawless protagonists or utterly villainous villains. A plaster-saint Washington or a basely murderous Aaron Burr, for example, have little chance to come alive vividly and truthfully on stage. Perceptive writers have discovered from human experience that there are no gods or devils on this earth, and that all men are a bit of both.

Fictional characters

Fictional characters can serve the same helpful functions in pageant-drama as in biography-drama. They are utilized less frequently owing to the pageant-drama's greater emphasis on re-creating historical events. Yet it is often overlooked that fictional characters, because of their flexible connection to facts of time and space, can aid the persistent problem of pageant-drama: the lack of unity of character and action.

Unity

The broad scope peculiar to pageant-drama tends to debilitate unity of action. The problem is intensified by the difficulty of concentrating on one or more characters that might link the action of the various scenes. But one way this problem can be met, at least partially, is for a writer to follow a community's development through the lives of one or more generations of the same family. This is apparent in *All Faces West*, discussed earlier. In *The Dream and the Deed*, author Glenn Hughes does this with some success. The drama encompasses Seattle history from approximately 1851 to 1951. The focal plot begins in Illinois with the pioneer family of Arthur and Mary Denny and their son David. The Dennys and several of their neighbors move west and settle the land where Seattle now stands. Subsequent scenes show the family experiencing the events of their new life—building a cabin, seeing David married and, as one of the first families, contributing to the growth of Seattle. Thus we also follow major events of the city's history, at least up to 1874, through the experiences of the Dennys. Focus on them lends a substantial sense of unity to most of the scenes. Of course, the comparatively short span of Seattle history makes possible a dramatic emphasis on one family. When a community's history does not offer such a possibility, a fictional group or personage can be used to good advantage. Or when one generation has passed from a community's story, the family of the second generation and/or one or more characters introduced earlier in the connective frame can link the subsequent scenes. Searching out the possibilities to focalize on a set of characters can result in a more dramatic and unified pageant-drama.

Types of connective frame

Unity is also aided by the use of a well chosen connective frame, which, other than furnishing accentuation of theme and necessary progressive exposition, also can provide a unity of action and/or character lacking in the focal plot. There are myriad types of such a device, but let us examine four general ones.

First, a frame can consist of interludes of allegorical action utilizing symbolic figures. More popular in past decades than today, this device must be freshly and skillfully handled in order to appeal to a modern audience now grown more sophisticated. Moreover, it does not easily facilitate the creation of characters or action fully capable of developing the necessary exposition from one focal plot scene to another. If a writer wishes to weave in some "symbolic dance" or allegorical action engendered by such interludes, he is wise to integrate the latter with the focal plot action as a montage, a dream sequence, or through an allegorical character appearing throughout the focal plot as an imaginative presence.

A second type of connective frame consists of interludes of realistic action. To give one common example, the pupils of a class are told the story of a community's history by a teacher or minister. The story provides the requisite exposition and introduction for the scenes of the focal plot. The interaction of the frame characters not only can embody the spirit and events of the day, but also can demonstrate the impact of the re-created history upon people today. (Of course, there are more exciting possibilities of realistic action interludes than this one cited.) A connective frame of this nature, moreover, can be fused into the focal plot when the latter's action arrives at the present day, thus up-dating the action in a dramatically smooth and consistent manner. And, also important, realistic interludes (and allegorical interludes as well) can furnish a cause and effect pattern lacking in the focal plot itself. In such cases the scenes of interludes of the frame are constructed on the same dramatic principles as those of the latter. Since such scenes normally represent a different plane of reality than those of the focal plot, they can effect a refreshing variety in the total progression of the action, namely, historical episodes of a stark or serious nature can be alternated with frame scenes that are light in mood. The only major caution about this kind of frame is that it should not replace in importance the focal plot.

A third type of connective frame is narration by one who may be realistic or abstract or allegorical, seen or unseen. He may be called a variety of names ranging from "narrator," "storyteller," "historian," "chronicler," to a specific character name like "Young America," "Knowledge," or "Mr. Jones." He may be one or more figures appearing within or between all or certain episodes to give information essential to understanding and linking together the episodes. Because the time span between focal plot scenes is often substantial, the narrator, when requisite, can be used to tell the audience the outcome of the re-created event it has just seen, the vitally important history occurring between one episode and another, and the information necessary to introduce the episode to come. Furthermore, he has, when well conceived, a compelling quality drawing spectators to identify with or participate through a figure who can lead them through the action and thus unify it for them. Overall, his chief function is to unify and clarify the focal plot action. And that is the function of any kind of connective frame.

Several problems can arise with the use of narration. First, there is a danger of overloading the narrator with historical exposition. The result can be a dull history lesson taking precedence over the focal plot's dramatic action. The speech of a narrator should be terse in offering only the most essential exposition, and, when the figure has identity as a character, should individualize the personage speaking. Second, the narrator should not be used as a crutch to do the work of the action episodes. The latter should be dramatic entities not requiring narration to tell what should be demonstrated in action. Third, a narrator should evoke the past through the power and beauty of his speeches which should not merely be recitation of historical facts. He sets the proper tone of the entire drama, often appearing as a prologue to the historical episodes in which he may suggest the theme, the significance of the site and the occasion, and so on. Fourth, the narrator ideally serves as the primary point of identification through which the audience witnesses the episodic story of the focal plot. In a sense, he carries the audience through the community's story. When a narrator is splintered into two, or three, or five narrators, or when he is unseen or merely an impersonal figure spewing out facts, this last function usually is nullified.

These problems, and several others, are in most cases best met by the use of the fourth type of connective frame, which is merely an extension of the narrator device. The greatest unity and the least distraction often are the result of utilizing historical or fictional characters who are directly involved in the action. (The pageant-drama scene at the end of this chapter illustrates this device.) Such characters can step in and out of scenes to give the necessary exposition and narration for events preceding or following their appearance. Because such characters form a part of the history they relate, their "first person" narration may be lent a sense of immediacy and meaningfulness. Perhaps the most effective focus occurs when the character-narrator is one person. Certainly, when the span of the dramatized history is extensive, it is difficult, if not impossible, to employ a historical character as narrator who will be logically and continuously involved in all the focal plot action. In this case, it is reasonable to consider creating a sufficiently flexible fictional character to step in and out of the focal plot (usually as a minor character).

Whatever means employed, the aim of the connective frame will be to bind together and elucidate the focal plot. Its other related functions can be summarized as follows. It can be used to provide: 1] exposition, 2] causal pattern of action lacking in the focal plot, 3] a frame for the action, entailing its appearance at the start and finish of the focal plot, 4] a reality different from that of the focal plot, 5] the setting of a proper tone and mood for the drama as a whole, 6] contrast and variety in relation to the focal plot scenes, and 7] adjustment for the technical needs of the drama, i.e. allowing time for scene and/or costume changes.[11]

Dialogue

Considerations regarding dialogue in biography-drama (see chapter ix) are similarly applicable in the case of pageant-drama and need no restatement here. However, several additional points should be mentioned.

First, in this form effective dialogue demands the use of simple, concrete, action-connoting words and phrases. When demands upon audibility and intelligibility are increased, the need for clarity in dramatic language is intensified. In Thomas Wood Steven's *The Pageant of Newark* an angry citizen, Amos Roberts, exhorts to action a New Jersey town rebellious against the unjust imprisonment of three peaceful townsmen by an overbearing British colonial rule.

AMOS ROBERTS. Men of Essex, Associators of East Jersey, the time has come tonight for a determined stroke. Three of our fellows, Nehemiah Baldwin among them, are in that jail charged with riot and insurrection. We have no wish for riot. We are peaceful men, but we have been driven too far by the Lords Proprietors and the Governor's Council of Tyranny. You know whence all this trouble springs. You know that two men, rich and understanding men, oppressors by nature, Morris and Alexander, have claimed the lands our fathers bought fairly of the Indians. They have set up again the grasping claim of the Lord's quit-rent, the ha'penny tax our fathers hated. They have ejected our people from their homes. . . . My friends, we have suffered enough. Tonight let us break down the jail doors and set our comrades free. Are you with us, men of the Essex Society? (*There is shout of approval.*) Those who are on my list, follow me.[12]

Notice the use of brief sentences, and concrete, action-connoting words in this direct speech.

A second consideration regarding dialogue for pageant-drama concerns the need to eliminate all lines easily subject to mushmouthed rendition. Writer Kermit Hunter points out that a typical phrase of the year 1800, such as, "Lord love us, this heel music'll ruin the young 'uns!" is improved when altered to say something like, "Looky, Tom, you quit scratchin' out that jumpy music; these boys and gals are getting the devil in 'em'!" [13] The second speech stresses consonant sounds and is easier for the ear to grasp. On this same point, the re-creation of speech patterns of past eras often is difficult for an audience to understand. It may be authentic for a character in 1800 to say, "Hit 'uz a-leanin' sigoddlin' yonder ferninst the barn." Yet the sentence makes more intelligible dialogue when broken up into several brief sentences containing only a few key words reminiscent of the period. "Hits over yonder." "Where?" "Ferninst the barn, like I said." [14] The adroit handling of a few colloquialisms will establish the flavor of the time and place.

Owing to emphasis on public events, dialogue in pageant-drama must be largely expository in nature. The form's emphasis upon expository dialogue represents a difference in degree rather than in kind in the common functions of dialogue. Here the playwright's task is to make such expository dialogue dramatic by remembering that audience interest lies not so much in the events themselves as in the effect they create on the people participating in them. And he also must remember that the *actions* of his characters are as effective as what they say. Therefore, lines can be brief and to the point. Involved, long speeches are both confusing and tiresome. Digressions or circumlocutions have no place. Terseness is a desirable characteristic.

Why is terseness so vitally important in this form, other than the fact that there is little time to spare for each scene? When presented outdoors or on a large indoor stage by amateur community actors, the pageant-drama raises certain considerations. First, as mentioned earlier, visual action normally ascends to a position of major emphasis. And, secondly, spoken lines are difficult vocally for untrained community actors to project meaningfully when there is considerable distance from actor to spectator. When the playwright realizes such conditions will occur, he is well advised to use the strictest economy in his dialogue. This does not mean that such questionable practices must be followed as having all scenes in dumb show with dialogue printed in a program, or having one to five readers giving *all* the dialogue over loudspeakers while the actors pantomime all the action. It merely means that the playwright realizes his dialogue is only part of a total work which depends largely on visual action.

By the same token, dialogue deserves no less attention than any other aspect of the drama and its production. No artistic standards will be met by a pageant-drama with badly-written and ineffective dialogue, no matter how excellent all its other aspects.

The development of a pageant-drama

This section outlines several major steps in the development of the pageant-drama *Hark Upon the Gale*. One scene from the drama appears at the end of the chapter preceded by a brief discussion of its evolution. As in the previous chapter, the intent here is to suggest to the writer several common problems encountered in the making of this kind of historical drama.

A playwright is commissioned by the College of William and Mary to write a script dramatizing its history. He learns that the dramatization will commemorate the institution's 254th anniversary and also will serve as part of the College's participation in the state-sponsored 350th anniversary year of the settlement at Jamestown, Virginia. It will be presented for a three-day run in the College's new indoor theatre possessing a spacious stage and the best of stage machinery and equipment. The stage production will be directed by a professor of theatre and enacted largely by student actors.

In addition to the requirements implied by this initial information, several specific demands are mentioned. The script must be historically accurate in its major details and must be approved by the College's senior historian. Also, certain events designated by the historian are to be included in the drama; however considerable freedom of choice is permitted the writer.[15] Only twenty-five student actors will be available to carry all the speaking roles, thus restricting the number of characters in each scene. Also it is implied that one large neutral unit probably will have to serve as the major setting in front of which are placed properties to "set" the many changing scenes as they appear. Finally, standard prerequisites for the script are assumed, such as maximum playing time of two and a half hours, provision for property and costume changes between scenes, and variety in audience appeals in the overall arrangement and depiction of the scenes.

An alumnus of the College, the writer begins with a certain preknowledge of its characteristic atmosphere and basic traditions. After preliminary discussions with the College historian and a review of the institution's general history, the writer finds this welter of major facts about the academic community's past:

THE COLLEGE of William and Mary was founded in 1693 by royal charter presented at the English Court of William and Mary to the Reverend James Blair, named as the institution's first president. Completed in 1697, the main college building was burned in 1705 following festive preparations for an anniversary celebration. Almost ten years went by before the building was completely rebuilt. Having continually clashed with British colonial governors over college administrative policy, President Blair was surprised that Governor Alexander Spotswood interceded on the institution's behalf to gain money from the English Crown for the reconstruction. In 1729 all departments of the College with its President and faculty were finally established. The years preceding the American Revolution brought young George Washington to the College to pass a required examination for county surveyor and Thomas Jefferson to matriculate as a student.

During the Revolution, a number of students and faculty joined local militia companies. The students who remained formed a company with the college president serving as captain. Also during this period, the Phi Beta Kappa Society was formed by several students; and the college became a university establishing a school of medicine and the first American chairs of law and modern languages. In 1781, British General Lord Cornwallis used the president's house as his temporary headquarters prior to the battle of Yorktown. After the Revolution, the institution's funds were diminished—its English endowments were halted—and the student body dwindled to fifty by 1806.

In the early nineteenth-century, after the state capital was moved from Williamsburg to Richmond, the College declined. Students in this period were fired by the ideals of the French Revolution and engaged in intense factionalism. An attempt to move the College to the new capital was thwarted, but its enrollment began to increase in the decade before the Civil War. The main College building in 1859 burned again, but was rebuilt in less than a year.

At the start of the Civil War, the president, faculty and students all entered the Confederate Army. The main building was used first as a Confederate barracks and later as a hospital. Union troops captured the town of Williamsburg in 1862, and their commanding officer established his headquarters at the College. That same year, the main build-

ing was set on fire by Union soldiers. After the war, classes resumed in the ruined College building, which had to be reconstructed for the third time. In 1881, the College was forced to close for lack of funds; it reopened in 1888 and slowly began to achieve prosperity. After 1934 its enrollment and holdings increased steadily to bring it to a state of current well-being. Among famous men educated at the College were Thomas Jefferson, James Monroe, John Tyler, John Marshall, and George Wythe.[16]

How does the writer approach this mass of facts? He first looks for a pattern of some sort. After studying this outline, which he fills out with his knowledge of the general historical background, he perceives that the College —the obvious hero of the pageant-drama—has encountered its greatest number of crises in the period from its founding to 1888. The institution striving for survival, is challenged by the constant ravages of fire, occupation by hostile troops in the course of two wars, and foreclosures due to destruction of property and lack of funds. The three greatest antagonists appear to have been fire, war, and insufficiency of funds. That the College has been able to surmount all these obstacles to regain its losses and build toward a slowly increasing property evinces its courage and perseverance. And herein lies the drama's theme: the imperishable spirit of the College has surmounted many obstacles to achieve not only a proud past and present but also the promise of a prosperous future. In a general way a broad pattern begins to emerge.

The key event around which the others may fall into place appears to be the College's reopening in 1888—which terminated the lowest point of its fortune, its closure for seven years. Realizing immediately the need to set some limits on the broad expanse of history to be covered, the writer determines to end the dramatization in 1888 when the institution again opens its doors—this time to a brighter future.

The next step for the writer is to learn from the historian those events which must be included. The latter urges the dramatization of seven particular events. Conceding their significance, the writer plans to incorporate them into the focal plot. To this group, he adds another. An early meeting of the Phi Beta Kappa Society has been one of the historical items selected. Its beginning years encompass the forming of the College militia company in 1777. Both events—which show colorful aspects of student life—can easily be compressed into one episode. The events, then, to be re-created in seven episodes roughly are set.

Because the material presents a good number of potential episodes no more than a maximum of ten minutes is estimated for each scene, thus permitting roughly a total of sixteen to seventeen scenes (to keep within two and a half hours). On the basis of this calculation, the writer estimates that material for nine to ten more scenes can be selected.

The writer allows historical significance to act as the next yardstick for selection, aided by the ever-present criterion of dramatic value. In addition to those already chosen, what other events fall into this category? Certainly the granting of the charter at the court of William and Mary in 1693 is one. Furthermore, it is rich in interest as further research reveals. Opposed by powerful officials, James Blair has been kept waiting in England two years for the charter to be granted. Here is material for a strong opening scene. Another important event is certainly the closing of the College in 1881, representing the nadir of the institution's career. And the closing of the College as most of the men leave to join the Confederacy is as dramatic as it is historically important. The subject matter of ten episodes, dealing with events of primary significance, has been selected.

The other focal plot episodes fall into place. The dramatic value and historical interest of five hitherto unchosen events render them apt material: the burning of the College building in 1705 and the governor's aid in getting money from England to rebuild it; the temporary occupancy of the College by General Cornwallis in 1781; the abortive attempt to move the College to Richmond in 1824 which sparks opposition from Thomas Jefferson as well as several faculty members; the burning of the College building in 1859; and the return of the President after the Civil War to reopen the College in 1865. All these events show the College encountering serious crises demanding struggle and destiny-affecting decisions on its part.

Time for one to two more episodes remains. The playwright sees the need for a few more scenes treating faculty and/or student life which will also help to picture the College in the periods between 1749 to 1760, and 1781 to 1824.

The comic and dramatic possibilities of an occurrence in 1758 suggest a colorful episode of faculty life between 1749 and 1760. At that time two professors violate the College rule that no faculty member except the President may marry, and they refuse the President's demand that they remove their families and depart from their College lodgings; the professors soon resign but appeal the rule which later is revoked. Also, another likely subject is discovered. To fill the need for a depiction of student life in the period following the Revolution when pro- and con-Jeffersonian feeling ran strong, an interesting account of two students expelled for dueling in 1806 furnishes the substance for a focal plot scene.

To be sure, when selecting the material for his focal plot the writer also considers, in addition to historical importance and dramatic value, such other factors as the sources available, and the potentialities for appeal of spectacle and variety (in contrast to other scenes).

Arriving at the maximum number of scenes possible, the writer considers the most workable alternative for a connective frame. He decides that specific characters in the scenes—presidents, faculty members, and students— can serve as narrators introducing the scenes in which they appear. This device, he feels, will enable the explanatory narration binding the various episodes to appear more a part of the focal plot action.

In order that the reader may better visualize the considerations affecting the arrangement and selection of pageant-drama scenes an outline of each focal plot episode in *Hark Upon the Gale* (each is actually used in the final script) follows, sketching its action and its essential characteristics. (Narration precedes each scene.)

ACT ONE

Scene 1: *The court of William and Mary at Whitehall in England. February, 1693. Focus: Historical event.*
Synopsis: *Despite a long delay and the opposition of important officials, Reverend James Blair receives a charter from the English monarchs for the establishment of the College. Elements: Spectacular appeal, comic and serious in tone, seven speaking roles and adjustable number of extras, interior setting, music and choral singing. Estimated playing time: Ten minutes.*

Scene 2: *The Great Hall of the Wren Building, Williamsburg, Virginia. May, 1699. Focus: Historical event.*
Synopsis: *At an assemblage of the Virginia General Assembly and Royal Governor, student orators give speeches requesting the assembly's support of the College. Elements: Spectacular appeal, largely serious in tone, eight speaking roles, and adjustable number of extras, interior setting. Estimated playing time: Ten minutes.*

Scene 3: *The President's home. Williamsburg. 1710. Focus: Historical event.*
Synopsis: *President James Blair is surprised to gain the unsolicited support of Governor Spotswood in getting money from England to rebuild the College building badly damaged by fire in 1705. Elements: Small*

scene, largely serious in tone, five speaking roles, interior setting. Estimated playing time: *Four minutes.*

Scene 4: *The Blue Room of the Wren Building. August, 1729. Focus: Historical event.*
Synopsis: *The President and the faculty meet to approve the transfer to them of the corporate authority of the College from the surviving trustees; the institution's departments and staff are finally established.* Elements: *Small scene, comic in tone, five speaking roles, interior setting.* Estimated playing time: *Three minutes.*

Scene 5: *The College yard. Autumn, 1749. Focus: Historical event.*
Synopsis: *Young George Washington is given an examination for country surveyor by the faculty and passes after showing up some lapses of knowledge in the examining committee.* Elements: *Small scene, comic in tone, five speaking roles, exterior setting.* Estimated playing time: *Eight minutes.*

Scene 6: *The College yard. February, 1758. Focus: Faculty life.*
Synopsis: *Having rebelled against the college rule that the faculty may not marry, two married professors question President Thomas Dawson's authority, refuse to immediately leave the campus, and make the President unwittingly admit that the anti-marriage rule is illogical.* Elements: *Comic in tone, nine speaking roles, exterior setting.* Estimated playing time: *Eleven minutes.*

Scene 7: *A clearing in the woods. Williamsburg. Spring, 1761. Focus: Student life and relationship of Jefferson and Professor William Small.*
Synopsis: *Student Tom Jefferson argues the fickleness of Virginia girls with fellow students, and fights one student in defense of a favorite professor; the fight is halted by the professor himself who makes Tom realize not only the importance of logic and reason but the responsibility of insuring man's freedom of mind.* Elements: *Small scene, comic and serious in tone, six speaking roles, exterior setting.* Estimated playing time: *Eight minutes.*

Scene 8: *The Apollo Room of the Raleigh Tavern. Autumn, 1777. Focus: Student life.*
Synopsis: *College President James Madison encounters some problems in training the student militia company whose drill inadvertently interrupts a debate meeting of the Phi Beta Kappa Society.* Elements: *Spectacular appeal, comic in tone, ten speaking roles and no extras, interior setting.* Estimated playing time: *Ten minutes.*

Scene 9: *The Blue Room of the Wren Building. December, 1779.* Focus: *Historical event.*
Synopsis: *Governor Thomas Jefferson proposes to his fellow members of the College's Board of Visitors that the institution change its traditional curriculum and become a university; despite some opposition, his proposal is accepted.* Elements: *Largely serious in tone, nine speaking roles and one extra, interior setting.* Estimated playing time: *Eight minutes.*

Scene 10: *The President's house. June 1781.* Focus: *Historical event.*
Synopsis: *General Cornwallis takes over President Madison's home as his headquarters but not without encountering defiance from the President and his family.* Elements: *Small scene, serious in tone, music, five speaking roles, interior setting.* Estimated playing time: *Ten minutes.*

ACT TWO

Scene 1: *A clearing in the woods. Williamsburg. Autumn, 1806.* Focus: *Student life.*
Synopsis: *A heated dispute over politics between two students leads to a duel which to their own relief is halted by College President Madison who expels them for engaging in a practice forbidden by College rules.* Elements: *Spectacular appeal, comic in tone, eight speaking roles, exterior setting.* Estimated playing time: *Ten minutes.*

Scene 2: *The Apollo Room of the Raleigh Tavern. Winter, 1824.* Focus: *Student life and historical event.*
Synopsis: *During a student ball College President John A. Smith argues with a faculty member the advisability of solving the College's enrollment problems by moving it to the state capital.* Elements: *Spectacular appeal, music, dancing, serious and comic appeal, five speaking roles and an adjustable number of extras, interior setting.* Estimated playing time: *Eight minutes.*

Scene 3: *The College year. February, 1859.* Focus: *Student life and historical event.*
Synopsis: *During preparation for an anniversary celebration featuring a debate between the two rival campus literary societies, the College Building catches fire but no lives are lost; not giving way to despair, President Benjamin Ewell vows to build again.* Elements: *Spectacular appeal, serious and comic, ten speaking roles and adjustable number of extras, exterior setting.* Estimated playing time: *Ten minutes.*

Scene 4: *The College yard. Spring, 1861. Focus: Historical event.*
Synopsis: *President Ewell leads the students and faculty off to war.* Elements: *Spectacular appeal, music, choral singing, largely serious in tone, seven speaking roles and adjustable number of extras.* Estimated playing time: *Six minutes.*

Scene 5: *The College yard. Spring, 1865. Focus: Historical event.*
Synopsis: *President Ewell and several students return to the war-ravaged campus; the President determines to reopen the College and build again on the old foundations.* Elements: *Small scene, serious in tone, three speaking roles, exterior setting.* Estimated playing time: *Four minutes.*

Scene 6: *The hall of the Wren Building. October, 1881. Focus: Historical event.*
Synopsis: *The College is forced to close owing to a lack of funds and students.* Elements: *Small scene, serious in tone, two speaking roles, choral singing, interior setting.* Estimated playing time: *Four minutes.*

Scene 7: *The village green and the College yard in Williamsburg. August, 1888. Focus: Historical event.*
Synopsis: *The College reopens after seven years and a festive celebration honors the occasion.* Elements: *Spectacular appeal, music, dancing, singing, light in tone, three speaking roles, and adjustable number of dancers and extras, seventeen nonspeaking montage figures representing famous alumni, exterior setting.* Estimated playing time: *Six minutes.*

The synopses and elements of the above focal plot scenes give some indication of the variety between them as arranged by the playwright. There is a commendable balance of scenes light to serious, long to short, large cast to small cast, exterior to interior, focusing on student life to those centering on a specific historical event. Also a positive feature is that the total running time estimated does not exceed two and a half hours.

The weaknesses of the whole appear to lie in the following areas: an insufficient number of "big" scenes with spectacular appeal and too many "small" scenes, the first four scenes in Act I are predominantly serious in tone and need to be relieved by a comic scene, and the number of speaking roles indicates that probably there is too much dialogue.

Nevertheless, the writer does select, use, and arrange his historical materials with conscious attention to the demands of the source material, the dramatic form, and the college community audiences for which he writes.

Development of a pageant-drama scene

A look at the evolution of one episode from *Hark Upon the Gale* (Act II, Scene 1) will discover the decisions regarding invention, and selection and arrangement of facts made by one writer in approaching his materials. This particular illustration of the creative process reveals several common considerations in forming a pageant-drama episode.

At one point in the drama there is a need for a scene depicting student life in the decades following the American Revolution. As the opening scene of Act II, it should be lively, visually exciting, and possess some comic possibilities. Because the liveliest student reaction to national politics occurred during Jefferson's administration—the nation's President being an alumnus and popular hero of the students—the scene is set in the early 1800's. Casting about for material, the writer encounters three factual items:

AN EFFECTIVE, although often criticized, method of raising funds in Colonial and post-Revolutionary America was the lottery. The College of William and Mary after 1781 had lost many important sources of revenue which affected its prosperity. Therefore, the College held one of several lotteries in 1805 for fund-raising purposes. The first prize was ten thousand dollars.[17]

The period 1790 to 1810 might be called the French Revolution period. William and Mary students, reacting to French writers and firmly remembered ideals of the American Revolution, were divided into two political camps. Four-fifths of the student body, supported the French Revolution and Jefferson, belonged to a party known in Virginia as the "Jacobins." This group of Republicans addressed each other as "Citizen" and sometimes wore the tricolor cockade as a sign of friendship for France. One-fifth of the students allied themselves with the more conservative Federalists, a group associated with George Washington and John Marshall—and accused by the "Jacobins" of being anti-French and therefore pro-British.[18]

After the state capital moved to Richmond the decline of Williamsburg, coupled with the influence of the French Revolution, led students to breaches of discipline. To limit ever-recurring dissipation and idleness, junior students were compelled to lodge at the College, devote stated hours to study, and remain in their rooms from early evening until morning. Yet this did not quell student spirits, which *found one outlet in the traditional but illegal practice of dueling. Despite a strict rule against dueling stipulating that the principals and seconds of a duel should be expelled, student dueling was not infrequent.*

A student duel in 1806 concerned a dispute between Armistead T. Mason and Bartholomew Henley which led to a challenge. They were to fight with two pistols each at only ten steps distance, and fire when they pleased. The seconds were getting the pistols ready in Mason's room when the College President James Madison, having heard of it, appeared suddenly with a magistrate. Mason escaped! A Williamsburg lawyer and friend of Mason's father named William Wirt had himself appointed a constable. He arrested Mason and became surety for $7500 for his good conduct. The affair was settled by friends of the two parties.[19]

After details on the period are filled in by several primary sources and by the historian, the playwright is ready to begin the saturation process by visualizing the major characters and their environment. The environment and general setting are known—the College in the early nineteenth century.

The incident of the duel immediately offers a dramatic situation for the episode. Two students about to engage in a duel are interrupted by the College President. The incident contains at the outset three major characters: students Mason and Henley, and President Madison. What does history tell us about them? Armistead T. Mason, the son of a United States Senator, was nineteen at the time of the duel. After completing an appointment to fill a vacancy in the United States Senate in 1816 to 1817, he was killed in a duel with his brother-in-law two years later at the age of thirty-two. Here was a person who evidently possessed some volatile characteristics and who well might initiate a challenge to duel. The writer is able to learn little of Bartholomew Henley. Neither Henley nor Mason appear in any other scenes of the drama and, therefore, must be introduced adequately to the audience in this episode. The Reverend James Madison, a cousin of the nation's future president, had been president of the College since 1777, staying at its helm during the difficult years of the American Revolution and the decades immediately following. He staunchly embraced the principles of American independence (in his public prayers it is said he replaced "kingdom of heaven" by "republic of heaven"). And he combated rising student tomfoolery and dissipation by establishing rules restricting the students' social life. The historical portrait shows an enlightened and politically passionate man, stern but not unkind, who enforced his rules. This characterization of Madison has been established by his presence in three scenes immediately preceding this one (the last in which the character appears). Because the audience will be familiar with the character when witnessing the second act, the writer can concentrate on developing the other stage figures. These three characters, then, would be a start. The others that will be needed probably will be suggested as the scene is progressively sketched out.

With three major characters taking shape, the writer is ready to further envision his action. He refers back to the account of the uncompleted duel. First, the latter's cause must be determined. Several alternatives are considered. A minor insult to a person's family or one of his relatives can be cause for a duel in 1806—and Mason is from a prominent family. Also in view of his later demise, he appears to be a logical challenger. Yet something is missing! Impugning the honor of a family no matter how lightly is neither ridiculous nor insignificant—yet an insignificant cause is desirable here since such duels probably stemmed most commonly from foolish remarks. Perhaps it will be helpful to reevaluate the purpose of the scene and its relationship to those scenes surrounding it. The purpose is to present a richly representative picture of student life in the period between the time of the previous scene (1781) and that of the scene following (1829). Because of the rich recount of a dueling incident in 1806 and the intense political feelings held by the students at this time, 1806 is chosen as the time of the scene. For the scene to be representative, the playwright realizes, both these aspects must be shown in the episode.

The writer also realizes that the scenes immediately preceding and following are largely serious in tone; therefore, definite comic qualities in this scene will be helpful to contribute variety. Certainly the imputation of an insult upon a family is not particularly comic nor would it suggest a typical student duel for the cause is perhaps too specific. Another alternative begins to form in the writer's mind. A representative aspect of this period is the factional feeling between the supporters of Jefferson and the French Revolution and those of the Federalist group. The cause of the duel, therefore, can stem from a political dispute between the two students. This will revivify more precisely and interestingly the spirit of the time and permit necessary exposition concerning the period's political background. This is a better choice. And since the "Republicans" are noted for hot-headedness and fervor for their cause, let the apparently more volatile Mason support the French Revolution and cast the initial challenge.

What aspect of the political dispute between the students will be sufficiently insulting to motivate the challenge? What will either consider the greatest affront to their beliefs? The answer comes quickly: both parties eulogized their leaders. The Jacobins held Jefferson almost as a deity and the Federalists held Washington in the same awe. When Washington died, it is reported that some Jacobins refused to wear black in his memory. If this taunt is thrown in the teeth of a Federalist, it can logically provoke a similar retort in reference to Jefferson. Such an exchange between the two students can lead to a challenge for a duel and also suggest the period's intense factionalism. The writer decides to hold onto this idea.

Having his chief characters and a basic action with a point of attack, the writer prepares to flesh out the situation and the other characters. The historical account involves four other characters in addition to the student duelists and President Madison: the students acting as seconds for Mason and Henley, the magistrate, and William Wirt. None of these characters appears elsewhere in the drama. The student seconds certainly are necessary—one for each principal. Customarily a duelist's second is a close friend. Perhaps these students can have respectively the same relationship to Mason and Henley. But here a problem arises. In a brief focal plot scene there will not be time to develop adequately the friendship between duelist and his respective second. It may be more effective if the seconds are not close acquaintances of their respective principals, but perhaps merely fellow students who are "roped in" to participating in the duel. Such a circumstance will have two advantages. The characters in question will require less delineation since close interrelationships need not be established. And if the two are *reluctant* seconds, comic possibilities are more clearly apparent.

The writer, pleased with his approach, now proceeds to the other two characters. The magistrate is an essential character since it is important to show that dueling was also against the law. The character will be needed only briefly, probably at the end of the scene. His characterization can be determined when the rest of the scene takes shape. What about the lawyer, William Wirt? Yes, he will be required to complete the resolution unless the boys are to be dragged away to jail by the magistrate. Since the playwright has been cautioned to be as accurate as possible in all major details, William Wirt will be kept in the scene. Now seven characters are beginning to take form. That may be enough unless one or two others will later come to be demanded by the action. Judgment will have to be reserved until later on this point.

The playwright now turns to the detail of the historical account. The President halted the duel in Mason's room before it even began, and apparently missed confronting Mason who "escaped." The incident as reported does not reach its maximum dramatic potential. How much more effective on stage it will be if Madison interrupts the duel at the moment when the boys have their revolvers in hand and are raising to take aim. This does not seriously distort the actual incident but merely moves the duel forward a bit in time, making it more dramatically interesting. Within this framework, the duel must take place in the out-of-doors—since duels are not fought generally in students' rooms (at least not with pistols or swords). There is no point, then, in using Mason's room as a setting. Since a focal plot scene in the interests of dramatic unity should generally have only one locale, the action can occur entirely outside. Remembering that the three preceding scenes and the next one following all are set in interiors, the playwright welcomes this opportunity for an exterior scene.

The writer now asks himself if the action of the scene can flow without interruption—which will demand that the challenge for the duel lead directly into the duel itself. He answers the self-asked question with a "no." It would be neither logical nor accurate for the duel to happen so quickly. (Such is only the case in television westerns.) Pistols will have to be prepared; the challenger according to the dueling code must set an hour which gives his opponent time to make his preparation. And according to the actual incident, President Madison must have had time to learn of the duel in order to halt it as efficiently as he did. Certainly, a passage of time is needed—perhaps from an afternoon to the dawn of the next day. This can be suggested by a simple lowering and raising of lights rather than by a curtain which always impedes the action. So far, so good. Yet another alteration in the historical account is demanded. If President Madison is to confront the duelists "at the ready," it will be unlikely that Mason can escape. The action must be such, furthermore, that the resolution be achieved swiftly after the climactic moment. Unless both duelists are on stage when confronted by Madison, the resolution will be difficult to "tie up" dramatically. It will be wise, therefore, to alter the detail of Mason's escape.

Now the basic action for the scene—the dueling incident already helpfully provided by history—has been filled out and its characters envisioned. But the environment for the action does not seem complete. The practice of the lottery comes to mind. Can it be made part of the action? Neither time nor pertinence will allow a scene focusing on student life to show College officials planning or executing a fund-raising lottery. Why can not it be placed in the context of student life by having the students conduct their own lottery? This may allow opportunity to inform the audience about this colorful practice of the College to raise money and also may serve as the background of the scene.

A student lottery can furnish a lively backdrop against which the prospective duelists may meet and against which some facts about contemporary student life may be revealed. Will additional characters be involved? At least one student is needed to operate the lottery. Such a character can be one of the duelists or one of the seconds. Or the character can be a student onlooker who does not become involved in the duel either as second or principal. The last idea gives the writer more latitude and is accepted tentatively.

After wrestling for a sufficient time with the saturation phase of molding his material, the writer drafts a synopsis of the dramatic action in which he takes opportunity to further round out his characters and concentrate on the most essential aspects of his scene. Then, after refining his action on the basis of his synopsis, he transforms the latter into a scenario. The writer now makes an evaluation of the dramatic action to test its completeness and structural strength. He applies to his scenario a check list composed of the basic units of a plot:

> *Exposition and preparation:* Essential background of student life and College history is presented by James Madison as narrator and by the lottery-operator and two other students who begin the scene.
>
> *Complication:* Armistead Mason interrupts the lottery drawing boldly announcing his Jacobin sympathies; Henley appears and antagonizes Mason by criticizing the latter's beliefs.
>
> *Point of attack:* Arguing over political allegiances, Mason challenges Henley to a duel.
>
> *Struggle:* The conflict between Mason and Henley culminates in a duel.
>
> *Major crisis:* Henley and Mason refuse to call off the duel and proceed to carry out the instructions of their seconds.
>
> *Major climax:* Henley and Mason turn to face each other with pistols leveled.
>
> *Outcome:* The duel is halted by President Madison and the boys are threatened with expulsion and arrest (by a magistrate). A friend of Mason's father offers surety for the boy's behavior. The duelists forego their enmity toward each other and shake hands.

According to the check list, the scenario's blueprint for dramatic action passes muster. Now the writer turns to making several drafts of the scene. His final result, a scene tested in performance and proven effective, appears in the following pages.

Hark upon the gale [20]

by Christian Moe

Act II, Scene 1

THE CHARACTERS OF THE SCENE

JAMES MADISON, *President of the College of William and Mary*
STUDENT BARKER, *the operator of a lottery*
FIRST STUDENT
SECOND STUDENT
ARMISTEAD MASON, *a student of Republican principles*
BARTHOLOMEW HENLEY, *a student of Federalist principles*
MAGISTRATE, *a local law official of Williamsburg*
WILLIAM WIRT, *a Williamsburg lawyer*

* * *

SETTING: *A clearing in the woods. Williamsburg. Autumn, 1806.*
(A spot of light discovers President MADISON, *clad in the clerical dress of the early nineteenth century, standing before the curtain.)*

MADISON. 'Tis the year 1806 now and the Revolutionary War is won. Aye, the war is won, but the College has lost in many ways. Our funds greatly diminish. Our state capital moves to Richmond. And our students dwindle to two score and ten. Yet we again steady ourselves on our feet *despite* the troublous acts of students set afire by the French Revolution. One revolution wasn't enough for them, it seems. And the nation's new President Thomas Jefferson is not one for pouring oil on troubled waters, I assure you. Throughout the land now the Jefferson Republicans are ramming into the Washington Federalists like John Paul Jones into a British man-of-war. And the Federalists are ramming back just as hard—even though President Washington is gone now, rest his soul! But, as to ramming, our students do a bit of that too.
    (During the last few sentences of MADISON'S *narration we hear student voices singing "Old Colony Times." The light fades out on* MADISON *as the curtain opens, and come up on the scene. A clearing in the woods not far from the College is seen. Three students stand singing before a small makeshift booth on the counter of which stands a*

rudely made lottery wheel. A banner which hangs over the booth announces LOTTERY. The boys finish singing.)

STUDENT BARKER *(going behind the booth).* I have not the time to spend singing. I have a business to manage. *(In the style of a carnival barker; ignoring the other two students and speaking to an invisible audience supposedly offstage.)* Step ye up to the booth, gentlemen, and buy a ticket for the lottery. If the College can conduct a lottery to raise money so can its students! Each ticket costs only ten pennies! Put your ticket in the wheel, and you may be the happy winner. The first prize will be a jar of homemade apple honey that tempts the gods and—

FIRST STUDENT. When the College held its lottery last year the first prize was ten thousand dollars.

STUDENT BARKER *(unperturbed).* Aye, and the tickets sold at three hundred dollars apiece, not ten pennies. *(Continuing his announcement.)* The second prize will be a bottle of exquisite wine from the Canary Islands. Come one and all, gentlemen. The drawing will take place in only a few minutes. *(He stops, discouraged that no new customers have appeared.)*

FIRST STUDENT. No one else is going to come, sir. On with the drawing!

SECOND STUDENT. We bought our tickets and we demand the drawing. Now!

STUDENT BARKER *(uneasily).* But I've only sold two tickets!

SECOND STUDENT. Good! Then we shall both receive the prizes.

FIRST STUDENT. I hope I win the wine, for now that all we junior students must lodge at the College and stay in rooms from nine o'clock till morning, we can no longer dissipate at the tavern. If a lad cannot pursue his pleasure outside he must pursue it in!

STUDENT BARKER. Gentlemen, excuse me! *(The students turn to him with annoyance.)* Perhaps if you would be so good as to allow me to postpone the drawing until—

FIRST STUDENT. Enough, sir! Turn that wheel, and let fortune fall where she may.

(Reluctantly the STUDENT BARKER *begins to turn the wheel slowly, when suddenly a student rushes in, sporting a tricolor cockade on his hat. His name is Armistead* MASON.)

MASON. Hold your wheel, Citizen, hold your wheel!

STUDENT BARKER *(eagerly).* Do you wish to buy a ticket, Armistead Mason?

MASON. Well—no, I have not the purse for it. But what else is there to do in Williamsburg with no gaming and no theatre, but to watch the lottery? Resume your drawing, Citizen.

STUDENT BARKER (*disappointed*). Oh. (*Hopefully.*) Is there anyone else coming?

MASON. No—unless there be some full-pocketed Washington Federalists about! Note the cockade on my hat, Citizen? I'm for the French Revolution, Thomas Jefferson, and the rights of the States, I am. We are all Republicans here, I take it?

STUDENT BARKER
FIRST STUDENT } (*a bit fearful of his enthusiasm*). That we are—Citizen!

(*Bartholomew* HENLEY, *a small but wiry student, enters.*)

HENLEY. Still this talk of citizen! Are we French Jacobins back in the reign of terror then?

STUDENT BARKER (*not concerned with politics*). Tickets for the lottery now on sale! Ten pennies each! (*With renewed hope.*) Bartholomew Henley?

MASON (*vehemently*). Jacobins we are, and proud of it, Master Henley, for it means the same as Republicans. 'Tis the party of our nation's President Thomas Jefferson.

HENLEY (*ignoring* MASON; *to the* STUDENT BARKER). I only come to see who wins the drawing.

STUDENT BARKER (*in anguish*). Please, I've sold but two tickets. Won't you—

MASON (*interrupting*). Do you hear me, Master Henley?

HENLEY. I am not deaf yet—Citizen Mason. Go back to your Rousseau and spare your shouts for other ears!

MASON. I speak for your ears, sir. You are one of the parcel of damn'd fools who call themselves the Federalists, I have no doubt. British Hirelings would be the better name!

SECOND STUDENT. Calm down, Master Mason! We are not politicians here.

MASON (*hotly*). I will not calm down.

HENLEY. A common failing for a son of sedition, I may say!

FIRST STUDENT. Now see here, Master Henley!

MASON. Let him rant on—he's a Federalist all right.

HENLEY. I favor no party, sir, but if I did I would prefer the camp of the late George Washington, John Marshall, and Patrick Henry. At least they wish a strong government to unite the nation.

MASON. Washington is it! A dead leader for a dead cause! Why, when he died in '99 I refused to wear crepe in his memory.

HENLEY. Do you so basely dishonor the dead, sir?

STUDENT BARKER. Gentlemen, the lottery! (*No one notices him.*)

MASON. I tell you, Master Henley—

HENLEY. And I tell you, Citizen Mason, that I might do the same were your precious Jefferson or James Monroe to join their Maker.

FIRST STUDENT (*a trifle shocked*). You forget, Master Henley, that both are William and Mary men!

STUDENT BARKER (*choosing the better of two evils*). I have decided to start the drawing of—

MASON. You insult Thomas Jefferson! That is an outrage not to be borne, ye damn'd rascal!

HENLEY. Anarchist! You have not the intelligence to be about a college.

MASON. I post you as a coward, sir!

HENLEY (*furiously*). I challenge you to a duel, sir! Choose your place and weapons!

MASON. Here at dawn tomorrow. The weapons to be two pistols each.

HENLEY. At ten paces!

MASON. And fire at will!

HENLEY. Agreed!

FIRST STUDENT. Gentlemen, dueling is forbidden by law!

SECOND STUDENT. And by the College!

STUDENT BARKER. The penalty is expulsion! Only a few years ago four students were dismissed!

MASON (*commandingly; to* FIRST STUDENT). Will you serve as my second, Citizen?

FIRST STUDENT (*regretfully*). Aye, Master Mason.

HENLEY (*to* STUDENT BARKER). Will you serve as my second, sir?

STUDENT BARKER (*terrified*). Oh, no—I couldn't—I—I have an appointment. (*Pointing to* SECOND STUDENT.) Perhaps this gentleman—

HENLEY (*to* SECOND STUDENT). Will you be my second, sir?

SECOND STUDENT (*regretfully*). Aye—it appears I'm the only one left.

HENLEY. See you prepare the pistols. (*To* MASON.) Until tomorrow then—at dawn. (*Exits.*)

MASON. My second and I will be there. (*Exits in the opposite direction.*)

STUDENT BARKER (*still terrified but springing into action, he reaches behind the booth, pulls out a bottle of wine and a jar of honey, and hands the wine to the* FIRST STUDENT). Let us dispense with formality. Here is your wine—(*Handing honey to* SECOND STUDENT.) And here is your honey—(*Grabbing his lottery box under one arm and a bundle of unsold tickets under the other, he dashes from behind the booth.*) And may God save you both! (*Exits running.*)

(*The lights lower to indicate the passage of time. The lights fade up again. The scene is exactly the same except that the lottery booth is absent. The two seconds stand on opposite sides of the stage, each load-*

ing two pistols. *It is dawn. We hear a whippoorwill plaintively singing
its song in the distance.)*

FIRST STUDENT. Politics is a silly thing to fight a duel over. A woman, yes, but
politics! *(Looking at the pistols.)* I wish it were swords. These pistols
are dangerous—they can kill people!

SECOND STUDENT. A remarkable observation!

FIRST STUDENT. Maybe someone will come and stop it.

SECOND STUDENT. 'Tis too late for that now.

*(HENLEY enters from R. One second later MASON enters from L.
They glare at each other for a moment. Then both men go to their respective seconds, take their pistols, move toward each other and then
turn back to back. The seconds cross to them.)*

FIRST STUDENT. In the absence of a third party, one of us will give the instructions. *(He looks hopefully to the* SECOND STUDENT, *who makes a gesture
of refusal; regretfully.)* Before we begin, I should like to ask each of you
gentlemen to reconsider this decision. I believe the entire matter can
be settled without bloodshed. If you have had a change of heart—?

MASON *(hesitantly).* No.

HENLEY *(also hesitant).* No. Get on with it.

FIRST STUDENT *(after a deep sigh).* You will proceed ten paces, turn at my command, then advance and fire at will. One volley only will be allowed.
Are you ready?

MASON. Ready!

HENLEY. Ready!

FIRST STUDENT. Proceed!

*(MASON and HENLEY raise the muzzles of their pistols upwards,
slowly walk ten paces in opposite directions, and arrive at their positions.)*

FIRST STUDENT *(nervously).* Turn!

*(The duelists turn to face each other and level their pistols. Sud-
denly President MADISON enters, followed by a MAGISTRATE.)*

MADISON. Lower your pistols at once! The duel is over, gentlemen!

(The surprised duelists do so—almost gratefully.)

SECOND STUDENT. Dr. Madison! Thank God!

MAGISTRATE. You are both under arrest.

*(The MAGISTRATE moves toward the duelists but MADISON halts
him.)*

MADISON. One moment, Magistrate. *(To the duelists.)* You are hereby expelled
from the College, gentlemen, until and unless your fathers bring you

back and offer surety for your behavior! Yet more important, do you realize that had I not fortunately learned of this duel, one or both of you might well have committed murder. The law would have hanged you for it.

FIRST STUDENT. We tried to make them change their minds, sir.

MADISON. To no avail, I see. (*To* MASON *and* HENLEY.) You are silent, gentlemen. Perhaps you are a bit thankful to have been spared the blood of a fellow student on your hands—and on your conscience.

HENLEY. I am, Dr. Madison.

MASON. And so am I.

MADISON. May I remind you of the duty you owe your College? She too has an honor that a pistol shot can kill.

(WILLIAM WIRT, *a resident of Williamsburg, enters.*)

MASON. Forgive us, Dr. Madison.

MADISON. I might, but the Magistrate cannot.

MAGISTRATE. Come with me, gentlemen.

WIRT (*stepping forward*). A moment, please.

MAGISTRATE. What brings you here, William Wirt?

WIRT. I have had myself appointed constable and should like to arrest Armistead Mason myself.

MAGISTRATE. That is an odd action and request from a Williamsburg lawyer, Mr. Wirt. Your reason?

WIRT. The boy's father is my good friend. I should like to offer surety for his son's good conduct in the future. Sir, I feel sure this matter can be settled by friends of the two parties.

MADISON. I hope you are right. I agree.

MAGISTRATE (*to* WIRT). Well—if you're a constable you had better make your arrest. I am certainly called upon to do peculiar duties here in Williamsburg. (*A bit exasperated.*) Good day, gentlemen. (*Exits.*)

The duelists exchange looks, throw down their pistols and shake hands. MADISON lightly grasps both boys and knocks their heads together. And then throws up his hands in a gesture of exasperation as the lights dim out.)

xi. The features of epic-drama

THE OPENING NIGHT audience at the Cort Theatre in New York is not prepared in the autumn of 1934 to see and hear what it does. *Roll, Sweet Chariot* offers a serious concern for Negro life in this country; an entire Negro village is presented as protagonist. Its playwright, Paul Green, chooses to project a group struggle through symbolic use of time and space and by flooding the stage with light and sound. In the orchestra pit there is a chorus of twenty-two voices, supported by timpani and clarinet, chanting the joy and grief of the dramatic action not in recognizable words but in musically notated sounds. At a particularly critical moment, unfortunately, a loud-speaker blows a fuse with an unpremeditated yowl, and thereafter all amplified voices loses their sense of gravity. Furthermore, Green has insisted that the performance be without intermission. Out in the lobby he paces, listening for audible reactions from the first-nighters. Suddenly, midway through the performance, out from the auditorium bursts critic-humorist Robert Benchley. The usually unruffled Benchley bears down on the playwright. "Intermission or not," he snaps, "I'm going to smoke! What's it all about, anyhow?" [1]

For a combination of reasons Green's "experiments" in *Roll, Sweet Chariot* leave most first-nighters either indifferent or confused; few of them apparently share Benchley's desire to know what it is "all about." Only a limited number of spectators have a chance to find out for themselves, because the production comes to an abrupt halt. Although two or three of the New York drama reviewers defend the production or at least its intent, the producer cannot ignore public apathy and so closes the operation at the end of the first week. A financial flop, *Roll, Sweet Chariot* yet serves to convince Green that, somehow, he is on the right road; under different conditions, perhaps, he might find answers to the artistic questions that challenge him.

What is epic-drama?

A "sounding together" of elements

In company with other native playwrights and kindred spirits of the twenties and thirties, Green is dissatisfied with the subject matter then being dramatized in the American theatre. Prompted by his own urgings and stimulated by what he experiences abroad, he searches for a personal means of expressing the changes and tensions in contemporary American life. He evolves a theory which he attempts to test in Roll, Sweet Chariot: the employment of theatrical elements such as "dance pantomime, poetry, mental speech, masks, choreography, story-line, sound and music," but beyond that, their synthesis into a meaningful dramatic unity. He labels the result "symphonic drama," based on the original Greek meaning of "sound together." To Green "symphonic" seems right for the expression of

> group life, of setting forth the relationships of individuals and their fellows, of masses and crowds affected, energized and motivated as they would be by some centripetal idea and dramatic intent—some story of traditions, of folk inheritance and legend, some famous native character or group of characters splurging themselves forth out of their heritage.[2]

The different conditions that Green hoped would allow him to experiment further with his concept emerge far from the Broadway market place. Members of an isolated fishing community on the Outer Banks encourage him to write a drama commemorating the three hundred and fiftieth anniversary of Sir Walter Raleigh's attempts at an English settlement in the New World. Keeping uppermost in mind the turmoil, longing, and suffering of the little band of some one hundred twenty colonists whose fate still remains a mystery today, Green "sounds together" the elements of a drama he calls The Lost Colony. It opens in 1937. Except for the war years, it is performed regularly on the same site every summer for more than twenty-five years. Its patterns of success, both in the writing and staging, provide a vigorous impetus to the production of historical drama in this country.

The elements of music and sound, dance, poetry, pantomime, and masks have for generations attracted playwrights. No matter what the source of their inspiration or their purpose in turning to the theatre, many imaginative playwrights have shared a common aim in integrating all of the theatrical elements at their disposal. This has been true whether their interaction with the turbulent twentieth century led them to adopt the cause of realism or various departures from it. Earlier periods of theatre history, from what we can piece together of performances in Sophocles' Athens, Shakespeare's England, and Moliere's France, as well as in Oriental traditions, utilized a wide range of theatrical elements. Whereas we cannot be always certain of the degree to which these elements were fused in the past, our impressions of modern drama are clearer. Green and his contemporaries have not only allied a wide range of elements but their purpose, however successfully achieved, has been a fusion of elements into a synthesis meant to be understood as an artistic whole. This

integration aims at "making familiar" to the audience an illusion of a particular world. It is especially in behalf of a world rooted in American history that
Green has so energetically practiced his ideal of "symphonic drama."

While Green continues to apply "symphonic drama" to his own plays
written for outdoor presentation, other playwrights, drama critics, and theatre
practitioners question the descriptive accuracy of the term. Some object that
it indicates much less importance placed on the spoken language than is actually borne out by current writing in this genre. Others point out that audiences unfamiliar with the term are led to expect not so much an enacted
"play" as waves of stereophonic sound. Still another view is that "symphonic"
infers something of the "operatic," which is of course not Green's intent.

There are obvious shortcomings to the invention of catchphrases applicable to this or any particular dramatic form; still we need to view the characteristics of the genre in their relation to those of biography-drama and pageant-
drama. For this purpose we propose the term epic-drama.

The world of the epic

Applying "epic" as a concept to the historical drama under consideration has its pitfalls. The association of "epic" as such with twentieth-century
European trends was formed even before the German poet-playwright Bertolt
Brecht in the twenties began announcing and testing his theories of dramaturgy. Brecht revolted against what was to him the vapidity of the old "dramatic" or so-called "Aristotelian" theatre, intended to arouse and then purge
the emotions of the audience through carefully arranged suspense and climax
sequences. This, according to Brecht, merely induces an emotional involvement in the spectator that prevents his critical faculties from participating in
the action. In theory the Brechtian theatre, by contrast, activates the judgment
of the spectator and enables him to relate his experience in the theatre to
social and moral conditions encountered outside. As one way of enhancing
this critical awareness the Brechtian theatre strives to treat its materials anti-
realistically, deliberately presenting only a segment or fragment of the story
or action. One of Brecht's original key terms, Verfremdung, is popularly ren-
dered as "alienation," but a more accurate translation would be "to make
strange." [3] This desired condition is partially attained, according to Brecht, by
such anti-illusory devices as music, dance, visual projections, amplified narration, and unconcealed mechanical devices of production. The similarity of
these elements is recognizable to those which Green wished to "sound together." In Brechtian dramaturgy, however, the elements are to remain as independent units rather than fusing with each other; their "separate sounding"

functions as another contributing means of enabling the spectator to view alertly and detachedly the action before him.

In practice Brecht's own plays sometimes failed to coincide with his dramatic theories. These, understandably, in turn underwent alteration as he tried to make them work in production.

We offer this brief description of Brecht's concept of "epic" mainly to avoid confusion with our own use of the term "epic-drama," which draws upon the commonly accepted meaning of the heroic world of the epic. In this respect, several features of the epic poem merit attention here. In extant examples the epic poem reflects a dependence on a tradition common to poet and audience. Based on a traditional story or legend, it concentrates on a predominant main subject not through accumulation of details but through emphasis on the generic rather than the particular. Moreover, it is organized into alternating sections of dialogue and narration, and the entire story is presented from the viewpoint of a single reporter or chronicler. The epic poem also encourages latitude in changing place and time; it casts some scenes into enactment while reserving others for description; and with swiftness it "accordionnizes" great passages of time in a brief narrative passage. Such features as those above are reflected in masterpieces (such as Homer's *Iliad, Beowulf,* and old Scottish ballads) inherited from various lands and past epochs.[4] While it is true that the epic poem was a *narrative* form, there are implications that might be fruitful in viewing epic-drama, a view idealized rather than practiced by writers of this form of American historical drama.

From leading practitioners comes support for the application of "epic-drama" in relation to what they conceive to be the idea behind and within their own plays and those they interpret. Green, in thinking back on the evolution of *Roll, Sweet Chariot,* declares that he set out to "write an epic drama on the Negro. . . ."[5] Kermit Hunter speaks of the form as "dealing with epic themes out of American history" and as "American epic theatre."[6] In believing that the imaginary scale of the historical dramatist's world transcends at every point that of ordinary life, Samuel Selden sees an "epic quality in all its parts."[7] And from a more detached vantage point, John Gassner sees in *The Lost Colony* the birth of a new American genre, "a native variant of the epic style developed by Brecht . . . in the Germany of the twenties."[8] Noting the elevated subject matter of the form, Gassner further avers that the resultant dramas, in spite of obvious shortcomings, are "constructed for broad effects on an epic scale to push home an epic theme."[9] It remains for us to ask: what are American playwrights seeking when they deal with "epic quality" and "epic theme"?

The ideal world of epic-drama is inhabited by characters scaled larger than in ordinary life. They demand amplitude in fulfillment of their existence. A central feature of an epic-dramatist's design is concern largely for the oneness of men rather than for any one man, where the group, as protagonist, takes on an elevation and magnitude by virtue of the situation in which its members (the Roanoke colonists or the defenders of the Alamo) find themselves struggling. Since all of the inhabitants are likely to share to some degree magnitude of deed if not thought, the struggle of the group demands a confrontation with foes worthy of its steel. Furthermore, the remoteness of time and place of epic-drama encourages the introduction of abstract or supernatural characters, such as Death, Satan, and other personifications.

In the world of epic-drama, the Patrick Henrys, Sam Houstons, Abraham Lincolns and their deeds are chosen for celebration because of their already existing fame among men. In consequence, the range of suitable subject matter is limited to the deeds and personages the community—whether it be national, regional, or local—considers worthy of celebration. In general, freedom in dealing with material is limited by the fact that the prospective audience, knowing the story by heart, would resent radical changes. Invention by the playwright (as Ramsey Yelvington in *A Cloud of Witnesses* demonstrates by his treatment of the siege of the Alamo) is likely, therefore, to be restricted to shifts of stress, elaboration, and variation of details. Because he does not have to invent a story, the playwright's creative powers are devoted in the main to *making an epic-drama* out of a story well-known if not famous in the community.

A well-known story does not assure an epic-drama of any predetermined form (see chapter vii). Immersion in and imaginative exploration of materials must first take place before dramatic action emerges as a structured shape befitting the aim of the playwright. Certain features of an American epic-drama, nonetheless, are discernible in scripts that have been written and performed. Continued experimentation is needed. Writers can search the materials of the epic world, with its inextricable patchworks of fact and fancy awaiting the skill of the dramatist to pattern them into meaning. He can be concerned with the epic figures and great events of our past, utilizing for instance all manner of technical devices for purposes of greater expressiveness. Through experience and insight a playwright will discover what means express most vividly and completely his view of history and its significance for the audience he has in mind.

Comparison of epic-drama with biography-drama and pageant-drama

Before turning to an appraisal of special features of the American epic-drama, it is profitable to glance at comparative uses of certain dramatic features by playwrights dealing with the three major forms of historical drama. General observations can be drawn regarding the importance such playwrights attach to: 1] the structural elements of plot, character, theme, and spectacle; 2] the adaptation of historical data; and 3] the extent of dramatic "characterization."

Emphasis given structural elements

The commemorative and social function underlying the pageant-drama lends primary emphasis, as Table 2 suggests, to the element of theme. Devising

2. *Relative emphasis given four structural elements.*

biography-drama	epic-drama	pageant-drama
Character	Plot	Theme
Plot & Theme	Theme & Character	Plot & Spectacle
Spectacle	Spectacle	Character

a plot consisting of a series of episodes, the writer deals with significant events in the history of a community. Placing much emphasis on broad effects of spectacle, this episodic structure affords a panoramic view of the community's growth and development. In most cases, a long chronology is covered, sometimes several generations, in order to give this expansive view. The "hero" of the pageant-drama is the geographic place or social organism. Thus, the individual character is subordinated to the group. In the extensive type of pageant-drama, particularly, he is minimized in importance also because of the form's lengthy time span which: 1] renders difficult, if not impossible, concentration on one central character or the same group of characters, and 2] renders the individual relatively transitory in nature, regardless of the weight of his contribution to the community.

Since the biography-drama concerns primarily the chronicle of an individual, it focuses intensively on the delineation of his character. In general, this means its scenes are causally—even if episodically—related and cover a relatively compressed chronology which usually is within the lifetime of an individual. Furthermore, the depiction of happenings in biography-drama, and the theme, while often clearly delineated, are secondary to the concentration on character—with fictional characters sometimes employed to show certain aspects of the biography and to lend unity to the central action. Spectacle is, correspondingly, reduced to fourth place on the scale of emphasis, below that of plot and theme.

Placed schematically between the pageant-drama and the biography-drama, the epic-drama has a main action which elevates plot to primary emphasis. Commonly, the story which the plot projects is familiar to and revered by a homogeneous audience, and often by a heterogeneous audience also. With structural units functioning in a focal plot and connective frame, a sequential scenic order normally outlines a chronological progression; but in this respect writers attach more importance to a dramatic progression gained through causal connectedness of scenes. The elements of theme and character share a secondary place since their import is likely to be dependent upon each other's magnitude and insight. Spectacle in epic-drama generally earns subsidiary emphasis.

Adaptation of historical data

An appraisal of Table 3 suggests comparative treatments of historical facts by the three forms. Pageant-dramas generally employ events primarily

3. *Relative emphasis in adaptation of historical data.*

biography-drama	epic-drama	pageant-drama
Historical figure's personal life	Historical figure's "public" life	Historical events
Historical figure's "public" life	Historical events	Historical figure's "public" life
Historical events	Historical figure's personal life	Historical figure's personal life

for their historical significance and secondarily for their intrinsic dramatic value. The essential facts of a community's history are presented with less rather than more adaptation and compression. For an epic-drama, the writer selects both human beings and events for their historical as well as their dramatic weight. In this form facts are observed and then adapted for the enhancement of dramatic expression. To a greater extent than is called for in pageant-making, the epic-dramatist telescopes historical events, translocates historical personages and incidents, and invents fictitious characters and incidents. The author of a biography-drama chooses to do the same thing to facts to an even greater degree. He selects them for their dramatic value and often for their relevancy to contemporary issues. It can be observed, in short, that among the three forms the adaptation of historical facts for dramatic purposes differs only in degree.

Since it is the historical events which are paramount in the pageant-drama, the writer follows the historical record closely in showing the external facts of what happened and when. And since the events in which the historical figure appears are of "public" significance, his actions and words are usually shown in the light of their "public" context. Here again the simple, outward facts are used. However, the indices of character, his deeds and words, are represented as the audience familiarly recalls them. Rarely does the pageant-writer penetrate deeply into the personal side of a character's life.

The writer of the biography-drama attempts to penetrate, more deeply than he would in the other two forms, the personal or inner life of his leading characters. He is less hesitant to delve into facts of personal relations which may not mesh with the preconceived image the audience has or with what it thinks ideal. Next in importance to his treatment of the personal aspects of his characters, the playwright places weight on the "public" career of his characters. He may go beyond the familiarly known facts, sometimes consciously deviating from them if he wishes to give contemporary meaning to broaden his thematic purposes. For this reason, the biographer-dramatist modifies incidents and invents fictional characters whenever they, without distorting historical truth, improve his dramaturgy.

When it comes to dealing with the basic events of history, the epic-dramatist is likely to hew less strictly to the line than does the pageant-writer. The historical character used by the former must be dramatically satisfying but he must, nevertheless, still be subject to the depiction of the community's history. Thus, here, but to a lesser extent than with the pageant-drama, the epic-drama gives prime emphasis to those actions and words of the character which are of significance in the community's history. The external facts are observed, but frequently, in order to enhance the dramatic story, they must be adapted. The adaptation, however, generally avoids violating limits imposed by the character's public image.

Extent of characterization

With the pageant-drama the writer finds it less possible, and necessary, to develop character complexity and growth. His historical character must be subordinate to the community, which is "hero," and to the depiction of significant events. Because he is important only insofar as he is related to the development of the community, little of the character's action will be self-revealing. Rather, the character will serve, as Table 4 diagrams, to exposit facts

4. Relative degrees of dramatic "characterization" (in no order of emphasis).

biography-drama	epic-drama	pageant-drama
Complexity	$\longrightarrow$	Simplification
Depth	$\longrightarrow$	Surface
Self-revealing	$\longleftrightarrow$	Exposited
Participant in events	$\longleftrightarrow$	Expositor of events
More development	$\longleftarrow$	Less development
More self-revelatory interaction with other characters	$\longleftarrow$	Less self-revelatory interaction with other characters

concerning events and predict their outcome. Time-consuming, character-revealing action within or among the episodes is not often possible. The writer is forced therefore to distinguish his characters by a few easily recognizable traits and no more. Collectively, then, the presentational and structural features of the pageant-drama form contribute largely to a simplified characterization rather than a fully dimensional "individual."

The historical character emerges in the biography-drama as a more complex and three-dimensional personality than that possible in the pageant-drama. The character voices more complex feelings and ideas; and general intensiveness of the plot in the biography-drama allows him character-revealing action through more intimate interrelationship with other characters. He is less obligated than in the other two forms to exposit events or predict their future significance. When famous historical events are shown, they are depicted with the aim of revealing the character's thoughts and beliefs, rather than for their own intrinsic historical interest. In sum, the presentational and structural idiosyncrasies of biography-drama influence the playwright to create a humanly expressive and well individualized character. He appears, then, as far more complex than the simplified historical character of the pageant-drama.

In the epic-drama the historical figure tends toward simplification, but less so than in the pageant-drama. He must often function, influenced by the pageant-drama, as an expositor of events and sometimes as a prognosticator of their future significance. Depth of characterization, somewhat restricted, is pulled away from biography-drama. The basic story of the epic, nevertheless, enables the hero's character to be delineated in action. He can also show development of character through interaction with carefully chosen characters, some of them fictitious, to bring out salient human traits, especially in the protagonist. With the epic-drama a writer is able to mold characters of more roundness and vitality than in the pageant-drama, but they are still likely to be a concentration of simplified traits and not, as in biography-drama, deeply plumbed.

Between the poles of pageant-drama and of biography-drama stands the epic-drama; it is helpful to regard it as an amalgam of both of these forms yet one possessing its own individuality. The pulls of both pageant-drama and biography-drama operate on the epic-dramatist: the demands for magnification and adherence to a preconceived image in the historical figure often result in idealization to a point where the character's individualization as a human personality is weakened; conversely, the demands for theatrical richness and appeal yield universal human qualities that serve to extend the characterization. In the hands of competent playwrights, characterization in the epic-drama can borrow the human vitality and expressiveness of the biography-drama and blend it with the magnification and typification of the pageant-drama. The result is a stage personality which has the strength and grandeur to inhabit the world of the epic.

Structural features of epic-drama

To examine more closely salient characteristics of the epic-drama form, four recent full-length works of American playwrights are analyzed: *The Common Glory* by Paul Green, *The Golden Crucible* by Kermit Hunter, *Dawn's Early Light* by Emmet Lavery, and *A Cloud of Witnesses* by Ramsey Yelvington. The playwrights selected offer variety in subject-matter, intent, methods of approach, and geographic location; they have in common considerable writing experience and skill, and individuality of outlook. A specific sponsoring group commissions each of the four playwrights to deliver a historical drama. Two of the four dramas are written to satisfy the conditions of outdoor performance, the other two being required to adjust to the physical environment of an indoor site. In addition, one of the dramas staged indoors is later taken into two separate outdoor theatres. As might be expected, the demands of spectacle and auditory projection vary markedly according to the physical site and production mode chosen. Important distinctions are therefore possible in comparing and contrasting the four dramas.

Following a structural analysis of the four dramas, *A Cloud of Witnesses*—written for an indoor theatre and then adjusted for open-air performance—will be used to illustrate a conjectured process by which the playwright may have composed his work. Because the general principles of such a process already have been established, discussion of the Yelvington drama's development will be somewhat modified.

Synopses of the four dramas

The Common Glory's longevity has been mentioned earlier as a long-run summer presentation in an outdoor setting in Williamsburg (see fig. 20). Green's drama records the efforts of American colonists, prior to and during the Revolution (1774–81), to lay the foundations of our national government. The colonists are shown going through seven long years of unrest, decision-making, Tory opposition, doubt, deprivation and death, and eventual victory following the Battle of Yorktown. All but one scene is laid in Virginia, at such places as the mansion at Monticello, the Governor's Palace at Williamsburg, and St. John's Church in Richmond, where Patrick Henry delivers his "Liberty or Death" speech. When Jefferson is presented in a rooming house in Philadelphia, he is shown drawing up the first draft of the Declaration of Independence and then testing it on Benjamin Franklin and John Adams. While representative patriots struggle to attain their independence, the centrality of the action resides in the fiery political leader Jefferson, who matures in wisdom and understanding under the burden of personal griefs, the duties of governorship, and the agonies of the Revolution.

The second example, *The Golden Crucible*, is tailored to the special requirements of the Pittsburgh Bicentennial Amphitheatre with its floating stage (see fig. 17). The drama shows how persons of different ethnic and economic backgrounds work together to build the city of Pittsburgh and then, when its metropolitan health is seriously endangered, rally in a cooperative campaign of rebuilding. A number of characters have a historical connection with the city's history—George Washington, Daniel Boone, General John Forbes, Mike Fink, Abraham Lincoln, and the scientist-educator John Brashear. A fictitious Scotch Presbyterian minister, Reverend MacDougald, traces the early history of the city for his classroom of immigrants desirous of becoming American

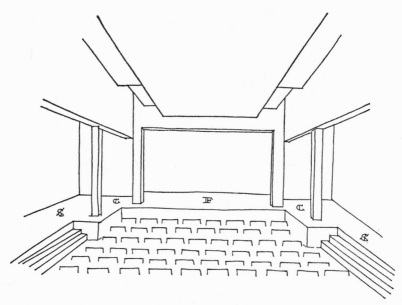

24. STUDIO ONE, AN INDOOR THEATRE at *Baylor University. In this playhouse, the audience is surrounded by stages. Five stages form a rough semi-circle around the acting area, and a sixth is located in the rear. The spectators are seated on swivel chairs, allowing them to turn and view any of the six stages. Shown are two side stages* **S,** *two corner stages* **C,** *and a front stage* **F.** *For arena presentation, the seats are moved from the floor center to its edge and to the stages, thereby enclosing the acting area.*

citizens. A fictional Frank Radekowski is the protagonist, a symbol of Pittsburgh's foreign-born. Although Frank is readily imbued with the ideals of democracy, he grows bitter over the death in childbirth of his young wife, with the bitterness increasing when his only son dies fighting for his country in World War II. Not until his declining years does Frank discover concretely how to fulfill his obligations as a citizen. He does this by offering his material assets and prestige to help speed the renaissance of the city.

As the third drama, *Dawn's Early Light,* written for production in a conventional proscenium theatre at the University of Oregon, focuses on the period prior to the American Revolution. It deals with some of the same principal characters as does *The Common Glory,* but catches them when they are younger. Although the locale is the English colony of Virginia, Lavery's drama is about the way all thirteen colonies come to be united. Its action embroils such diverse personalities as Patrick Henry, Thomas Jefferson, George

25. TEXAS HISTORIC THEATRE at *Mission San Jose, San Antonio. This amphitheatre, modifying the Studio One concept of enveloping stages (fig. 24), has a variable capacity of 1000–1500 seats. A side stage* S *is slightly ramped and joined with the front stage* F *by a corner stage* C. *A light tower* T *offers positions for instruments to illuminate* S, C, *and* F. *A stockade fence* SF *blends into a grove of trees and shrubbery.*

Washington, James Madison, George Wythe (Jefferson's mentor), and Edward Pendleton in conflict over the meaning of political tyranny and individual freedom. Also prominently involved are Henry's mother and his two wives, and Martha Washington, giving the momentous issues confronting the leaders a distinctly human cast. It is Pendleton, particularly, who at first opposes the severance of ties with England; but it is he who, in the critical hours, overcomes his personal dislike for Henry and begs the latter's forgiveness in order that there be unanimity in the Virginia legislature for adoption of the Declaration of Independence. The drama demonstrates that freedom grows even among those who do not agree with each other.

A *Cloud of Witnesses* has its initial presentation indoors at Baylor University (see fig. 24). Because of its favorable reception in Waco, the drama is repeated the following summer outdoors within the confines of the San Jose Mission in San Antonio. Then, after a year's intermission, another production of it is prepared for performance in a nearby amphitheatre constructed and owned by the state park system (see fig. 25). Taking the historical incident of the siege and fall of the Alamo, Yelvington dramatizes the twelve-day ordeal for a band of persons portrayed with weaknesses as well as strengths. Although the author establishes Colonels Travis, Crockett, and Bowie as the leaders of the contingent, he has wider interests; he wishes to weigh the cost of freedom involved for all those who sacrificed their lives against great odds in defending the Alamo. How he manages to do this will be the subject of discussion later.

Four structural patterns

In the previous chapter the terms *focal plot* and *connective frame* have been discussed. Paralleling their use in the pageant-drama, these terms have in the epic-drama the same general meaning. A focal plot embraces structural units demonstrating the central dramatic story, which is depicted in a series of scenes. A connective frame is comprised of those actions and devices which the playwright finds necessary in explaining the focal plot and expressing his view as a whole. As exemplified in *The Common Glory, The Golden Crucible, Dawn's Early Light,* and *A Cloud of Witnesses,* units of the connective frame may be devices such as prologues, epilogues, narrations, retrospective (looking backward) or prospective (looking forward) "dream" sequences, or sequences stressing dance and/or music, both choral and instrumental. As an effective theatrical principle, the focal plot and the connective frame are frequently juxtaposed to suggest distinct and separate planes of reality, imagined by the playwright as being different in time, or in place, or in the realm of plausibility.

To understand the structural patterns of these epic-dramas, the sequential order of scenes is listed as the respective scripts indicate they have been performed. Connected where possible with matters of presentation, these factors of structure are considered in order: 1] the number of structural units per act,   2] the length of time covered by the action,   3] the time-lapse between scenes,   4] the ratio of "interior" to "exterior" scenes,   5] the frequency of "spectacle" or crowd scenes, and   6] the use of framing or connective devices in the plot.

The Common Glory
by *Paul Green*

written for performance in the Lake Matoaka Amphitheatre at Williamsburg, Virginia, beginning in the summer of 1947
(*indicates a connective frame unit; units not so indicated are components of the focal plot. ***indicates narration.)

TIME OF ACTION: the latter part of the 18th century
PLACE OF ACTION: Virginia and Philadelphia

ACT I

*Prologue: Narrator with Choir interlude

Scene 1: The terrace at Monticello, an autumn afternoon, 1774

> ***

Scene 2: The ballroom at the Governor's Palace at Williamsburg, a January night, 1775

> ***

Scene 3: St. John's Church, Richmond, March, 1775

> ***

Scene 4: The House of the Burgesses in Williamsburg, May, 1776

> ***

Scene 5: Before the gaol in Williamsburg, the same day

> ***

Scene 6: The garden of Robert Gordon's plantation house on the James River, the next night

> ***

Scene 7: A rooming house in Philadelphia, summer, several weeks later

> ***

Scene 8: The Palace Green in Williamsburg, a July afternoon, 1776

ACT II

*Narration

Scene 1: A montage sequence, Virginia, summer, 1779

***

Scene 2: An inner office in the Governor's Palace at Williamsburg, winter,
1779

***

Scene 3: A ruined churchyard at Jamestown, a winter night, 1780

***

Scene 4: A montage sequence, Virginia, September, 1781

***

Scene 5: A farmhouse near Yorktown, a few days later

***

Scene 6: A battlefield at Yorktown, October, 1781

***

Scene 7: Somewhere in Virginia, sometime later
*Epilogue: Narrator

The Golden Crucible
by Kermit Hunter

written for performance in the Pittsburgh Bicentennial Amphitheatre at
Pittsburgh, Pennsylvania, during the summer of 1959
(*indicates a connective frame unit; units not so indicated are components
of the focal plot.)

TIME OF ACTION: from 1753 to 1946
PLACE OF ACTION: Western Pennsylvania, what is now Allegheny
County

ACT I

*Prologue: Voice of The River, and dance ceremony to The River
*Scene 1: Seneca village, mouth of the Youghiogheny River, late December
1753
Scene 2: Schoolroom at the home of Rev. MacDougald, Pittsburgh, July 5,
1891
*Scene 3: Fort Duquesne, July 6, 1755
*Scene 4: Braddock's defeat, a few hours later
*Scene 5: Gist plantation (near Uniontown), that night
Scene 6: The schoolroom, a few minutes later than Scene 2

*Scene   7: Fort Duquesne, November 28, 1758
Scene   8: The schoolroom, a few minutes after Scene 6
*Scene   9: The Point, July 4, 1810
Scene 10: The schoolroom, a few minutes after Scene 8
Scene 11: Street before Frank Radekoski's house, Pittsburgh, a few minutes
later
Scene 12: Porch of Frank's house, a year later, night of July 5, 1892
*Scene 13: The Monongahela House, Pittsburgh, February 14, 1861
Scene 14: Porch of Frank's house, a moment after Scene 12

ACT II

*Prologue: Voice of The River
Scene   1: Mill Yards, Homestead, afternoon of July 6, 1892
Scene   2: Porch of Frank's house, later that evening
Scene   3: Office of H. C. Frick, Pittsburgh, July 23, 1892
Scene   4: Porch of Frank's house, later that evening
Scene   5: Garden of Jane's house, Pittsburgh, early summer, 1910
Scene   6: Terrace at Jane's house, a few minutes later
Scene   7: Porch of Frank's house, summer of 1917
Scene   8: Office of the Allegheny Conference, summer of 1946
Scene   9: Porch of and street before Frank's house, three hours later
*Epilogue: Voice of The River

Dawn's Early Light
by Emmet Lavery

written for first performance at the University of Oregon Theatre, Eugene,
Oregon, in August, 1959.
(*indicates a connective frame unit. **indicates scenes that in the Oregon
première were staged on the apron of the University Theatre.)

TIME OF ACTION: from 1765 to 1776
PLACE OF ACTION: Williamsburg, Monticello, Philadelphia

PART I

*Scene   1: ** Prologue—Address of welcome given by Washington
Scene   2: The Williamsburg Race Track, noon, May, 1765

Scene 3: ** The House of Burgesses, the following day
Scene 4: The Raleigh Tavern, evening, the same day
*Scene 5: ** Series of scenes (1765–1769)
Scene 6: Hilltop at Monticello, sunset, May, 1769
Scene 7: ** The House of Burgesses, 1769
Scene 8: The Raleigh Tavern, evening, 1769
*Scene 15: ** The General Court, April, 1770

PART II

Scene 10: The Palace Green, evening, April, 1770
*Scene 11: ** Series of scenes (1770–1774)
Scene 12: Hilltop Cemetery, Hanover, January, 1775
Scene 13: ** St. John's Church, March, 1775
Scene 14: Terrace at Monticello, morning, May, 1775
Scene 9: ** Pendleton, 1776
Scene 16: The Chamber of the House, Williamsburg, May, 1776
Scene 17: ** Philadelphia, July, 1776

A Cloud of Witnesses
by Ramsey Yelvington

written for first performance at Baylor University at Waco, Texas, in November, 1954
(*indicates a connective frame unit.)

TIME OF ACTION: from February 18, 1836 to March 5, 1837; and indefinite time since then
PLACE OF ACTION: outside and inside the Alamo Chapel; and in the memory of Texan and Mexican women and their men

ACT I

*Prologue

*Scene 1: A Dark Place, sometime after the Alamo
*Scene 2: Outside the Alamo Chapel, sometime after the Alamo
Scene 3: Inside the Alamo Chapel, mid-morning, February 23, 1836
*Scene 4: Memory sequence

Scene 5: *Inside the Alamo Chapel, the next afternoon, February 24, 1836;
Memory sequence*

ACT II

*Prologue
Scene 1: *Inside the Chapel, evening, March 1, 1836*
*Scene 2: *Memory sequence*
Scene 3: *Inside the Chapel, continuous time from March 3 to March 5,
1836*
*Scene 4: *Memory sequence*
*Epilogue

Number of structural units

Each of these exemplary dramas has a two-act structure. The total
number of scenes in them varies from nine in *Witnesses* to twenty-three in
Golden Crucible, with *Glory* and *Light* divided into fifteen and sixteen, respectively. A meaningful breakdown is the proportionate pattern of scenes
appearing in the printed or typed script. (A more meaningful index, admittedly, is the time actually clocked in performance, but pagination offers an

5. *Total number of scenes in focal plot and connective frame (excluding prologue
and epilogue). Shortened titles are used in the text.*

	Glory			Golden Crucible			Light			Witnesses	
acts	scs.	pgs.	acts	scs.	pgs.	acts	scs.	pgs.	acts	scs.	pgs.
I	8	64	I	14	44	I	8	57	I	5	54
II	7	40	II	9	28	II	8	70	II	4	35
total —	15	104		23	72		16	127		9	89

acceptable substitute.) Roughly sixty per cent of the dialogue in *Glory,
Golden Crucible,* and *Witnesses* precedes the intermission. In *Light* a little
more than sixty per cent of the dialogue is placed in Act II, a division justified
by Lavery's decision to reveal after the intermission the ever-increasing complications of youthful leaders finding resistance to their ideals. Increased involvement demands extended development.

The general practice of structuring the epic-drama form, however, for
one intermission coming about or shortly past the half-way mark in playing

time has much to commend it. Such a scheme enables the dramatist to dwell
sufficiently on exposition, preparation, and development while audience attention is still fresh; following the intermission, the playwright can then "accor-
dionize" action and heighten tensions for the greatest effect in the shorter
Act II division.

Note that the total number of twenty-three scenes in the *Golden
Crucible*, fourteen of which appear in Act I, is determined in part by author
Hunter's decision to chronicle the influence of many diverse personalities in
the two-hundred-year history of Pittsburgh. Although the focal plot spans
only the 1891–1946 period, a connective frame of "flashbacks" presents historic
events dating back as early as 1753.

Length of time of action in focal plot

The time span of the focal plot for *Light* and *Glory* overlaps somewhat:
in the case of the former, eleven years prior to 1776 are treated; in the case of

6. *Length of time of action in focal plot.*

Glory	Golden Crucible	Light	Witnesses
[1774–1781]	[1891–1946]	[1765–1776]	12 days and indefi-
7 years	55 years	11 years	nite "memory" span

the latter, seven years from 1774 to 1781 are covered. Author Lavery comments
in the preface to *Light* that

> few liberties (if any) have been taken with the chronology of the years
> 1765–1776. The facts remain the same as they have always been and
> so do the (established) attitudes to these facts. This, however, is not
> a biography of the period: it is a dramatization and as such it does not
> hesitate to deal imaginatively with the private lives of many of the
> characters.[10]

To do this he moves toward biography-drama by compressing eight scenes into
five years in Act I, and eight scenes into six years in Act II. In *Witnesses*
Yelvington telescopes a focal plot into the twelve critical days leading to the
fall of the Alamo, meanwhile weaving through the action an imaginatively
conceived "memory span" extended indefinitely. In this drama standard measures of time are irrelevant.

The focal plot span of *Golden Crucible* reaches fifty-five years. This
mirrors the relatively extensive coverage of subject matter and the play-

wright's aims: to give a panoramic view of the founding and growth of a great city; to allow his protagonist, a steelworker who teaches citizenship to immigrants such as he once was, to discover after fifty-five years what the practice of democracy really involves. With epic-dramas in general a strict adherence to chronology is not as important as the means by which focal plot and connective frame combine to contribute a progressive forward thrust to the action.

Time-lapse between scenes

A contributing factor to the extensive or intensive nature of a play's structure is the interval of time observed between scenes of its focal plot.

7. *Average time-lapse between scenes in focal plot.*

Glory	Golden Crucible	Light	Witnesses
3	4	1	2
months	years	year	days

Considerable lapse of time may take place, thus giving an episodic or extensive design to the play. In the four examples, the average length of time between scenes ranges from roughly four years in *Golden Crucible* to two days in *Witnesses*, and spreads between one year in *Light* and three months in *Glory*. As a general rule the more concentrated the overall time-span in epic-drama, the stronger the sense of unification. In this regard, one critical factor is how well the connective frame succeeds in relating what is past with what is anticipated. Tensions are maintained, new perspectives gained by the urgency with which time is measured in the framing device. The average four-year span in *Golden Crucible* furthers the pageant-like features of that play; the blurring of time in the connective frame of *Witnesses* accounts for some of that play's unusual impact.

Unless there are greater values to be gained in more diffusion of content, the epic-dramatist, like the pageanteer, will find merit in the tightest possible relationship between his focal plot and an effective connective frame.

Ratio of interior to exterior scenes

The specificity of locale in epic-drama, whether interior or exterior, is relatively unimportant. In respect to these four plays, however, note that *Glory* and *Golden Crucible*, both specifically written for outdoor production, clearly favor the use of exterior scenes. Glory has reference to a half dozen locales in and around Williamsburg, and does specify Monticello, Richmond, and Philadephia as distinct settings. Green calls for six separate interior scenes and nine separate (but vaguer) exterior scenes; usually he alternates an exterior scene with an interior one, although with the regular use of narration in the connective frame he has a reliable control for gaining contrast. This scope in choice of setting makes for variety of visual effects as the production shifts its focus. When managed with technical skill, scenic designs for multi-set productions lend theatrical excitement at the same time they help realize dramatic potentials.

8. Ratio of interior to exterior scenes.

Glory	Golden Crucible	Light	Witnesses
6 interiors/	6 interiors/	8 interiors/	no clear-cut dis-
9 exteriors	17 exteriors	5 exteriors	tinction

Because of his subject matter's spread and the severe voice projection problems connected with the actor-to-audience distance in the large Golden Crucible amphitheatre, Hunter—not surprisingly—specifies seventeen exterior settings to six interior ones (one of the latter, a schoolroom central to the focal plot, is repeated three times). In the outdoors realistic interior settings are likely to afford less acting space and be more restrictive than exterior ones. Furthermore, they also are likely to be more costly to construct and shift than exterior settings.

Lavery's assignment, on the other hand, calls for an indoor production for Light. The increased intimacy between stage and audience accounts in part for his favoring eight interior scenes (five in ACT I, three in ACT II) to five exterior ones (two in ACT I, three in ACT II). Large numbers of actors do not have to be accommodated in acting space. One of Light's particular strengths, moreover, resides in the deliberative skills and rhetorical resources of its principal characters, powers which flourish best in the legislature forum and caucus room; hence, the action of the play is more congenial to the atmosphere of the indoors. When Lavery does turn to exterior settings, he capitalizes on the color and mass movement possible in such sites as the Williamsburg racetrack, the garden at Monticello, and the village common just outside the Williamsburg Theatre.

Lastly, Witnesses makes little distinction between physical interiors and exteriors. For reasons discussed later, the climate of probability in Yelvington's drama is appropriately nonrealistic and unlocalized in the memory of dead people, witnesses all to the heroic stand at the Alamo in 1836.

Use of "crowd" scenes

Of the fifteen scenic units in the focal plot of *Glory*, nine may be regarded as utilizing the visual and auditory effects of crowds for their spectacular values. Green employs patterns of mass movement and contrasting color in scenes varying from the glitter of a formal ball in the Governor's Palace to the confused violence of a battlefield at Yorktown. Other units suggesting eighteenth-century Virginia qualities include a street gathering outside the Williamsburg gaol; a garden party interrupted by a gang of Liberty Boys; assorted patriotic rallies supporting the appearance of Patrick Henry, General Washington, and Thomas Jefferson; and a montage sequence abstracting, in turn, choreographed actions of reapers-sowers, of convicts digging for iron, and of weary and sick soldiers.

9. *Ratio of "crowd" to total scenes.*

Glory	Golden Crucible	Light	Witnesses
9/15	11/23	3/16	"Crowd" always present; 4 scenes use mass movement

Of the twenty-three scenic units in *Golden Crucible*, eleven are designed to capture the expressive qualities of mass movement, speech, and, sometimes, song. Hunter's drama gains visual and auditory appeal through scenes ranging from the peacefulness of Senecan Indian pastoral life and of 1910 lawn parties hosted by Pittsburgh steel barons to the viciousness of the Homestead Steel Strike. Other crowd scenes include the capture by British troops of a French-held fort with an accompanying victory dance by Scottish Highlanders; a Fourth of July picnic and steamboat race; a street dance representing various European nationalities; and a political parade welcoming Abraham Lincoln.

The multi-stage spatial resources of the outdoor amphitheatre at both Williamsburg and Pittsburgh accommodate readily to the broad historical perspectives of playwrights Green and Hunter. Contrariwise, the authors of

Light and *Witnesses* gauge their production sights originally on indoor theatre objectives, but with differences. A proscenium arch stage with some apron thrust serves the University of Oregon presentation of *Light*. Lavery wisely reduces the element of the spectacle to a minimum, using few characters beyond the fourteen principal ones, and raising his off-stage sound patterns to a high level of importance. In the two-act structure of *Light* there are only three "crowd" scenes. These are: a racetrack scene, with the excitement of its special occasion enkindled by band music and fanfares; a festive gathering before the Williamsburg Theatre having a Virginia reel interrupted by overture music to *The Beggar's Opera*; and, finally, the legislature assembly where Patrick Henry rises to move the momentous adoption of the Declaration of Independence.

When he writes *Witnesses* Yelvington has Baylor University's Studio One staging resources in mind (see fig. 24). An intimate indoor auditorium, its flexible staging devices make possible the enclosure of members of the audience who swivel their chairs around in various directions to follow the ever-changing patterns of action. In this way the congregation of "witnesses" always present in the play may be emphasized or de-emphasized by light even though they are relatively static. The scenes in which physical crowd action is marked are proportionately few in number; they are associated importantly, as might be expected, with the focal plot. All four of them occur "inside the Alamo Chapel": an exodus of the Mexican populace and the arrival of Texan soldiers, followed by a "memory" sequence of Mexicans dancing the fandango to clicking castanets; a convocation of Alamo defenders to decide whether to stay and fight; a lively, friendly dispute between bagpipers and fiddlers which ends in a wild, happy processional throughout the Chapel as reinforcements arrive; and, climactically, a scene that telescopes time into three increasingly turbulent waves of battle, the first two seeing the Mexican soldiers repulsed, the final one resulting in the annihilation of all male defenders.

Some adaptation of Yelvington's script and its presentation is necessary when going from the indoor to the outdoor situation. When *Witnesses* moves to its first outdoor site, actors play against the high walls of the San Jose Mission chapel on a patio measuring 30 by 150 feet. Satan appears on the high enclosing wall, impressively contrasting with the other actors below him. Because the Mission itself is so isolated and free of city traffic noises, it seems necessary to make only the most minor changes—mainly cutting a line here and there—in the script. In this quiet place the intimacy possible in the indoor situation at Waco carries over, the actors achieving similar subtlety in handling the author's blank verse and with such sound effects as simulated gunfire rather than real ammunition.

In moving to the second outdoor situation, much more adaptation becomes necessary. A specially constructed one thousand-seat amphitheatre is built, patterned after the Baylor concept of enveloping stages around the audience (see fig. 25). Whereas the *general* mode of the production is preserved, values of intimacy are reduced considerably as the audience is distanced from the action and city noises set up distracting competition. The chief changes in the script are two: first, to shorten some of the extended poetic speeches; and secondly, to add visually a fandango dance that the soldiers recall in the daydream, and an elaborate, although brief, dance accompanying a speech of Crockett's when he recalls impressions of his Irish forebears. In the original version at Baylor these spectacular components are not included. As language nuances, especially in choral sequences, become lost outdoors, the playwright and director compensate for the losses by adding visual color and movement.

Connective frame, including prologue and epilogue

The authors of the four exemplary dramas employ the connective framing device effectively and in fertile ways. The Glory establishes an appropriate tone initially through an organ prelude, a visible singing choir, and a Narrator lending dignity and elevation to the proceedings. It is chiefly the Narrator, dressed as an eighteenth-century gentleman, who functions as expositor, reporter, and commentator of the main action (a narration follows each focal scene except the Battle of Yorktown), unifying the diffuse structure of the focal plot, and affording an olympian detachment for the struggles of the early

10. *Types of units used in connective frame (including prologue and epilogue).*

Glory	Golden Crucible	Light	Witnesses
organ music	recorded music	prologue	prologue
narrator	narrators	direct address to	omnipresent chorus
singing choir	dance ritual	audience	retrospective
choreography	retrospective	nonrealistic	"flashbacks"
"mental speech"	"flashbacks"	scenery	various levels of
dream sequence	fusion of frame	off-stage music	fusion with focal
supernatural being	with focal plot	and sound	plot
	prologue		nonrealistic
	epilogue		lighting
			nonrealistic
			sound

patriots. The Narrator also controls and interprets, by an omniscient and omnipresent amplified voice, two important "mental speech" sequences. One is in Act I when Jefferson, alone in his room in Philadelphia, composes silently the Declaration of Independence; the other is during a "dream" sequence in Act II when a despondent Jefferson encounters the figure of Death and, as a result of this confrontation with the supernatural, gains a mystic affirmation and renewal of spirit strong enough to sustain him in the struggle with the problem of the War. Green uses theatrical elements of music, singing, choreography, amplified thought, and pantomime to define a plane of reality in Glory different from that of everyday life. Reaction to the presence of the separate elements would probably lessen identification with their human relevancy; and so it is the Narrator who restores a synthesis of the strange and the familiar.

Hunter's employment of narration as a connective frame in Golden Crucible seems less arbitrary and more fluid in this drama than it does in Glory. He conceives a personification closely associated with the history of Pittsburgh, the Voice of The River, to establish immediately the appropriate tone; an opening spoken sequence is followed by an Indian dance ceremonial to The River ("the giver of life"). On an abstract level the Voice of The River is heard again at the beginning of Act II and at the end of the drama. In relation to the connective frame, the character-narrator Reverend MacDougald functions importantly. Vitally involved in the focal plot, it is he who, in order to prepare his immigrant students for citizenship, recalls some significant moments and men in the early history of the city. By means of "flashbacks" in the connective frame, these evocations impress the minds of Frank Radekowski, the fictional hero, and his laboring-class friends. With Act I, scene ten, the focal plot and the connective frame merge as one, moving forward chronologically except for the final "flashback" that constitutes Act I, scene thirteen. After this scene, all structural units—with the exception of the prologue and epilogue of Act II—proceed as focal plot. In Act I the dual handling of time is skillfully dramatized, appearing to grow out of the character-situation necessities of the drama. An orchestral score serving to punctuate dramatic ideas, make transitions, and enhance emotional states helps to unify the diffuse structure of the play.

The playwright's use of the connective frame in Light is straightforward and functional. A prologue consists of the character of Washington welcoming the audience to Virginia. Even though the chronology of historical events is restricted to the period 1765–76, Lavery prefers modern dress and modern speech. These are playwriting signals to a contemporary audience to regard familiar heroes and events with a critically fresh detachment. Following the prologue, the focal plot is uninterrupted in Act ɪ except for scene four, when a series of vignettes ("apron scenes," so named by the author) presents six different characters commenting on events and relationships thus far revealed. Act ɪɪ, however, frames the focal plot with two scenes: scene two, being a series of direct addresses by six characters; scene six, being part commentary and part exposition by Pendleton, Patrick Henry's chief opponent in the crucial showdown that follows in the next scene in the Chamber of the House. No epilogue is required, for the final scene in the play finds Jefferson reading a draft of the Declaration of Independence to the Congress assembled in Philadelphia, a Congress that is joined spiritually by members of the theatre audience.

The theatrical premises of *Witnesses* are swiftly exposed in a prologue spoken by Dr. Amos Pollard, an army physician involved as a minor character in the focal plot. Dr. Pollard explains to the audience that the author wishes not only to demonstrate what it already knows (the legend of the Alamo) but also to apply its meaning to the human condition now. The doctor further makes acknowledgment of the play's technical indebtedness to the choric aids found in classic Greek and Japanese drama and to a stock character type found in the morality play of the Middle Ages. This last reference is preparation for the introduction of Satan who also doubles as a character in the focal plot. Nonrealistic use of sound and lighting effects, abrupt interruptive illusion-breaking devices, subtly introduced retrospective "visions," the ever-present chorus of women, sometimes narrating, sometimes commenting collectively or individually—all of these and other devices make for a complex presentational mode. Yelvington structures theatrical experience for the purpose of startling the audience "into a keener, sharper sort of recognition—to make an old story fresh and vital." [11]

Collective and individual heroes

Assuming that he has freedom of choice in shaping his materials, a writer dealing with the epic-drama form should recognize important differences operating when his protagonist is single, as in *Glory* and *Golden Crucible*, and when it is a group, as in *Light* and *Witnesses*. In the case of the latter pair of plays, the appealing strength of the action results from a struggle in part elevated and magnified by the sight of many individuals sharing a commonly desired goal. For the occasion regarded worthy of celebration, the group has a single purpose and distinctive identity. With *Glory* and *Golden Crucible* this insistence on group unity, in comparison with *Light* and *Wit-*

nesses, is neither emphatic nor sustained; still the protagonist in each case (Jefferson in the former, the imaginary Frank Radekowski in the latter) serves as a representative of his fellows in a large community involvement. This type of dramatic emphasis calls for a character of recognized stature to lead his fellows as he personifies ideals which they respect if not, indeed, cherish.

Distinction between outdoor and indoor production

Related closely to subject matter and central focus is the distinction between outdoor and indoor production. The limitations of each type need to be recognized, their assets capitalized on. Conceived initially by their authors for indoor presentation—in intimate circumstances seating, respectively, about two hundred and four hundred persons—*Witnesses* and *Light* could consequently afford to have more complex characterization and subtlety in language than if they had been planned for theatres out-of-doors. (Large indoor auditoriums seating thousands would, of course, be a different matter.) But when playwrights visualize their dramas for open-air production in amphitheatres accommodating eighteen hundred to twenty-four hundred persons, as in the case of *Glory* and *Golden Crucible*, respectively, they must respond to the inherent demands for spectacle on the one hand and vocal projection on the other. In the main, exterior scenes more easily reinforce these presentational factors, but this statement must be qualified—as was pointed out in Chapter vi—on the degree of specificity agreed upon by the theatre architects and the production mode desired by the director and designer. As outdoor performance demands colorful and large visual effects, and as it is customarily less effective to render these in interior scenes, most playwrights favor a substantial number of exterior scenes which can accommodate the spectacular aspects of American epic-drama.

Directing and acting in the open-air theatre

The outdoor stage, with from one to as many as five potential acting areas, is well suited to the fluid, expansive, and often episodic action of the epic-drama, with its frequent scene changes, just as it is to the pageant-drama. In part because of the physical conditions of production, a director's staging of such dramas emphasizes the spectacular elements intrinsic in mass groupings and action, colorful costumes, lively group dances, and music. Enlarged, these elements serve to 1] make the action visible and meaningful to an audience often distant from the stage, 2] vivify the individual scenes, 3] fill the expansive stage space, and 4] gratify the spectator's sensory urge for spectacle. Conspicuous use, therefore, is made of crowds, dance groups, and/or choruses. The frequently elevated relation of the audience (in a well-planned auditorium) to the space for action usually encourages the director to weave intricate patterns of color and movement over a large area which the spectator can appreciate as an interestingly-designed mosaic. Out-of-door production elements are scaled upwards, broadly and vividly.

The greatest impact an alfresco production has on an audience lies in generous employment of vividly costumed groups demonstrating some physical action within the scene. A director's success in achieving this depends on his skill in getting the individual actors in the crowd to move and react meaningfully and with strong expressiveness. The experienced director of dramas seen out-of-doors must convince his actors that the large-scale effect required places distinct obligations on them. In most cases they will find that realistic acting conventions, nuances, and the sense of intimacy often effective inside no longer work for them. Large strokes of movement, gesture, and vocal delivery are instrumental in projecting unmistakably the intended meaning. The distance from the actor to auditor necessitates, of course, this magnified style, in which large gesture, long and easy stride, and broad stance convey the character's expression, whereas small gestures, hesitant steps, and random movement blur and negate the characterization.

In casting for outdoor production, a director looks for physical vigor and grace and listens for vocal power and clear articulation. Physical vitality must support the voice, particularly when a performance is to be repeated for any length of time. Audibility and intelligibility are paramount factors on the expansive open-air stage with its increased actor-audience distance. These are even more important factors when sound amplification systems are rejected by directors because of the inhibiting and artificial results created by dependence on microphones.

The magnification of acting that open-air theatre conditions frequently require often shows up bodily awkwardness, ineptitude of technique, or distracting personal mannerisms which may be overlooked (and which are sometimes regarded as effective) in an indoor performance. An adaptable, resourceful actor will always wish to replace strain by control. He will learn how best to use his vocal equipment; he will know how to master his full resonant powers, projecting his voice to the last row of spectators. He will know how to conserve his vocal energies, mindful that if he shouts or yells, they will fail him before the performance ends. He will know how to articulate carefully, yet keeping the individual word subject to the meaning of the phrase as a whole if he is not to sound stilted and self-conscious. Appropriate and full meaning is mainly a matter of relative emphasis within the connected speech whether the spectator is twenty or two hundred feet distant. The actor has, moreover, a double challenge in projecting this appropriate and full meaning while he must at the same time contend with such hazards as nature's wind, drizzle, and insect noises. That the open-air can, contrariwise, serve as an incentive to the actor is summed up in the following advice given by the British director E. Martin Browne:

> Breadth and depth are the right qualities for open-air acting. Let the air fill your lungs and let your body expand its movements to the size of its surroundings. . . . Breadth does not mean slowness, nor does depth mean dullness. Open-air acting should be as athletic as open-air sport, and its emotion should have the extra strength of passion that the freedom of the air can release.[12]

Development of an epic-drama: a cloud of witnesses

As a playwright, Ramsey Yelvington writes in a wide variety of styles to suit his particular material and viewpoint. His personal method of creating historical drama, he testifies, demands his seeking out all the information possible. He must know the information whether he uses it explicitly in the action or not; and in all important details he feels that his finished product must conform to that knowledge. Such an approach imposes something of a burden, he admits, but he feels that it increases his authority over his material and helps him to solidify his interpretation.[13] Our conjectured description of his method of developing A Cloud of Witnesses depends heavily on his apparent authority over all pertinent material.

Historical background of a cloud of witnesses

When Yelvington decides to write a drama about the siege and fall of the Alamo, he is far along the way of preparation. As a fourth-generation Texan on both sides he comments:

> I was already imbued with the spirit of the event and much of the lore because I had lived in San Antonio from the sixth grade through high school, and my father had been born less than twenty miles away. I had visited the place many, many times. As a school boy I had witnessed the laying of wreaths there, heard famous men orate there. I knew a great deal about the fall of the Alamo from a kind of osmosis.[14]

Possessing an emotional saturation with deeds so closely associated with the "Cradle of Texas Liberty," Yelvington seeks authentic detail and discovers very little. From the director of the Texas State Historical Association, he learns of one particularly valuable source: "A Critical Study of the Siege of the Alamo and of the Personnel of its Defenders" by Amelia Williams, published in five issues of the *Southwestern Historical Quarterly*. This publication the playwright resorts to almost exclusively. He encounters the issue of whether or not one frontiersman named Moses Rose actually averted death by fleeing the Alamo. He confers with the historical association director who believes that the men of the Alamo, reacting as any group of frontiersmen of the period would have done, "simply did not believe in running away." [15] Yelvington also quizzes the noted Texan historian-folklorist J. Frank Dobie on the Moses Rose question. While Mr. Dobie does not vouch for the authenticity of the story, he tends to believe it.[16] The playwright decides to straddle the issue and still make use of it (which he does in the concluding scene of Act 1).

Yelvington again delves into Amelia Williams' study of the Alamo and its defenders in which she established a reliable list of those who had actually died there and who had not. To this list Miss Williams had added whatever biographical information she could find. For most of the names there was a slim body of confirmable data; for the leaders such as Colonels William B. Travis, James Bowie, and David Crockett there was considerably more. The profiles of these leaders are studied by the playwright who looks first at a description of Travis.

At the time of death Travis was in his twenty-seventh year. "In person he was," as Williams describes him,

> about six feet tall and weighed about 175 pounds, being inclined to be sinewy and raw-boned. . . . With intimates the young man was genial, often jolly, but he was given to reverie, and toward mere acquaintances he often appeared stern. His temper was quick and only fairly well controlled.[17]

Travis was doing well in a law practice in Alabama when a marital blight struck him: he was led to believe that his young wife was unfaithful to him. Leaving her and his two children, he went to Texas. There he proved that he "was pre-eminently the good soldier, for while it is probable that no man in Texas did more than he did to initiate the revolution, certainly none fought more bravely, served more faithfully, or died more heroically." [18]

A transplanted Tennessean, James Bowie was a tall, well-built frontiersman, self-made, ambitious and wealthy; he was happily married to a beautiful

Mexican woman and living in San Antonio when his wife and their two children suddenly died of cholera. "Self-controlled and calm as Bowie habitually
was, the death of his family seemed to upset the foundations of his life." [19] In
1830 Bowie had been elected a colonel of the Texas Rangers, and in the
Ranger service he won the confidence and loyalty of his men because of his
kindness to them and his unvarying fairness to friend or foe. Stricken with
"typhoid-pneumonia" on the second day of the siege, Bowie was forced to
relinquish command over his volunteers during the remainder of the siege,
thus easing the internal discord that developed over the command of the
garrison. The volunteers, who outnumbered the regulars, elected Colonel
Bowie as commandant, objecting to Travis on grounds of his being a regular
officer. But after February 24, Bowie was too ill for active service, and from
that date Travis had sole command at the Alamo.

Well known and popular as a national figure, David Crockett was as
shrewd and clever as he was honest. His defeat in 1835 when he stood again
for congressman from Tennessee weighed heavily on his spirits and he decided
to move on West, to begin a new life. He was attracted by the news from
Texas. "At Nacogdoches he found himself elected colonel of a company of
Tennessee volunteers on its way to San Antonio. . . . Possibly twelve of them
entered the Alamo with Crockett, although one or two others of the company
. . . went into the fort a few days later." [20] Crockett was well received by Travis,
and was offered a command, which he refused. Crockett was very popular with
the soldiers and "after the siege began, constantly cheered and encouraged the
men. . . . He often played tunes on his fiddle when the fighting was not
brisk; and . . . sometimes he played in competition with [Sergeant] John
McGregor's bag-pipes." [21]

Before moving next to considering the physical characteristics of the
Alamo and the siege itself, the playwright's interest is caught by a particularly
brave group incident in the defensive operation. On March 1 thirty-two men
from near-by Gonzales entered the fort. In answer to Travis' widespread calls
for help, these men rode to San Antonio, slipping past the Mexican troops to
enter the Alamo. "They well knew that there was little hope that the Alamo
would be strongly reinforced, but they went with the determination to sacrifice
their lives, if need be, in order to encourage and strengthen their friends and
compatriots." [22] This incident is well remembered by Yelvington, who now
turns to surveying the historic building known as the Alamo (from the Spanish
word for "cotton wood").

Originally the Alamo was the chapel of the Mission San Antonio de
Valero, founded in 1718 by Franciscans. Upon the disappearance of the In-

dians from the vicinity the mission was abandoned but after 1793 it was some-times used as a fort.[23] At the time of the heroic defense in the war between Texas and Mexico, the architectural complex consisted of the chapel with walls twenty-two and a half feet high and four feet thick, a convent yard, a small two-story building, the upper story being used as a hospital, the lower floor serving as an armory and barracks. The main area, enclosed by these buildings and walls, was little more than a two-acre plot "that would have required more than a thousand men to defend with the kind of fortifications the Texans had." [24] The old buildings had been constructed for a mission rather than a fortress, and while strong enough for ordinary defense, the thick walls were without the necessary redoubts or bastions for efficient protection. When the siege began on February 23, the defenders had mounted approximately eighteen guns of assorted age and capacity. By this time a breach had been made in one of the walls, and Colonel Travis put an eight-pounder there to protect that weakness. After the siege ended, Travis' lifeless body was found slumped on this gun.

The playwright considers also the general facts relevant to the Alamo's gallant stand. In December, 1835, when San Antonio fell into the hands of the Texans, that event meant not only that the Mexicans had lost their last military base in Texas which could be advantageously used against the rebellious colonists, but also the humiliation of surrendering a stronghold held by Mexico for more than one hundred years. Consequently, the Mexicans made elaborate preparations to field a force of some five thousand well-equipped soldiers with the express purpose of recovering the Alamo and their prestige. To assure this, General Santa Anna, the Mexican dictator, personally commanded the Alamo's siege and final assault.

The defenders, who never totalled more than one hundred and eighty fit combatants, were composed of Texas regulars, Texas volunteers pledged to follow Bowie, and Tennessee volunteers whose main allegiance was to Crockett. In sum, the defenders of the Alamo were bound together by ties other than those of a strictly military organization. They succeeded in withholding Santa Anna's well-equipped force until the thirteenth day of siege, March 6, when a breach was made in the walls. The Mexicans then overpowered and slaughtered the garrison in a hand-to-hand combat; five male survivors were subsequently killed in cold blood by order of Santa Anna. All the bodies were stripped and mutilated. Three pyres were built of alternate layers of wood and dead bodies. Then grease and oil were poured over the pyres and the torch applied. "To the modern mind," Williams observes, this seems a more humane way to dispose of great numbers of dead bodies than was the fate meted out to Santa Anna's own dead soldiers. But in 1836 cremation on a funeral pyre at the order of the victor was regarded as the greatest cruelty and dishonor that could be shown a fallen foe.[25]

After the citadel's fall, "Remember the Alamo" became the rallying cry of Texans who, under San Houston at San Jacinto on April 21, 1836, defeated and captured Santa Anna. Texas independence of Mexico was complete.

The playwright, having investigated the limited data of the Alamo, continues with the composing of his drama.

Creative approach to playwright's problems

Even before saturation with his materials, the playwright resolves to make the Texan sacrifice of 1836 meaningful in our times by ways other than a straightforward retelling of the *legend* of the Alamo. From this premise comes the idea of the returning "witnesses," a congregation of dead persons connected in one way or another with the historic siege. Then gradually he evolves the concept of the entire action as a lyrical paean to freedom; as a companian thought, a verse, sometimes singing, metre suggests itself to him. He makes further decisions toward the final mode of the play by settling on a choric ode structure, after the Greek dramatic form with which he has some familiarity. Finally, to implement these ideas, he sees the advantages in envisioning the effect of the Alamo's fall on those thirty-two women left widows in the settlement at Gonzales. What better way to express the human realities of pioneer life than to have these bereft women, as an all-feeling and ever-present chorus, lament their sorrow, doubt, and bitterness on being left alone? What better way to gain perspective and to comment on the implications of sacrificing for an abstract ideal? In addition, their supernal presence in the company of the other "witnesses" will make time and place dissolve with swift ease, a prime consideration in a world of "memory."

Analysis of scene relationships

Lack of space prevents reproducing *A Cloud of Witnesses* in its entirety. In order to suggest some major dramatic relationships in the action, Yelvington's drama is synopsized, except for a portion of two scenes in dialogue form (the final scene of Act I and scene one in Act II). (* indicates a connective frame scene; units not so marked may also include fragments of a connective frame, e.g. Scene three.)

*Prologue: *Quite casually and directly, Dr. Amos Pollard, the army physician* attached to Travis' company, introduces himself and the drama's intent. He advises the audience that the playwright is using unconventional techniques borrowed from the theatres of the past.

ACT I

*Scene 1: The scene opens with "the sound of wings in the darkness over-head, descending." Assorted voices, male and female, speak in English and Spanish from all sides of the stage, making gradual adjustments to this place they find themselves in. These voices, belonging to the dead, have been summoned to witness the enactment of the siege and fall of the Alamo. Their mission is to "try again to reach the Ear of Man." Then Satan comes into visibility to mock them all for dying on behalf of a cause that is no longer fashionable; freedom, he insists, is currently in a vulnerable position. He boasts that before the evening is over the theatre audience will diminish the size of the heroes of the Alamo. As the Witnesses plead for support from their unseen audience, Satan disappears, scoffingly.

*Scene 2: The Witnesses are now brilliantly lighted in gold. Satan, invisible, taunts Crockett into defending his past actions as a statesman, husband, and father. The women of Gonzales challenge Crockett, but his gift of oratory stands up well for him. Satan disappears entirely, apparently, for his voice is no longer heard. Then Travis' qualifications to lead men are examined freely by the Witnesses. Before long Bowie is involved with Travis and others in a discussion over the relative merits of their religious biases. Bowie then defends his past actions as a land speculator and slave dealer, finally personalizing his great love for his Mexican wife, dead with the cholera. A distant bell begins to toll as the quality of light changes into the next scene, the first one of the focal plot.

Scene 3: It is a cold and dark morning, February 23, 1836. The audience is aware that its point of vantage is inside the Alamo chapel. The last of the Mexican populace hurriedly leaves the Alamo compound as soldiers drive cattle into it. Two young soldiers begin to respond to the bell tolling, which they take to be the signal that warns of the approach of the Mexican army. A fragmented "memory" scene enables the young soldiers to recall their amorous exploits, only to be reprimanded by the chorus of Women, who accuse the soldiers of faithlessness. This blends into a lament by the Women for their dead husbands. At its conclusion Travis and Crockett enter to hear the report of the two scouts who had sighted Santa Anna's troops on the move. Travis dispatches pleas for help to Gonzales and Goliad as Crockett reassures him of the active

support of his Tennessee volunteers. A red flag is reported sighted atop
the Cathedral, a sign that no quarter will be given by the Mexican
commander. Defiantly, Travis answers this sign with a cannon shot just
as he discovers a Texan marching towards the Mexican lines, white
flag in hand. Infuriated, particularly when he learns that Bowie ordered
the messenger to be sent, Travis determines to settle once and for all
the matter of authority in the fort. He goes looking for Bowie, who is
reported sick, as the scene shifts into another "memory" sequence.

*Scene 4: This is a "flashback" in which the contents of three messages are
revealed: Bowie's inquiry about a parley with the enemy; its disdainful
rejection of negotiations by Santa Anna's aide-de-camp; and Travis'
declaration of "no surrender" in the appeals for assistance sent to the
the people of Texas. The Women read more personalized meanings
into the messages than their authors intended. The lights change again
as the next focal scene begins.

Scene 5: It is afternoon of February 24, 1836. All the defenders are gathered
for conference. Bowie, resting on a cot, is pale with illness. He acknowl-
edges openly the clear-cut authority of Travis as commanding officer,
and urges all men to respond. Whereupon Bowie turns his sword over
to Travis, retaining his "Bowie knife." Travis uses the sword to apos-
trophize the soul of the new nation they are forging. Growing out of
this emotional appeal comes the group's determination to stay and
fight. The dialogue of the last three pages of Act I suggests the Cas-
sandra-like warning against the exhortations of Travis. Then suddenly
there is a deliberate "flatting" of the emotional effect created: Satan
steps forward to suggest why the legend of Moses Rose—the one man
who may have fled the Alamo—could not have happened; Satan also
reminds the audience, by this frank theatrical interruption, to maintain a critical detachment.

The final portion of the scene follows. We hear Travis address-
ing the assembled defenders.

TRAVIS

... Men! The Mexicans have handed us a coward's choice
Of living under a despot without a governing voice,
Or running away.
Everything dear to our conscience they've sought to gag,
And now they taunt us with a blood-red flag.
Will we run away?

TEXANS
No! No!

TRAVIS
Will we stay?

TEXANS
Yes! Yes!

WOMEN
        (*softly under as Travis continues
            to exhort*)
Like a camp-meeting
In a brush arbor
The men are swayed
By Travis' ardor.
Cling! Clang!
Clong! Clong!
Beating steel
On an anvil gong.
Beating you
On His anvil gong!
Do they know
What he's doing?
Do they know
Death they're wooing?
Now they sway
To and fro . . .
        (*louder*)
*Tapley Holland's
The first to go!*
        (*swiftly*)
Some step quickly
And some step slow,
Some take a dare
Some say a prayer
Some smirk
And some just don't care!
        (*a pause, then slower, softer*)
Isaac. Isaac Millsaps,
You with seven children and a blind
        wife—

TRAVIS
See this sword?
A drawn sword!
Unsheathed, naked,
To be clothed in blood!
Look at it!
Look at it long!
You are this blade
And God made you strong!
Who will follow me?
Follow the sword?
Follow the sword
Of our precious Lord!
Here I draw a blood-red line
For you to cross

What did you think when pledging
    your life?
    MILLSAPS
Why, it happened quick as a wink.
Fact is—I guess a man didn't have
    time to think!
    WOMEN
And the Taylor boys
George, Edward, James,
Eighteen, twenty, twenty-two—
Boys, what prompted you?
    TAYLOR BROTHERS
We don't know.
We don't know.
We can't seem to remember.
All we know is
We looked at George, our older
    brother,
And then we looked at one another,
And George said:
"Let's go."
    SATAN
    (Disguised as one of the colonists on stage, he now steps forward. The
    actors stop and stare at him in wonder, sensing his identity.)
And now may I have just a moment to explain why I didn't cross over the line?
Because, like all myths and legends that spring up without corroboration from
the most unlikely situations, this scene never happened. It's rank fiction. It's
pure myth. There was never any line to cross over!
    WOMEN
    (they are outraged)
Oh is that so?
Well, we know you,
And even if what you said were true,
We know our men
And we say, true or untrue,
It would have been just like them!
    Lights go up immediately.[26]

Or stay behind.
Who will be first
To follow me,
To throw down his life
For Liberty?

End of Act I

ACT II

Prologue: The women Witnesses offer expository material: it is now the eighth day of the siege during which there has been sporadic fighting; mostly it has been just waiting, and thinking about dying. But, in another mood, the Women, recalling that it is also the first of March, start thinking of watching things grow in their gardens. Here in the Alamo things are slow.

Scene 1: *It is ten o'clock in the evening of March 1, 1836. Guitar music is heard softly in the enclosure, and a soldier repeats the same ballad. Two soldiers and a sentry exchange impressions of their fatigue and their hunger. This admission of physical weariness is interrupted by the entrance of Crockett, Dr. Pollard, Private Reynolds, and Sergeant Mac-Gregor, all interested in knowing if reinforcements have been sighted by the sentry. The latter reports that he has not seen anything. Reynolds expresses the view that there has been plenty of time for people to respond, if they were going to do so. Dr. Pollard agrees. Whereupon, Crockett, trying to ease the mood of despair, explains why help is slow in arriving.*

CROCKETT

Maybe they're holding a farewell ball before the soldiers take off. MacGregor, speaking of balls, where's that instrument o' yours, if instrument it be!

MACGREGOR

Instrument it is and a noble one, too, Colonel. Besides the hunting horn, the bugle, and perhaps the ram's horn o' Joshua, there be none so manly as the bagpipe.

CROCKETT

And none so hard to coax a tune from?

MACGREGOR

The tunes are there. They but require a Scot's ear to detect 'em.

CROCKETT

The sounds you get on it, it seems to me, would better suit the fiends o' hell.

MACGREGOR

If the pipes do better seem to suit the fiends o' hell, sir, then 'tis all to my instrument's credit, and to me. That is that for which it was constructed: to summon the clans to war. And what, might I ask, would the playin' o' your fiddle bring, the scrapin' o' the gut? A host o' howlin' tomcats, like as not!

CROCKETT

I like the sauce of your remarks, MacGregor, if not the wail o' your pipes. And I'm thinking it might stir our boys' faltering blood if we was to fight—the fiddle, that is, against the pipes. What do you say we try it? A contest. Right now. Tonight.

MACGREGOR

I accept the challenge. The contest will be unequal, o' course, but . . . don't you worry. I'll not play me best.

CROCKETT

Then get your weapon, mon, and if it's dreadful noise we're judgin' on, then I'm agreed—you've already won!

MACGREGOR (as he goes for bagpipes)

If you fiddle like you talk, Crockett, then I'm already lost!

CROCKETT

It could be a musical duel would stir up the coals in our boys and add a mite o' warmth for another long night's watch.

DR. POLLARD

Our fires could use some stirring.

REYNOLDS

They're low tonight.

CROCKETT

Aye. But not burnt out!

REYNOLDS

No. Not out.

CROCKETT

All they need is to be poked about.

DR. POLLARD

Men can go just so long without sleep.

CROCKETT

How long?

DR. POLLARD

And be effective? Three days—four—in rare men, five.

CROCKETT

In rare men—five.

REYNOLDS

And we're already into the seventh!

DR. POLLARD

But you couldn't say we were altogether effective.

CROCKETT

No. But dead from the neck up and walking in their sleep I'll take our boys one against any ten of Santa Anna's Mexicans.

DR. POLLARD

Ten? One against ten? They'll have to do better than that. Santa Anna may have as many as five thousand men out there. No, one to ten won't do, Colonel. It'll have to be nearer one to thirty-three. Unless we get reinforcements.

REYNOLDS

That's pretty long odds on men dead for sleep, with no coffee, not enough ammunition, and not much to eat.

DR. POLLARD

Mighty long.

CROCKETT

But not too long!

DR. POLLARD

I hope you're right. But I'd feel a lot better if Fannin came.

REYNOLDS

Yes. And a hundred or so from Gonzales.

DR. POLLARD

I was wondering if we hadn't better bring Jim Bowie in here. The men have got their hands full. He's running a high fever and a lot of the time he's out of his head. I thought maybe the women here might look after him. He'd be a lot better off.

CROCKETT

Yes, he would. I'd plum forgot about there being any women here. (*He sees them, huddled with the children and two Negroes, at the far side of the stage.*)

DR. POLLARD

I hesitated bringing him in here because what he's got could be contagious. It has the look of typhoid, with other complications.

CROCKETT

At any rate we can feel out their attitude. (*They walk toward the women, about half way.*) Ladies, are all of you well?

MRS. DICKINSON

We're making out. About as well as the men.

DR. POLLARD

Mrs. Dickinson, Colonel, wife of the Captain of Artillery.

CROCKETT

Yes, I know Mrs. Dickinson . . . and the other ladies, who are they?

DR. POLLARD

Mrs. Alsbury I know. The others . . . I'm sorry, I don't.

MRS. DICKINSON

Mrs. Esparza, Mrs. Losoya, and Miss Navarro. And the children. They do not all speak English.

CROCKETT

I see. Ladies, although I regret it, we have need of your services. Colonel Bowie, as you may know, is very sick. Dr. Pollard is of the opinion his disease may even be highly contagious. However, the soldiers have as much as they can do, and we were wondering if you could possibly relieve them of looking after the Colonel. You would, of course, be running some risk.

MRS. DICKINSON

We are running a bigger risk just being here. Bring him to us. We'll put him in a room to himself and keep the children away.

(Sound: The playing of the bagpipes, at a distance.)

DR. POLLARD (to Reynolds)

Purdy, get some of the men to help you bring Bowie into the chapel.

(Purdy Reynolds goes; Crockett is already striding away, calling:)

CROCKETT

All right, boys! Get ready for the battle of the century: John MacGregor versus me! A fight to the finish between the fiddle and the pipes! Concert tonight! Everybody gather round except them that's walking post or on the lookout! Gather here!

(growing fainter)

Gather here for the fight between the fiddle and the pipes! First, my honored opponent, Sergeant John MacGregor!

(In the distance may be heard the skirl of the bagpipes, followed by a weak response, a few halfhearted yells and laughter; then Crockett plays, and again the response is weak. As he fiddles a hoedown, the dialogue below continues, over:)

SOLDIER ONE (at cannon on wall)

Did you hear what Doctor Pollard said just now?

SENTRY

How could I? I was walking my post. Or reckon I was. I could have been asleep.

SOLDIER ONE

He said the odds was one to thirty-three.

SENTRY

He did?

SOLDIER ONE

Yeah. He said there was one of us to maybe every thirty-three of them. About
a hundred and fifty to five thousand. If'n we don't pretty soon git some
more men.

SENTRY

I don't look for none. Not now. (pause) Do you?

SOLDIER ONE

I don't know. But I do wish they'd come on if'n they're coming. Either them
or the Mexicans, one. I just wish *something* would git done!

SENTRY TWO (after a moment of listening)

Listen to that!

SOLDIER TWO (after another pause)

It'll take a devil of a lot better'n that to light a fire under me.

SENTRY TWO

I figure our fire's about out.

SOLDIER TWO

You know what? I was just thinking.

SENTRY

What?

SOLDIER TWO

If'n these fellers can come through the Mexican lines *this*-a-way, it's a cinch
we could go through them Mexicans *that*-a-way! Ain't it?

SENTRY (considering)

Yeah. Them scouts come in and go out all the time.

SOLDIER TWO

You know, we could just take off and leave this place. Walk right off. Couldn't
we? Run away.

SENTRY

(a pause, uncertainly)

We could.

SOLDIER TWO

A mile from here a man could lie down in some brush, or maybe a barn even,
and sleep a week with nobody being the wiser.

(They are silent, thinking of it)

Only, we ain't the runnin' kind.

SENTRY (*rising a little, but still under the spell*)
A cup o' coffee and a warm feather bed.

SOLDIER TWO
We fired a couple o' times at old Santy Anna's headquarters today, and hit it,
too—but he wasn't to home, they say.

SENTRY
I heard 'em cheer.
(*a pause*)
Well, I reckon I best make me another round.
(*He is on the point of departure when, from the southeast side of the fort,
there comes a distant shout. Then others, coming closer and closer.*)

SOLDIER TWO
What you reckon it is?

SENTRY
I don't know but I'm going to see!
(*He goes at a trot. The women in the chapel wake and whisper excitedly.
the women Witnesses also begin to stir.*)

MRS. DICKINSON
Is it the Mexicans coming?

SOLDIER
I don't know. I don't hear no guns. But I can't see!

SENTRY (*bursting into chapel*)
Hurrah! Hurrah!

SOLDIER
What is it, man? Who is it?

SENTRY
The men from Gonzales! They got here! They got here!
(*He rushes back outside*)

SOLDIER
Thank God. Thank God.
(*Now the women Witnesses sit up in alarm. They speak:*)

WOMEN
Our men. Our men.
(*Now Crockett and MacGregor lead a joyous march about the enclosure,
playing the bagpipes and the fiddle, the men shouting wildly, happily. In
the course of their marching they do a turn through the chapel, and
Crockett shouts:*)

CROCKETT
Dr. Pollard! Dr. Pollard! These are your rare men! We are your rare men!
(*Dancing in single file, they wave their rifles and exit whooping.*)
SOLDIER (*at cannon, after a pause*)
I wonder how many there are. They don't look very many to me . . .
Lights fade on stage center as music continues briefly, then out.[27]

*Scene 2: The women Witnesses are galvanized into action at the thought of their men entering the Alamo: to the Women the sound of the closing of the gate after the entrance of the men is the sound of a lid on a coffin. Their strong protestations soften into an attitude of prayer, and the Women are on suppliant knee as the scene fades.

Scene 3: Inside the chapel the mood is drearier, the area is in greater disarray than before. The time period within the scene is telescoped from the evening of March 3 to the evening of March 5, as the defenders become more haggard. Their movements and speech are increasingly more trance-like. A distant cannonade begins. Travis orders the Texans to hold their retaliatory fire, because they'll need it; he has a feeling that this is the beginning of the end. The cannonade builds to a terrifying climax, then stops abruptly. In the hush that follows, the worn-out besieged, who have been for eleven days and nights at their posts, fall fast asleep near the wall, their weapons in their hands. Then in the distance the sound of a harsh bugle call awakens Travis; he sounds the alarm that an attack is underway. The Texans successfully repulsed the first attack. There is no jubilation when the second attack is turned back, at great cost to lives and ammunition. The third attack is the final one, the battle din deafening, as Mexicans in great profusion swarm over the walls into the enclosure. The fighting is hand to hand, with the Texans, no longer able to fire their arms, resorting to knife and butt of gun. Finally, Santa Anna enters to inspect the carnage. Finding the body of Crockett, he touches the famous frontiersman with his boot, snorting derisively. The last Texans to die are five men, found in the barracks hospital in a sick and wounded condition. Brought before the Mexican dictator, they are bayonetted in cold blood on a signal from him. Santa Anna leaves.

*Scene 4: The Women comment on the events just observed in a quiet matter-of-fact tone. Then Francisco Ruiz, the alcalde of San Antonio, and other dignitaries enter, he to give his report on the battle. As he speaks, the Mexicans gather up dead bodies and carry them off beyond the Alamo façade. There, they are stacked in piles. Soon a torch is applied to the stacks and for awhile they burn brightly. It is the news of this deed, observe the Women, that erupts into San Jacinto. This observation stimulates Vicente Filisola, an Italian serving as a mercenary general in the Mexican Army, to step forward. Although he says he is impressed with the heroism of the defenders, Filisola raises the question of why they did not withdraw the better to fight some other day (isn't this what Houston did?). Did they not die fruitlessly? This, in turn, elicits from the Texans a sober question: what is Man to do? What are they to do?

*Epilogue: To this question comes an arbitrary and, in realistic terms, interruptive device. Satan appears, disguised as the mythical Moses Rose; he offers the cynical view that the audience, at least, should learn what Moses Rose did in 1836 or any year: Man should champion no cause that does not produce for him material gain. The Witnesses, he says, died uselessly for an abstraction no longer taken for granted. With the question, "Hasn't Freedom changed?" Satan leaves. The Texans, confused, cannot at first remember a Moses Rose. Guided by the Women, the Texans finally recall the condition of the Alamo and the reason for which they died. Freedom, they conclude, is the same as before: it has not changed. The Witnesses, turning to the audience, call Man fortunate to be able to make a choice, he can decide for himself if Freedom is worth dying for. The play ends as the lights descend and the sound of ascending wings fades out.

XII. Epilogue

WE LIVE in an age when, in an immediate sense, history is made every hour. We see it made before our eyes. On a television screen we watch astronauts rocketing off for space outer and unlimited, political conventions nominating their candidates, pickets demonstrating against alleged injustices, or a self-appointed assassin-slayer shooting a man who two days before has killed the President of the United States. The speed with which such events occur in our space-exploring not so peacefully coexistent age often leaves us bewildered enough to thirst for their meanings in the slower moving rivers of the past. Under its deceptively quiescent surface, the past does have a "moving" vibrant life waiting to be plumbed. When that life is effectively brought to the surface in a biography, history, novel, or drama, a creative event occurs signaling artistry and achievement. And those who bear witness may be granted a clearer perspective of human experience. The past will not uncover answers to all the terrifyingly swift events of our own lives, but when it is vividly re-created it can bestow gifts on both giver and receiver.

Historical drama holds horizons without limit. Throughout our land there is an ever-increasing consciousness that the richness of our heritage needs to be revivified. A developing realization that our history deserves re-creation offers an open door to talented artists, organizers, and other leaders, with power to bring forcefully to life yesterday's personalities and events for today's interpretation.

For the community and the individual eager to meet the challenge of dramatizing history, there are, in the words of poet Robert Frost, "promises to keep." Desire and good intentions are not enough. Resources and purposes must be wisely evaluated and all efforts, carefully organized, put into skilled action. Genuine talent must be searched for and trained by the most experienced specialists available. Finally, achievement must be significant in the areas of artistic performance, service to the community, and managerial responsibility. Only then will the "promises" be kept.

To the community and individual desirous and capable of creating historical drama in any of its aspects, and willing to accept the responsibilities of doing so, we wish good fortune and Godspeed.

APPENDICES/NOTES/BIBLIOGRAPHY/INDEX

APPENDIX A

Selected list of produced historical dramas in the United States

(Includes titles other than those mentioned in text, but is not intended to be an exhaustive record; classified according to forms defined in text. Dramas that, to the authors' knowledge at the time of this writing, still are performed or are scheduled are indicated by *. Population of communities is indicated to nearest hundred based on the 1960 census.)

Biography-Drama—

(o) *indicates outdoor performance*

Title and Author(s)	Location of Community	Sponsor(s)	Subject	Performance Date
Abe Lincoln in Illinois by Robert E. Sherwood	New York, N.Y. (7,782,000)	The Playwrights' Co.	Abraham Lincoln	1938–39
	Springfield, Ill. (83,300)	Springfield Theatre Guild (forms Abe Lincoln Players, Inc.)		1947
	(o) Petersburg, Ill. (2,400)	Abe Lincoln Players, Inc. of Springfield, Ill.		*1947–
Abe Lincoln of Pigeon Creek by William E. Wilson	Bloomington, Ind. (31,400)	Univ. of Indiana	Abraham Lincoln	1962
American Portrait by Emmet Lavery	San Francisco, Cal. (740,000)	Missionary Soc. of St. Paul the Apostle	Father Isaac Hecker, founder of the Paulist Fathers	1958

Title and Author(s)	Location of Community	Sponsor(s)	Subject	Performance Date
Andersonville Trial, The by Saul Levitt	New York, N.Y.	William Darrid, Eleanore Saidenberg, Daniel Hollywood	Trial of Henry Wirz, Civil War prison superintendent	1959–60
Anvil, The by Julia Davis	Charleston, W. Va. (3,300)	Local Civil War Centennial Com.	John Brown	1961
Banners of Steel by Barrie Stavis	Carbondale, Ill. (14,700)	Southern Illinois Univ.	John Brown	1962
Bloody Tenet, The by James Schevill	Providence, R.I. (207,500)	Central Congregational Church	Roger Williams	1956
Caleb Hopkins Story, The by Ruth Post with a group of high school students	Penfield, N.Y. (16,100)	Dramatic Club of Senior High School	Caleb Hopkins & early Penfield history	1959
Cardiff Giant, The by A. M. Drummond and Robert E. Gard	Ithaca, N.Y. (28,800)	Cornell Univ.	1869 hoax of New York State's Cardiff Giant	1939
Count Philippe's Wild Orange Tree by Sydney and Marjorie Barstow Greenbie	(o) Philippe Park, Pinellas County, Fla. (374,700)	Pinellas County Park System & Univ. of Tampa	Count Odet Philippe	1951–52
Crossing, The by Howard Fast	Dallas, Tex. (679,700)	Dallas Theater Center	George Washington	1962
Crucible, The by Arthur Miller	New York, N.Y.	Kermit Bloomgarden	Salem witch trials	1953
Cry of the Jay, The by Mary Ellis	Hattiesburg, Miss. (35,000)	Mississippi Southern Coll.	Local Civil War events	1961

Title and Author(s)	Location of Community	Sponsor(s)	Subject	Performance Date
	Jackson, Miss. (144,400)	Mississippi Economic Council		1961
Curate's Play, The by Nathaniel Banks	New York, N.Y.	St. George's Episcopal Church	The Nativity within a modern allegory	1961
Damien Letter, The by Aldyth Morris	Honolulu, Ha. (294,100)	Honolulu Community Theatre	Father Damien and Robert Louis Stevenson	1964
Defiant Island by James Forsyth	Washington, D.C. (785,000)	Howard Univ.	Henry Christophe	1962
Early Days in Tin Top by Community committee advised by Junius Eddy	Tin Top, Tex. (100)	Community members and Baylor Univ.	Tin Top	1951
Ezekiel's Nose by Idaho Historical Soc. Staff	Boise, Idaho (34,500)	Boise Junior League and Idaho Historical Soc.	Discovery of gold in Idaho	1961
Fiorello! by Jerome Weidman and George Abbott	New York, N.Y.	Robert E. Griffith and Harold S. Prince	Fiorello LaGuardia	1959–61
Flowering Peach, The by Clifford Odets	New York, N.Y.	The Producers Theatre	Noah and his family	1954–55
Gideon by Paddy Chayefsky	New York, N.Y.	Fred Coe and Arthur Cantor	Biblical Gideon	1961–62
Harriet by Florence Ryerson and Colin Clements	New York, N.Y.	Gilbert Miller	Harriet Beecher Stowe	1942–43
Impeachment by Jack LaZebnik	Columbia Mo. (36,600)	Stephens Coll.	Andrew Johnson and Thaddeus Stevens	1962

Title and Author(s)	Location of Community	Sponsor(s)	Subject	Performance Date
Inherit the Wind by Jerome Lawrence and Robert E. Lee	New York, N.Y.	Herman Shumlin and Margo Jones	Scopes trial in Dayton, Tenn.	1955–57
John Brown by Jack LaZebnik	Athens, Ga. (39,600)	Univ. of Georgia	John Brown	1961
Journey to Jerusalem by Maxwell Anderson	New York, N.Y.	The Playwrights' Co.	Jesus as a boy	1940
Last Days of Lincoln, The by Mark Van Doren	Tallahasee, Fla. (48,200)	Florida State Univ.	Abraham Lincoln	1961
Man Who Never Died, The by Barrie Stavis	New York, N.Y.	Irving Strouse	Joe Hill, American labor movement poet	1958
Mehitabel Wing by Isobel Rose Jones and Geoffrey O'Hara	Pawling, N.Y. (1,700)	Starlight Playhouse	Mehitabel Wing	1958
Mighty Fortress, A by Jane Erickson	(o) Portland, Ore. (522,800)	Reed Coll.	Whitman Massacre	1952
Miracle Worker, The by William Gibson	New York, N.Y.	Fred Coe	Helen Keller and Anne Sullivan	1959–60
	(o) Tuscumbia, Ala. (9,000)	Starmaker Community Theatre and AAUW		*1962
More Love, Brother by Miriam Anne Cramer	Cleveland, Ohio (876,000)	Western Reserve Univ.	Shaker settlement at North Union, Ohio in 1864	1944
One For the Lord's Day by Fred Carmichael	Sturbridge, Mass. (3,600)	Old Sturbridge Village, Inc.	Early New England treatment of the poor	1963

Title and Author(s)	Location of Community	Sponsor(s)	Subject	Performance Date
On Hemlock Brook by Arnold Sundgaard	Williamstown, Mass. (5,400)	Williamstown Bicentennial Com.	Hoosac Valley in 1756	1953
Pangs of Liberty, The by Priscilla A. Alexander	Sturbridge, Mass.	Old Sturbridge Village, Inc.	New England village's reaction to Hartford Convention of 1814	1961
Patriots, The by Sidney Kingsley	New York, N.Y.	The Playwrights' Co.	Thomas Jefferson	1943
Prologue to Glory by E. P. Conkle	New York, N.Y.	Federal Theatre Project	Lincoln's early years in Illinois	1938
Rivalry, The by Norman Corwin	New York, N.Y.	Cheryl Crawford, Joel Schenker	Lincoln–Douglas debates	1959
Sergeant Molly by Mrs. Donald English and Mrs. Emery Wingerter	Monmouth County, N.J. (334,400)	Junior Service League of Red Bank, N.J.	Molly Pitcher and Battle of Monmouth	1961–62
Sunrise at Campobello by Dore Schary	New York, N.Y.	Theatre Guild and Dore Schary	Franklin D. Roosevelt's battle with polio	1958–59
Trial of John Brown, The by Richard F. Stockton	Lawrence, Kan. (32,900)	Univ. of Kansas	John Brown	1961
Triple-A Plowed Under by Staff of Living Newspaper	New York, N.Y.	Federal Theatre Project	American agricultural problems	1936
Unsinkable Molly Brown, The by Meredith Willson	New York, N.Y.	Theatre Guild and Dore Schary	Molly Tobin Brown	1960–62

Title and Author(s)	Location of Community	Sponsor(s)	Subject	Performance Date
Valley Forge by Maxwell Anderson	New York, N.Y.	Theatre Guild	Washington as commander-in-chief	1934
Who Ride on White Horses by Richard Breen and Harry Schnibbe	New York, N.Y.	Fordham Univ.	Edmund Campion, Jesuit martyr	1939
Young Abe Lincoln by Richard Bernstein, John Allen, & Arnold Sundgaard	New York, N.Y.	Little Golden Theatre, Inc.	Lincoln's early years at New Salem	1961

Pageant-dramas—

(I) *indicates indoor performance*

Title and Author(s)	Location of Community	Sponsor(s)	Subject	Performance Date
Air Power Pageant by Ruth & Val Rosing	Los Angeles, Cal. (2,479,000)	U.S.A.F.	Military aviation	1951
All Faces West by Roland & Helen Parry	Ogden, Utah (70,200)	Ogden Pioneer Days, Inc.	Mormons' great trek to the West	*1951–
America's Witness for Christ: Hill Cumorah Pageant by H. Wayne Driggs & Harold Hansen	Palmyra, N.Y. (3,400)	Eastern States Mission of the Church of Latter Day Saints	Book of Mormon	*1937–
Appropriation, The by Louis P. Peck	Montpelier, Vt. (8,800)	Vermont Historical Soc.	Vermont's entry into Civil War	1961
As Long as the Grass Grows by Bert Hansen	Missoula, Mont. (27,100)	Missoula Kiwanis Club and Salish Indians Tribal Council	Missoula and Salish Indians	1949
Birth of Yellowstone National Park by Bert Hansen	Madison Junction, Yellowstone Park, Wyo. (300)	National Park Service	Origin and development of	1957–58, 1960

Title and Author(s)	Location of Community	Sponsor(s)	Subject	Performance Date
			Yellowstone National Park	
Black Hill Passion Play by Joseph Meier (translator and adapter)	Spearfish, S.D. (3,700)	Passion Play Corp.	Life of Christ	*1939–41, 1946–
	Lake Wales, Fla. (8,300)			*1953–
Bon Homme Pageant by Hazel Abbott	Bon Homme, S.D. (100)	Old Settlers Assoc., Bon Homme County	Bon Homme County	1953
Castine by Sydney and Marjorie Barstow Greenbie	(1) Castine, Me. (500)	Castine Pageant and Players Assoc., Inc.	Castine	1946–50, 1952–53
Century of Progress by Charlotte McLeod	Carbondale, Ill.	Southern Illinois Univ.	Carbondale	1952
Control: A Pageant of Engineering Progress by George Pierce Baker	Hoboken, N.J. (48,400)	Stevens Inst. of Technology	Development of Mechanical Engineering	1930
Corridor of Empire by Bert Hansen	Three Forks, Mont. (1,200)	American Pioneer Trail Assoc., Three Rivers Chapter	Lewis and Clark Expedition	1950
Dekandawida by Robert E. Moody	Naples, N.Y. (1,200)	Nundawaga Soc. chartered by N.Y. Dept. of Educ.	Iroquois Confederacy	1957
Dolgeville by Eleanor Franz	(1) Dolgeville, N.Y. (3,000)	Dolgeville Central School Library Council	Dolgeville	1959
Dream and the Deed, The by Glenn Hughes	(1) Seattle, Wash. (557,100)	Univ. of Washington	Seattle	1952
Elk Story by Ruth & Val Rosing	Los Angeles, Cal.	B.P.O.E.	B.P.O.E.	1954
Ft. Laramie Treaty Pageant by Will Robinson	Cheyenne Agency, S.D. (2,700)	Sioux Cheyenne River Agency and Tribal Council	Ft. Laramie	1951–52

Title and Author(s)	Location of Community	Sponsor(s)	Subject	Performance Date
Freeport Pageant of the Blackhawk Country by Ethel Theodora Rockwell	Freeport, Ill. (26,800)	Freeport Chamber of Commerce	Freeport	1915
Gift of the Waters by Marie Montabe	Thermopolis, Wyo. (4,000)	Gift of Waters, Inc.	Shoshone Indians	*1950–
Golden Prairie, The by Kermit Hunter	Decatur, Ill. (78,000)	Decatur-Macon County Fair Assoc., Inc.	Decatur-Macon County	1960
Gunboats 'Round the Bend by Torrey McKenny	(1) Vicksburg, Miss. (29,100)	Vicksburg Civil War Centennial Com.	Vicksburg in 1862	1960
Hark Upon the Gale by Christian Moe	(1) Williamsburg, Va. (6,800)	Coll. of William and Mary	Coll. of William and Mary	1957
Hiawatha by Robert E. Moody	Naples, N.Y.	Nundawaga Soc.	Iroquois confederacy	1956
Kansas Story, The by Ruth and Val Rosing	Wichita (254,700) and Topeka, Kan. (119,500)	Wichita Chamber of Commerce and Kansas Centennial Com.	Kansas	1961
Legend of Rawhide, The by Eva Lou Paris	Lusk, Wyo. (1,900)	Chamber of Commerce	Local legend of Rawhide Buttes	*1946–
Lexington by Sidney Howard	Lexington, Mass. (27,700)	Pageant of Lexington, Inc.	Lexington	1925
Magnolia Pageant by Guyla Moreland	Cairo, Ill. (9,300)	Cairo Historical Assoc.	Cairo	1955
Maifest Pageant by Anne Hesse (a new pageant offered annually varying from (0) to (1) production)	Hermann, Mo. (2,500)	Brush and Palette Club, Inc.	Aspects of Hermann history	*1952–
Manhattan Story, The by Bert Hansen	(1) Manhattan, Kan. (23,000)	Kansas State Coll.	Manhattan	1955
Nundawao by Robert E. Moody	Naples, N.Y.	Nundawaga Soc.	Iroquois nation	1954–55

Title and Author(s)	Location of Community	Sponsor(s)	Subject	Performance Date
Pageant and Masque of St. Louis, The by Thomas Wood Stevens and Percy MacKaye	St. Louis, Mo. (750,000)	St. Louis Pageant Assoc.	St. Louis	1914
Pageant of Illinois, The by Thomas Wood Stevens	Evanston, Ill. (79,300)	Northwestern Univ.	Illinois	1909
Pageant of Newark, The by Thomas Wood Stevens	Newark, N.J. (405,200)	Committee of 100 for Newark's 250th Anniversary	Newark	1916
Pageant of Virginia, The by Thomas Wood Stevens	Richmond, Va. (220,000)	Virginia Historical Pageant Assoc.	Virginia	1922
Penfield Portraits by William DeRitter	(1) Penfield, N.Y.	Penfield, N.Y.	Town of Penfield	1960
Quashquema to Nauvoo by Paxton J. Lewis	Nauvoo, Ill. (1,000)	Nauvoo Grape Festival Assoc.	Nauvoo	*1951–
Raleigh, Shepherd of the Ocean by Frederick H. Koch	Raleigh, N.C. (93,900)	North Carolina Literary & Historical Assoc.	Sir Walter Raleigh	1920
Road to Orange, The by John Ehle	Hillsboro, N.C. (1,300)	Orange County Bicentennial Committee	Orange County	1953
Sand in Their Shoes by R. Don Oscarson	Provo, Utah (36,000)	Brigham Young Univ.	Mormon Battalion in Mexican War	1957–61
Sense of Destiny, A by Esther Jones and Naomi Pyle	(1) Richmond, Ind. (44,100)	First Friends Church of Richmond	Local Quaker history	1959
Sketches in the Life of Daniel Penfield by Mrs. William Clark and Mrs. Rona Emory	(1) Penfield, N.Y.	Penfield Sesquicentennial Com.	Daniel Penfield	1960
Song of Hiawatha, The adapted from Longfellow's poem	Pipestone, Minn. (5,300)	Pipestone Hiawatha Club	Longfellow's Hiawatha	*1948–
Strangers Come to Nunadawo by Robert E. Moody	Naples, N.Y.	Nundawaga Soc.	Iroquois confederacy	1958

Title and Author(s)	Location of Community	Sponsor(s)	Subject	Performance Date
Streight's Dash Through Cherokee by Thelma Slone	(1) Cedar Bluff, Ala. (700)	Cedar Bluff High School	Confederate General Nathan B. Forrest's defeat of Colonel Streight	1943
Those Who Bear the Torch Horace Mann Schools	(1) New York, N.Y.	Horace Mann Schools	Great teachers and thinkers throughout history	1937
Thunder on the River by Kermit Hunter	Peoria, Ill. (103,200)	Arts & Science Fed. of Peoria	Peoria	1961
To Arms in the Valley by Eleanor Holder	Tuscumbia, Ala.	Tennessee Valley Historical Soc.	North Alabama Civil War history	1961
Twin Titans by Ruth and Val Rosing	(1) Los Angeles, Cal.	Dept. of Water and Power, City of Los Angeles	Public utilities	1952
Uniting a Nation by William Blake Hindman	Farmington, Pa. (200)	Allegheny Mt. Fall Foliage Festival Association	George Washington and the Battle of Ft. Necessity	*1965

Epic-dramas—

(1) *indicates indoor performance*

Always Acadia by Clinton W. Bradford	St. Martinville, La. (6,500)	Acadian Bicentennial Celebration	Acadian "promised land"	1955
Aracoma Story, The by Thomas M. Patterson	Logan, W.Va. (3,800)	The Aracoma Story, Inc.	Aracoma and her	1953

Title and Author(s)	Location of Community	Sponsor(s)	Subject	Performance Date
			father, Chief Cornstalk Shawnee leader	
Bell and the Plough, The by Kermit Hunter	(1) Tucson, Ariz. (240,000)	Univ. of Arizona	Gadsen Purchase territory	1954
Book of Job, The arranged by O. R. Corey	Pineville, Ky. (3,200)	Kentucky Mt. Theatre, Inc.	Old Testament Job	*1959–
	(1) New York, N.Y.	Drama Committee, Christ Church Methodist		1962
Bound for Kentucky! by Kermit Hunter	Louisville, Ky. (395,000)	Bound for Kentucky, Inc.	George Rogers Clark and Louisville	1961
Chucky Jack by Kermit Hunter	Gatlinburg, Tenn. (1,800)	Great Smoky Mts. Hist. Assoc.	John Sevier and Tennessee	1956–59
Cloud of Witnesses, A by Ramsey Yelvington	(1) Waco, Tex. (104,000)	Baylor Univ.	Siege of the Alamo	1954
	(o) San Antonio, Tex. (612,000)	San Antonio Conservation Soc.		1955, 1957–60
Common Glory, The by Paul Green	Williamsburg, Va.	The Jamestown Corp.	Thomas Jefferson and War of Independence	*1947–63 1965–
Confederacy, The by Paul Green	Virginia Beach, Va. (114,500)	Tidewater Historic Drama Assoc.	Robert E. Lee and the Civil War	1958–59
Cry of the Wild Ram, The by Frank O. Brink	Anchorage, Alaska (44,200)	Anchorage Community Theatre and Alaska Methodist Univ.	Alaskan history	1960

Title and Author(s)	Location of Community	Sponsor(s)	Subject	Performance Date
Dawn's Early Light by Emmet Lavery	(1) Eugene, Oregon (59,000)	Oregon Centennial Com. and Univ. Theatre	National events leading to 1776	1959
Eleventh Hour, The by Kermit Hunter	Staunton, Va. (23,000)	Chamber of Commerce	Woodrow Wilson	1956
Faith of Our Fathers by Paul Green	Washington, D.C.	National Capitol Sesquicentennial Com.	George Washington as President	1950–51
Florida Aflame by John Caldwell	Lake Wales, Fla.	Florida Outdoor Drama Assoc.	Seminole Indians	1953–55
Forever This Land by Kermit Hunter	Petersburg, Ill.	New Salem Lincoln League	Lincoln's New Salem years	1951–52
Founders, The by Paul Green	Williamsburg, Va.	The Jamestown Corp.	Founding and settlement of Jamestown	1957–58 *1964–
Golden Crucible, The by Kermit Hunter	Pittsburgh, Pa. (676,800)	Pittsburgh Bicentennial Com.	Pittsburgh	1959
Highland Call, The by Paul Green	(1) Fayetteville, N.C. (50,500)	Fayetteville Historical Celebration, Inc.	Pioneering Scots in Carolina	1939
	(1) Chapel Hill, N.C. (12,600)	The Carolina Playmakers		1939
	Hartnett County, N.C. (48,200)	Harnett County Centennial Celebration		1955
Home is the Hunter by Robert Emmett McDowell	Harrodsburg, Ky. (6,100)	Fort Harrod Drama Prod., Inc.	Settlement of Kentucky frontier	*1963–
Honey in the Rock by Kermit Hunter	Beckley, W.Va. (18,000)	W.Va. Historical Assoc.	Attainment of West Virginia statehood	*1961–

Title and Author(s)	Location of Community	Sponsor(s)	Subject	Performance Date
Horn in the West by Kermit Hunter	Boone, N.C. (3,700)	Southern Appalachian Historical Assoc.	Daniel Boone and other hardy pioneers	*1952–
In White America by Martin B. Duberman	(1) New York, N.Y.	Judith Rutherford Marechal	Documented Negro history from slavery to Little Rock	1963–64
Let Freedom Ring by Rose K. Banks	(1) Hopewell, Va. (17,900)	Jamestown-Williamsburg-Yorktown National Celebration Committee	National independence	1957
Lost Colony, The by Paul Green	Manteo, N.C. (587)	Roanoke Island Historical Assoc.	First English colonists	1937–41 *1946–
Man's Reach by Gladys L. Hoover	Ambridge, Pa. (16,400)	Harmonie Associates, Inc.	"Father" Rapp and Harmonist Society	1956–61
Next Day in the Morning by Kermit Hunter	(1) Jacksonville, Fla. (200,000)	Ribault Quadricentennial Corp.	French Huguenot's attempt to establish colony	1962
Out of the Wilderness by WPA Writers	Petersburg, Ill.	State Parks and Memorials Div.	Lincoln's years in New Salem	1940
Prophet, The by Wallace Dace	Harpers Ferry, W.Va. (700)	Harpers Ferry Civil War Centennial Assoc.	John Brown and Harpers Ferry	1959

Title and Author(s)	Location of Community	Sponsor(s)	Subject	Performance Date
17th Star, The by Paul Green	Columbus, Ohio (495,000)	Ohio Sesquicentennial Com.	Ohio's rise to statehood	1953
Shadow of an Eagle by Ramsey Yelvington	(1) Dallas, Texas	Dallas Theater Center	Sam Houston	1962
Shout Freedom by Legette Blythe	Charlotte, N.C. (201,600)	Mecklenburg Declaration Centennial Committee	Mecklenburg "Declaration of Independence"	1948
Stars in My Crown by Kermit Hunter	Murray, Ky. (10,500)	West Kentucky Prod. Assoc.	Alben Barkley and TVA	1963–64
Stephen Foster Story, The by Paul Green	Bardstown, Ky. (4,800)	Stephen Foster Drama Assoc., Inc.	Stephen Foster and his melodies	*1959–
Sword of Gideon, The by Florette Henri	Kings Mountain, N.C. (8,000)	Kings Mountain Little Theatre, Inc.	Battle of Kings Mountain	1952–55
Theodore Roosevelt's Life in North Dakota (originally titled Old Four-Eyes) by Thomas M. Patterson	Medora, N.D. (100)	Theo. Roosevelt National Memorial Park & Badland Assoc.	Theodore Roosevelt	*1958–
Third Frontier, The by Kermit Hunter	(1) New Bern, N.C. (16,200)	New Bern & Craven Co. 250th Anniversary Committee	Founding of New Bern	1960
Thunderland by Robert Hayes	Asheville, N.C. (60,200)	Sunset Mountain Attractions, Inc.	Daniel Boone	1952–53
Thy Kingdom Come by Kermit Hunter	Salem, Va. (1,600)	Roanoke Valley Drama Assoc.	Saul's conversion to the Apostle Paul	1957–60
Toward the Western Sky by Lynn Riggs	Cleveland, Ohio	Western Reserve Univ.	Western Reserve Territory	1951

Title and Author(s)	Location of Community	Sponsor(s)	Subject	Performance Date
Trail West by Frederick Walsh and W. T. Chichester	Mandan, N.D. (11,000)	Mandan Historical Development Assoc.	George Armstrong Custer	1959–61
Unto These Hills by Kermit Hunter	Cherokee, N.C. (500)	The Cherokee Historical Assoc.	Cherokee nation	*1950–
Voice in the Wind by Kermit Hunter	Tampa, Fla. (275,000)	Florida Outdoor Drama Assoc.	Andrew Jackson and Seminole Indians	1956
Wilderness Road by Paul Green	Berea, Ky. (4,300)	Berea Coll.	Anti-slavery movement; founding of Berea Coll.	1955–57

Appendix B

List of selected terms and concepts

The selection of entries in the following list is based on the desire to provide the nonspecialist with a simple working vocabulary. Pertaining largely to either dramatic structure or technical theatre, the terms are meaningful only through application and practice. The italicized terms are defined in their alphabetical positions.

AESTHETIC DISTANCE. In the theatre, the spectator's maintenance of artistic ILLUSION by physical or other means of detachment or separation.

ANTAGONIST. A principal figure in a dramatic work opposed to the PROTAGONIST.

APRON. The forestage, a section of the PROSCENIUM STAGE between the front curtain line and the audience.

ATMOSPHERE. The dominant emotional quality or spirit of a drama, in part or as a whole; sometimes called mood.

ATTACK. The moment when a force is introduced that initiates the STRUGGLE.

CHARACTER. One of the dramatis personae; also, a type of personality portrayed on the stage. The sum total of characters in action is the PLOT.

CHARACTERIZATION. The process of portraying the imagined personality of the CHARACTER.

CLIMAX. A peak of DRAMATIC TENSION released by a CRISIS. Also, any high point in a scene or speech. The major climax is the maximum peak of intensity possible in a given STRUGGLE.

COMPLICATION. The introduction of a new force, mainly through INCIDENT or CHARACTER, to develop dramatic action.

CONFLICT. A dramatic tension between two or more characters leading to a CRISIS. A sustained series of conflicts results in STRUGGLE.

CONVENTION. An accepted usage; in the theatre, a common agreement between playwright and audience as to the manner in which the ELEMENTS are to be interpreted.

CRISIS. A decisive moment of uncertainty, clash, or danger posing alternative courses of action for a CHARACTER, any one of which has important consequences for him. The major crisis is the most crucial moment in the DRAMATIC ACTION.

DEVELOPING ACTION. The DRAMATIC ACTION preceding the major climax.

DIALOGUE. The imagined speech exchanged between characters; used to advance PLOT and disclose the personality of each speaker, as well as his station, environment, and emotional state.

DRAMATURGY. The art of writing plays.

DRAMATIC ACTION. Broadly viewed, the forward movement of a play, wholly or in part, by means of speech, physical, or subjective behavior.

DRAMATIC STRUCTURE. In playwriting, the arrangement of structural ELEMENTS.

DRAMATIC SUSPENSE. Anxiety provided as to the outcome of the DRAMATIC ACTION.

DRAMATIC TENSION. The emotional intensity created by the opposing drives of CHARACTERS involved in the DRAMATIC ACTION.

ELEMENT. One of the seven essential components of DRAMATIC STRUCTURE; these components are conventionally known as PLOT, CHARACTER, THEME, DIALOGUE, ATMOSPHERE, SOUND, and SPECTACLE.

EMPATHY. The process of "feeling into" the object or action viewed; in terms of the theatre, the spectator's imitative response to the DRAMATIC ACTION.

EMOTIONAL IDENTIFICATION. Harmonious or sympathetic relationship; in the theatre, the spectator's experiencing vicariously the emotions of a stage character.

EXPOSITION. Information connected with events preceding the beginning of a drama, given to an audience so it may understand further developments.

FALLING ACTION. DRAMATIC ACTION following the major climax.

FLASHBACK. A dramatic technique which carries the spectator back to an earlier event, thereby interrupting the chronological development of the PLOT.

FLOODLIGHT. A lighting instrument without a means of focusing, used to illuminate a large area diffusely. Also, to illuminate the stage with such a light.

FRENCH SCENE. A division of structural unit marked (as in French drama) by the entrance or exit of any CHARACTER.

FULL-LENGTH PLAY. A play long enough for a full program, conventionally from one and a half to two and a half hours.

GERMINAL IDEA. In playwriting, the beginning of a process that may develop into substantial DRAMATIC ACTION; the nucleus, the seed, the jumping-off place for testing the dramatic potentials inherent in much of life's materials.

ILLUSION. The voluntary acceptance by the audience of a simulated reality in the PLOT, CHARACTER, and other ELEMENTS being presented; an artistic method or style which attempts to create this simulated reality.

INCIDENT. Any small event forming a component of the DRAMATIC ACTION.

MULTIPLE SETTING. A stage setting showing more than two locales simultaneously.

OFF STAGE. Outside the playing area.

ON STAGE. Within the playing area.

ONE-ACT PLAY. A play in one act, usually longer than a SKETCH, concentrated, economical of detail, unified in effect.

OPEN STAGE. A stage which uses various physical means of breaking down the PROSCENIUM STAGE separation between audience and playing space. (see figures 2 and 25.)

OUTCOME. The resolution of the DRAMATIC ACTION.

PERMANENT SETTING. A stage setting in which the chief scenic units remain fixed for an entire performance.

PLOT. The order of the presented happenings, the succession of unfolding COMPLICATIONS, in a drama.

PREPARATION. Any means used by a dramatist to prepare the audience for something which will later be introduced into the DRAMATIC ACTION; by such means a CHARACTER becomes credible, DRAMATIC TENSION is heightened, and DRAMATIC SUSPENSE is increased.

PROSCENIUM STAGE. A stage with a permanent arch or "picture frame" through which the audience views the actor in the playing space.

PROTAGONIST. The central figure in a dramatic work; usually, the hero, who may be an individual or a group.

REVOLVING STAGE. A circular stage pivoting at the center and on which two or more sets can be constructed; a turntable, either permanent or portable, adding quick changes of setting.

SIGHT LINE. A line of vision from any audience seat to the playing area; in common usage, the line of vision from the worst seat in the auditorium.

SITUATION. An arrangement of INCIDENTS which arrests the attention of the audience and stirs its curiosity as to what will happen to the characters.

SKETCH. A playlet in one scene; a short dramatic episode usually farcical or humorous.

SOUND. Broadly conceived, the ELEMENT including all the auditory material of performance: tonal patterns of the human voice; instrumental and vocal music; nonmusical mimetic sounds and abstract noises.

SPECTACLE. The ELEMENT including everything in performance appealing to the eye through mass, proportion, color, and movement.

SPOTLIGHT. A lighting instrument which can provide intense illumination upon a limited area. Also, to illuminate the stage with such a light.

STORY. A narration from which a PLOT may be developed; sometimes, misleadingly, called the plot itself.

STRUGGLE. The sustained conflict from which the DRAMATIC ACTION grows.

THEME. The principal thought or organizing view of the drama, as differentiated from the elements of PLOT or ATMOSPHERE. This term designates or implies the playwright's perspective on life that he wishes to express.

WAGON. A low platform on wheels, casters, or rollers, upon which settings may be mounted, so that shifting can be quickly done; sometimes operates on permanent tracks.

WINGS. The OFF STAGE space to the side of the acting area.

APPENDIX C

Reference list for further information

(Please refer to the current edition of *Literary Market Place* for changes in name and/or address of publishers.)

A. BOOKS

General

Tilden, Freeman. *Interpreting Our Heritage: Principles and Practices for Visitor Services in Parks, Museums, and Historic Places.* Chapel Hill: University of North Carolina Press, 1957.

> Informally outlines the new approach among workers in historic sites, parks, and museums which is making interpretation of our history so attractive to many Americans. Contains effective techniques for community sponsors of historical drama.

Reference

Simon, Bernard (ed.). *Simon's Directory of Theatrical Materials, Services, and Information.* New York: Package Publicity Service, Inc., 1963.

> Invaluable guide to where to buy, rent, lease, or find out about materials or equipment necessary for theatrical production and playhouse management. Classified by states. Most complete listing of this nature published to date. Can be ordered directly from Package Publicity Service, Inc., 247 West 40 St., New York 36, N.Y. $3.60.

Production

Albright, H. D., Halstead, William, and Mitchell, Lee. *Principles of Theatre Art.* Boston: Houghton Mifflin Company, 1955.

> Presents aesthetic and practical principles of the various arts of the theatre. Includes clearly synthesized approach to principles of design in directing, scenery, costumes, and make-up. Well illustrated.

Brockett, Oscar G. *The Theatre: An Introduction.* New York: Holt, Rinehart, and Winston, 1964.

Well-rounded introduction to the theatre including sections on theatre history from classic to modern times, and the responsibilities and practices of the theatre artist from playwright to choreographer.

Gassner, John. *Producing the Play, with the New Scene Techician's Handbook* by Philip Barber. Rev. ed. New York: Holt, Rinehart & Winston, Inc., 1953.
Aspects of modern play production are discussed by leading theatre practitioners. Included handbook for technicians offers information on technical theatre practices.

Heffner, Hubert C., Selden, Samuel, and Sellman, Hunton D. *Modern Theatre Practice.* 4th ed. New York: Appleton-Century-Crofts, 1959.
Comprehensive handbook for play production. Includes valuable annotated bibliography and helpful appendix on costume and make-up by costume designer Fairfax Proudfit Walkup.

Open-air production

Bailey, Howard. *The ABC's of Play Producing. A Handbook for the Non-professional.* New York: David McKay Co., Inc., 1955.
Includes brief but helpful section on basic considerations for open-air productions.

Free, William J. and Lower, Charles B. (eds.). *History Into Drama: A Source Book on Symphonic Drama.* New York: The Odyssey Press, 1963.
Articles by experienced practitioners on producing historical dramas out of doors accompany the complete text of Paul Green's *The Lost Colony* with historical and critical materials relating to the Green drama.

Parker, Anthony. *Pageants: Their Presentation and Production.* London: The Bodley Head, 1954.
Production guide for open-air pageant-dramas in Great Britain by an experienced British "pageant-master." Practices recommended, while not directly applicable to American production, provide enlightening suggestions.

Selden, Samuel, and others. *Producing America's Outdoor Dramas.* University of North Carolina Extension Bulletin, XXXIII, No. 4 (March, 1954). Chapel Hill: University of North Carolina Press.
Articles on producing historical drama out of doors by experienced practitioners.

Children's theatre

Citron, Samuel J. *Dramatics for Creative Teaching.* New York: United Synagogue Commission on Jewish Education, 1961.
Details practices for teaching children an active appreciation of drama and

history. Contains valuable section on advantages and techniques of dramatizing history in the school.

Davis, Jed H. and Watkins, Mary J. L. *Children's Theatre, Play Production for the Child Audience*. New York: Harper & Brothers, Publishers, 1960.
> Recommends principles and practices in writing and producing dramas for child audiences.

Religious drama

Chapman, Raymond (ed.). *Religious Drama: A Handbook for Actors and Producers*. London: Published for the Religious Drama Society of Great Britain by S.P.C.K., 1959. Distributed in United States by Baker's Plays.
> Brief manual giving British views of producing chancel drama. Suggestions on acting, staging, and lighting are applicable to American production.

Ehrensperger, Harold. *Religious Drama: Ends and Means*. New York: Abingdon Press, 1962.
> Discusses purposes of religious drama and its means of presentation. Large section devoted to helpful appendices which include play lists and annotated bibliography.

Theatre architecture

Burris-Meyer, Harold and Cole, Edward C. *Theatres & Auditoriums*. New York: Reinhold Corp., 1949.
> Graphic and authoritative analysis of principles and problems involved in planning physical structure of modern theatres.

Cogswell, Margaret (ed.). *The Ideal Theatre: Eight Concepts*. New York: American Federation of Arts, 1962.
> Eight imaginative concepts of proposed buildings for one or more of the performing arts. Stimulating for planning new theatres.

Organization and management

Plummer, Gail. *The Business of Show Business*. New York: Harper & Brothers, Publishers, 1961.
> Problems and effective procedures for publicity, promotion, and box office management.

Rappel, William J. and Winnie, John R. *Community Theatre Handbook*. Iowa City: Institute of Public Affairs, State University of Iowa, 1961.
> Covers community theatre: organization and management, personnel, and available production centers. Appendices contain sample constitutions and bylaws for three types of theatre organizations.

Selden, Samuel (ed.). *Organizing a Community Theatre*. Cleveland: National
Theatre Conference, 1945. Distributed by Theatre Arts Books.
> Articles by theatre specialists on various aspects of community theatre or-
> ganization and management. Sample constitutions and bylaws are included
> in appendices.

Playwriting

Busfield, Roger M., Jr. *The Playwright's Art*. New York: Harper & Brothers,
Publishers, 1958.
> Practical treatment of playwriting principles and techniques including exer-
> cises compiled with the aid of many playwriting teachers.

Garrison, Roger H. *A Creative Approach to Writing*. New York: Henry Holt
and Co., 1951.
> Suggests methods designed to stimulate creative writers to see, feel, hear, be
> aware, and express themselves accurately and imaginatively. Applicable to
> the playwright as well as other writers.

Grebanier, Bernard. *Playwriting*. New York: Thomas Y. Crowell Co., 1961.
> Presents a workable, comprehensive approach to composing a play.

Selden, Samuel. *An Introduction to Playwriting*. New York: F. S. Crofts & Co.,
1946.
> Brief but easily understandable guide to dramatic writing.

Directing and stage management

Boyle, Walden P. *Central and Flexible Staging: A New Theatre in the
Making*.
Berkeley: University of California Press, 1956.
> Well illustrated advice on the staging, technical consideration, and possible
> physical arrangements of arena-style production.

Canfield, Curtis. *The Craft of Play Directing*. New York: Holt, Rinehart &
Winston, Inc., 1963.
> Examines the director's necessary qualifications and methods from the
> analysis of a script to its actual performance.

Dietrich, John E. *Play Direction*. Englewood Cliffs, N.J.: Prentice-Hall, Inc.,
1953.
> Comprehensive, practical presentation of the basic principles and methods
> involved in stage direction.

Gruver, Bert. *The Stage Manager's Handbook*. New York: Harper & Brothers,
Publishers, 1953.

Describes responsibilities of stage management. Contains diagrams and charts for running a performance.

Oxenford, Lyn. *Playing Period Plays*. London: J. Garnet Miller, Ltd., 1958. Distributed in United States by Coach House Press.

> Parts 1 and 2: Medieval (1066) through Stuart (1649); Parts 3 and 4: Restoration (1688) through Edwardian (1910). Treats manners, customs, dress of four historical periods. Useful guide for directing and acting of historical dramas.

Acting

Albright, H. D. *Working Up a Part: A Manual for the Beginning Actor*. 2nd ed. Boston: Houghton Mifflin Company, 1959.

> Practical analysis of approaching a role from rehearsal to performance. Includes exercises and practice scenes.

Oxenford, Lyn. *Playing Period Plays*. See Directing.

Selden, Samuel. *First Steps in Acting*. 2nd ed. New York: Appleton-Century-Crofts, 1964.

> Basic manual emphasizing combined use of voice and body to create a dramatic role. Includes exercises and practice scenes.

Strickland, F. Cowles. *The Technique of Acting*. New York: McGraw-Hill Book Company, 1956.

> Advances a method for approaching a role. Includes exercises and suggestions to stimulate the actor's creative imagination.

Stagecraft, properties, scene design, lighting, sound

Bowman, Wayne. *Modern Theatre Lighting*. New York: Harper & Brothers, Publishers, 1958.

> Practical and comprehensive handbook of lighting practice in the school or community theatre. Suitable for beginning and experienced workers.

Burris-Meyer, Harold and Mallory, Vincent. *Sound in the Theatre*. Mineola, N.Y.: Radio Magazines, Inc., 1959.

> Authoritative treatment on the production and control of sound. Includes sections on sound's relation to architecture and scenery, sound systems and equipment, installation, operation and maintenance.

Conway, Heather. *Stage Properties*. London: Herbert Jenkins, Ltd., 1959.

> Brief but helpful handbook recommending materials and techniques in constructing stage properties.

Fuchs, Theodore. *Home-Built Lighting Equipment for the Small Stage*. New York: Samuel French, Inc., 1939.

Detailed instructions for building lighting equipment with materials at hand. Good working drawings.

Hake, Herbert V. *Here's How! A Basic Stagecraft Book.* rev. ed. Evanston: Row, Petersen, Publishers, 1958.
Practical treatment of the essentials of stagecraft. Includes sections on painting techniques, sound effects, and lighting. Text and diagrams on facing pages. Easy to use.

Napier, Frank. *Noises Off: A Handbook of Sound Effects.* 4th ed. London: J. Garnet Miller Ltd., 1962.
Valuable handbook on how to produce different kinds of sound effects.

Nelms, Henning. *Primer of Stagecraft.* rev. ed. New York: Dramatists Play Service, Inc., 1955.
Concise and well illustrated explanation of methods of building theatre sets. Includes an appendix detailing approximate costs of materials.

Parker, W. Oren and Smith, Harvey K. *Scene Design and Stage Lighting.* New York: Holt, Rinehart & Winston, Inc., 1963.
Authoritative exposition of scene design and stage lighting principles and practices. Most suitable for the person with some experience or training.

Philippi, Herbert. *Stagecraft and Scene Design.* Boston: Houghton Mifflin Company, 1953.
Includes an excellent chapter on properties.

Rubin, Joel E. and Watson, Leland H. *Theatrical Lighting Practice.* New York: Theatre Arts Books, 1954.
Contains valuable sections on arena, outdoor production, and television as well as standard stage lighting.

Costume and make-up

Barton, Lucy. *Historic Costumes for the Stage.* Boston: Walter H. Baker, 1935.
Comprehensive guide to costume and costume accessories throughout history. Detailed sketches of costumes and accessories of all periods furnish extensive reference.

Corson, Richard. *Stage Make-up.* 3rd ed. New York: Appleton-Century-Crofts, 1960.
Detailed text on stage make-up techniques. Includes color chart and more than 275 illustrations.

Melvill, Harald, *Magic of Make-up.* New York: Citadel Press, 1957.
Stresses simplicity in dealing with practical problems of make-up in contemporary theatre.

Paterek, Josephine D. *Costuming for the Theatre*. New York: Crown Publishers, Inc., 1959.
> Emphasizes the importance of studying the character thoroughly in discussing the design and construction of stage costumes. Includes the use of color and accessories.

B. AGENCIES

American Educational Theatre Association, INC. (AETA)

Well-established national organization includes divisions of American Community Theatre Association, Children's Theatre Conference, and Secondary School Theatre Conference. Has annual convention, and publishes annual directory and quarterly, the *Educational Theatre Journal*, with articles on a wide variety of theatre subjects, together with much helpful information on production. AETA operates a contact placement service for trained personnel wishing to direct, design, and administer in producing theatre organizations connected with educational or community institutions. In addition, AETA publishes regularly as part of its service such helpful bulletins or pamphlets as these:

> Bidulph, H. R., Mailer, J. H., and Kamarck, Edward. *Bibliography of Books, Pamphlets and Magazines Relating to Community Theatre*. Free to members of AETA.
>
> Hobgood, Burnet M. (ed.). *Directory of American College Theatre*. AETA members $2.00; nonmembers $3.00.
>
> Bowman, Ned A., and Engel, Glorianne (eds.). *Recent Publications on Theatre Architecture*. AETA members $1.00.
>
> National Education Association, Division of Adult Education. *The Education Theatre in Adult Education*. AETA members $1.00, nonmembers $1.50.

For information regarding individual or group membership in AETA or to order any publications, address: Melvin R. White, Executive Secretary, AETA, John F. Kennedy Center for the Performing Arts 1701 Pennsylvania Avenue, N.W. Washington, District of Columbia 20006.

American National Theatre and Academy (ANTA)

Nationally chartered by Congress to extend the living theatre. Supplies to members theatre information and advisory service, placement and job counseling, photo loan and script service, etc. Membership open in a variety of individual and group classifications. Among ANTA's services is the distribution of such helpful bulletins and pamphlets as these:

Board of Standards and Planning for the Living Theatre.

Open Stage Theatre Check List.

Proscenium-Type Theatre Check List.

Theatre-in-the-Round Check List.
    All three booklets contain valuable check lists of basic minimums in planning the physical structures of proscenium, open-stage, and arena theatres. Extensively illustrated with diagrams and photographs. Compiled by a committee of theatre specialists organized by the Greater New York Chapter of ANTA.

Goodman, Randolph (ed.). *Bibliography of Arena Theatre.* Free to ANTA members; nonmembers $0.60.

Miller, James Hull. *Initial Factors in Theatre Planning.* Free upon request. Rubin, Joel (ed.). *Basic Technical Bibliography.* $0.40.

Theatre Architects Project of AETA. *Suggested Readings in Theatre Architecture.* Free upon request.

Verbecke, W. E. *Community Theatre Structure.* Free to ANTA members; nonmembers $0.15.

Individual and group memberships invited. For information regarding membership or to order any publications, address: Stanley Young, Executive Director, American National Theatre and Academy, 245 West 52 Street, New York, N.Y. 10019.

American Symphony Orchestra League (ASOL)

Influential in spreading cooperative arts approach. Helpful in founding CACI and continues to provide valuable service and information. ASOL distributes printed material such as:

Governing Boards of Symphony Orchestras. $1.75.
    Although focus is on the selection of members of symphony orchestra governing boards, many points in book apply to personnel and procedures applicable to community theatres.

Legal Documents of Symphony Orchestras. $1.25.
    Though aimed at symphony orchestras, information in book applicable to community theatre producing groups. A necessity for writing charters and bylaws.

Individuals and groups should address inquiries or book orders to: American Symphony Orchestra League, P.O. Box 164, Charleston, W.Va.

Community Arts Councils, INC. (CACI)

CACI holds annual convention, issues bulletins to members on such topics as fund-raising methods, arts calendars, festival promotions, and other cooperative arts projects. Also aids arts councils in finding trained executives. Has two membership classifications: Council Members, organizations engaged in promotion and encouragement of the arts; Associate Members, all other organizations and individuals. CACI distributes instructive materials such as:

Burgard, Ralph. *Study of Arts Councils* (1963). $1.75.
    A report on the structure and operating procedures of over one hundred arts councils in United States and Canada.
Winston-Salem Arts Council. *The Arts Council Handbook, 1965 edition.* $1.75.

Individuals and groups should address inquiries or book orders to: Community Arts Councils, Inc., 300 Maine Street, Quincy, Ill.

The Institute of Outdoor Drama (IOD)

Founded by the University of North Carolina, under direction of the Department of Dramatic Art and the Carolina Playmakers, IOD serves as central agency for groups interested in producing dramas out-of-doors. Services available to individuals and groups on national basis. Resources include a library of scripts, promotional materials, architectural plans, financial and management counsel, and other aids. Sponsors conferences to bring about exchange of information. Supplies names of experienced personnel in various sections of country qualified to advise on artistic, technical, and operation matters. For information address: Mark R. Sumner, Director, The Institute of Outdoor Drama, The University of North Carolina, Chapel Hill, N. C. 27515.

National Council on the Arts and Government, INC. (NCAG)

Provides information on impending and enacted government legislation to encourage and support the arts. Publishes NCAG *Annual Report*, a survey of federal legislation affecting the arts, with summaries of accomplishments and plans at state and county levels. For free copy of report address: National Council on the Arts and Government, Inc., 22 West 54 Street, New York, N.Y. 10019.

New York State Council on the Arts

Experiment at state level in encouraging and supporting the arts which may point important directions for other states and smaller communities. Its publication, *New York State Council on the Arts, a Report on Activities for 1960–64*, contains a statement of the council's initiation and development, varied programs, plans for the future, and present organization structure. Copies of the report are free upon inquiry to: New York State Council on the Arts, 250 West 57 Street, New York, N.Y. 10019.

New York State Community Theatre Association (NYSCTA)

Coordinating agency for community theatre groups in New York has state-wide representation, annual conference, regional meetings, a playwriting contest, a quarterly journal, and other helpful services not limited to New York Staters. Among recommended NYSCTA pamphlets available are three pertaining to community theatre organization and administration:

Dicker, William, and Heller, Sanders, *Incorporation of Little Theatre Groups*
Sample Constitution of Little Theatre of Binghamton
Sample Constitution of Little Theatre of Watertown

These and other pamphlets are distributed free upon request to: Edward J. Mendus, Administrative Secretary, New York State Community Theatre Association, State University of New York at Albany, 135 Western Avenue, Albany, N.Y. 12203.

Wisconsin Idea Theatre

Coordinating agency, similar to NYSCTA, that has made theatre a community force in state. Sponsored by Department of Speech and the University Extension Division, its activities include development of rural drama program, indigenous writers movement, and children's theatre activities. Each summer it draws upon experts to staff the lecturers of the National Community Theatre Center, designed to train local leaders in the regional theatres of the country. For information regarding the Center and other available services address: Edward L. Kamarck, The University of Wisconsin, Extension Building, Madison 6, Wis.

FOUNDATION INFORMATION

The resources of private and semi-private foundation aid are covered in these three publications:

Foundation Library Center. *Foundation News*, published six times a year. $3.00 per year.
> Contains information on grants to the arts as well as other activities. Address orders for subscriptions to: The Foundation Library Center, 428 East Preston Street, Baltimore 2, Md.

National Council on Community Foundations. *Community Foundations in the United States and Canada, 1914-61.* 2nd ed. 1961. $2.50.
> A guide to the organization, development, and operation of foundations. Address inquiries and book orders to: The National Council on Community Foundations, 345 East 46 Street, New York, N.Y. 10017.

Walton, Ann D., and Lewis, Marianna D. (eds.). *The Foundation Directory.* 2nd ed. (New York: The Russell Sage Foundation, 1964).
> An excellent and comprehensive encyclopedia of foundations, describing their purposes and special areas of interest. $10.00. Address inquiries and book orders to: The Russell Sage Foundation, 230 Park Avenue, New York, N.Y. 10017.

Notes

Chapter I

1   George Pierce Baker, *Dramatic Technique* (Boston: Houghton Mifflin Co., 1947), p. 43.

2   Hervey Allen, "History and the Novel," *Atlantic Monthly,* CLXXIII (February, 1944), 119–21.

3   Specific information about historical dramas mentioned in the text is given in Appendix A.

4   The term "epic" is associated in our age with the theories and work of the late German playwright Bertolt Brecht (1898–1956). Our own use of the term considers a more traditional concept than that of Brecht as Chapter XI will illustrate.

5   Robert Littell, "History Brought to Life," *The Reader's Digest,* LXXVIII (May, 1961), 193–96. Boscobel Mansion overlooking the Hudson River near Garrison, New York, and Independence Hall in Philadelphia are two of the small but growing number of American historic sites which have featured such "Sound and Light" productions.

6   "The Field of Travel," *New York Times,* March 22, 1964, Sec. 10, p. 8.

7   This group of museums includes: Colonial Williamsburg, Fort Ticonderoga, Henry Ford Museum and Greenfield Village, Mystic Seaport, National Baseball Hall of Fame and Museum, Farmers Museum and Fenimore House, Old Sturbridge Village, and Shelburne Museum. A comparative list of museum attendance figures compiled by Old Sturbridge Village was released in July, 1961.

8   Figures supplied by the National Park Service, U. S. Department of the Interior.

9   Allan Nevins, " 'An Idea Whose Time Has Come'," *New York Times,* October 18, 1959, Sec. 2, p. 7.

10   Statement made by Louis C. Jones, Director of the New York State Historical Association in "History for Everyman," a radio broadcast on February 15, 1952.

11   American Heritage (eds.), *The First Year of American Heritage* (New York: American Heritage Publishing Company, Inc., 1958), preface.

12   Information furnished by Ray C. Dovell, President of the History Book Club, Inc., February 29, 1960.

13   John P. Sisk, "American Best Sellers," *Commonweal,* LXVIII (July 11, 1958), 373.

14   *The Americana Annual: 1964* (New York: Americana Corporation, 1964), p. 448.

15   "The Talking Discs," *Holiday,* XXIX (May, 1961), 179–83.

16   Letter from Robert E. Seaver, Director of Religious Drama Program at Union Theological Seminary, October 7, 1959.

17   Civil War Centennial Commission, "State Centennial Commissions at Work." A report issued by the Civil

War Centennial Commission, January 4, 1961.

18   From a public printed message from Arthur Miller on the occasion of World Theatre Day, March 27, 1963.

19   Louis Jouvet, "Notes on the Role of the Theatre," *New York Times*, April 8, 1951, Sec. 2, p. 3.

Chapter II

1   Harold Newcomb Hillebrand, *Writing the One-Act Play* (New York: F. S. Crofts & Co., 1925), p. 79.

2   *Encyclopaedia Britannica*, 14th ed., *s.v.* John Brown.

3   *Ibid.*, *s.v.* Paul.

4   Carl Carmer, *The Hudson* (New York: Farrar & Rinehart, 1939), pp. 81–89.

5   The authors are indebted to Samuel Selden's discussion of the qualities of the dramatic in his book *An Introduction to Playwriting* (New York: F. S. Crofts & Co., 1946), pp. 1–28.

6   Howard Lindsay, "Some Notes on Playwriting," *The Theatre Arts Anthology*, ed. Rosamond Gilder, *et al.* (New York: Theatre Arts Books, 1950), p. 124.

7   Helene Hanff, " 'The Footnote-and-mouth disease'," *Harper's*, CCXXIII (July, 1961), 59.

8   Investigative procedures and types of source materials are discussed in Chapter IX.

9   Lee appears as a character in Stephen Vincent Benét's *John Brown's Body*, Acting ed. (New York: Dramatists Play Service, 1961), and in Paul Green's *The Confederacy* (New York: Samuel French, 1959).

10   Two Washington plays of recent years are worthy of mention. Howard Fast's *The Crossing* depicts Washington just before his crossing of the Delaware. The drama projects a rough-swearing Virginian who not only likes wine and the companionship of a pretty Pennsylvania farm girl, but also has strong inward doubts of his capacity as general of the Continental forces. In his effort, however, to present a very human Washington who somewhat shatters the myth, the writer has been unable to bestow his character with sufficient nobility to render him fully believable to spectators anticipating at least a strong glimmer of the Stuart portrait. An earlier version is published under the following title: *General Washington and the Water Witch* (London: The Bodley Head, 1956).

Ramsey Yelvington's *The Marble Horseman* shows Washington immediately after the British surrender at Yorktown. Pondering a decision to halt or approve the execution of a Tory prisoner, the victorious but tired Commander-in-Chief recalls incidents in his past which as brief flashback scenes are interwoven with the main action. While a human Washington—and the man of the Stuart portrait—is delineated in the retrospective sequences, the character is not dramatically realized in terms of action.

11   William Archer, *Play-Making: A Manual of Craftsmanship.* (Boston: Small, Maynard and Co., 1912), pp. 157–58, 251.

12   *Home Is the Hunter* by Robert Emmett McDowell is an epic-drama presented annually in the summer at Harrodsburg, Kentucky, since 1963.

13   Robert   Emmett   McDowell,

"Home Is the Hunter," *Home Is the Hunter* 1964 Souvenir Program, pp. 22–23.

14   With such considerations in mind, several recent regionally produced dramas have seized upon John Brown, the Apostle Paul, and Mehitabel Wing as leading characters. The actions of Brown, for example, form the basis of: Barrie Stavis' *Banners of Steel*, Wallace Dace's *The Prophet*, Jack LaZebnik's *John Brown*, Richard F. Stockton's *The Trial of John Brown*, and Julia Davis's *The Anvil. The Moon Besieged* by Seyril Schochen, another Brown drama has been produced off-Broadway. Kermit Hunter's *Thy Kingdom Come* centered on Paul. The Quaker heroine is dramatized in *Mehitabel Wing* by Isobel Rose Jones and Geoffrey O'Hara. In most instances, these dramas are written by regional writers.

Other noted figures out of our past thought sufficiently dramatic to qualify as central characters of American dramas over the last two decades have been: Thomas Jefferson, George Washington, Patrick Henry, Daniel Boone, Fiorello La Guardia, Commandant Wirz of Andersonville Prison, Theodore Roosevelt, George Armstrong Custer, Franklin D. Roosevelt, Abraham Lincoln, Stephen Douglas, Woodrow Wilson, Benjamin Franklin, and others.

15   Federal Writers' Project, *Utah: A Guide to the State* (New York, Hastings House, 1941), pp. 201–8.

16   The story of the Mormons' great trek to the West is dramatized in the musical pageant-drama *All Faces West* by Roland and Helen Parry.

17   Quoted in John P. Shanley, "Grant's Story on Television," *New York Times*, February 21, 1960, Sec. 2, p. 15.

18   Mrs. Will Griffith, "A Capsule History of Carbondale," in *Century of Progress*. A centennial souvenir program issued by the Carbondale Chamber of Commerce.

19   Charlotte McLeod's *A Century of Progress*—a pageant-drama of Carbondale's past—did discover and utilize such dramatic materials.

20   This aspect of dramatic writing is treated at greater length in Chapter VIII.

21   Federal Writers' Project, *New York: A Guide to the Empire State* (New York: Oxford University Press, 1940), pp. 624–25.

22   E. M. Forster, *Aspects of the Novel* (New York: Harcourt, Brace & Co., 1927), p. 72.

Chapter III

1   Bert Hansen, "Sociodrama in a Small-Community Therapy Program," *Sociatry*, I (March, 1947), 92.

2   Sydney Greenbie and Marjorie Barstow Greenbie, "Preface," *Castine: A Dramatized Biography of a Town* (Penobscot, Maine: Traversity Press, 1948), p. 7.

3   Comments reported in *Conference Notes from the First National Outdoor Drama Conference* (Chapel Hill, North Carolina: Institute of Outdoor Drama, 1963), p. 37.

4   For further details see Milton Esterow, "Dramatic Bootstrap," *New York Times*, August 6, 1961, Sec. 2, p. 1.

5   Paul Green, *Drama and the*

Weather (New York: Samuel French, 1958), p. 35.

6 Samuel Selden, *Outdoor Historical Dramas*, a report to the University of North Carolina Trustees, November, 1955.

7 "The Grand Tour," *Newsweek*, XLIX (June 17, 1957), 118–19.

Chapter IV

1 The formation of such an advisory group for the "institutional" or "organizational" community is patently unnecessary, of course, since there already exists in the standard school and church situation motivation and procedural means for the sponsorship of dramatic events.

2 A partial listing of such drama educators includes the names of Alexander Drummond and Mary Eva Duthie of Cornell; Alfred Arvold and Frederick G. Walsh of North Dakota State College; Ethel Theodora Rockwell and Robert Gard of Wisconsin; Thomas Wood Stevens of Carnegie Institute of Technology and Goodman School of Drama; Frederick H. Koch, first of North Dakota and then North Carolina, where his influence radiated from Chapel Hill through Samuel Selden, Paul Green, and Kermit Hunter; Alexander Dean of Montana State and Yale University; Paul Baker of Baylor and Trinity University, and Horace Robinson of Oregon.

3 To avoid unnecessary confusion, we are using the terms "sponsoring" and "producing" interchangeably, fully aware that some theatrical enterprises receive support from two different kinds of groups: one, the *producing* unit,

committed to legal and financial involvements and artistic decisions in the presentation; two, the *sponsoring* unit, committed to nothing more than general advice and the weight of its prestige. An example of such division is the production of *The Miracle Worker*, "produced" in Tuscumbia, Alabama, by the Starmaker Community Playhouse in "cooperation with" the Helen Keller Property Board, and "sponsored" by the local chapter of the American Association of University Women.

4 The Producers Association for Young America in New York makes locally available to interested groups productions of this and such other musical historical dramas for children as John Allen's *Young Ben Franklin* and *Young Jefferson* (with music by Albert Hague), and Robert K. Adams' *Young Tom Edison* (with music and lyrics by Martin Kalmanoff). The Association is located at 506 East 89 Street, New York, New York 10028.

5 Letter from Leighton Ballew, March 30, 1961.

6 Not to be minimized in this respect is the leadership of the Department of Worship and the Arts, National Council of the Churches of Christ, and the Program of Religious Drama at Union Theological Seminary. Across the Atlantic, the Religious Drama Society of Great Britain has pointed the way for international exchanges of ideas, practices, and scripts.

7 Letter from Mrs. J. N. Newcomer, President, Harpers Ferry Area Foundation, November 8, 1960.

8 Formed in 1946, the Jamestown Corporation opened *The Common Glory* in 1947. The idea for a historical

drama at Jamestown began to germinate around 1942. This information and its statement of operations are contained in a mimeographed report distributed by the Corporation in 1959.

9   Richard Hoover, "The Business Manager," Theatre Arts, XXXIII, December, 1949, 55–56.

10   Christopher Crittenden, "History: Germinal Ideas for Playwrights," a talk to the Carolina Dramatic Association, Chapel Hill, April 14, 1956. Mr. Crittenden is Director, Department of Archives and History, State of North Carolina.

Chapter V

1   Conference Notes from the First National Outdoor Drama Conference (Chapel Hill, North Carolina: Institute of Outdoor Drama, 1963), p. 40.

2   Gail Plummer, The Business of Show Business (New York: Harper and Brothers, 1961), pp. 11–16.

3   John H. MacFadyen, "State Programs for Support of the Arts—a General Outline." A report issued by the New York State Council on the Arts, April 19, 1963, Appendix C.

4   Ralph Burgard, "Arts Councils: New Approach to Cultural Leadership," Arts in Society, II (Fall–Winter 1962/63), 120–31. See also Charles Mark, "Common Sense about Citizen Support for Arts and Culture," Arts in Society, II (n.d.), 4–11.

5   Arts Management, published monthly by The Radius Group, Inc., New York, No. 16 (May, 1963); No. 17 (June, 1963).

6   Harold Burris-Meyer and Edward C. Cole, Theatres & Auditoriums

(New York: Reinhold, 1949), p. 215.

7   Conference Notes from the First National Outdoor Drama Conference, p. 18.

8   Ibid., p. 6.

9   "1963 Annual Report of the National Council on the Arts and Government, Inc." (New York, 1963), pp. 4–6.

10   New York State Council on the Arts Newsletter (published monthly by Arts Management), July, 1963; also The Arts Council Handbook, 1963 ed. (published by the Winston-Salem Arts Council, Winston-Salem, North Carolina).

11   Junius Eddy, Drama and Leisure Time: A Report on the Two-Year General Education Board Study at Baylor University on the Integration of Dramatic Activities with Community Leisure Time Programs. (Waco, Texas: Baylor University, Aug., 1951), p. 62.

Chapter VI

1   This procedure was effectively used by the general manager of Kentucky's Home Is the Hunter at Harrodsburg before the drama opened in 1963. A sample format of a feasibility study is made available to interested communities through the Institute of Outdoor Drama at Chapel Hill, North Carolina.

2   For a full description of the Hermann Maifest, see Vivian Hansbrough, "The Woman Behind the Maifest," The Missouri Farmer, May, 1961, 36–37.

3   For a detailed list of audience-related and other specifications pertaining to the open-air theatre—many can be applied to the indoor theatre as well

—see Samuel Selden, "A Theatre for Outdoor Plays," *Producing America's Outdoor Dramas,* Samuel Selden, et al. (Chapel Hill: University of North Carolina Press), Extension Bulletin, XXXIII, No. 4 (March, 1954), 26–34.
4   James R. Carlson, "The play's the thing," *International Journal of Religious Education,* XXXVII (February, 1961), 9–12. This article contains many helpful suggestions on the staging of drama in the church.
5   Walden Boyle, *Central and Flexible Staging: A New Theatre in the Making* (Berkeley: University of California Press, 1956), p. 23.
6   *Ibid.,* p. 26.
7   For a description of the needs of flexible staging in the social or multi-purpose room, see Arthur C. Risser, "Building and equipment for drama," *International Journal of Religious Education,* XXXVII (February, 1961), 22–23.
8   James Laver, *Drama: Its Costume and Décor* (London: The Studio Ltd., 1951), p. 67.
9   Ward Wagnon, "Evening with an Aura," *Holiday Inn Magazine* (April, 1963), 11. Mr. Wagnon capitalizes on the historic identity of a colonnaded ante-bellum mansion called Forks of Cypress, near Florence, for the staging of his own play, *This Land, This Dream.* The action witnessed by the audience seated on the lawn of Forks of Cypress is based, in part, on events which transpired there in Alabama's past.
10   For its 1964 presentation, *The Founders* moved to the "nonspecific" staging patterns of the Lake Matoaka Amphitheatre (Fig. 20).

11   A helpful discussion regarding selected characteristics of five outdoor theatres appears in Philip G. Hill, "A Theatre for the Outdoor Historical Drama," *Educational Theatre Journal,* XIV (December, 1962), 312–17.

Chapter VII

1   With essentially the same Lincoln "facts" available to them, the following playwrights have written and had produced dramas conceiving significant human differences in the historical figure: Robert E. Sherwood, *Abe Lincoln in Illinois;* E. P. Conkle, *Prologue to Glory;* Kermit Hunter, *Forever This Land;* John Allen, Richard Bernstein, and Arnold Sundgaard, *Young Abe Lincoln;* W. P. A. Writers Program, *Out of the Wilderness: The New Salem Years of Abraham Lincoln;* Norman Corwin, *The Rivalry;* Mark Van Doren, *The Last Days of Lincoln;* Nat Sherman, *The Washington Years;* Arthur Goodman, *If Booth Had Missed;* and John Drinkwater, *Abraham Lincoln.* The first five plays mentioned depict Lincoln before assuming the Presidency, the last four plays mainly treat his life after 1860. Differences in approach to the same personage are also marked in dramas about John Brown (see chapter II, note 14).
2   Roger H. Garrison, *A Creative Approach to Writing* (New York: Henry Holt and Co., 1951), p. xvi.
3   It is interesting to compare the number of words used in dramatizations of novels and the number used in the novels themselves. Kathryn Forbes, Herman Melville, Thomas Wolfe, Arthur Koestler, and James Agee in the novels

mentioned used from 100,000 to 200,-000 words. The dramatized versions of each were reduced to anywhere from 25,000 to 30,000 words.

4   Thornton Wilder, "Some Thoughts on Playwriting," *Aspects of the Drama*, ed. Sylvan Barnet, Morton Berman, and William Burto (Boston: Little, Brown and Co., 1962), p. 10.

5   The four plays are Friedrich Schiller's *The Maid of Orleans*, George Bernard Shaw's *St. Joan*, Maxwell Anderson's *Joan of Lorraine*, and Jean Anouilh's *The Lark*.

6   Kenneth Thorpe Rowe, *A Theater in Your Head* (New York: Funk & Wagnalls, 1960), pp. 220–26.

7   The story of Narcissa Whitman and her family is dramatized by Jane Erickson in *A Mighty Fortress*.

8   Herbert Halpert, "Aggressive Humor on the East Branch," *New York Folklore Quarterly*, II, No. 2 (May, 1946), 94.

9   Emelyn E. Gardner, *Folklore from the Schoharie Hills* (Ann Arbor: University of Michigan Press, 1937), pp. 314–17.

10   *Ibid.*, pp. 36–38.

11   Halpert, p. 94.

12   Charles Coleman Sellers, *Lorenzo Dow, The Bearer of the Word* (New York: Minton, Balch & Company, 1928), p. 4.

13   *Ibid.*, p. 5.

14   *Ibid.*, p. 4.

15   Roughly one minute of playing time is customarily allotted to each 8½" x 11" manuscript page typed in standard form. For acceptable examples, the reader is referred to Kenneth Macgowan, *A Primer of Playwriting* (New York:

Random House, 1951), pp. 192–98, or Bernard Grebanier, *Playwriting* (New York: Thomas Y. Crowell Co., 1961), pp. 362–65.

16   Roger M. Busfield, Jr., *The Playwright's Art* (New York: Harper & Brothers, 1958), pp. 120–21. For the purposes of the present work, the material cited is somewhat modified. The material, *The Playwright's Art*, is partially based on Samuel Selden, *An Introduction to Playwriting* (New York: F. S. Crofts & Co., Inc., 1946), pp. 50–64. By permission of Appleton-Century-Crofts, Inc.

17   Robert Gard, "Raisin' the Devil," *The Lake Guns of Seneca and Cayuga*, ed. A. M. Drummond and Robert E. Gard (Ithaca, New York: Cornell University Press, 1942), pp. 179–98. By permission of Cornell University Press.

Chapter VIII

1   Naomi Mitchison, "Writing Historical Novels," *Saturday Review of Literature*, XI (April 27, 1935), 645.

2   Boyd B. Stultler, "The Hanging of John Brown," *American Heritage*, VI (February, 1955), 4–9.

3   Louis A. Mallory, "Patrick Henry," *A History and Criticism of American Public Address*, ed. William Norwood Brigance (New York: Russell & Russell, 1960), II, p. 590.

4   Theodore Ward, "Our Lan'," *A Theater in Your Head*, Kenneth Thorpe Rowe (New York: Funk & Wagnalls, 1960), p. 262.

5   Letter from Ramsey Yelvington, March 16, 1964.

6   Emmet Lavery, *The Magnificent*

Yankee (New York: Samuel French, 1946), p. vii.

7 Robert Emmet Sherwood, "The Substance of 'Abe Lincoln in Illinois'," *Abe Lincoln in Illinois* (New York: Charles Scribner's Sons, 1939), pp. 191–92. See also Benét's handling of historical narrative in "John Brown's Body," *Selected Works of Stephen Vincent Benét* I (New York: Farrar & Rinehart, Inc., 1942).

8 Letter from Kermit Hunter, September 16, 1957.

9 Letter from Sidney Kingsley, March 28, 1957.

10 William Gibson, "Prefatory," *Dinny and the Witches; The Miracle Worker* (New York: Atheneum, 1960), pp. 6–10.

11 From two letters in Paul Leicester Ford, ed., *The Writings of Thomas Jefferson* (New York: G. P. Putnam's Sons, 1892), I, pp. 347, 353.

12 Letter from Paul Green, April 22, 1957.

13 Maxwell Anderson, Preface to "Journey to Jerusalem," *Three Plays by Maxwell Anderson*, ed. George Freedley (New York: Washington Square Press, 1962), pp. 214–16.

14 Letter from Ethel Theodora Rockwell, February 1, 1958.

15 *Chicago Daily Press and Tribune*, September 1, 1858, p. 2.

16 *St. Louis Post-Dispatch*, March 11, 1962, Section J, p. 4.

17 Barrie Stavis, *The Man Who Never Died* (New York: Haven Press, 1954), p. ix.

18 Held in 1957 at Jamestown, Virginia.

19 The reader will enjoy Catherine Bowen's enlightening experiences with librarians recounted in her book *Adventures of a Biographer* (Boston: Little, Brown and Company, 1959), pp. 138–51.

Chapter IX

1 Stephen Leacock, "Historical Drama," *Laugh with Leacock* (New York: Dodd, Mead & Company, 1930), pp. 323–25. Reprinted by permission of Dodd, Mead & Company.

2 To cite one illustration, several drama critics commenting on Raymond Massey's portrayal of the titular character in *Abe Lincoln in Illinois* noted the effectiveness of the actor's facial expression in suggesting the character's inner conflicts. In a large outdoor theatre this kind of detail cannot be seen except by persons sitting in the first few rows.

3 George Middleton, *These Things Are Mine* (New York: Macmillan Company, 1947), p. 144. The dramatist has written several biography-dramas of which *That was Balzac* is one of the best known.

4 Robert Emmet Sherwood, "The Substance of 'Abe Lincoln in Illinois'," *Abe Lincoln in Illinois* (New York: Charles Scribner's Sons, 1939), pp. 190–91.

5 C. V. Wedgwood, "Art, Truth and History," *Biography as an Art*, ed. James L. Clifford (New York: Oxford University Press, 1962), p. 217.

6 *Ibid.*, p. 217.

7 Christopher Fry, *Curtmantle* (New York: Oxford University Press, 1961), p. vii.

8 Carl Sandburg, *Abraham Lincoln: The Prairie Years* (New York:

Harcourt, Brace & Co., 1926), II, p. 278.

9   This information in the main is drawn from Sandburg's *Abraham Lincoln: The Prairie Years,* II.

10   Stark Young, "The Patriots," *New Republic,* CVIII (February 15, 1943), 211, [review].

11   From a statement accredited to Levitt in *The Andersonville Trial* 1963 Souvenir Program (road company production).

12   Elmer Rice, "A Personal Memoir: Tribute to Robert E. Sherwood," *New York Times,* November 20, 1955, Sec. 2, p. 1.

13   Letter from Barrie Stavis, March 15, 1962. Stavis' other plays all deal with such historical figures: labor leader Joe Hill in *The Man Who Never Died,* Galileo in *Lamp at Midnight,* the biblical Joseph in *Coat of Many Colors.*

14   Sherwood, "The Substance of 'Abe Lincoln in Illinois'," p. 220.

15   *Ibid.,* p. 189.

16   Based on Louis Ruchames (ed.), *A John Brown Reader* (New York: Abelard-Schuman Limited, 1959), and Oswald Garrison Villard, *John Brown: 1800–1859: A Biography Fifty Years After* (Boston: Houghton Mifflin Company, 1910).

17   In speaking of his own efforts to write historical drama, playwright Christopher Fry admits: "It is tempting to make a misleading simplification. In the absence of any other household-god, simplification becomes a gross superstition. It gives us the security of 'knowing,' of being at home in events. We even call it reality or getting down to the truth. But everything that we ignored

remains to confute us." Fry, *Curtmantle,* pp. vii–viii.

18   This point is implied in the advice of nineteenth-century German critic-playwright Gotthold Lessing: "From the stage we are not to learn what such and such an individual has done, but what every man of a certain character would do under certain given circumstances." Gotthold Ephraim Lessing, Extract from "Hamburg Dramaturgy," *European Theories of the Drama,* ed. Barrett H. Clark, rev. ed. (New York: Crown Publishers, 1947), p. 259.

19   For an interesting discussion of this problem, see Nathaniel Wright Stephenson, "History and the Playwright," *Drama,* no. 6 (May, 1912), 191–209.

20   Leacock, "Historical Drama," p. 323.

21   Sherwood, "The Substance of 'Abe Lincoln in Illinois'," p. 203.

22   John Drinkwater, *Abraham Lincoln* (Boston: Houghton Mifflin Company, 1919), p. vii.

23   Edith Mirick, "Storm" (Notes to unpublished manuscript circulated by the American Educational Theatre Association's Manuscript Play Project, copyright 1944 by the author).

24   Barrie Stavis, "Banners of Steel" (Unpublished manuscript circulated by the American Playwrights Theatre, Ohio State University, Columbus, Ohio), pp. 7–8.

25   George Bernard Shaw, *Our Theatre in the Nineties* (London: Constable and Co. Ltd., 1932), II, p. 45.

26   Maxwell Anderson, "Valley Forge," *Three Plays by Maxwell Anderson,* pp. 106–7. Copyright 1934 by

Maxwell Anderson. Copyright renewed 1962 by Gilda Anderson, Alan Anderson, Terence Anderson, Quentin Anderson and Hesper A. Levenstein. All rights reserved. Reprinted by permission of Anderson House.

27 Ibid.

28 Jared Sparks (ed.), The Writings of George Washington (Boston: 1834), V, p. 290.

29 John Gassner, The Theatre in Our Times (New York: Crown Publishers, Inc., 1954), p. 486.

30 Wolcott Gibbs, "Birth of a Nation," The New Yorker, XVIII (February 6, 1943), 31.

31 John Bartlett, Familiar Quotations, 10th ed. (Boston: Little Brown and Company, 1920), p. 1047.

32 An outstanding example of effectively integrating quoted material with a playwright's own words is found in the last scene of Sherwood's Abe Lincoln in Illinois. Sherwood has taken remarks from three of Lincoln's speeches and joined them with his own to create the stage figure's farewell speech at Springfield in 1861. See Sherwood, Abe Lincoln in Illinois, pp. 182–84.

33 Letters from Fred Carmichael, August 23 and September 19, 1963, and from Catherine Fennelly, Research Director of Old Sturbridge Village, October 21, 1963.

34 Based on an explanatory summary from the program of One for the Lord's Day, 1963, Old Sturbridge Village, Sturbridge, Massachusetts, and on Alice Felt Tyler, Freedom's Ferment: Phases of American Social History to 1860 (Minneapolis: University of Minnesota Press, 1944), pp. 291–92.

35 Based on Noah Parker, "The New England Meeting House," Tercentary Commission of the State of Connecticut, Pamphlet 18 (New Haven, Yale University Press, 1936), pp. 1–5.

36 Fred Carmichael, One for the Lord's Day. All rights are reserved. By permission of the author. Fred Carmichael has written other biography-dramas produced at Old Sturbridge Village. He also is the author of the following plays published by Samuel French, Inc.: More Than Meets the Eye, Inside Lester, The Night Is My Enemy, Petey's Choice, Luxury Cruise, The Pen Is Deadlier, Exit the Body, The Robin Hood Caper, and Any Number Can Die.

Chapter X

1 Booth Tarkington, Penrod (New York: Grosset and Dunlap, 1914), pp. 41–42. From "The Pageant of the Table Round" copyright 1913 by Booth Tarkington. Reprinted by permission of Doubleday & Company, Inc.

2 Ethel Theodora Rockwell, Third Episode from The Freeport Pageant of the Blackhawk Country, Pageants of Our Nation, ed. Anne P. Sanford and Robert Haven Schauffler (New York: Dodd Mead, 1929), II, p. 32.

3 Foster Fitz-Simmons, "Choreography in The Lost Colony," History Into Drama: A Source Book on Symphonic Drama, ed. William J. Free and Charles B. Lower (New York: Odyssey Press, 1963), p. 152.

4 Charlotte McLeod, "Century of Progress," (Unpublished manuscript), p. 34.

5 Sydney and Marjorie Barstow Greenbie, Castine: A Dramatized Biog-

raphy of a Town (Penobscot, Maine: Traversity Press, 1948), pp. 88–89.

6   Thomas Wood Stevens, The Historical Pageant of Illinois (Chicago: Aldenbrink Press, 1909), p. v.

7   This event furnishes the substance of a scene in The Pageant of Newark by Thomas Wood Stevens.

8   William Chauncy Langdon, "Compass Points in the Festal Drama," The Drama, No. 27 (August, 1917), 408.

9   Esther Willard Bates, George Washington of Young America (Boston: Walter H. Baker Co., 1931).

10   The author mentions Lodge as a chief source for her Washington pageant-drama. Letter from Esther Willard Bates, August 26, 1957. The commentary on Washington's qualities is based on Henry Cabot Lodge, George Washington, 2 vols. (New York: Houghton Mifflin Co., 1889).

11   Various possible functions and types of framing devices in modern drama are cogently discussed in Barnard Hewitt, "Some Uses of the 'Frame' in Playwriting," The Quarterly Journal of Speech, XXXII (December, 1946), 480–84.

12   Stevens, The Pageant of Newark (Newark, New Jersey: The Committee of One Hundred, 1916), p. 42.

13   Kermit Hunter, "Oral Interpretation in the Outdoor Theater," The Southern Speech Journal, XIX, No. 2 (December, 1953), 133.

14   Ibid.

15   For a previous discussion of the relationship between writer and historian in this instance, see chapter ix.

16   College Library Staff, compilers, Vital Facts of the College of William

and Mary in Virginia (Williamsburg, 1955), 5–12.

17   "Notices," The William and Mary Quarterly, 2nd Series, Vol. V (April, 1925), 121–24.

18   Based on E. G. Swem, "Kentuckians at William and Mary College Before 1861 with a Sketch of the College Before that Date," Filson Club History Quarterly, XXIII (July, 1949), 185–86.

19   Ibid., 188.

20   Copyright 1956 by the author.

Chapter XI

1   Paul Green, "Symphonic Drama," Ten Talents in the American Theatre, ed. David H. Stevens (Norman: University of Oklahoma Press, 1957), p. 256.

2   Ibid.

3   Oscar G. Brockett, The Theatre: An Introduction (New York: Holt, Rinehart and Winston, 1964), p. 311.

4   Encyclopaedia Britannica, 14th ed., s.v. Homer.

5   Conference Notes from the First National Outdoor Drama Conference (Chapel Hill, North Carolina: Institute of Outdoor Drama, 1963), p. 24.

6   Kermit Hunter, "Outdoor Dramas," New York Times, July 18, 1954, Sec. 2, p. 1.

7   Samuel Selden, "Making the Outdoor Play," Producing America's Outdoor Dramas, Samuel Selden et al. (Chapel Hill: University of North Carolina Extension Bulletin, XXXIII, No. 4, March, 1954), 18.

8   John Gassner, "Broadway in Review," Educational Theatre Journal, V (October, 1953), 237.

9   ———, taken from a lecture given at a conference of the New York State Community Theatre Association, Ithaca, New York, October 20, 1956.

10   Emmet Lavery, "Dawn's Early Light." (Unpublished MS., 1957), p. 3.

11   Ramsey Yelvington, A Cloud of Witnesses: The Drama of the Alamo (Austin: University of Texas Press, 1959), p. 17. Copyright 1959 by the University of Texas Press.

12   E. Martin Browne, "Acting Out of Doors," Drama, No. 49 (Summer, 1958), 26.

13   Letter from Ramsey Yelvington, March 16, 1964.

14   Ibid.

15   Ibid.

16   Ibid.

17   Amelia Williams, "A Critical Study of the Siege of the Alamo and of the Personnel of Its Defenders, Part III," Southwestern Historical Quarterly, XXXVII (October, 1933), 84.

18   Ibid., 84.

19   Ibid., 97.

20   Ibid., 108.

21   Ibid., 109.

22   Williams, Part IV, XXXVII (January, 1934), 161.

23   Encyclopaedia Britannica, 14th ed., s.v. Alamo.

24   Williams, Part II, XXXVII (July, 1933), 18.

25   Williams, Part IV, XXXVII (January, 1934), 173.

26   Ramsey Yelvington, A Cloud of Witnesses: The Drama of the Alamo (Austin: University of Texas Press, 1959), pp. 71–73. By permission of the University of Texas Press.

27   Ibid., pp. 77–84.

General Bibliography

Books

The Americana Annual: 1964. New York: Americana Corporation, 1964.

American Heritage (eds.). A Treasury of American Heritage. New York: Simon and Schuster, Inc., 1960.

Archer, William. Play-Making: A Manual of Craftsmanship. Boston: Small, Maynard and Co., 1912.

The Arts Council Handbook. Winston-Salem, N.C.: Winston-Salem Arts Council, 1963.

Baker, George Pierce. Dramatic Technique. Boston: Houghton Mifflin Co., 1947.

Bates, Esther Willard. The Art of Producing Pageants. Boston: Walter H. Baker Co., 1925.

Beegle, Mary Porter and Crawford, Jack Randall. Community Drama and Pageantry. New Haven: Yale University Press, 1916.

Bowen, Catherine Drinker. Adventures of a Biographer. Boston: Little, Brown and Company, 1959.

————. The Writing of Biography. Boston: The Writer, Inc., 1952.

Boyle, Walden. Central and Flexible Staging: A New Theatre in the Making. Berkeley: University of California Press, 1956.

Brockett, Oscar G. The Theatre: An Introduction. New York: Holt, Rinehart and Winston, 1964.

Burris-Meyer, Harold and Cole, Edward C. Theatres & Auditoriums. New York: Reinhold, 1949.

Busfield, Roger M., Jr. The Playwright's Art. New York: Harper & Brothers, 1958.

Carmer, Carl. The Hudson. New York: Farrar & Rinehart, 1939.

Casey, Francis J. Staging the Bible. Westminster, Md.: Newman Press, 1962.

Chapman, Raymond (ed.). Religious Drama: A Handbook for Actors and Producers. London: Published for the Religious Drama Society of Great Britain by S.P.C.K., 1959. Distributed in United States by Baker's Plays.

Cheney, Sheldon. The Open-Air Theatre. New York: Mitchell Kennerly, 1918.

Cherokee Historical Association. A Community Effort. Cherokee, N.C.: Cherokee Historical Association, Inc., 1952.

Clark, Barrett H. (ed.). European Theories of the Drama. rev. ed. New York: Crown Publishers, 1947.

Clifford, James L. (ed.). Biography as an Art. New York: Oxford University Press, 1962.

College Library Staff, compilers, *Vital Facts of the College of William and Mary in Virginia*. Williamsburg: College of William and Mary, 1953.

Cunliffe, Marcus. *George Washington: Man and Monument*. Boston: Little, Brown and Co., 1958.

Dickinson, Thomas H. *The Case of American Drama*. Boston: Houghton Mifflin Co., 1915.

Ehrensperger, Harold. *Religious Drama: Ends and Means*. New York: Abingdon Press, 1962.

Esslin, Martin. *Brecht, a Choice of Evils*. London: Eyre & Spottiswoode, 1959.

Federal Writers' Project. *New York: A Guide to the Empire State*. New York: Oxford University Press, 1940.

————. *Utah: A Guide to the State*. New York: Hastings House, 1941.

Fishwick, Marshall. *American Heroes: Myth and Reality*. Washington, D.C.: Public Affairs Press, 1954.

Fitzpatrick, John C. (ed.). *The Diaries of George Washington: 1748–1799*, I. Boston: Houghton Mifflin Co., 1925.

Ford, Paul Leicester (ed.). *The Writings of Thomas Jefferson*. New York: G. P. Putnam's Sons, I, 1892.

Forster, E. M. *Aspects of the Novel*. New York: Harcourt, Brace & Co., 1927.

Free, William J. and Lower, Charles B. (eds.). *History into Drama: A Source Book on Symphonic Drama*. New York: The Odyssey Press, 1963.

Gard, Robert. *Grassroots Theatre: A Search for Regional Arts in America*. Madison: University of Wisconsin Press, 1955.

Gardner, Emelyn E. *Folklore from the Schoharie Hills*. Ann Arbor: University of Michigan Press, 1937.

Garrison, Roger H. *A Creative Approach to Writing*. New York: Henry Holt and Co., 1951.

Gassner, John. *The Theatre in Our Times*. New York: Crown Publishers, Inc., 1954.

George Washington Bicentennial Commission. *The History of the George Washington Bicentennial Celebration*. "U. S. Government Publications: Literature Series," II. Washington, D.C.: Government Printing Office, 1931.

Gilder, Rosamond, et al. (eds.). *The Theatre Arts Anthology*. New York: Theatre Arts Books, 1950.

Grebanier, Bernard. *Playwriting*. New York: Thomas Y. Crowell Co., 1961.

Green, Paul. *Drama and the Weather*. New York: Samuel French, 1958.

————. *Dramatic Heritage*. New York: Samuel French, 1953.

————. *Plough and Furrow*. New York: Samuel French, 1963.

Hillebrand, Harold Newcomb. *Writing the One-Act Play*. New York: F. S. Crofts & Co., 1925.

History Through Drama: A Manual for the Writing and Production of Historical Drama. Minneapolis: Drama Advisory Service of the University of Minnesota and the Minnesota Statehood Centennial Commission, 1958.

Laver, James. *Drama: Its Costume and Décor.* London: The Studio Ltd., 1951.

Leacock, Stephen. *Laugh with Leacock.* New York: Dodd, Mead & Company, 1930.

Lodge, Henry Cabot. *George Washington.* 2 vols. New York: Houghton Mifflin Co., 1889.

Macgowan, Kenneth. *A Primer of Playwriting.* New York: Random House, 1951.

MacKaye, Percy. *Community Drama; . . . an Interpretation.* New York: Houghton Mifflin Co., 1917.

Mersand, Joseph. *The American Drama: 1930–1940.* New York: The Modern Chapbooks, 1941.

Middleton, George. *These Things Are Mine.* New York: Macmillan Company, 1947.

Nannes, Caspar H. *Politics in the American Drama.* Washington, D.C.: Catholic University of America Press, 1960.

Parker, Anthony. *Pageants: Their Presentation and Production.* London: The Bodley Head, 1954.

Parker, Noah. *The New England Meeting House.* Tercentenary Commission of the State of Connecticut, Pamphlet 18. New Haven: Yale University Press, 1936.

Parris, John. *The Cherokee Story.* Asheville, North Carolina: The Stephens Press, 1950.

Playground and Recreation Association of America. *Community Drama: Suggestions for a Community-Wide Program of Dramatic Activities.* New York: Century Co., 1926.

Plummer, Gail. *The Business of Show Business.* New York: Harper and Brothers, 1961.

Ribner, Irving. *The English History Play in the Age of Shakespeare.* Princeton, N.J.: Princeton University Press, 1957.

Rossiter, Clinton. *The American Presidency.* New York: Harcourt, Brace & Co., 1956.

Rowe, Kenneth Thorpe. *A Theater in Your Head.* New York: Funk & Wagnalls Co., 1960.

Ruchames, Louis (ed.). *A John Brown Reader.* New York: Abelard-Schuman Limited, 1959.

Sandburg, Carl. *Abraham Lincoln: The Prairie Years.* 2 vols. New York: Harcourt, Brace & Co., 1926.

Selden, Samuel. *An Introduction to Playwriting.* New York: F. S. Crofts & Co., 1946.

———. (ed.). *Organizing a Community Theatre.* Cleveland, Ohio: National Theatre Conference, 1945. Distributed by Theatre Arts Books.

———. *The Production of Local History Plays and Pageants.* "Bulletins of the American Association for State and Local History," I, No. 6. Washington, D.C.: American Association for State and Local History, 1943.

————, and others. *Producing America's Outdoor Dramas.* University of North Carolina Extension Bulletin, XXXIII, No. 4 (March, 1954). Chapel Hill: University of North Carolina Press.

Sellers, Charles Colemon. *Lorenzo Dow, The Bearer of the Word.* New York: Minton, Balch & Company, 1928.

Shaw, George Bernard. *Our Theatre in the Nineties.* II. London: Constable and Co. Ltd., 1932.

Shirk, Samuel Blaine. *The Characterization of George Washington in American Plays Since 1875.* Published Ph.D. dissertation. Philadelphia: University of Pennsylvania, 1949.

Smith, Robert Metcalf (ed.). *Types of Historical Drama.* New York: Prentice-Hall, Inc., 1928.

Spalding, Lucile, et al. *Why Not Write a Documentary Play.* London: University of London Press Ltd., 1961.

Sparks, Jared (ed.). *The Writings of George Washington.* V. Boston, 1834.

Stevens, David H. (ed.). *Ten Talents in the American Theatre.* Norman: University of Oklahoma Press, 1957.

Taft, Linwood. *The Technique of Pageantry.* New York: A. S. Barnes and Co., 1921.

Tilden, Freeman. *Interpreting Our Heritage: Principles and Practices for Visitor Services in Parks, Museums, and Historic Places.* Chapel Hill: University of North Carolina Press, 1957.

Tyler, Alice Felt. *Freedom's Ferment: Phases of American Social History to 1860.* Minneapolis: University of Minnesota Press, 1944.

Villard, Oswald Garrison. *John Brown: 1800–1859: A Biography Fifty Years After.* Boston: Houghton Mifflin Company, 1910.

Virginia's Opportunity: The Civil War Centennial: A Manual for Its Observance. Richmond, Virginia: Virginia Civil War Commission, 1961.

Waugh, Frank Albert. *Outdoor Theatres.* Boston: Richard G. Badger, 1917.

Wedgwood, C. V. *Truth and Opinion.* New York: Macmillan Company, 1960.

Williams, T. Harry. *Abraham Lincoln: Selected Speeches, Messages, and Letters.* New York: Rinehart and Co., 1957.

Withington, Robert. *English Pageantry: An Historical Outline.* 2 vols. Cambridge, Mass.: Harvard University Press, 1918–1920.

————. *A Manual of Pageantry.* "Indiana University Extension Bulletin," XIII, No. 7. Bloomington: Indiana University Extension Division, 1915.

Articles and Periodicals

Allen, Hervey. "History and the Novel," *Atlantic Monthly,* CLXXIII (February, 1944), 119–21.

Arts Management, published by The Radius Group Inc., New York. No. 16 (May, 1963) and No. 17 (June, 1963).

Atkinson, Brooks. "Hunter's 'Forever This Land'," *New York Times*, June 30, 1952.
———. "The New Play: 'The Common Glory'," *New York Times*, July 19, 1947.
———. "Sherwood's 'Abe Lincoln in Illinois'," *New York Times*, October 17, 1938.
———. "Virginia's 'Glory'," *New York Times*, July 27, 1947.
Baker, George Pierce. "Pageantry," *Art and Progress*, IV (January, 1913), 831–35.
Brown, Frank Chouteau. "The American Pageant Association," *The Drama*, No. 9 (February, 1913), 178–88.
———. "The 'Book of the Pageant': And Its Development," *The Drama*, No. 18 (May, 1915), 269–83.
Browne, E. Martin. "Acting Out of Doors," *Drama*, No. 49 (Summer, 1958), 26–28.
Burgard, Ralph. "Arts Councils: New Approach to Cultural Leadership," *Arts in Society*, II (Fall–Winter, 1962/63), 120–31.
Carlson, James R. "The play's the thing," *International Journal of Religious Education*, XXXVII (February, 1961), 9–12.
Carroll, Walter. "Quiet Please—The Stars Are Out," *Theatre Arts*, XXXIV (July, 1950), 53–55.
Chicago Daily Press and Tribune, September 1, 1858.
Corey, Albert B. "Year of History Dramas," *New York State Folklore Quarterly*, XXVI (Spring, 1960), 3–5.
Crittenden, Christopher. "Theatre under the Stars," *American Heritage*, V (Summer, 1954), 16–23.
DeVoto, Bernard. "Fiction and the Everlasting If," *Harper's Magazine*, CLXXVII (June, 1938), 42–49.
Doan, Barbara. "Hark Upon the Gale," *The Alumni Gazette of the College of William and Mary*, XXV (December, 1957), 6–7.
Drinkwater, John. "Historic Figures on the Stage," *Theatre Magazine*, XXXIII (June, 1921), 394, 448.
Ellison, Jerome. "Churches Take Up Show Business," *The Saturday Evening Post* (September 22, 1962), 60–61.
Esterow, Milton. "Dramatic Bootstrap," *New York Times*, August 6, 1961. Sec. 2, p. 1.
"The Field of Travel," *New York Times*, March 22, 1964, Sec. 10, p. 8.
Gassner, John. "Broadway in Review," *Educational Theatre Journal*. V (October, 1953), 233–39.
———. "Dangers of the History Play," *Theatre Arts*, XXXVII (April, 1953), 78–81.
———. "Jefferson and Hamilton in Drama," *Current History*, IV (March, 1943), 88–91.
———. "Outdoor Pageant-Drama: Symphony of Sight and Sound," *Theatre Arts*, XXXVIII (July, 1954), 80–83.

Gaw, Allison. "Centers of Interest in Drama, Dramatic Tension, and Types of 'Conflict'," *Schelling Anniversary Papers*. New York: The Century Co., 1923. 151–72.

Gibbs, Wolcott. "Birth of a Nation," *The New Yorker*, XVIII (February 6, 1943), 31.

Gilder, Rosamond. "Broadway in Review," *Theatre Arts*, XXVII (April, 1943), 201–11.

"The Grand Tour," *Newsweek*, XLIX (June 17, 1957), 118–19.

Green, Paul. "The Lost Colony," *Theatre Arts*, XXXVI (July, 1952), 72–73.

Grein, J. T. "Biography on the Stage," *Illustrated London News*, Vol. 182 (April 15, 1933), 522.

Griffith, Mrs. Will. "A Capsule History of Carbondale," in *Century of Progress*, a centennial souvenir program issued by the Carbondale (Illinois) Chamber of Commerce, 1952.

Halpert, Herbert. "Aggressive Humor on the East Branch," *New York Folklore Quarterly*, II (May, 1946), 85–97.

Hanff, Helene. " 'The Footnote-and-mouth disease'," *Harper's*, CCXXIII (July, 1961), 58–61.

Hansbrough, Vivian. "The Woman Behind the Maifest," *The Missouri Farmer* (May, 1961), 36–37.

Hansen, Bert. "Sociodrama in a Small-Community Therapy Program," *Sociatry*, 1 (March, 1947), 92–96.

Hesse, Anne. "This Is Our Heritage," *The American-German Review*, XXVII (April–May, 1961), 28–31.

Hewes, Henry. "Optimism under the Pines," *Saturday Review*, XXXIX (August 4, 1956), 30–31.

Hewitt, Barnard. "Some Uses of the 'Frame' in Playwriting," *The Quarterly Journal of Speech*, XXXII (December, 1946), 480–84.

Hill, Philip G. "A Theatre for the Outdoor Historical Drama," *Educational Theatre Journal*, XIV (December, 1962), 312–17.

Hoover, Richard. "The Business Manager," *Theatre Arts*, XXXIII (December, 1949), 55–56.

Hunter, Kermit. "History or Drama?" *South Atlantic Bulletin* (May, 1953), 3–4.

———. "Oral Interpretation in the Outdoor Theater," *The Southern Speech Journal*, XIX (December, 1953), 133–39.

———. "Outdoor Dramas," *New York Times*, July 18, 1954, Sec. 2, p. 1.

———. "The Outdoor Historical Drama," *The North Carolina Historical Review*, XXX (April, 1953), 218–22.

———. "The Theatre Meets the People," *Educational Theatre Journal*, VII (May, 1955), 128–35.

Jouvet, Louis. "Notes on the Role of the Theatre," *New York Times*, April 8, 1951, Sec. 2, p. 1.

Kernodle, George R. "The Outdoor Setting," Theatre Arts, XI (July, 1937), 558–61.

Koch, Frederick H. "Amateur Values in Pageantry," The Quarterly Journal of Public Speaking, No. 1 (October, 1915), 288–97.

Langdon, William Chauncy. "Compass Points in the Festal Drama," The Drama, No. 27 (August, 1917), 404–24.

Lerner, Max. "The Lincoln Image," The New Republic, XCVIII (March 8, 1939), 134–36.

Littell, Robert. "History Brought to Life," The Reader's Digest, LXXVIII (May, 1961), 193–96.

"The Lost Colony," The Reader's Digest, XXXVII (July, 1940), 30.

Mallory, Louis A. "Patrick Henry," A History and Criticism of American Public Address, ed. William Norwood Brigance. New York: Russell & Russell, Inc., 1960. II, 580–602.

Mark, Charles. "Common Sense about Citizen Support for Arts and Culture," Arts in Society, II (n.d.), 4–11.

McCalmon, George and Moe, Christian. "The Dramatic in the Historical Character," The Southern Speech Journal, XXVIII (Winter, 1962), 85–97.

McDowell, Robert Emmett. "Home Is the Hunter," Home Is the Hunter 1964 Souvenir Program, 22–23.

Mitchison, Naomi. "Writing Historical Novels," Saturday Review of Literature, XI (April 27, 1935), 645.

Nathan, George Jean. "Art of the Night," Saturday Review of Literature, XV (January 2, 1937), 18.

Nevins, Allan. " 'An Idea Whose Time Has Come'," New York Times, October 18, 1959, Sec. II, p. 7.

New York State Council on the Arts Newsletter, published by Arts Management, July, 1963.

"North Carolina: Tourists Line Up at the Box Office," Business Week (July 12, 1952), 90–92.

"Notices," The William and Mary Quarterly, 2nd Series, V (April, 1925), 120–24.

Putsch, Henry E. and Stanhope, S. Browne. "Masks in the Chancel," The Episcopalian, CXXVIII (April, 1963), 14–19.

Rankin, Allen and Martha. "How the Lost Colony Was Found," Theatre Arts, XL (July, 1956), 69–70, 84, 95.

Rice, Elmer. "A Personal Memoir: Tribute to Robert E. Sherwood," New York Times, November 20, 1955, Section 2, p. 1.

Risser, Arthur C. "Building and equipment for drama," International Journal of Religious Education, XXXVII (February, 1961), 22–23.

Rockefeller, John D., 3rd. "The Arts and the Community," Music Journal, XXI (September, 1963), 27, 86–88.

St. Louis Post-Dispatch, March 11, 1962, Sec. J, p. 4.

Selden, Samuel. "America's Open-Air Dramas," *State Government*, XV (April, 1952), 86–87, 94–95.

———. "America's Outdoor Dramas," *Players Magazine*, XXXI (February, 1955), 106–7.

Shanely, John P. "Grant's Story on Television," *New York Times*, February 21, 1960, Sec. 2, p. 15.

Sisk, John P. "American Best Sellers," *Commonweal*, LXVIII (July 11, 1958), 373–75.

Stephenson, Nathaniel Wright. "History and the Playwright," *Drama*, No. 6 (May, 1912), 191–209.

Stultler, Boyd B. "The Hanging of John Brown," *American Heritage*, VI (February, 1955), 4–9.

Swem, Earl Gregg. "Kentuckians at William and Mary College Before 1861 with a Sketch of the College Before that Date," *Filson Club History Quarterly*, XXIII (July, 1949), 173–98.

"The Talking Discs," *Holiday*, XXIX (May, 1961), 179–83.

Tourtellot, Arthur Bernan. "History and the Historical Novel, Where Fact and Fancy Meet and Part," *Saturday Review of Literature*, XXII (August 24, 1940), 3–4, 16.

Trumbo, Charles R. and Pollyann. "History of Pageantry," *Dramatics*, XXX (October, 1958), 14–15.

Wagnon, Ward. "Evening with an Aura," *Holiday Inn Magazine* (April, 1963), 11.

Wedgwood, C. V. "History and Literature," *Fortnightly*, CLXX (October, 1951), 679–84.

Wilder, Thornton. "Some Thoughts on Playwriting," *Aspects of the Drama*, ed. Sylvan Barnet, Morton Berman, and William Burto. Boston: Little, Brown and Co., 1962, 1–11.

Williams, Amelia. "A Critical Study of the Siege of the Alamo and of the Personnel of Its Defenders," *Southwestern Historical Quarterly*, XXXVI (April, 1933), 251–87; XXXVII (July, 1933), 1–44 (October, 1933), 79–115 (January, 1934), 157–84 (April, 1934), 237–312.

Young, Stark. "The Patriots," *New Republic*, CVIII (February 15, 1943), 211, [review].

Dramas

Published

Anderson, Maxwell. *Three Plays* by Maxwell Anderson. Ed. George Freedley. New York: Washington Square Press, 1962.

———. *Valley Forge*. Washington, D. C.: Anderson House, 1934.

———. *The Wingless Victory*. Washington, D.C.: Anderson House, 1936.

Anouilh, Jean. *Becket*. New York: New American Library, 1964.

Baker, George Pierce. *Control; A Pageant of Engineering Progress*. New York: The American Society of Mechanical Engineers, 1930.

Banks, Nathaniel. *The Curate's Play*. New York: Dramatists Play Service, 1962.

Bates, Esther Willard. *George Washington of Young America: A Pageant in Honor of the Father of His Country*. Boston: Walter H. Baker Co., 1931.

Benét, Stephen Vincent. *John Brown's Body*. New York: Dramatists Play Service, 1961.

————. *Selected Works*. New York: Farrar & Rinehart Inc., 1942.

Chayefsky, Paddy. *Gideon*. New York: Random House, 1962.

Corey, Orlin. *The Book of Job*. Anchorage, Kentucky: Children's Theatre Press, 1960.

Corwin, Norman. *The Rivalry*. New York: Dramatists Play Service, 1960.

————. *The World of Carl Sandburg*. New York: Harcourt, Brace & World, 1961.

Davis, Julia. *The Anvil*. Evanston, Illinois: Harper and Row, 1963.

Driggs, H. Wayne and Hansen, Harold. *America's Witness for Christ*. Provo, Utah: Brigham Young University, 1957.

Drinkwater, John. *Abraham Lincoln*. Boston: Houghton Mifflin Company, 1919.

Duberman, Martin B. *In White America*. New York: Samuel French, 1964.

Fast, Howard. *General Washington and the Water Witch*. London: The Bodley Head, 1956.

Fry, Christopher. *Curtmantle*. New York: Oxford University Press, 1961.

Gard, Robert. "Raisin' the Devil," *The Lake Guns of Seneca and Cayuga*, ed. A. M. Drummond and Robert E. Gard. Ithaca, New York: Cornell University Press, 1942.

Gibson, William. *Dinny and the Witches; The Miracle Worker*. New York: Atheneum, 1960.

Goodman, Arthur. *If Booth Had Missed*. New York: Samuel French, 1932.

Goodrich, Frances and Hackett, Albert. *The Diary of Anne Frank*. New York: Random House, 1956.

Green, Paul. *The Common Glory*. Chapel Hill: University of North Carolina Press, 1948.

————. *The Confederacy*. New York: Samuel French, 1959.

————. *The Founders*. New York: Samuel French, 1957.

————. *The Lost Colony*. Chapel Hill: University of North Carolina Press, 1937. Memorial edition, 1946.

————. *Wilderness Road*. New York: Samuel French, 1956.

Greenbie, Sydney and Marjorie Barstow. *Castine: A Dramatized Biography of a Town*. Penobscot, Maine: Traversity Press, 1948.

Halverson, Marvin (ed.). *Religious Drama*. 1 ("Living Age Books") New York: Meridian Books, 1957.

Horace Mann Schools. *Those Who Bear the Torch*. Washington, D.C.: National Education Association, 1937.

Howard, Sidney. *Lexington: A Pageant-Drama of the American Freedom.* Lexington, Mass.: Lexington Historical Society, 1924.

———. *Yellow Jack.* New York: Harcourt, Brace and Co., 1934.

Hughes, Glenn. *The Dream and the Deed.* Seattle: University of Washington, 1952.

Hunter, Kermit. *Unto These Hills.* Chapel Hill: University of North Carolina Press, 1950.

Kingsley, Sidney. *The Patriots.* New York: Random House, 1943.

Lavery, Emmet. *American Portrait.* New York: Samuel French, 1959.

———. *The Magnificent Yankee.* New York: Samuel French, 1946.

———, and others. *Theatre for Tomorrow: Damien, Savonarola, Who Ride White Horses.* New York: Longmans, Green and Co., 1940.

Lawrence, Jerome and Lee, Robert E. *The Gang's All Here.* Cleveland, Ohio: World Publishing Co., 1960.

———. *Inherit the Wind.* New York: Random House, 1955.

Levitt, Saul. *The Andersonville Trial.* New York: Random House, 1960.

McCaslin, Nellie. *Pioneers in Petticoats: Dramatized Stories and Legends of Heroic American Women.* Evanston, Illinois: Harper and Row, 1960.

Miller, Arthur. *The Crucible.* New York: Viking Press, 1953.

Morris, Richard. *The Unsinkable Molly Brown.* New York: G. P. Putnam's Sons, 1961.

Riggs, Lynn. *Toward the Western Sky.* Cleveland, Ohio: Western Reserve University Press, 1951.

Rohan, Pierre de (ed.). *Federal Theatre Plays: Prologue to Glory, One-Third of a Nation, and Haiti.* New York: Random House, 1938.

———. *Federal Theatre Plays: Triple-A Plowed Under, Power, and Spirochete.* New York: Random House, 1938.

Rutenborn, Guenter. *The Sign of Jonah.* New York: Thomas Nelson and Sons, 1960.

Ryerson, Florence and Clements, Colin. *Harriet.* New York: Charles Scribner's Sons, 1943.

Sanford, Anne P. and Schauffler, Robert Haven (eds.). *Pageants of Our Nation.* 2 vols. New York: Dodd, Mead and Co., 1929.

Schary, Dore. *Sunrise at Campobello.* New York: Random House, 1958.

Sherwood, Robert Emmet. *Abe Lincoln in Illinois.* New York: Charles Scribner's Sons, 1939.

Stavis, Barrie. *The Man Who Never Died.* New York: Haven Press, 1954.

———. *Lamp at Midnight.* New York: Dramatists Play Service, 1955.

Stevens, Thomas Wood. *The Pageant of Newark.* Newark, New Jersey: The Committee of One Hundred, 1916.

———. *The Historical Pageant of Illinois.* Chicago: Aldenbrink Press, 1909.

Van Doren, Mark. *The Last Days of Lincoln.* New York: Hill and Wang, 1959.

Yelvington, Ramsey. *A Cloud of Witnesses: The Drama of the Alamo*. Austin: The University of Texas Press, 1959.

————. (ed.). *Dramatic Images: Plays for the Church*. (Baylor Theatre Church Play Series, I.) Waco, Texas: Baylor University, 1959.

Unpublished

Dace, Wallace. "The Prophet." MS. in Public Library, Harpers Ferry, West Virginia.

Erickson, Jane. "A Mighty Fortress." MS. in Reed College Library, Portland, Oregon.

Hunter, Kermit. "Forever This Land." MS. in possession of New Salem Lincoln League, Petersburg, Illinois.

Lavery, Emmet. "Dawn's Early Light." MS. available through Brandt & Brandt Dramatic Department, Inc., New York 17.

Lazebnik, Jack. "Impeachment." MS. in Stephens College Library, Columbia, Missouri.

————. "John Brown." MS. in Stephens College Library, Columbia, Missouri.

McDowell, Robert Emmett. "Home Is the Hunter." MS. in possession of Fort Harrod Drama Productions, Inc., Harrodsburg, Kentucky.

McLeod, Charlotte. "A Century of Progress." MS. in Southern Illinois University Library, Carbondale, Illinois.

Moe, Christian. "Hark Upon the Gale." MS. in College of William and Mary Library, Williamsburg, Virginia.

Parry, Roland and Helen. "All Faces West." MS. in possession of Ogden Pioneer Days, Inc., Ogden, Utah.

Stavis, Barrie. "Banners of Steel." MS. circulated by American Playwrights Theatre, Ohio State University, Columbus, Ohio.

Stockton, Richard F. "The Trial of John Brown." MS. in University of Kansas Library, Lawrence, Kansas.

Sundgaard, Arnold. "On Hemlock Brook." MS. in Williams College Library, Williamstown, Massachusetts.

WPA Writers Program. "Out of the Wilderness: The New Salem Years of Abraham Lincoln." MS. in University of Illinois Library, Urbana, Illinois.

Yelvington, Ramsey. "The Marble Horseman." MS. in possession of Dallas Theater Center, Dallas, Texas.

————. "Shadow of an Eagle." MS. in possession of Dallas Theater Center, Dallas, Texas.

Reports

Civil War Centennial Commission. *State Centennial Commissions at Work*. A report issued by the Civil War Centennial Commission, Washington, D.C., January 4, 1961.

Eddy, Junius. *Drama and Leisure Time: A Report on the Two-Year General Education Board Study at Baylor University on the Integration of Dramatic Activities with Community Leisure Time Programs.* Waco, Texas: Baylor University, August, 1951.

Institute of Outdoor Drama. *Conference Notes.* A report from the First National Outdoor Drama Conference. Chapel Hill, North Carolina: Institute of Outdoor Drama, 1963.

Jamestown Corporation. "Statement of Operations." Williamsburg, Virginia, 1957.

MacFadyen, John H. *State Programs for Support of the Arts—A General Outline.* A report issued by the New York State Council on the Arts, April 19, 1963.

National Council on the Arts and Government, Inc. *1963 Annual Report.* New York, 1963.

Selden, Samuel. *Outdoor Historical Dramas.* A report to the Trustees of the University of North Carolina, November, 1955.

Other Unpublished Material

Leggette, L. Poe. "Festival Drama." Doctoral dissertation, Teachers College, Columbia University, 1956.

Lokensgard, Maurice Foss. "A Study of Some Aspects of Bert Hansen's Pageant-Dramas." Master's thesis, Department of Speech, Montana State University, 1959.

Mallery, Mary Louise. "Pageant-dramas in the United States Today." Master's thesis, Syracuse University, 1952.

Nary, Bruce LeRoy. "A Study of the Major Lincoln Dramas in Relationship to Selected Lincoln Biographies." Doctoral dissertation, Department of Speech, University of Michigan, 1956.

Walsh, Frederick H. "Outdoor Commemorative Drama in the United States 1900–1950." Doctoral dissertation, Department of Dramatic Arts, Western Reserve University, 1952.

White, Nathaniel Stell, Jr. "Theatre Management in Three Outdoor Theatre Projects." Master's thesis, Department of Dramatic Art, University of North Carolina, 1951.

Williams, Anne St. Clair. "Theatre Promotion in North Carolina." Master's thesis, Department of Dramatic Art, University of North Carolina, 1952.

Wilson, Barry Preston. "Paul Green: Evangelist for Democracy." Master's thesis, Department of Speech and Drama, Cornell University, 1955.

Index